Critical Acclaim for

IN THE HANDS OF
THE GREAT SPIRIT

"Page covers it all . . . he rema[...]
Indian life today . . . a well-re[...]
reader."

—The Weekly Standard

"[A] lively and readable compendium in a single volume of what we know about native history, *Great Spirit* is an excellent choice. . . . [It] has much to teach."

—The Washington Times

"Page [writes] with a storyteller's flair and a historian's regard for demonstrable facts."

—Kirkus Reviews

"[S]uperb."

—Library Journal

"Page does well to inform his audience of . . . the archaeology and historiography of the subject."

—Booklist

"[A] terrific primer."

—The Denver Post

"Jake Page has written a truly interesting and important book. . . . The mastery of historical detail never overwhelms the majesty of the story. Indeed, the individual human experience emerges as the central element of *In the Hands of the Great Spirit*."

—Rennard Strickland, author of *Tonto's Revenge: Reflections on American Indian Culture and Policy*

"A splendid achievement."

"A marvelously readable mosaic. . . . Sympathetic without being mawkish, comprehensive without being tedious, authoritative without being pompous, probing without being preachy, Page paints a compelling panorama of 20,000 years of American Indian experience. . . . Moreover, he accomplishes all of this with a stylistic flair and literary flow that draws in and engages the reader from beginning to end."

Also by Jake Page

JAKE PAGE

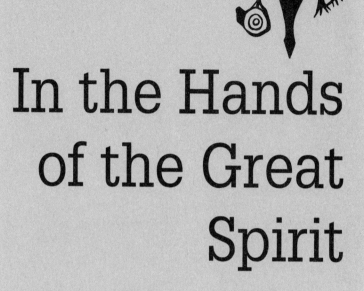

In the Hands of the Great Spirit

THE 20,000 YEAR HISTORY OF AMERICAN INDIANS

FREE PRESS

NEW YORK   LONDON   TORONTO   SYDNEY

*f*P

FREE PRESS
A Division of Simon & Schuster, Inc.
1230 Avenue of the Americas
New York, NY 10020

First Free Press trade paperback edition 2004

For information regarding special discounts for bulk purchases,
please contact Simon & Schuster Special Sales:
1-800-456-6798 or business@simonandschuster.com

Designed by Karolina Harris

Manufactured in the United States of America

20   19   18

The Library of Congress has catalogued the hardcover edition as follows:
Page, Jake.
In the hands of the great spirit : the 20,000-year history of American Indians/Jake Page.
    p. cm.
Includes bibliographical references and index.
1. Paleo-Indians. 2. Indians of North America—History. I. Title.
E77 .P14 2003
973.04'97—dc21   2002035266

ISBN-13: 978-0-684-85576-9
ISBN-10:   0-684-85576-3
ISBN-13: 978-0-684-85577-6 (Pbk)
ISBN-10:   0-684-85577-1 (Pbk)

*In homage to Susanne Page
and the memory of Abbot Sekaquaptewa*

Shoshone crane head on dance wand

We are still here.

WORDS ON A PLAQUE IN THE NATIONAL MUSEUM
OF THE AMERICAN INDIAN, IN NEW YORK CITY

I have been asked, how do you define an Indian, is it a matter of blood content? I say no, an Indian is someone who thinks of themselves as an Indian. But that's not so easy to do and one has to earn the entitlement somehow. You have to have a certain experience of the world in order to formulate this idea. I know how my father saw the world, and his father before him. That's how I see the world.

N. SCOTT MOMADAY, KIOWA

"When the legends die,
dreams die also,
And when dreams die,
there is no greatness."
And when there is no greatness,
who will suffer the most?
Well, I will tell you, the people.
The people who don't know their own shadows,
And cannot see their visions clearly,
And the ones who don't know themselves pretty well,
But someday when you stop and think,
You'll see the real image
of yourself and the ones
that were before you
and then you'll see.

ANONYMOUS ZUNI STUDENT

Southern Sierra

CONTENTS

Part Five: New Deals 334

Nakataya split willow figurine

INDIAN COUNTRY

A wonderful T-shirt used to appear at powwows and other Indian gatherings. It is black, with the silhouette of North America emblazoned in red and a simple caption: *Indian Country.* I have seen it worn by equal numbers of Indians and non-Indians.

Like all superior graphics, its message is clear and simple. This vast region of the globe was once Indian country. All of it. Its message is also complex, bearing a suggestion of the word "ought," the notion that this should still by right be Indian country, except for the inappropriate intervention of history in the form of wayfaring Europeans. Philosophers can argue whether history has an essential moral component or is, like the biological process of evolution, something more neutral than that. The Hopi linguist and anthropologist Emory Sekaquaptewa points out that his people have always known the Hopis' path through time would be littered with new things, new events. Some of these would be opportunities, some obstacles—in fact, usually both at the same time. The question for the Hopis has always been whether they could take advantage of the opportunities proffered and avoid the obstacles—incorporate the good and avoid the bad. This is a very practical way to look at history, and perhaps more useful in the long run if history is to teach any of us very much, to serve as a landform we can keep in sight as we all navigate our way across the uncharted ocean that is the future.

Today, some 2 million people who are Indians inhabit the United States, less than 1 percent of the nation's population. A widely held notion is that they are mostly rural people, living on reservations that are located, for the most part, west of the Mississippi. This is not true: almost three quarters of Indian people live off-reservation, chiefly in cities. The cities with the largest Indian populations are Los Angeles, Tulsa, New York, Oklahoma City, San Francisco, and Phoenix. Though these Indians live in the midst of American society, they are less visible in many ways than their relatives on the reservations. Two million people may seem like a large number, but the Indian population has been far greater (before European contact) as well as far smaller (a hundred years ago).

Today, there are more than five hundred different federally recognized Indian groups, each with its own culture and past. Another hundred or so tribes are currently seeking federal recognition. (As many as two hundred tribes may have gone extinct since Columbus's arrival.) Tribal size today ranges from two or three individuals to more than 250,000 (the Navajos). In addition, estimates exist of as many as 15 million other Americans who have a discernible degree of Indian blood but who long ago lost any tribal connection. Indian reservations range in size from a quarter of an acre (in a New England town) to an area the size of West Virginia.

Taken together, the Indian tribes represent the most unusual ethnic group in the United States. Unlike all others, the recognized tribes enjoy special political rights—as nations (the tribes) dealing with another nation (the United States). This unique and extremely complicated situation (a matter of being both a part and apart) is referred to as *sovereignty* and will be one theme in this book. The Indian tribes, collectively, are also unique as an ethnic group in this country in that for many of them, their ethnicity is rooted in particular plots of ground, however shrunken now or different from the land they once called their homeland. Tying any other ethnic group in the United States to a place would be taken as the grossest discrimination.

This peculiarity can be looked at from another angle. A few years ago, before apartheid was ended as official policy in South Africa, a group of African journalists were invited to meet with a group of American Indians in Albuquerque, New Mexico, chiefly members of the various Pueblo tribes. The Africans were astonished to learn that while Indians lived on reservations, they were free to come and go whenever and wherever they wished.

A great legal scholar in the 1930s and 1940s, Felix Cohen, had yet another angle on the peculiar—or special—position of the American Indian in the larger society of the United States. "Like the miner's canary," he wrote, "our treatment of Indians, even more than our treatment of other minorities, reflects the rise and fall in our democratic faith."

These few thoughts are, perhaps, sufficient reason to try to understand the history of the American Indians. There are others that are equally compelling, which will emerge as the story proceeds.

For reasons that might be taken as obvious, since history is generally considered that part of the past for which written documents exist, most histories of the American Indians begin with the arrival in this hemisphere of Columbus. But Indians do not make the same distinction between prehistory and history, and neither does this book—it begins some seventeen thousand years ago, the earliest date at which we know people were present in North America. Probably they were here earlier. In any event, without the first 16,500 years of at least partially known accomplishment and loss, the last five hundred years of loss and accomplishment cannot be seen with anything approaching wholeness. Just as it is impossible to understand what has happened in a chemistry experiment without knowing the initial conditions, so it is unlikely that we will get a true picture of modern Indian history without being aware of what preceded it—life before Columbus. Thus, archaeology plays a major role in the first part of this book. As for Indian history as such, it has been known largely from accounts written by only one side in a long-running conflict. In the past few decades, a new generation of historians has arisen, determined to look more closely at the available records, and these more recent researchers have cast an array of new lights on the general history of American Indians. It is part of the purpose of this book to make these new scholarly insights more broadly known.

The story of the Indian people, in their own eyes, is all one continuing story—or stories—and Indians arrive at their past differently than non-Indians, and think of it in entirely different ways. The European mind calls such stories *mythology,* which is a snobby sort of word for someone else's religion and history. But all mythology, including that of the Judeo-Christianized West and the Islamicized Middle East, is the primary, even only means by which all humans until very recently have endeavored to understand the paradoxes and mysteries of the universe: the existence of what appears to be order from an original chaos; the meaning and value of human life and other forms of life; the nature of good and evil; and—importantly— in the face of all this, how human beings are supposed to behave. Most Indian histories—their own histories—are of this kind. Whether these tales are local metaphors, archetypal human dreams, imaginative versions of actual events, or faithful renditions of real occurrences is really of no concern to those who do not share them as belief systems. They simply *are,* just as the events of the past simply are. Historians and archaeologists sift through whatever they can confirm as facts and tend to seek some sort of meaningful pattern in them—chronologies and more complex matters. This is essentially the opposite of the traditional Indian way. Indians' history is a story as well, but story comes first—that is, the meaning of a story is its originating core. The facts follow the meaning.

One of the most important things to learn about Indian people, their cultures, and their history is that they too, like all of us with feet of clay and dreams of perfection, are human. This means that American Indians are capable of both acts of great sacrifice and acts of great self-ishness, of nobility and of mean-spiritedness. They can demonstrate an ability to take responsibility for their acts and decisions, as well as an inability to predict the future results of those same acts. They possess all the attributes of human beings everywhere. Some histories have romanticized the Indians; this one tries to avoid that temptation.

Indian traditions can be just as confining as any other traditions— and just as sustaining—but Indian people, like many others, are per-fectly capable of shedding shopworn ways, of remaking their cultures, and of spinning the truth as well as perpetuating stereo-types about their neighbors. They have been doing all of these things, on and off, for longer than human memory. The point is that both Indian people and non-Indian people in the United States these days entertain a great many silly misconceptions about each other and our joint history together.

No one can deny that the impact of European arrivals on Indian tribes and individuals has mostly been tragic. From the point of view of Indian peoples alive today, the story of that encounter is one of astonishing staying power amid vast and devastating change and loss. When Europeans arrived on these shores, they generally agreed that the wilderness was a place of dark and mysterious dangers, a place to be tamed, cut back, reduced to civilized plots of farmland and towns. It was assumed that the Indians—savages—lived in the untamed woodland wilderness among all of Satan's plots and schemes. Today in America, vast hordes of European-derived citizens flock to the wilderness, grow angry at any invasion of the wilderness (such as a cow pod) besides their own, and consider such places almost sacred. In this, they often invoke the benign ecological presence of the Native Americans, to whom many plots of land are indeed sacred. The notion of wilderness in American minds has changed by approximately 180 degrees, and perhaps some of this is thanks to the Indian population.

I owe my existence here in part to the early arrival on the continent of European ancestors whose Puritan ways are extremely opaque to me today—a different culture altogether from my own. I grew up with all the common Indian stereotypes of my time fully in mind, not that I ever believed John Wayne movies were intended as models of historical accuracy. I spent the sixties, when imperialist attitudes were so forcefully challenged, learning what every other sentient American did—namely, that minorities and women had gotten a rotten deal and their points of view had been almost systematically ignored. In that period, as editorial director of *Natural History* magazine, I published a number of articles on the then-current status of American Indians. But until 1974 I never met one.

Then, in that year, the woman I would soon marry, Susanne Anderson, was invited by the Hopis to photograph their daily lives—which the tribe had expressly forbidden since the turn of the century, when it had become clear to them that anthropologists and missionaries with cameras had ripped them off, publishing photographs of altars and other ceremonial matters that were private. For the next eight years, Susanne and I made some thirty trips from Washington, D.C., to the Hopi Reservation in northeastern Arizona, publishing the book *Hopi* in 1982. And that invitation issued in 1974 resulted, in due course, in our move to the Southwest, to what is often called Indian Country, where thirty years later we still live.

As a science writer and editor at the time, I found myself increasingly immersed in a world so utterly different from mine as to make me wonder if I was traveling not two thousand miles in space but five hundred years in time. I asked very few questions. Instead, I listened as carefully as I could to what the Hopis told me about themselves, what they wanted the world to know about them. (Of course, by just being there I learned a few things they would probably not want the world to know about them, but they didn't seem to mind when I pointed such things out in the book. They laughed when they encountered Page's Law of Hopi, for example, which states that if you find two Hopis agreeing with each other for fifteen minutes, one of them is lying.)

One of the things I learned was that Indian people do not necessarily hold their Indian neighbors in particularly high esteem. The Hopis and the surrounding Navajos were engaged at the time in a wracking land dispute, with a great deal of mutual suspicion and downright hostility erupting, occasionally, into outright violence—an ancient pattern. Another thing I learned was to take seriously and with respect what I was told of the metaphysical world—and this was not something I, the science buff, was accustomed to doing. Not particularly entranced by the religious world of my own culture, I was not at any time tempted—as some quixotically have been—to try to become a Hopi religionist. But from what I came to understand about the Hopi worldview and the ways it forms the basis of Hopi society, polity, family, and even humor, I found it to be a far more *coherent* religious tradition than my own. In short, over the years, I came to feel comfortable among these particular Indian people, more so in fact than among many groups of my own people. It is also true that they, like all of us, are perfectly capable of creating a slightly idealized notion of themselves and passing it along to outsiders.

The same, of course, goes for the Navajos, who asked Susanne and me to produce a similar book about them. Here were two utterly different and often antagonistic cultures, cheek by jowl, which never-theless, in many important ways, had far more in common with each other than either had with me—and I was privileged to glimpse both for long periods. Susanne and I were well aware, during all this time, that we were whites—respectively *pahanas* (Hopi) and *billeganas* (Navajo)—undertaking tasks that might more appropriately be done by members of the two tribes themselves. But they asked us, and we were happy to oblige.

Certainly, my life and my outlook on the world has been greatly changed by my experiences among these Indians—and others in the Southwest, where we moved in 1988. Had they not, I would never have been able to summon up the nerve (gall, some might say) to attempt this volume. Just as no book can explain all of Hopi life, no book about the American Indians can explain (or even mention) all of their histories—each one an epic of its own. But in attempting such a book, as selective as it must be, I have hoped to cast new light on this segment of the American past, and perhaps help to put to rest some misconceptions that still exist. In doing this, I have taken courage from my experiences among the southwestern Indian people, who have taught me so much, who have been forthright, honest, and thoughtful. I have happily sought to leap up onto the shoulders of many scholars and other observers—particularly those who have contributed so much in this realm in the past two decades or so. They will find themselves listed in the bibliography at the end of the book, and my debt to them is immeasurable.

In this regard, I have tried here to tell a story in a narrative form, but not slavishly—sometimes backtracking in time, sometimes leap-ing ahead. I have also tried to tell this history without dwelling on how historians, scientists, and others have arrived at their conclusions. But there are exceptions. Some matters covered are deeply laden emotion-ally and highly controversial, such as the time of the earliest arrival of people on this continent, who they were, and the numbers present when Europeans arrived, as well as several other difficult topics. Here I have felt it necessary and useful to report *how* the scholars have arrived at their conclusions.

Although I have relied on sources that are preponderantly of recent origin—from the 1980s and 1990s, as well as a few books published in this new century—my story may strike some people as a bit old-fash-ioned in that it is not ethnohistory or social history. It is an atttempt to put the grand sweep of more than seventeen thousand years into one volume, and as a result there is little time to pause and look intimately into the daily lives or the worldviews of the people who have lived this history. Instead, it is mostly an overview, what I hope is a judicious rendering of some of the main events that have shaped this history. I have also chosen to restrict myself to the history of those Indian people in the lower forty-eight states.

A brief comment on terminology. As you have no doubt already noticed, I use the word "Indian" freely. Other terms also appear in this book, such as "indigenous people," "nations," "tribes," and "native people." The problem with the word "Indian" is twofold. One, it is the result of an enormous geographical misperception. Two, and worse, it generalizes several hundred different cultures into a single unit. As such it is resented as a vestige of colonialism by some Indian people and their friends. On the other hand, as David E. Wilkens, a member of the Lumbee tribe and a political scientist at the University of Arizona, has written in his monumental study of Indian sovereignty and the U.S. Supreme Court, "*Indian* or *American Indian* is the most common [appellation] used by many indigenous and non-indigenous persons and by institutions, and so it will be used in the text when no tribe is specified."

The term "Native American," Wilkens points out, as others before him have, includes native Hawaiians, Indians, Eskimos, Aleuts, and in fact, all the descendants of all immigrants to these shores (which ultimately means everyone born in this hemisphere), and thus is more confusing than the term "American Indian." In my experience, which is largely anecdotal and far from exhaustively scientific, reservation Indians and Indian scholars tend to use the phrase "American Indian," while urban Indians and those who are of multitribal origins and many non-Indian scholars use "Native American," but no generalization holds here. Certainly, I regret that the familiar labels can be upsetting, but as even a practical matter, wordy and elaborate circumlocutions are not an attractive option in an enterprise that must cover an enormous amount of material in one volume, or to someone with any sense of a language's music.

Yet another matter of usage. It was common practice for many years to refer to a tribe's members in the singular—such as, "The Hopi are agriculturalists." Recently one of the leading historians of the Indian experience on this continent said he would not go along with that practice *unless* we were all willing to refer to the collective German or the collective Canadian, or to say, "The Brazilian are a sensuous people." Suddenly it sounds awfully condescending, doesn't it? So it's Hopis and Navajos, Pequots and Cherokees (but *not* Iroquoises or O'odham).

The part-opening maps are intended to give a general overview of Indian disposition and movement at the various points in time covered by each part. They are by necessity incomplete—exhaustive maps of all Indian groups would be impossibly detailed and inaccurate. Nonetheless, the information contained herein is as accurate as possible.

In addition to the T-shirt with which this preface began, I also admire and often wear a less frequently seen one, designed by a Navajo friend from Fort Defiance, a Vietnam War veteran named Al Slinkey. It bears a drawing of a caped European standing on the beach, his square-rigger slightly offshore. He faces several Indians improbably arrayed in elaborate Plains headdresses. The caption says: *Columbus sought India and called us Indians. Glad he wasn't seeking Turkey.*

Mindful of that spirit, I have been pleased and honored to write this book.

PART ONE

Initial
Conditions

Beringia

Cordilleran

Exposed land

Glacial sheets

CHAPTER ONE

ARRIVAL

Origins

In the late 1970s, one of the nation's leading anthropologists visited the Hopis and, in a meeting, set out to explain the latest archaeological findings as to their origins. A Hopi man who was, among other things, a successful entrepreneur and world traveler, as well as a snake priest, rose to object, saying that was all very well, but the Hopis, to a person, knew that the real truth of their origins lay in their migration through three previous worlds into this one, aided along the way by Spider Grandmother. The hole from which they emerged, called the *sipapu*—located not far off, near the confluence of the Little Colorado and Colorado Rivers—was a site well known to the Hopis, and they often made pilgrimages to it. Once in this world, the man said, the people who would become the Hopis went off in all the directions, but eventually returned in the Gathering of the Clans, forming the Hopi people. Each clan brought with it some particular talent that could help everyone, and those clan talents are still honored today.

Similarly, in the lands along the upper Rio Grande, many *sipapu*s exist, secret places that might be thought of as the earth's navel and, in a sense, the center of the universe. Every tribe on the continent has honored such places, where this world came about and where the people learned, through long and arduous challenges and with the aid of the spirit world, how to conduct life.

The Osages of the Plains once lived in the sky way beyond the earth. They were the children of the Sun (their father) and the Moon. Told by their mother to go live on the earth, they did so and found the earth covered entirely by water. Desperate, they turned to the stately Elk, who let himself fall into the water and sink. From below the water, the Elk called to the winds, which came from all directions and blew away most of the waters. First rocks were exposed, then soft earth, and the Elk, delighted with his work, rolled about, his loose hairs sticking to the soil and becoming beans and corn, grasses and trees.

The Yokuts, a California tribe that lived in the San Joaquin Valley, also tell of a world covered with water, from which a tree grew one day. In it was a nest containing Eagle and several other animal people. All they could see from this high perch was water. But Eagle began to think, "We will need some land." He sent a little duck down into the water to bring up some soil, but the little duck couldn't reach the bottom and perished in his quest. Another kind of duck was dispatched. It reached the mud but it too died, floating up to the surface.

Eagle noted some dirt under the duck's fingernails. He took it and mixed it with seeds into a kind of dough, and put the concoction in the water. The dough began to spread out everywhere around the tree they sat in. When the morning star came out the next day, Wolf shouted and all the earthly dough vanished. Again, Eagle mixed up some dough and placed it in the water. The next day, as the morning star rose, he told Wolf to shout three times. Wolf's shouting caused an earthquake but the earth remained. Then Coyote shouted as well, and the earth remained. And the animals left the tree to live on the ground.

For the Creeks, who lived in the southeast portion of what is now the United States until they were forcibly removed to the Oklahoma Territory, it was Crawfish who dove to the bottom of the ubiquitous water and found mud, which he proceeded to stir up, annoying the Mud People. But Crawfish was too fast for them and he kept stirring up the mud, making more and more land. This new earth needed drying, and Buzzard soared over it, flapping his wings. Where he swept his wings downward, valleys came into being; where he raised his wings, mountains occurred. It was still dark, so Star, and then Moon, tried to provide light. Finally Mother Sun began her daily rounds. From a drop of her blood that fell on this new earth the first people were born.

The Senecas of the northeast woodlands tell how the daughter of the Great Chief fell through a hole during the time when the whole world was water, plummeting into empty space. Birds flew up, making a nest for her with their wings. Finally growing tired, they placed the girl on the back of Turtle. Turtle soon got tired from this burden, and the birds knew that he would need something to rest upon. They persuaded Toad to dive into the water and bring back some mud, which he put on Turtle's back. Soon the earth—and Turtle—began to spread out in all directions. Before long, there was plenty of land and the girl, now known as Star Woman, had children.

These events occurred, of course, at a time when animals and people shared many characteristics, including speech, and could understand each other pretty well, a time that has for various reasons passed. But the animals all still retain the original spark, their spirit. No traditional Indian culture denies them this.

For some American Indians, the continent of North America is known as Turtle Island. Even more widespread is the theme of the earth diver, the figure who must dive into the depths of the primeval, undifferentiated world of water and bring up the makings of earth to provide a place for the creatures to live. Thus was primal order created from primal chaos, the void. The earth diver is common among the Inuits (Eskimos) and the Athapascan people of the Arctic and far north; among many tribes of the Plains, the Southeast, and the Northeast; as well as among many tribes of California and western Arizona. It is a common theme also in central Asia, Mongolia, and Siberia, as well as among the Ainu of Japan and some of the northernmost peoples of Europe. This suggests that the essential features of this version of creation are something those who would become American Indians brought with them. Some Indian people simply say that is backward: quite obviously it all originated here and spread to other lands.

Another element common to many such stories and virtually omnipresent in American Indian cultures is the trickster—who appears as Raven, Hare, Coyote, Spider, and in other forms. The trickster is a dangerous character, usually capable of transforming himself into any form he chooses, in order to wreak what is usually a certain amount of havoc. For example, when the Navajo's First Man was methodically placing stars into the sky, forming the seven basic constellations, Coyote came along and impatiently threw the rest randomly into the sky, where they remain in disorderly fashion. The trickster is also a collection of base appetites and no scruples, going through all sorts of calisthenics and cons to take the major share of food and to make love with any and all who catch his fancy. Ribald, humorously scandalous, slippery, the trickster is also quite often in on the original creation, sometimes its chief agent, and with predictable results. For a California group called the Maidus, Coyote played a major and not salubrious role in the origins of things, once Turtle and a figure called Earth Initiate had created some land out of a world that was merely night and water:

Raven mask, Northwest coast

Before long, Coyote emerged of his own accord and watched as Earth Initiate created all the animals out of clay, along with First Man and First Woman. Trying to do the same thing, Coyote botched the job because he laughed while making them. Earth Initiate scolded him, saying that he had told Coyote not to laugh. And Coyote replied that he hadn't laughed—the world's first lie.

Where does the trickster come from? Scholars of comparative religion report that the trickster in whatever form is an element common to many cultures—African and Asian, for example, as well as North American. They see in him an analogue of the shaman, the magical one who can disappear into the world of spirits, defy time and space, change form, challenge the towering forces of evil, and enlist the forces of good—the healer in many ancient cultures. What may be depictions of the shaman occur in the famed caves of France dating back some twenty thousand years. Such healers are often loners: given their ability to deal directly with the supernatural, to wrestle with both evil and good, they may also be sorcerers and are widely respected, even feared, as such. Many Indian people who have seen their cultures, their lives, change in order to survive identify closely with this shape-changing figure, the trickster.

An altogether different explanation of how this world came to be is found chiefly in the Southwest, primarily among the more settled, pueblo-dwelling tribes along the upper Rio Grande in New Mexico and, to the west, among the Hopis, though elaborate versions exist among the neighboring Apaches and Navajos and elsewhere. The Hopis today live in twelve separate villages and count some thirty clans among them. Each clan has its own version of the same basic creation story, what scholars call *emergence stories*. One version, here much abbreviated, goes like this:

> In the beginning there was endless space in which nothing existed but Tawa, the sun spirit, who gathered the elements of space and added some of his own substance, thereby creating the First World. This world was inhabited by insectlike creatures who lived in caves and squabbled with one another ceaselessly. Dissatisfied, Tawa sent a new spirit, Spider Grandmother, to lead them on a long journey, during which they changed form and grew fur like dogs, wolves, and bears.
>
> They arrived in the Second World but still didn't understand the meaning of life, so Tawa created a Third World, lighter and moist, and sent Spider Grandmother again to lead them. By the time they arrived in the Third World, they had become people, and Spider Grandmother told them to renounce evil and live harmoniously with one another. They built villages and planted corn, and Spider Grandmother taught them to weave and make pots. But it was cold in the Third World: the pots didn't bake and the corn didn't grow.
>
> Sometime later, a Hummingbird arrived, telling of yet another world, above the sky, ruled by Masauwu, who was owner of fire and caretaker of the place of the dead. The Hummingbird taught the people to make fire with a drill, and left. The people learned to bake pottery in the fire and warmed their cornfields with fires.
>
> Things went well in the Third World until sorcerers began turning the people's minds from virtue. Men gambled, women revolted, rains failed, and so did the corn. Again Spider Grandmother arrived, saying

that it was time to leave this world and go forth to the Upper World. The chief and some wise men sent a Sparrow up into the sky, and he found an opening there but was blown away by the winds. Next a Dove was sent, flew through the opening, and found a lifeless world spreading out in all directions. He flew back and made his report.

The wise men then sent a Hawk, who reported the same thing, and then a Catbird, who returned saying that the people had been invited to come up by Masauwu. But how were they supposed to reach the hole in the sky? Spider Grandmother again intervened, reminding them that Chipmunk planted seeds that grew into trees. So they enlisted Chipmunk, who planted several different trees that didn't grow tall enough, and finally he tried a bamboo reed, which reached through the hole. This was called the *sipapuni*, and Chipmunk explained that they could climb up through it because it was hollow.

The wise men drew four lines in the ground and said that any sorcerers crossing the lines would perish. Then, led by Spider Grandmother and her twin sons, the people climbed up the reed into the upper world, the present Fourth World of the Hopis.

It can be difficult for non-Indian people to comprehend that for Indians brought up in their own peoples' traditions, history is more than a sequence of events objectively recounted. History is the story of one's people's past, to be sure, but also the story of one's personal identity. And beyond that, history is also something akin to Aesop's *Fables*—moral lessons, a blueprint for conducting a proper life. In such a complex realm, chronology is not of paramount importance, nor is it important to adduce connective tissue between accounts of significant events. Perceiving, however dimly, such a different style of thinking, many non-Indian scholars—anthropologists and historians—have concluded that preliterate people whose creation stories are what we call myths have a minimally developed sense of time's arrow flying from the past toward a future, but instead think of time as a cyclical matter. Time seen as an endlessly repeated cycle is a difficult concept for most non-Indian Americans to grasp, except for those who, like the American Indians during most of their existence, have been tied—even shackled—directly to the land, making a living only by carefully heeding the cycles of the year and its seasons.

To suggest, however, that such preliterate people had no real concept of the passage of years is, at best, condescending. In the long, involved creation story of the Navajos—indeed, what could be thought of as a major epic poem—chronological events are carefully recited when needed: for example, to explain the order in which the first people proliferated into the different Navajo clans. Many if not most tribes have mnemonic devices—such as the Iroquois' belts of wampum (beads)—with which they have long kept track of the complex chronologies of their past, both distant and recent. In another example of non-Indian confusion about all this, a respected linguist, Benjamin Whorf, pointed out in the early years of the twentieth century that the Hopis made essentially no distinction (in tenses) between the past and the present, and spoke of the future as a matter of individual and group urges. This was then expanded into the notion that Hopi language and thought patterns were the linguistic equivalent of quantum mechanics! The Hopis think all that is pretty silly: they have extremely long memories, more tenses available to them than the English language has, and a thoroughly developed notion of historical chronology. And when a chronological account is important, such as in an argument over rights to a particular piece of land, they trot it out with great precision. Even so, tension continues to exist between Indian and non-Indian versions of history—tensions that may well not be reconcilable but that, instead, will continue to exist as a paradox. The world is aswarm with paradoxes, however. They are the plague of reason.

Virgin Country: Pleistocene America

What awaited people when they emerged onto this continent, indeed this hemisphere? Nothing all that surprising—at least to begin with. In Siberia they would have already learned to follow the big grazing animals of northern Asia. Early Siberians seem to have used mastodon bone for fuel and for home construction, but in their middens were mostly the remains of rabbit and fox, which could also supply needed furs. By some twenty thousand years ago, and probably earlier, bands of Stone Age hunters and gatherers had extended their range throughout Europe and most of Asia, reaching as far as eastern Siberia. These people, operating at the ultima Thule of human habitation at the time, were accustomed to the cold, to seasons of the year when it was almost always dark (or always light), to cracking flakes off cold rocks with cold hands to make weapons. Following their prey eastward, they had passed mountainous horizons of ice glaciers that possessed much of the north country—and no doubt knew that enormous floods of water could explode from under them unpredictably, so they probably kept their distance. Surely they did not bother to challenge these great walls of ice, for they were as lifeless as the driest desert.

Moving eastward from Siberia, they encountered not a frigid sea but more of the same—steppelike land covered mostly with grasses, sparse to be sure but sufficient to support game animals, especially near watercourses that crossed this landscape and in marshy areas. This was Beringia, a mass of land about a thousand miles wide from north to south that led eastward to Alaska, where the greatest glacier in the world had reached its westernmost configuration. Some two miles thick at its maximum points, this great blanket of ice had taken up the oceans' waters and, at its height in this period some twenty thousand years ago, lowered the sea level by as much as five hundred feet in some areas, more than sufficient to expose the huge land bridge that today lies under the Bering Sea. It was dry land from about twenty-five thousand years ago to about 14,500 years ago; and until ten thousand years ago the seas there were shallow enough to freeze over, allowing for passage between the continents. In the long interval when the land bridge was exposed, the Aleutian Islands were no fogbound archipelago but an icebound thumb projecting into the sea. This was part of an ice sheet, called the Cordilleran, that followed the southern coast of Alaska and turned southward down the west coast of Canada, extending as far as Washington State. It was a relatively minor glacier compared to the Laurentide ice sheet, which covered most of northern North America well into the Arctic, all of Canada and Greenland, and land as far to the south as New Jersey. The enormous glacier's vast grinding processes were gouging out what would become the Great Lakes, which would fill with water when the glacier finally receded. From there it swept northwestward through the Missouri River drainage into the Yukon and up along Alaska's Brooks Range. Between this unimaginably vast ice sheet and the smaller Cordilleran, a narrow corridor opened and closed, from time to time providing a (forbidding) way south from the wedge of open land that persisted across Alaska.

South of the ice, the climate was generally wetter and overall somewhat colder. What we think of today as northern deciduous forests—oak, hickory, beech—lined the Gulf coast, and blue spruce grew in the

Great Basin, which today is a sagebrush desert. Moderated (oddly enough) by the ice, the seasonal variation in temperature was slight. Winters were in fact slightly warmer than today, and the plenitude of forage for grazers was constant. These were the herds of woolly mammoths grazing on grasses, loner mastodons browsing on twigs and spruce needles, great assemblages of caribou, gigantic sloths weighing up to three tons, beavers weighing two hundred pounds or more, camels, horses, peccaries, herds of giant bison. They were preyed on by the likes of saber-toothed and other cats, long-legged eagles, and short-faced bears that were larger than grizzlies and fast as horses. Enormous vultures swung through the skies, peering earthward for carrion, for which they competed with dire wolves and other scavengers. Even the land itself was larger then: the east coast was hundreds of miles farther east than today, parts of the west coast some fifty miles farther west. Teeth of mammoths have been dredged up far out on today's continental shelves. Beringia was, of course, a two-way street: horses and camels, which evolved in the Western Hemisphere, would find their way to Asia and beyond, while (but for llamalike descendants) dying out here in due course.

The birth, life, and death of glaciers remains something of a mysterious dance, involving the precessional bowing of the earth over time in its orbit, the conga-line sway of the jet streams, the slow minuet of ocean currents, and a host of other performances. They come into being when the accumulation of snow exceeds its melting at sites called domes, gravity making ice of snow, and its weight forcing the ice out from the bottom to spread across the land. Twenty thousand years ago, the Laurentide ice sheet contained one-third of all the glacial ice on the planet. Three thousand years later, it had begun to decay around the edges, and unimaginable amounts of meltwater were streaming away from it, rearranging the landscape, producing and enlarging such vast river systems as the Mississippi. The weight of the ice had lowered the continent's surface itself and gouged out vast depressions that became lakes. A glacier-torn path eastward from the Great Lakes became today's Saint Lawrence River, sending icy meltwater toward the north Atlantic. Desert conditions began to inch northward from the Gulf of California, and as the American Southwest began to warm up, the subarctic plant life there found a haven only on the tops of some higher mountains. Silt-laden waters flowing seaward produced sandy littorals—beaches—and marshlands that moved ever inland with the rising seas. Here and there, salt water would invade the land as inland seas, until glacial meltwater filled them at least partially with silt and cut them off; such a place was Lake Champlain.

By 13,500 years ago, glaciers were mostly a thing of the past in today's lower forty-eight of the United States. By ten thousand years ago, the Laurentide ice sheet had withdrawn entirely into Canada, and the Cordilleran was found only in mountain highlands. The earth's axis had tilted to its greatest angle: summers were growing hotter (hotter than today) and winters colder. In a grand patchwork, southern plants were marching north, and with them, food chains were forging new links. The landscape and the climate of the continent were changing as rapidly and as profoundly as they ever had before. This was the beginning of what is called the Holocene era (in which we live today), and of course, people had long since arrived here.

The First Americans: Who Were They and When Did They Come?

To begin with, the first humans to arrive on this continent would almost surely not have considered themselves the first Americans (assuming for the sake of argument that they could have imagined that this new land would be called America). For these were people who felt akin to other creatures in a way that few people alive today can imagine—and the other creatures were here already: *they* were the first Americans. The first humans here came from a tradition perhaps as old as the dawn of *Homo sapiens sapiens,* some one hundred thousand years ago, but surely a tradition present some twenty thousand years ago, when people made magnificent pictures, in caves, of animals and people and of beings who were partly both. These latter were—we can imagine—animal masters, shamans who could enter the hidden world of spirits and essences and converse with all the beings that arose from and returned to the motherlike earth: one interdependent family. Though driven by the same physiological and mental urges that we all still share today, these people probably made few prideful distinctions between themselves and the other creatures who sustained them. Nowhere in today's world do fellow creatures—such as ravens, coyotes, turtles, bears, deer—play a larger role in a people's origin stories than among American Indians.

■ ■ ■

Just who these first American humans were and when they arrived is one of the great, and most controversial, questions that confront the modern archaeologist (not to mention the Indian descendants of these pioneers), and has confronted people of such mind for hundreds of years. Were the Indians encountered here the progeny of the lost tribes of Israel? Or, it has been asked in more recent times, could some of them at least have arrived in boats made of straw, drifting across the ocean from Phoenicia on accommodating currents? Or from Europe? Or the South Seas? Could the Negroid features of the monumental stone heads of the Olmecs mean that Africans visited here anciently? Such questions tantalize, fascinate, and make headlines, as does any sign that humans may have been here for longer than previously or currently supposed. Some Indian people today—Sioux political scientist Vine Deloria Jr. among them—say that humanity arose here, in this hemisphere, in the first place and spread around the world. Others, both Indian and non-Indian, have an urge to press ever backward the time when humans crossed Beringia (or paddled here in boats or waded through shallow seas).

It is by no means clear why many non-Indian Americans are so anxious to establish ever-earlier dates for the arrival here of the ancestors of the American Indian. After all, the very newness of the United States has always been one of its greatest causes of self-congratulation. That a nation could have accomplished so much in so short a time is taken as a plus: why not, then, for the native population? Against romantic notions of origins and claims of great ancientness—some reaching as far back as two hundred thousand years ago—the plodding, systematic, cautionary archaeologist whisking away the dust from old and mute moments encased in the earth can seem the stuffiest of fuddy-duddies, and a spoilsport to boot. Until only the final years of the twentieth century, the vast majority of archaeologists agreed that the earliest definitive and unarguable sign of humanity on this continent dated to about 11,500 years ago. Over the years, and even in the past decade, there have been claims by individual archaeologists—announced to the press with an enthusiasm that matches that of NASA when it finds what it hopes are signs of life in a Martian meteorite in Antarctica—that human artifacts from layers dating back, say, thirty-five thousand years have been found. On closer (and peer) inspection, such finds have typically been found to be overly enthusiastic, often the result of any number of natural processes that rearrange layers of earth, or contaminate artifacts like hearths, or push stone tools up or down through layers, changing age estimates greatly.

For nearly seventy years, the earliest unambiguous sign of human habitation in North America was a projectile point found in 1932, embedded among the ribs of a woolly mammoth near the town of Clovis, New Mexico. (The date of 11,500 years ago awaited the development of radiocarbon dating techniques in the 1950s.) The find followed the discovery in 1927 of a similar but smaller and finer projectile point at Folsom, New Mexico, also associated with the remains of an animal—a species of bison long since extinct. The

Clovis point

Clovis projectile point soon became the signature artifact of a culture that, in this general period of time, inhabited most of the continent, however sparsely—across the Plains and as far east as Florida—and signs of what was thought to be Clovis work have been found as far south as Tierra del Fuego. Clovis Man was taken to be a highly skilled culture of hunters who preyed on mammoths and other gigantic herbivores of the time.

The Clovis-style point may well be the most famous such point in the world and is certainly among the most beautiful and beautifully crafted—it was a thrusting blade for a spear or javelin, and it was made by percussion, the banging of rock. It also remains among the most puzzling. For one thing, it is extremely elaborate. Not only did the maker have to knock away tiny flakes from both sides to make the

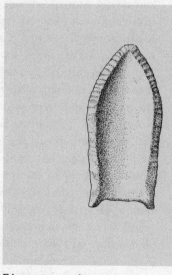

Folsom point, actual size

two sharp edges, but once that very arduous (and parlous) task was accomplished, he had to break off the ridges on either side to provide the point with its famous fluted configuration—the channel running about halfway up the point on each side. (Fluting is unique to the Americas, totally unknown elsewhere.) The slightest slip of the hand would ruin the entire piece, with hours of labor lost. And yet no one can figure out what advantage the fluted sides conferred on the point. They are not needed to fit the point firmly to a shaft. Some wonder if the fluting may have been a ritual matter of some kind that spread, along with the hunting culture, rapidly through the land. Also puzzling is that there appears to be no direct antecedent to this technology, no evolutionary steps leading to Clovis points, and such changes usually take place over long, long intervals. But not the Clovis points. They and their makers appear to have simply burst upon the scene as if from nowhere. Less sophisticated points have been found in Alaska, more or less contemporary with the Clovis era, that are much thicker in cross section than the elegant Clovis points.

Along with the distinctive Clovis points was a tool chest that consisted of various scrapers, knifelike artifacts, wrenchlike bone tools supposedly used for straightening spear shafts, and amazingly fine bone needles, presumably used for sewing hides together for clothing and shelter. More puzzling Clovis artifacts are enigmatic rods of bone, beveled at both ends and crosshatched, perhaps used in some manner to attach points to shafts. Clovis points ceased being made about five hundred years after they appeared—ending at the same time that the last of thirty-six *genera* (not species but genera) of North American mammals also disappeared from the paleontological record. Most of the creatures that went extinct were large—from 110 pounds to more than four tons among the elephantine animals. No such rapid mammalian extinctions occurred on any other continent at this time; here, in a few thousand years (what amounts to a trice in geological time), some 80 percent of the continent's megafauna were gone. And soon after the dates of his time here were firmly established by radiocarbon dating, Clovis Man, the only candidate then known for first American, would be accused of bringing about this mass extinction, a controversy to which we will return in the next chapter.

In the last decade of the twentieth century, the Clovis bar, as it has been called, has been lifted, and the Bering land bridge called into question as the sole or even main route to the New World. Numerous sites over the years since the 1930s had been proposed as pre-Clovis, but all of them had failed for one reason or another to convince the field of archaeology. On the other hand, in the 1960s, several sites in Tierra del Fuego were reliably pegged as human settlements and convincingly dated to about eleven thousand years ago. The notion that people (with a limited tool kit of stone and bone) could have made it overland from Alaska to the southernmost tip of South America in about five hundred years seemed to many to be asking too much of these ancestral people, however athletic and skilled they may have been.

Speculation of that sort, however, gave way to actual archaeological evidence in the late 1990s, based on two major excavations that began in the 1970s, thousands of miles apart—one in South America and one in North America.

In January 1998, a group of distinguished and skeptical archaeologists (what one wag called the "paleopolice") trooped down to south central Chile. There, in a marshy area along a creek, a multidisciplinary team under the leadership of Thomas D. Dillehay of the University of Kentucky had long been digging a site called Monte Verde. After careful, on-the-ground checking of their colleague's two-decades-plus of work, the distinguished panel agreed that here, about ten thousand miles south of Beringia, people had lived some 12,500 years ago.

Monte Verde is an area of sandy hillocks and damp forest and, importantly, bogs. The bogs covered the old settlement with peat, preserving it like a specimen in formaldehyde, and water provided anaerobic conditions in which bacteria could not thrive. Once excavated, the site provided not only remains of stone and bone tools, often the only remaining artifacts from such early sites, but also wooden structures, hunks of meat, and even partially chewed vegetable matter. Radiocarbon dates established an early date for this settlement of some 12,500 years ago; five hundred years after that, what may have been a young adult walked across some soft clay that had been imported to make improvements in one of the village's hearths. The clay hardened, preserving three of this person's footprints, one of them showing the heel, toes, and arch. These people lived (Dillehay reported), many of them year-round, in a sixty-foot-long building with a frame of wooden planks and logs and walls of poles covered with hides, all of this tied together with string made from reeds. Inside, separate quarters were marked off with planks and poles, each having a hearth in a clay-lined pit—in all, enough residential space for some twenty to thirty people. Outside were communal hearths, supplies of firewood, and a nearby cache of mastodon meat.

Another feature of the village was a building made of wooden uprights in a foundation of gravel and sand that had been hardened with animal fat. Here they butchered mastodon, prepared hides, and made tools. This, Dillehay suggested, may well have been the shaman's healing center as well, for the structure also contained the remains of some thirty-five plants still in use locally to cure such ailments as stomachaches, rheumatism, and various infections. Many of these plants are found only thirty-five miles away, on the coast, from which these people also imported various kinds of edible seaweed, salt, wave-smoothed pebbles, and bitumen for attaching stone tools to wooden shafts.

The Monte Verdeans ate mastodon and early forms of the llama, but also smaller animals, freshwater shellfish, local wild potatoes, as well as plants from local marshes and other, more distant areas. (There is no reason to think that the nomadic Clovis hunters did not take smaller animals and gather plant food when the opportunity presented itself—a situation far more frequent than the availability of killable large mammals.) It appears that some of the Monte Verdeans specialized in collecting coastal resources (certain fruits and tubers), which they pre-pared with special tools made of quartz, while others specialized in preparing animal skins with stone scrapers. Their tools were quite sim-ple, nothing as sophisticated as the Clovis point. Instead, along with wooden digging sticks and some bone tools, they mostly used frac-tured stone pebbles for many tasks.

Another site, in Brazil, may be of similar age, and in North Amer-ica, a rock shelter in Pennsylvania has yielded evidence that conclu-sively indicates pre-Clovis habitation by human groups. This is the Meadowcroft Rockshelter, located some thirty miles southwest of Pittsburgh, a place that was inhabited—on and off—until historical times. Beginning in the 1970s, it has been thoroughly excavated by a team led by James M. Adovasio, now of Mercyhurst College, in Erie, its astonishing eleven separate levels being carbon-dated (in all, some fifty-two dates were established). One of these layers, noted as stra-tum IIA, contained three sublayers, the lowest (and therefore earliest of the three) being sealed off from the late ones by a layer of rock that simply fell from the roof of the shelter, a process called spalling. The

sublayer below the spalling contains
an array of clearly man-made stone
artifacts that could have been made
over a period of six thousand years;
they yielded an *average* date of about
14,500 years ago, with the oldest date
being about sixteen thousand years
ago. Early critics noted that this site
was in a rich coal-bearing area and that
the artifacts—hearths in particular—
could have been contaminated, but
Adovasio's meticulous analyses, and
those of others expert in such matters,
have shown no sign of anything that
might have contaminated the samples
used for carbon dating.

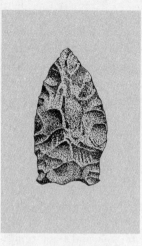

Meadowcroft Rockshelter point

Another criticism arose from a ques-
tion of timing. Fourteen to sixteen thousand years ago, the southern
edge of the Laurentide ice sheet lay a mere hundred miles north of
the Meadowcroft Rockshelter, and presumably it was a place of violent, swirling, icy winds that plummeted downslope off the glacier,
a region that would be forbiddingly cold at the very least. The
ground underfoot, it was said, would have been tundra, maybe even
permafrost, and at least a subarctic forest. Yet no sign of such ecosystems have been found in stratum IIA. Instead, the archaeologists
identified charcoal from oak and hickory trees and the remains of
deer and passenger pigeons—temperate creatures all. On the other
hand, Adovasio answered, the rock shelter itself is lower in elevation
than those sites where earlier scientists have established an allegedly
uniform tundra-type ecosystem for the edge of the glacier. Also, the
shelter faces south and, obviously, did harbor a temperate-zone
ecosystem despite the relative proximity of the glacier's edge.
Indeed, it is a fallacy that the glaciers brought with them, to their
edges, all of the features of the Arctic. Permafrost, for example, and
even tundra conditions would not necessarily occur at the glacier's
edge, particularly if it was melting.

By the end of the twentieth century, Meadowcroft was almost
universally taken as the earliest confirmed site of human habitation
in North America, clearly pre-Clovis by as much as three to five

thousand years. Like the Monte Verde site, Meadowcroft also turned up some tantalizing signs of even earlier habitation—for example, a fragment of a basket that was dated to at least seventeen thousand years ago, and perhaps two or three thousand years earlier.

Given these secure pre-Clovis dates, archaeologists began to explore alternate modes of arrival to hiking over Beringia. It was not unreasonable to imagine that people in hide boats followed the Pacific Ocean's version of the Gulf Stream to the north and then east, down the coast of the Americas. Or they might have made their way by foot *before* the last glacial maximum, about twenty thousand years ago, snaking down through the westernmost mountains, where the glacier was not a solid sheet but was confined to the mountaintops.

There, at the turn of the twenty-first century, the matter rested: still an enigma, and a question that will remain wide open for some years, if not decades. It is always useful to remember that science is not designed to produce absolute knowledge, eternally true once found; for the most part it simply pushes back the frontier of that vast realm called ignorance.

Who were these first inhabitants? Did they come in the form of a small group whose descendants populated the hemisphere, or in separate waves of people? And how did they—whoever they were—manage to adapt to conditions that ranged from the Arctic steppes of Alaska to the subtropical swamps of the Everglades, from the heavily canopied forests of the east to the arid deserts and canyon lands of the Southwest? These latter questions—how these first American humans went about conducting their lives in this new world—is the subject of ensuing chapters. But as for the question of who they were, recent evidence from a strange alliance of disparate fields of science has begun to piece together a coherent story.

In the first place—to dwell again on the time that native populations arrived in North America—most linguists would be greatly pleased to have it shown that people have been here far longer than fifteen thousand years. That is because they have identified about three hundred different spoken North American Indian languages in use at the time of European contact, these deriving from six or (as some argue) eight different root, or basic language, stocks, called *phyla*. For example, one phylum is called Macro-Siouan and it includes the languages of such Plains tribes as the Crows, Mandans, Omahas, Winnebagos, and of course, Sioux, but also the languages of the Mohawks and other Iroquoian tribes of New York State and Canada, along with the languages of the Cherokees (who were from the Carolinas) plus—in other, separate subgroupings, or families— the Catawbas, the Caddoan tribes, and the Yuchis. By much linguistic reckoning—of such matters as how long it takes for a fundamental root word such as that for "mother" or "sun" to change from a mother tongue—fifteen thousand years seems too short to account for such remarkable linguistic diversity.

One of these phyla includes the ten languages of the Eskimos and Aleuts of the far north; another includes the thirty-eight languages called Athapaskan (mostly northern Canadian, but including the Apache tribes and the Navajos, as well as some California groups). It has long been taken as sure that the Athapaskan-speaking people— also called Na-Denes—were relatively late arrivals on the continent, followed yet later by the Eskimos and Aleuts. If that is true, it leaves well over two hundred languages spoken by other American Indians at the time of Columbus's voyages, which represent a great deal of linguistic evolution (though nothing like the polyglot world of New Guinea, where some seven hundred languages existed). Could some of the linguistic diversity of America, therefore, have taken place in Asia? Could that diversity suggest that several different groups of people arrived here, presumably at different times? Or was it essentially one group of people who wandered out on the steppes of Beringia and wound up populating a hemisphere? In the late 1980s, a controversial linguist named Joseph Greenberg announced that all the languages of the entire hemisphere except Na-Dene and Eskimo-Aleut arose from a single root language he called Amerind. Among his reasons was that all of the Amerind languages—some nine hundred in the entire hemisphere—share about 280 words and a few grammatical forms (most notably, and uniquely among the languages of the world, the first person pronoun beginning with n and the second person with m). This was strong evidence for a single group of people who shared a single language being the first arrivals, particularly when it was added to other evidence, arising from such disparate fields as genetics and the study of teeth.

All humans share the same basic dental patterns, but different groups share certain minor, or secondary, dental characteristics. All humans, for example, have thirty-two adult teeth, including first molars, but some groups have different numbers of roots on the first molar. In all, there are more than twenty different secondary characteristics to human teeth. Christy Turner of Arizona State University made a study of two hundred thousand teeth from nine thousand prehistoric American Indians, along with thousands of teeth from Siberia, Asia, Africa, and Europe. Based on all these secondary characteristics, it is possible to distinguish Asian teeth from African and European, and to separate the Asian into two separate groups. One of these is called *sundadont* and characterizes populations from Southeast Asia. These people show up in the fossil record perhaps thirty thousand years ago. From this group, the second—called *sinodonts*—evidently evolved into most northern Asians and *all* the native populations of the Western Hemisphere. One of the traits of sinodonty, which arose in Asia about twenty thousand years ago, is extra ridges on the insides of upper incisors, which give them a distinctive shovel shape. Another, perhaps most telling, trait is that sinodonts possess three roots on the lower first molars. Of course, there is variation among sinodonts. Na-Dene teeth are different from Eskimo-Aleut teeth, and both types differ from those of the rest of the Indian people of the hemisphere. All told, paleodentistry matched the evidence of Greenbergian linguistics, and added an approximate timescale.

Over the years, geneticists have found a somewhat hazy picture when confronting the ultimate source of hereditary features—which is hardly surprising, given the millennia of gene exchange from mating, inbreeding, and random changes, or mutations, of genetic material (DNA). But mitochondrial DNA is inherited exclusively from the mother and it changes, or mutates naturally, five or ten times faster than the DNA in the cell's nucleus. Scientists have been able to clock such changes: on average, every 1 million years, between 2 and 4 percent of mitochondrial DNA will have mutated of its own accord. Groups of Indians widely separated geographically had nearly identical variations in mitochondrial DNA, which means that the ancestral group of all of them had to be very small. Further, since the variations common to native people in this hemisphere share only a very few characteristics with Asians' variations, it is clear that the clock began, in effect, to tick once they arrived here. And by this kind of reckoning, that moment was sometime between twenty-one thousand and forty-two thousand years ago. The more recent date would, of course, accord more or less gracefully with the sort of dates that archaeologists are turning up in places like Monte Verde; meanwhile, this biochemical measure also suggests that there might have been a second pulse of people arriving about the time of the Clovis culture, and then the Na-Denes and then the Eskimo-Aleuts.

The single story told by genes, teeth, and language immediately ran into problems. There arose a storm of criticism of Greenbergian linguistics, generally arguing that it oversimplifies things, disguising differences and overemphasizing similarities. More recently, linguist Johanna Nichols of the University of California believes she has uncovered a way of tracing languages back further in time than the six thousand years most historical linguists say is the limit beyond which the roots of languages disappear into the mists. She looks at underlying grammatical building blocks, rather than sounds and syllables and words, assuming that such basic features hark further back in time. The position of a verb in a sentence (at the end, in the middle, or up front) is such a marker, as is the attachment of a prefix to a verb to register tense. She has mapped these building blocks in the lands surrounding the Pacific Ocean, and her researches, in short, suggest that numerous groups of people migrated in waves to this hemisphere over many thousands of years, leaving plenty of time for people to have fetched up in southern Chile and near Pittsburgh.

Similarly, molecular geneticists have found several mitochondrial DNA lineages present in native populations—the lineages are called haplogroups—four of which, labeled A, B, C, and D, are found only in Asians and not anywhere else. A few other haplogroups are also found in Indian populations, but in smaller numbers, including one labeled X, which occurs minimally in Europeans but more fully in people from the Indian subcontinent.

To complicate matters yet further, in the public mind at least, some skeletal remains turned up in the 1990s of what seems to be a Caucasoid individual who may have been here as early as some nine thousand years ago, or even earlier—a skeleton found in the state of Washington and called Kennewick Man. To the dismay of many Indians, the fourth estate leapt upon these nine-thousand-year-old bones, speculating that Europeans were the first to come upon the new world (ignoring the already established earlier dates), and evidently a group of Norway lovers in California soon tried to claim some Indian lands in court as a result. At the same time, to the dismay of the archaeologists, the

Indian tribe on whose reservation lands the Kennewick skeleton was found sought to withdraw it from further scientific scrutiny. And some archaeologists themselves have suggested that Caucasoids (not necessarily European ancestors but people genetically like the aboriginal Japanese—the Ainu) arrived here from Europe bearing a Clovislike tool culture called Solutrean (which is known from southwestern Europe twenty to thirty thousand years ago), having sailed or drifted across the Atlantic Ocean to be among the first on the continent. And here, on the east coast, they would have (for reasons unexplained) developed the fluting common to Clovis points and spread this technology to the *west*. Yet other archaeologists are calling such notions nonsense, not to mention a more scatological term deriving from livestock industry waste products.

For now, then, who exactly the first Americans were and when exactly they arrived remains a tantalizing mystery—in science if not among the Indian people themselves.

CHAPTER TWO

HUNTERS AND GATHERERS

A Magical Bear

The Cherokee tell a story about a young hunter:

> A man trekked up into the mountains bent on killing a bear. Eventually he saw one and shot it with an arrow from his bow. The bear spun around and ran noisily into the sun-dappled forest, crashing through the underbrush. The hunter followed, loosing arrow after arrow at the bear, but the wounded bear would not fall.
>
> Finally, the bear stopped and pulled the hunter's arrows from its body, and held them out to the man.
>
> "There's no use shooting these arrows at me," the bear said. "You cannot kill me." The hunter realized that this was a medicine bear, protected by magic. "Come to my house," the bear said. "We can live there together."
>
> The hunter immediately feared for his life, but the bear knew his thoughts. "No, no," it said. "I won't hurt you." The hunter next wondered to himself what he would eat if he lived with this magical bear. And the bear said, "There will be plenty to eat."
>
> So the hunter followed along until they came to a hole in the side of the mountain.
>
> "This isn't where I live, but there will be a council here, and we should attend it to see what they do."

Inside, the hole widened out into a vast cave with houses ringing it. Many bears had assembled there already—old and young bears, bears of all colors—and the chief of all the bears was a huge white one. The hunter and his companion slipped into a corner to wait for the council to begin, but the bears began sniffing the air and complaining of a bad smell. Hearing this, the chief bear said, "Don't make rude comments. It is only a stranger who has joined us. Leave him alone."

The council meeting concerned the growing scarcity of food in the mountains, but some bears had found a new feeding ground where the chestnuts and acorns were plentiful, so the bears held a dance of celebration and went home. The hunter and his companion bear left as well, and eventually came to another hole, the bear's home, and went in.

Knowing the hunter was hungry, the bear rubbed his stomach and his paws filled up with food—huckleberries, blackberries, and acorns— enough for the hunter and the bear to live through the cold sleep of winter, when time stands still. As the winter wore on, the man grew long hair on his body, like that of bears, and learned the ways of bears.

Spring came and the earth began to warm, and the bear said, "Your people down below, they are getting ready to come into the mountains for a big hunt. They will find this cave and kill me. They will take away my clothes and cut me into pieces. No, no, they will not kill you. They will take you home with them. Don't be fearful."

And soon, when the earth was a little warmer, the bear said, "This is the day they come. Their dogs, the split-noses, will find me, and the men will drag me out and skin me and cut me up. You must cover my blood with leaves and go with them. But when they are taking me away, look back and you will see something."

Soon enough, dogs approached and barked, the men shot arrows into the cave, killing the bear, and they dragged him outside, skinned him, and quartered him. Then they looked back in the cave, thinking they saw another bear in the shadows. The hunter quivered in fear, but the men realized that, under the long bearlike fur, it was the hunter who had disappeared a year earlier. They invited him to come home with them.

Before leaving, the hunter piled leaves over the bloody spot where his bear companion had been skinned and butchered. Sadly, he set off after the men, but paused and turned around. And from under the leaves the bear rose up on his hind legs and shook his great shoulders. Then he dropped to the ground and disappeared into the warming forest.

Zuni bear fetish

Thus, a young man is initiated into the shamanistic mysteries of the hunt and the relationship of man and prey. The bear reads minds, creates food from nothing, and transcends death. The initiate can now speak to the bear, the bear spirit, who will provide many things, including food, so long as the proper negotiations are made. And the initiate will be able to intercede with the bear in his people's behalf. So it almost surely was for the earliest humans in North America, for whom the hunt was so central a feature of life.

We know Clovis Man largely, almost exclusively, from what appear to be kill sites. Typical is a place called Murray Springs, in southern Arizona's San Pedro Valley. Here, at a water hole, a mammoth and eleven bison died, not at the same time, making the site a palimpsest (a literary term for a document that has been written over one or more times). Clovis tools and thousands of stone flakes littered the bone beds, the flakes suggesting that butchering these carcasses called for a great deal of on-the-spot resharpening. Interestingly, spear points associated with the bison here and at other sites tend to be more damaged, with flakes broken off backward from the tip, suggesting that they struck bone on a charging animal. Mammoths seem to have been killed once mired or otherwise immobilized in the muck of water holes—the points involved in such kills usually show little damage and were presumably thrust with great accuracy between the animals' ribs. Most mammoth kills we know of were of juvenile animals, Clovis hunters following the age-old pattern of all predators—that is, to take the easiest prey.

The hunters may often have merely hidden beside such water holes, awaiting the unwary young mammoth, practicing an opportunistic kind of scavenging. A poignant moment may well have occurred at the Murray Springs site, for mammoth tracks lead up to and away from the skeleton: like elephants today, which live in matriarchal herds, the mammoth may have approached its dead relative, inspected it, and gone off in a dim form of grief.

Once successful, the Clovis hunters typically camped near the site, butchering the kill and repairing their tools. Usually, the hunters butchered only part of the carcasses. But success was by no means guaranteed, and even severely wounded animals could get away. For example, several mammoths bearing as many as eight Clovis points, made from the same stone as the Murray Springs points, got away and died later of natural causes, to be found nearby largely intact millennia later. By far, most mammoth remains are of animals that died naturally and not at the hands of human hunters (and this is even more pronounced among mastodons). At a spring near one Clovis site, archaeologists found that someone had carefully deposited a collection of Clovis points, conceivably a shaman's offering against the waywardness of the hunting life, but more likely merely a cache of useful tools, secreted there for future use.

Pleistocene Overkill?

By about 10,800 years ago, most of the larger mammals of North America were extinct, and the Clovis point vanishes from the record. In the 1960s, Paul Martin, a paleobotanist from the University of Arizona, suggested that it was the Clovis hunters who were responsible for this simultaneous calamity. At some point around 11,500 years ago, he said, a band of perhaps one hundred hunting people emerged into the ice-free realms of North America to discover a world teeming with herds of great beasts, none of which had learned to be wary of small, two-legged creatures bearing spears. The hunters experienced stunning, even profligate success in bringing down these beasts and grew rapidly in numbers, spreading with great speed across the continent in a five-hundred-year orgy of killing and feasting. This scenario was called *Pleistocene overkill,* and as can be imagined, it was not well received by those, including Indian people, who were in the 1960s beginning to see Indians and presumably their ancestors as natural ecologists. It did seem to explain the disappearance of those thirty-five genera of mammals, but as H. L. Mencken said, in a wholly unrelated matter, "For every complex problem, there is a solution which is simple, neat, and wrong."

Timing is, if not everything, an important coefficient of the Pleistocene overkill scenario. It depends, first of all, on Clovis Man hunters erupting onto this part of the continent around 11,500 years ago—the first confrontation between *Homo sapiens* and the American megafauna. This no longer seems tenable, given the finds at Monte Verde and Meadowcroft. The scenario depends also on the nearly simultaneous extinction of all that megafauna—the basic question in the first place. But more precise dating in recent years has shown that by twelve thousand years ago, only eight of the missing thirty-five genera still existed, the mammoths and mastodons among them. The others were already gone, having dropped off, species by species, over a good many millennia. This, too, was an era when the Pleistocene was merging into the Holocene, the end of the ice, and with that came more extreme seasonality—hot summers, colder winters—with major shifts in the biotic communities south of the receding glaciers. Indeed, there was a bewildering array of rapidly changing local climate and weather patterns all across the continent, as well as a general drying out, and these were sufficient to have extinguished the likes of sloths and horses and camels of North America, well before Clovis Man or even his ancestors made an appearance.

That hunters may have participated in the final extinction of dwindling numbers of the remaining large-animal types is likely, but these creatures would almost surely have been already on the way out. In fact, what have been seen as mastodon and mammoth kill sites all have been dated to the final centuries of their existence in North America. It is highly likely that Clovis Man simply preyed, occasionally and in an almost scavenging way, on a species that was on its last legs. Once an animal population becomes isolated and small enough, its chances of survival are slight in the best of circumstances. Mastodons, for example, were found mostly in the eastern part of the continent, where they fed chiefly on spruce trees. As the spruce forests were reduced to islands among north-moving deciduous forest, the mastodon population would have been splintered into isolated groups, subject not just to loss of habitat but also to the silent stalker of such populations— inbreeding, which can weaken a species' reproductive capacity in a few generations to the point of dysfunction. The mastodon would have disappeared whether mankind delivered the coup de grâce or not. Such was the fate, after all, of innumerable species and genera in all the preceding ice ages over the previous million years before humans existed. It seems, then, that Clovis Man and his successors are largely off the hook. Indeed, given the rather small number of genuine mammoth kill sites (at last estimate, maybe sixty) and the single known mastodon kill site, some archaeologists suggest that a handful of hunters among the Clovis people may have killed a single mammoth or mastodon in each generation and then talked about it for the rest of their lives.

In any event, people stopped making the leaflike Clovis points, replacing them in the western Plains at least by smaller fluted points (named for the one found in Folsom, New Mexico, a few years before the first Clovis find—see the illustration in the previous chapter). Smaller points were adequate, perhaps even better, for smaller game such as deer and bison; bison were evolving into a smaller version, like today's, in response to changes in the grasslands from tall- to short-grass prairie. Folsom points were pressure-flaked: pieces were flaked off by virtue of pressing a piece of stone or ivory against the point in a subtle manner. This is a more difficult craft than creating a point by just banging rocks together. Folsom points may have been the first points in North America designed to be used with a spear-thrower, what is called an *atlatl*. Folsom points persisted in use chiefly on the Plains for another thousand years, but just why the people who used them, presumably descendants of the Clovis people, made the effort to fashion points of such refined elegance is anybody's guess.

(One might wonder if Clovis peoples' contests with such awesome beasts as the mammoth would not have been passed along through time in stories, and continue however dimly in tribal tradition. At least one possible example of this exists: in the 1930s, the Naskapis of northeastern Labrador told an archaeologist about how their culture hero, a bit of a trickster, managed to slay some monsters that had huge teeth, large heads, and long, trunklike noses.)

Throughout the continent, peoples' lifeways began to differentiate along with the rapidly changing ecosystems where they lived and with the food resources they were left with. Some tools, and particularly points, began to differentiate regionally, and details of clothing might have done the same. Thus might ethnicity have begun in North America, but more likely it was already present in the differing bands of people who came to the new world millennia earlier. In any event, the notion held by wave after wave of Europeans that Indians constituted a single people, and (as is still heard in Washington, D.C.) that there could be a single policy to cover all the American Indians, was surely out of date ten thousand years before Columbus arrived.

Most of us today live in a world that changes so fast that many things disappear from use before they become familiar enough to generate a tradition. In 1998, a Frenchwoman died at age 119; she was born before the invention of the Internet, the computer, the liver transplant, the laser, the jetliner, the atom bomb, TV, radio, the typewriter, the telephone, the automobile, even electric light. It is therefore almost impossible for us to imagine the slow pace of technological change among those whom archaeologists call Paleo-Indians and Archaic Indians (Archaic generally being those who came to rely on smaller game and more plants than Paleo-Indians—a fuzzy border to be sure). It is nearly impossible to imagine the continued, almost religious adherence to a single design of a spear point over five hundred or more years, generation after generation for twenty or more generations.

Of course, change came—impelled by long-term and short-term changes in local, regional, and also global climate, and changes in population numbers. (In some areas, though, what is called the Archaic lifestyle persisted well into the historic, post-Columbian era—indeed, in some places into the twentieth century.) The most direct result of a change in climate is a change in the amount of available biomass that can be exploited—food and, to a lesser extent, fiber. An example of how a subtle change in weather can have a complex and important effect is to be found today in the ranch lands of southeastern Arizona, where for twenty years, beginning in the late 1970s, slightly more rain has fallen in winter than before and the winter temperatures have been slightly higher. Weedy and woody plants like mesquite are favored in such a situation because they are cold-season active, and they have spread at the expense of grasses, which are warm-season active. Similarly, the pine and juniper woodlands above the grasslands are cold-season active and have spread downhill at the expense of grasses. This puts limits on cattle grazing and, over a relatively short time—just a few decades—can put a rancher out of business. Such short-term local shifts have been taking place over eons, and with each shift, local populations had to adapt or move. At a certain point, moving was not an option, thanks to population growth. The most direct result of expanding human populations in a given area is, of course, a change in the amount of food available per person.

People for whom mere subsistence is the main business of each and every day have a limited range of options when the food supply changes significantly, and most of these options were taken up in one place or another in the long prehistory of the American Indians. Another way to think of this all-important matter of food and particularly foraging is that people tend to exploit locally available food sources that provide the most nutrition for the least effort. Taken together, food and population go a long way to explain at least the basics of life as lived during the prehistory of North America.

Beyond the basics, however, lie mystery and speculation. Archaeology can go only so far in explaining what life was like, and old stories passed on for many generations may or may not apply to times that lie far beyond memory and the ability of a spoken tale to remain unchanged. One thing is certain: in many parts of the continent (though not all), vast changes in the basics of life took place during the last centuries *before* Europeans came face-to-face with native populations, and tumultuous, even shattering change took place immediately upon contact. We can only guess at the content of rituals, the nature of child care, feelings (and manners) regarding in-laws, the purpose of a given petroglyph, the ranking of people in a given group or society, or what people found beautiful in the world they inhabited. Exactly how did a favored design for pottery arise, or the striking heraldic emblems of the people of the northwest coast? How sensitive were people about such things as killing and blood? What made people laugh? Was the Creator thought of as female, or male, or both, or neither? In such things, who now is to say?

Nevertheless, the archaeological record of the United States is dauntingly vast, full of material details painstakingly arrived at and thoughtfully considered. It provides an increasingly full outline of how the continent was populated, and how what we call cultures rose and fell (or changed)—each one an experiment in living. Lifetimes of scholarship have been devoted to even the least of these cultures, and any general summary of so long and varied a process is bound to be too short, too limited. The remainder of this chapter shows some of the major patterns of culture that arose in response to the conditions prehistoric people found—particularly environmental conditions, which are something we can know about with great certainty, as opposed to other conditions, like worldviews, which tend to leave fewer clear traces in the ground. What follows can best be thought of as a series of snapshots of life in various relatively distinct areas of the continent through a very long period of time.

Bison Hunting

For thousands of years, until the end of the nineteenth century, people followed the seasonal movements of the great herds of bison that flourished on the short-grass prairies that stretched eastward from the great rain shadow of the Rocky Mountains across the one hundredth meridian to the moister, long-grass prairies that ended west of the Mississippi River. Greater in north-south length than in width, this prairie began well into Canada and extended far south, into Texas and New Mexico. This is an enormous region, seemingly featureless to the unpracticed eye—a sea of grass, covering rolling or dead flat countryside, with a few trees restricted to watercourses, a region where most of the visible world is overhead, the big sky. The people who made a living on the Plains could hunt pronghorn, deer, elk, bear, and other, smaller animals, and they could forage for seasonal foods like prairie turnips, groundnuts, sunflowers, and Jerusalem artichokes. But the prize if not the staple was the bison *(Bison bison bison)*, which was smaller than its Pleistocene ancestors but still a hefty beast at about a ton or more in weight. Hunting such an animal, picking one out from a huge herd and dispatching it on foot with a stone-tipped spear, was

Painting on Sioux buffalo robe, 1884

certainly a parlous art, but it was done—along with the more dramatic, perhaps, but (to us) better understood process of running bison herds over cliffs or into natural corrals.

One hunting place was near Casper, Wyoming, where, some six thousand years ago, hunters made use of a large, parabolic dune of loose sand and steep sides. Probably from a watering hole nearby, they drove the animals into the curve of the sand dune, and as the bisons' hooves sank into the loose sand, the hunters moved in to kill them, each hunter selecting a single animal and ramming a spear through its ribs, into the heart. In another such site, in Colorado, they built a special corral and stampeded the bison into it. Archaeologists found what they took to be a shaman's paraphernalia near the corral—a pole, a flute made from an antler, and a miniature arrowhead. Quite likely, such hunts were organized or at least carefully watched over by someone who could exert some helpful power in the more magical realm of the bison.

Once such a stampede and slaughter was over, the carcasses had to be moved so that they could be butchered. The hunters rolled them onto their stomachs and split the hide down the back, yanking it down onto the ground. The choice cuts thus exposed could be sliced away and eaten or dried. Such drives were communal affairs, when people who normally lived and hunted in what were probably small family groups came together not only for mass hunts but for social purposes such as the choosing of mates. Such a life needed to change very little over time. Improvements (or elaborations) came slowly. By 300 A.D. people on the northwestern Plains were building elaborate corrals at such sites, made of poles set deep into the ground and horizontal timbers wedged between them. In one such place, called the Ruby Corral, near Wyoming's Powder River, the corral was built in a low-lying streambed. Using natural features of the land like ridges and arroyos, the hunters drove bison stampeding toward the corral, which they could not see until it was too late. Here again, it appears that a shaman was looking after his side of things: near a huge processing area up the streambed, archaeologists found the remains of a solid structure of posts with two separate rooms, of which at least one was roofed. In one room were eight skulls of male bison.

As time went by, elaborate bison jumps became more common, good sites being used over and over even for millennia. In such places, archaeologists have found rock cairns forming great Vs stretching from miles away to a cliff or a bluff, boulevards down which the animals were stampeded to their doom. Nearby, below the jump site, temporary camps housed the hunters and their families as the butchering and feasting and processing of meat into pemmican (what we call jerky) took place.

These had to be controlled stampedes, of course, and were accomplished by people on foot. Many drives probably failed since bison are extremely uncooperative beasts. In good times, when the grasses were rich locally and the herds were large and less nomadic, communal hunts were more effective and more common, and the people stayed together in more complex groups for longer periods of the year. But if times were poor, the grass less thick, and the bison moving over greater areas, people had to break up into smaller groups again and life became more nomadic, less socially complex—and presumably lonely. The introduction of the bow and arrow, during the first centuries A.D., probably made buffalo hunting more efficient, but otherwise not much different. The introduction of the horse—and the firearm—would change all that, and change the nature of life on the Plains in other ways as well. But at least on the periphery of this vast ecosystem, changes of an entirely different sort had long been under way.

Hot Rocks and Hostile Plants

Sometime around six to eight thousand years ago, in many parts of North America (and in some areas even earlier), some people began to make a crucial change in lifestyle that, in hindsight, we can say presaged the agricultural revolution. While important, it was not recognized by archaeologists until recently and remains largely unexplored. One place where it has been intensively studied is in south Texas, particularly near the confluence of the Pecos River and the Rio Grande, an area called the Lower Pecos. Today this is an unpromising, desertlike terrain, stretching away endlessly in every direction, covered with hostile and thorny plants—agave, sotol, prickly pear cactus—along with acacia and mesquite. The dry soil is littered with chunks and pebbles of white limestone that give the landscape a bleached, dead appearance. It has looked much like this for a very long time, suffering a continuing cycle of drought and less drought for thousands of years.

In mid-Holocene times, around ninety-eight hundred years ago, the climate in the Lower Pecos was relatively mild and not so dry; grasses covered the rolling terrain, however sparsely, and herds of bison grazed there at least seasonally. In a canyon that winds past today's town of Langtree, Texas (where only a hundred years ago a legendary saloon keeper named Roy Bean declared himself the law west of the Pecos), some people lived seasonally in a rock shelter under a large overhang. It is clear that they used to run bison up a rise to cascade over the edge directly above the overhang. Instead of crashing to the canyon floor, the huge creatures would hit a large outcrop and bounce handily into the rock shelter just below the canyon rim, where they would be promptly butchered—surely a grand, noisy melee. The bones of old bison still litter the outcrop.

Not long afterward, the climate of the Lower Pecos began growing warmer and drier, with a warming trend peaking around six thousand years ago. Grasses gave way to the desert plants common to the landscape today, along with such woody plants as juniper. Presumably, the bison came no more. At about this time, people began digging large pit ovens in their rock shelters and invented (or maybe borrowed from neighbors) a method of cooking that was far more elaborate than the simple spit over a fire needed to roast bison or deer meat. Around such pit ovens are hundreds and hundreds of burnt chunks of limestone, rocks that have been cracked by fire and thrown aside. Evidently, these people lined their pit ovens with arduously collected rock, built fires on the rock lining, added the food they wished to bake, and then covered the pit with more rocks and dirt. What necessitated all this effort?

Presumably, with the bison gone and the climate changing for the worse for most other meat-bearing prey such as deer, the people had to increase their consumption of plants. But in their part of the world, the plants don't just look hostile, they are hostile. Lechuguilla, for example, is a kind of agave (or century plant) that has thick bayonetlike leaves thrusting up from the ground. The steroid-rich sap from the leaves can be used as poison for an arrow tip or to kill fish in a creek. The people of the time knew to use dried strips from the leaves to make sandals, and more than likely they made a scalp-tingling shampoo from the plant's roots. Careful examination of some three hundred coprolites (ancient or fossilized turds) in one such canyon at a place called Hind's Cave showed that, beginning about six thousand years ago, lechuguilla was among the most commonly eaten foods. Also commonly eaten were sotol (another agave), prickly pear cactus pads, and wild onion, along with some fifty other plant foods, including seeds.

Texas archaeologists found that the lechuguilla plants were uprooted and the thirty-odd leaves cut off at a precise forty-five-degree angle, much as a chef trims an artichoke, leaving the large central stem where the plant stores carbohydrate. Forced either by population pressure or climate change or both, people learned that with use of rocks in a pit oven they could bake this exposed stem at high enough temperatures to eliminate the steroids and leave a rich, sugar-filled remnant. But this was an extremely energy-intensive affair. Hauling rocks, foraging for lechuguilla plants and onerously preparing them, collecting juniper wood for the fire, clearing out the old pit oven and refurbishing it, and covering it once the fire and food were in it—this was all a great deal of work for little return in sustenance. And there was no immediate gratification. Archaeologists have learned by doing this themselves that a plant like lechuguilla needs to be baked in this fashion for about two full days. Any less, say only thirty-six hours, and it works as a powerful emetic. What was happening here, then, was more than just people resorting to increasingly costly food-processing practices, learning among other things how big or small a rock should be to be an optimal heat sink. They were also presumably arriving at a lifestyle less mobile than that of the usual roaming hunter and gatherer. The ovens were probably in use from late spring well into the early fall. Some of the ovens are especially large—up to twelve feet across. A plausible picture emerges.

A band of people, probably closely related, sends a few young boys out to alert relatives living here and there around the landscape. Meanwhile the adults have dug a large pit oven and, for several days earlier, have been out collecting lechuguilla and other plants. The extended family soon gathers from far and wide, the oven is filled, and they talk about what is going on in the landscape and with the weather—where the deer are now, where the acacias are beginning to put out seed, where the food is. It would be a feast and a time of sharing critical information.

The switch to this kind of laborious food preparation seems humble enough. We know virtually nothing else about the people involved, but even these homely researches put a slightly more familiar face on them, a notion of what was driving human families at the time. As anthropologist Ralph Linton pointed out in 1944, "It seems to be a general rule that sciences begin their development with the unusual. They have to develop considerable sophistication before they interest themselves in the commonplace."

The Great Basin

Perhaps nowhere did a basic way of life persist for such a long period of time as in the vast region of sagebrush desert, high mountains, and rocky canyon lands called the Great Basin, which lies between the Rocky Mountains and the Sierra Nevada in California, and stretches from southern California as far north as southern Idaho and Oregon. In the early Holocene, this was a far different place. The Bonneville Salt Flats, so perfectly horizontal now that automobile speed records are set there, was formerly one of many lakes that existed in the region, perhaps some 150 all told. They filled with meltwater from glaciers and later mountain runoff that coursed downhill in rivers and streams to the low lake basins. None of these lakes drained to the sea; instead, they simply sat there until the climate changed and most of them (and most of the rivers) dried up, and the lush river and lake vegetation disappeared, a process that was well under way by 8000 B.C. Since that time, the climate has remained generally the same— alternating between dry and drier—and the region (some four hundred thousand square miles) has been but minimally hospitable to human life.

To live in this region called for a deep and subtle understanding of all of its life forms and a high degree of flexibility. People first came to this region before 10,000 B.C., exactly when is not clear, and they took up life along the watercourses and beside the lakes, more abundant then. Here camels, horses, mammoths, and bison flourished, and so did people, though never in great numbers. Another great source of food then might well have been—as it was later—waterfowl, among the most traditional of creatures, which migrate with stunning regularity through this region still, settling down here and there en route in spectacularly large flocks. By about 9000 B.C., these people netted land and water birds here, and even constructed duck decoys from reeds. Once the megafauna were gone and the world more arid, people relied more on seeds and nuts, living—at least many of them—in a rock shelter here for a while, then moving to another with the seasons. Recent evidence shows that even life along the watercourses and lakes was short-

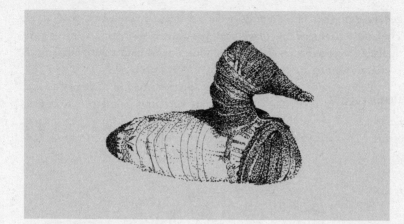

Tule canvasback decoy, Lovelock Cave, Nevada, 1000–500 B.C.

term and seasonal, shore dwellers leaving for long periods for such purposes as harvesting piñon nuts on higher ground. Everywhere in the Great Basin, through time, local conditions changed. In a land where game was sparse, except locally, and the weather could change drastically from year to year, people had to rely on a wide variety of food sources both vegetable and animal, including rabbits, reptiles, and even insects, and (in the somewhat wetter western part of the Great Basin) marsh plants on the dwindling lakes' shores—whatever was present momentarily. One way or the other, there was usually plenty to eat, at least for a relatively small population. Their most important implements (or at least most common) were wooden digging sticks for such tasks as digging up tubers and roots, baskets for gathering seeds from grasses and roasting them, and flat grinding stones called metates (still in use today). In the southern part of the region particularly, people became especially adept and (judging from the quantity) very enthusiastic artists, leaving signs, symbols, and animal and human figures etched into and painted on local rock faces. Rock art, common throughout much of the continent and possibly, at least in some cases, a kind of common symbolic language, flourished here as nowhere else.

By about 500 B.C., the bow and arrow replaced the spear and atlatl (or spear-thrower), pottery appeared here and there, and small game and seeds played a bigger role in the diet. Most people continued their seasonal rounds, but a few lived in places, such as central

Nevada, where piñon nuts were sufficiently abundant that year-round settlement may have been possible. Elsewhere, in one or two places, people began irrigating stands of wild plants with occasional stream waters, another local bit of opportunism.

Around 400 A.D. a shift in the approach to life took place here and there in Utah and its immediate surround. Some people began

Pit house

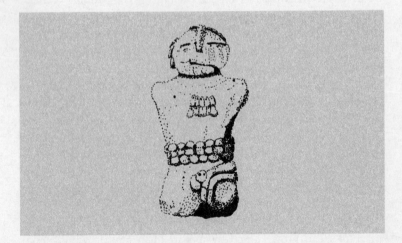

Fremont figurine

living in pit houses, and later stone buildings, cultivating maize and making pottery—traits that were already relatively common in the nearby Southwest.

Many such places were found along Utah's Fremont River, which gave this culture its name. Its several variants probably derived from the local base of hunters and gatherers as a result of the infusion of southwestern domesticated plants (like maize) into the region. The sites vary in small stylistic matters, and some were founded as late as 800 A.D. In any event, around 1250 A.D., severe and prolonged drought set in, perhaps associated with the global Little Ice Age that persisted into the eighteenth century. Growing corn in the Great Basin was no longer viable, and within a short time all the so-called Fremont sites were abandoned. This timing also coincides with the arrival in the area of people who came to be known as Paiutes, Shoshones, and Utes—all speakers of languages known as Numic.

By the time Europeans first entered this region, they found people living much as people always had here—except for the Fremont interval—subtly and cleverly eking out a fairly simple subsistence from the ever-changing and parsimonious bounty of an unforgiving land. These were Numic-speaking people who traveled in bands or small family groups with little recognition of any tribal membership.

The Pacific Coast

An entirely different world existed west of the Great Basin, along the Pacific coast and inland in such great valleys as those we call the Sacramento and San Joaquin. In this region, once the ice had moved north out of what is today Washington State, prehistoric people were virtually guaranteed a good living once they learned a few important tricks. The coast, from southern California to southern Alaska, was one of the richest places in the world for marine mammals, fish, and shellfish. At one time, one could catch a five-hundred-pound halibut in the waters offshore. The rivers teemed with a variety of fish, and in the north they were almost literally plugged up annually by one or another of five species of salmon headed upstream to spawn and die. In central California, oak and grassland covered much of the land, providing seeds and, importantly, acorns, which if properly leached become a tasty and

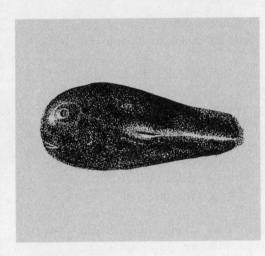
Island Chumash whale effigy

nutritious food and indeed served as the staple for many of the California tribes once the mortar and pestle came along, around 4000 B.C. In the highlands where chaparral led up to conifer-filled forest, deer, rabbit, bear, and a host of other species abounded. North, these creatures shared the redwood forests and the rain forests with elk and beaver. Virtually everywhere one could find tuberous roots in a pinch.

Human habitation came early to this blessed strand, much of it probably taking place before the sea level rose from its Laurentide low to its present configuration, obliterating numberless future archaeological sites as it rose. Over the millennia in California, hunting land animals gave way to more use of plants and the consumption of shellfish, then more hunting of marine mammals and fishing, with the processing of seeds becoming less important when acorns could be ground up with the new mortars and pestles. Kelp beds grew larger and diminished with climatic changes, as did the fish that depend on them. People rarely starved as different food sources rose and fell in importance. Acorns and offshore fishing in canoes came into fashion when populations had begun to grow, perhaps making hunting land mammals like deer less rewarding, and making the building of canoes and the tedious processing of acorns worth the

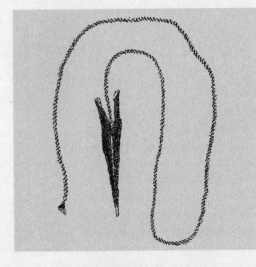
Shasta fish harpoon point

effort. People learned early on that setting fire to the chaparral and other ecosystems promoted the growth of plants they (and deer) knew were desirable, and a good deal of this sort of land management was practiced over the centuries.

This Pacific region came to be populated by almost countless tribal units, one of the most polyglot regions of the continent. In certain inland parts of California, bands of people could live for generations with little contact between them, sticking instead to their own generous patches of territory. In general, over the millennia, the climate remained relatively salubrious, and making a living was probably never especially strenuous except in the desert areas of southern California, where lifestyles were closer to those of the people of the Great Basin. Our current notion, so widely held until recently, that California is a kind of lotus land where the living is easy has origins in prehistoric reality. No doubt, there were severe problems from time to time, with too much rain all at once or too little. There were long periods of drought, for example, and from time to time the offshore waters warmed up—not good for fish populations and the marine mammals that feed on them.

Particularly along the coasts, people over time began to live in more and more settled and socially complex villages, such as the ancestors of the Chumashes who inhabited the Santa Barbara area, along with the Channel Islands and areas inland. The coastal and the inland areas each had its own benefits and costs. For example, a diet given over largely to gathered plants can lead to a high incidence of dental caries (cavities, in other words), which is avoided with a concentration of marine food. On the other hand, a preeminently marine diet can lead to arthritis. Such conditions have been noted from burials of early Chumash people, as well as periods of malnutrition, often associated with climate change. In about 1100 A.D., with the onset of a long drought period, larger numbers of people began to die from arrow wounds. Even a place as rich in resources as the California coast had its limits. It seems likely that as the population grew, these limits hove into sight. This presumably is a factor in the gradual rise of ranked societies and the concentration of political power in the hands of chiefs and lesser elites, who could organize hunting and fishing expeditions and the allotment of food resources, as well as run whatever military operations were needed as the world became more competitive. One sign of this ranking was the existence of certain kinds of shell beads that became a kind of gen-

eral currency for trading or, in effect, buying and selling, even by commoners. But yet another kind of bead was evidently a second and special form of currency, or at least status indicator, restricted to members
of the elite—whether these were lineage-based elites or simply those
people who were chosen as noble allies by whoever had risen, in a given
generation, to a position of leadership: in short, an early version of
either nepotism or meritocracy. In any event, on the whole, conditions
up and down the Pacific coast were sufficiently comfortable over the
millennia, and resources so varied, that some of the most sophisticated
and thickly populated hunter and gatherer societies ever known came
about there. In recent years, scholars have called such societies by the
more elegant rubric *affluent foragers*. Except in the southernmost parts
of California, agriculture would not emerge as a needed option
throughout the entire prehistoric period and well afterward.

A not dissimilar pattern over time occurred along the coast from
northern California all the way to Alaska. What were once relatively
small coastal and riverine hamlets located in good to marginal areas
later became fewer, larger villages where evidently people of many different lineages lived together.

By as early as 1100 B.C., people in this area were living in large
plank houses, labor-intensive structures that lasted for hundreds of
years, suggesting a good deal of cooperative effort and perhaps also the
concentration of political power among a few. Coastal villages grew in
size and importance with population growth, and specialized techniques for harvesting the ocean's and the rivers' bounty came into
being. By about 1000 A.D., whaling took on a greater role in many of
these northern societies, and no doubt among the specialists in these
northwest coast villages were those particularly adept at building the
great canoes, exquisitely crafted harpoons, and other paraphernalia
required for such an arduous enterprise. Large canoes were also used for
warfare. In part, the growing concentration of people in settlements
was for defensive purposes (some of these towns were fortified, and
many were located on long straight shorelines where surprise attack by
sea was less likely). But even with local hostilities erupting from time
to time, there were also, it seems, very strong linkages between these
numerous groups that were emerging into linguistically different peoples. These linkages, among other things, were for the exchanging of
food and other items as needed but probably had some political role as
well. The waxing and waning of subtle diplomatic and trade relations

between far-flung groups, the rise and fall in status of particular lineages, the eruption of hostilities and the making of peace—these must have been common practices, much of it lost and unrecoverable now. No doubt, however, the machinations so common to the courts of European kings and queens were not a bit more constant or complex than those of the Pacific Northwest.

The East

East of the Mississippi River, the world tends to be moister than to the west, and so it has been for a very long time—certainly as long as people have lived there. For most of that time, once the glacier began shriveling, it has tended to be a place of forest, intersected by innumerable streams and rivers draining toward the Mississippi and the Gulf of Mexico or, east of the Appalachians, to the Atlantic. Dampness is not good for archaeology, as a rule, and neither are forests, where the floor is filled with organic detritus and infinite numbers of microorganisms that devour things. As a result, the archaeology of the eastern half of the country lagged behind that where such destructive forces are sparser, as in the far West. The ruts of the Oregon Trail, in use far more than a century ago, are still to be seen here and there, and the tracks of various off-road vehicles in the Mojave Desert may puzzle archaeologists a century from now. In the East, archaeologists long for more sites, more artifacts, though most modern archaeologists know that it is what you make of artifacts, not their sheer quantity, that is important. In this regard, the evidence of human life in much of the Archaic period in the eastern woodlands was long restricted mostly to arrowheads, which are bacteria resistant and which occurred in a considerable array of styles geographically and over time, each style being thought of as a *culture*.

People hunted deer and other game, perhaps fished along rivers, and took shellfish and the like along the coasts—and that was about that, over the eons. Eventually they made pottery. More recently, it has come to light that hunters and gatherers tend to operate over large pieces of territory, pursuing different activities in different places. For each of these activities, different tools are usually required, just as we today would keep one set of tools in the bathroom and another set in a kitchen drawer. Thus what once seemed a huge array of mini cultures (based on the variety of arrowhead shapes) may, instead, have been groups of people who, not being witless, made different tools to suit the subtle differences in their seasonal rounds and tasks. Yet part of the same picture is certain *similarities* over space and time, perhaps most notably the use of similar materials over large areas despite the fact that the source of those materials is restricted in locale. This suggests trading over long distances, meaning a good deal of contact between local bands of people.

In all, a picture emerges of people in groups of fifty to 150 learning to make ever more various use of their local ecological situations (such as river drainages). They used what could be called base camps (for example, on the floodplains east of the Appalachians) for increasingly long periods of the year, decamping in smaller numbers in season to hunt and gather on higher ground. Over the eons, they began to return each year to the same base camps—some of these sites, for example, show shell middens that would have taken far more than one season to accumulate. Periodically, they also came together in larger groups for communal hunts, for trade in valued exotic materials like marine shells from the Gulf coast or copper from Lake Superior, or jasper from Pennsylvania, and for social and probably ceremonial purposes. It is possible that throughout most of prehistory, up until perhaps some four thousand years ago, the people of the woodland East spoke the same language, or at least dialects of the same language, perhaps an aboriginal Algonquian tongue.

By about 5500 B.C., people living at least part of the year in places like one site near Titusville, Florida, not far from Cape Canaveral, made a good living from the fish and shellfish that were themselves flourishing as the sea level rose and rivers settled down a bit, creating marshes, swamps, and shoals and the accumulation of silt. The first known use of gourds as containers in the East is known from Titusville in this period, among some people who were also expert weavers, making clothes, bags, and matting from strips of sabal palm and palmetto at thirty strands per inch, which, given the materials, is remarkably fine work.

A halting trend toward permanent settlements in places that had a sufficient abundance of varied food resources gained momentum as the overall population began significant growth—around 4000 B.C. At about this time, an increased reliance on storage appears to have begun—baskets and pits to hold the likes of seeds and hickory nuts— which indicates surpluses. By 2500 B.C., people along the South Carolina coast were making rough clay containers, the idea no doubt springing from the fact that a hearth built in clay will bake itself hard, particularly with the ashes mixed in. This is the first sign of pottery in North America, and it spread westward into the Mississippi Valley in relatively short order. Pots, of course, are better for a number of things than baskets, such as boiling water to leach the bitter toxins from acorns. But pots are harder to carry around, and are usually taken as a sign of a more sedentary lifestyle. The question arises: did a growing population with its pressure on food resources lead to these advances in technology, or did the advances in technology make increased population possible?

Early woodland relief, detail from gorget

This is a matter of greater concern to present-day scholars than it was to the people involved. They, meanwhile, had other things that needed inventing besides the tools for a more complex material life. They needed to invent new social systems for larger and larger congregations of people to live successfully together for longer and longer periods of time.

Reasons exist to think that groups of people up to about five hundred can live an egalitarian life without the emergence of social ranking and political office. In a group of five hundred or fewer, virtually everyone knows what everyone else is doing. Tasks can be shared as needed among people who all know one another. Beyond that number, however, constant and easy communication is less possible. Some people know more than others, and not everyone is a familiar. In such situations, typically, hierarchies arise. The number five hundred seems to be something of a social constant, similar to a constant in physics equations. It is borne out in numerous ethnographic studies and in other, perhaps surprising circumstances. Akbar the Great, supreme ruler of sixteenth-century India, allowed his far-flung nobility (the administrative class) to reach no more than five hundred, and subsequently the British Raj was operated by almost exactly five hundred British officers. It has been found, also, that the human brain can typically manage in its short-term memory about five hundred items. Beyond that, it needs to break those items down into categories—like *animal, vegetable,* or *mineral* in the old children's game of twenty questions, or like *we* and *they.*

It would be some time before people in the eastern woodlands began living in groups of more than five hundred, but even before that time arrived, social invention was under way. Around 4000 B.C., some people began to bury their dead in groups on ridge tops, bluffs, and soon in mounds, placing with the dead their daily tools and accoutrements. In essence, these were cemeteries, noticeable places that may have served as markers, denoting and even celebrating a particular lineage of people (something like a clan) and perhaps also letting the world know that a particular lineage was associated with and had certain rights to a particular territory. By about 2000 B.C., regional variation in styles of dart points and so forth became more pronounced; this perhaps suggests that ethnicity, which had presumably been present from Paleo-Indian times, was intensifying. (On the other hand, many more archaeological sites have been found dating to a period after 2000 B.C. Their number makes regional variations easier to detect, and therefore appear more pronounced than earlier.) Certainly trade in exotic materials was becoming increasingly important as well, and some people in the cemeteries were buried with more elaborate products made of these valued materials—adornments and other signs of rank or particular esteem. These individuals were probably social arbiters—a group's wise men—or ritual leaders, or those who embodied both roles and began as well to represent the group in its necessary dealings with neighboring groups.

At the same time, people here and there in the East had begun to take more active advantage of certain edible plants, cultivating them. People living in more permanent sites would tend to disturb the ground underfoot, leading to colonization by opportunistic weedy plants (as every lawn tender knows). Some of these weedy plants would prove more useful than others—gourds, for example, which may well have spread from their native Mexico through Texas to the eastern woodlands. People probably learned quite quickly that these useful plants did better if the less useful weeds were pulled up. Sunflowers and Jerusalem artichokes may have been cultivated in this manner as early as 2200 B.C. Given such opportunities, some plants evolved yet more useful features on their own, such as larger seeds—a kind of inadvertent synergy had begun.

Other plants that became widely cultivated, even domesticated, were goosefoot, a kin of lamb's-quarter, which provides edible seeds but also edible leaves; knotweed, with long stems that are rather like asparagus; and maygrass, a long-leaved inhabitant of marshy areas that was soon propagated by deliberate planting of seeds. These cultivated and domesticated wild plants provided a hedge against a bad year for hickory nuts or other resources. When maize (corn) was introduced into the eastern woodlands much later, it would be taken as just one of many helpful but not crucial food plants that could be encouraged or deliberately grown. On the whole, it was usually easier to harvest the region's wild bounty. And indeed, not everyone was settling down. Many in the East continued much the same lifestyle as had existed for millennia.

Something odd took place, beginning about 1700 B.C., on the banks of the lower Mississippi River, where numerous small rivers join it, and along the nearby Gulf coast, reaching its peak after 1000 B.C. At a place now called Poverty Point in Louisiana, some two to five thousand people eventually lived in an area of some five hundred acres and built an enormous and enigmatic series of earthworks. In all, more than 1 million cubic feet of earth were heaped up into six concentric semicircular rings, each about eighty feet wide and ten feet high—the total configuration consuming almost one square mile. What purpose these artificial ridges served remains a complete enigma—they were not burial sites. One suggestion is based on the existence of a single, taller mound on the western (open) side of the earthworks: standing on that mound and sighting directly across the semicircle to the east, one can sight the rising of the sun at precisely the vernal and autumnal equinoxes. But what value such a sighting would be to a society that lived much as other, less sophisticated ones did remains a question. The people at Poverty Point had no great agricultural system but depended on hunting and gathering for the most part, while cultivating gourds and some wild food plants as a backup. It appears that Poverty Point was a great distribution center, importing materials such as copper and slate and quartz from hundreds of miles off and making finished tools for distribution among the like-minded people of the region. In all, some ten lesser sites have been found associated with the Poverty Point florescence. Intriguingly, archaeologists reported in 2001 on a nearby mound site that could be almost two thousand years older than Poverty Point—a place called Watson

Brake, located near the Arkansas River, where people came at least seasonally to fish, though they hunted small game and ate copious amounts of aquatic snails. They had no pottery but did bake clay into little cubes, for what purpose no one can even imagine, and they made beads unlike those found at the much younger site of Poverty Point. Thus large mounds, one of which was twenty-five feet high, were being built into a large circular arrangement probably a thousand years before.

By 700 B.C., whatever was going on at Poverty Point ceased and the great earthworks were abandoned. Sorting through the ruins, archaeologists have found that the artifacts located in the north side of the semicircle were of one sort, while south-side artifacts were of another sort, which suggests the possibility that this society consisted of two halves, or moieties, each with different status or functions. Beside these few speculations, Poverty Point is a mystery—the first experiment in inventing a truly complex social organization in North America north of Mexico, if indeed a social scheme that lasted about a millennium can be called an experiment.

Meanwhile, elsewhere throughout much of the eastern woodlands, people with many different cultures or lifestyles had several things in common. One of these was increasingly widespread and intensive trade. Another was an increasingly elaborate concept of the role of the dead, this being reflected in ever more elaborate burial practices, particularly the construction of larger burial mounds. Centered in the Ohio Valley, where perhaps this overriding preoccupation originated, the trend spread throughout most of the eastern woodlands all the way into New England. More and more, mounds served as graves for numerous people, some cremated, some buried whole. In other cases just bundles of bones were interred, as if the person had died elsewhere and was brought back for interment—or as if the corpse was defleshed before interment. People were buried with copper bead necklaces, various tools, carved stone pipes, their bodies painted with red ocher and sprinkled with other colored minerals. By two thousand years ago, large burial chambers, sometimes made of logs, were common, often found lying below the floors of circular houses that were set on fire before the mound was built or added on to. This suggests a practice akin to a body lying in state before interment.

The largest of these mounds, in the approximate middle of the Ohio Valley, is the Grave Creek mound, a structure that reached nearly seventy feet in height. Grave goods continued to proliferate in kind, with some important burials containing what appear to be trophy skulls and ornaments like copper bracelets and rings, neck pieces called gorgets, and carved animal effigies, all made of materials from far-off sources—presumably signs of the death of an especially important individual. The trend in funerary customs spread widely and across otherwise quite distinct culture groups; it has been called the Adena Complex where it occurred in the Ohio Valley, and by other names elsewhere. Most likely, it testifies to the growing importance of lineages and clans, and

Maize from Bat Cave and Tularosa Cave

the need to celebrate important kin leaders. A funeral would have been a long, drawn-out affair, bringing together many people from far and wide—an event during which the participants received gifts of ornaments and redistributed food, all promoting a solidarity among people. The trend would only accelerate in the East as the world entered the so-called present era, which is the more politically correct way of expressing the time since the birth of Christ.

The Coming of Agriculture

What we think of as agriculture, the deliberate planting and harvesting of plants for food or fiber, was not a revolution, though its effects would come to be revolutionary. As noted, it came in fits and starts, here and there, in large part due to a series of inadvertent actions like trampling or disturbing an area, inviting weeds. Digging up tubers with a wooden digging stick aerates the soil and promotes the growth of seeds one might have tracked in on one's sandals. More deliberate tending of such wild plants included the use of fire, as noted among the Californians. Weeding and clearing areas not only affect the plot of ground in question but its edges. Certain kinds of berry-bearing shrubs do better at the edge of the woods, becoming not only more abundant but closer by and easier to harvest. Archaic Indian populations had profound if local effects on the landscape, and as we have seen, people in the East and elsewhere actively cultivated increasingly tamed plants for thousands of years, continuing long after the introduction of that sine qua non of American Indian nutrition (and what we think of as actual agriculture), maize.

Maize arrived in the American Southwest about 1000 B.C., making what could be called a pretty small splash among the people there, who lived in much the same way as their neighbors to the north in the Great Basin. It had been intensively cultivated in northern Mexico for more than five thousand years and was, along with beans and squash, a main staple there. At this time in the Southwest, there was what archaeologists call an imbalance between population and resources: food resources were pretty well stretched out. Lowland areas were producing less then by way of abundance, and the highlands were more seasonal and unpredictable than before. But these foraging people already knew about seeds—they had a complete tool kit for processing them. The first maize to appear was a puny strain, the ears hardly more than a couple of inches long. From sites such as Bat Cave, in central New Mexico, it appears that people planted this new cultigen in the spring and then went on to make their seasonal rounds, hunting and gathering, to return to Bat Cave and harvest whatever maize plants had survived, along with the other opportunists. Maize was a bit of a hedge, a supplement, and also was storable, as were other seeds for use in the early spring before the world again sprouted. Over time, people could take it or leave it, and did, depending on what else was happening in their ever-changeable locale. It was not until a thousand years after its first appearance in the Southwest that maize became an important part of the diet, along with squash and beans (which, among other things, provide the necessary amino acid,

Iva xanthifolia (marsh elder)

lycine, that corn lacks and that makes corn more digestible).

At some point, perhaps around the beginning of the present millennium or slightly before, a new strain of maize appeared, called *maíz de ocho*. It had more rows of larger kernels and it was adapted to very dry conditions, possibly a hybrid that arose in the Southwest itself rather than being an import from Mexico. It spread throughout the Southwest and to points beyond, profoundly affecting the way of life of most native people. This strain of corn and myriad other hybrids that arose were something worth settling down for, particularly when grown alongside

Helianthus annuus (sunflower)

beans, which complement corn and also resupply the soil with nitrogen.

Corn arrived in the eastern woodlands by at least 400 A.D., if not earlier, again making no great difference in life there. It was not until about 900 A.D. that it came into its own as a major part of the diet. It had a profound effect on the Plains, often thought of as the exclusive home of bison-hunting people and not the sort of place where agriculture could flourish until Europeans brought a plow capable of turning the thick mat of prairie grasses over to expose the topsoil. But the Plains produced some of the continent's most important native farming communities long before European contact.

Agriculture on the Plains

By about the beginning of 1000 A.D., maize and beans were being grown in small, semisedentary villages on the central Plains, even as far north as North Dakota, which is about as far north as maize can be grown. The villagers also made pottery and buried their dead in small mounds, traits probably taken on from their eastern woodland neighbors. They also hunted bison, as did their neighbors on the Plains to the west. Over the centuries, village life became more widespread, with villages now permanent habitations, usually on terraces and bluffs above rivers. Corn and beans were the staples, and the farmers lived in substantial single-family dwellings with ample storage pits, the village or hamlet of fifty to seventy-five people typically being surrounded by stockades or moats. Seasonally these people gathered wild plants and trekked westward to hunt bison. Here, then, were people who lived between two quite different worlds—that of the new, elaborate farming societies of the woodlands and that of the ancient, still basically archaic nomads of the dry Plains—taking from each world what they deemed useful and ignoring the rest. They were the putative ancestors of the northern tribes (Hidatsas, Mandans, Arikaras), the central tribes (Pawnees and Wichitas), and the Caddos of Oklahoma and Texas.

The Caddos abutted yet a third world—that of the Southwest—and took on some traits from there as well, such as houses built, at least in part, from adobe. To the north, houses were built of poles, round lodges replacing rectangular ones over time. At the same time, the Caddos took on rather more of the culture to their east, which included larger aggregations of people in villages and more elaborate burials in great mounds. From north to south, the Plains villages were relatively self-contained societies, typically ruled (if that is the word) by chiefs, with ceremonial matters—such as ensuring a successful bison hunt and ushering in the spring season of rebirth and fecundity—left in the hands of priests. Trade with the nomadic hunters to the west was a continuing feature of life, the villagers exchanging their produce for meat, hides, and pemmican. In fact, overall, the Plains afforded relatively few places where such village life could be lived satisfactorily, and with changes in the climate, these places either grew in number (and population) or shrank. A thousand years ago, a long dry spell began, and this, probably coupled with previous population growth, led to a fair amount of competition for good places, competition that included intervillage warfare. In one site, called Crow Creek, five hundred people were buried in a mass grave, no doubt overwhelmed and massacred by a rival village.

While life proceeded thus on the Plains—a developing tradition that began approximately two thousand years ago and lasted well into historic times—the agricultural life as practiced east of the Plains and to the southwest of them would show a different trajectory, in due course helping to create what are the most elaborate and astonishing societies in native North America. To varying degrees, these would all be a result of the adoption of maize as the chief staple and a central and sacred gift of the earth to the people. The attitude to this gift, probably widely held though expressed in as many ways as there were separate groups of people, can be glimpsed in a tale told by the Ojibways.

Mondawmin

When the youth called Wunzh reached the right age, his father built him a lodge in a far-off place where he could live alone for a while and find his guardian in life. At first, Wunzh walked in the woods each morning, thinking about the first shoots of plants that were coming alive in the warming earth of spring. This, he hoped, would give him pleasant dreams at night. Sometimes he found himself wondering how the plants grew, some sweet and edible, some bitter and poisonous, yet others bitter and full of medicine. Perhaps, if he could learn how the plants grew, he could help his people, who had to rely of the luck of the hunt.

Time passed and Wunzh grew too weak for his daily strolls, so he lay in his lodge. Growing dizzier each day, he allowed himself the thought that the Creator had made all things, including the people, but could have made life a little easier for them. On the third day, he saw a figure descend from the sky. It was dressed in yellow and green, with a plume of golden feathers waving on its head. It floated into Wunzh's lodge.

"The Creator sent me to you, my friend," the figure said. "Your prayers are unusual, and he heard them." The figure went on to explain that it was possible Wunzh could do something for his people—if he would wrestle with his visitor. Wunzh's heart sank. He knew he was already too weak to wrestle anyone. But he summoned up his courage and what was left of his strength and began to wrestle the figure, soon falling utterly exhausted on the ground. "You did well," the figure said, smiling. "I will come again." With that, he ascended a beam of light to the sun.

The next day, he came again and challenged Wunzh, who was, if anything, weaker than before. But the weaker his body was, the greater, it seemed, was his courage. Again they wrestled and again the figure finally broke it off, promising to come again for the third time, the final trial, leaving Wunzh in an exhaustion near death. The next day, after the third and final match began, the figure broke it off, saying that he was beaten. He sat down next to Wunzh and told him the Creator was pleased and impressed by the youth's courage. Now he would receive the instruction he had been praying for.

"Tomorrow," the visitor said, "is the seventh day of your fasting. Your father will come with some food to give you strength and I will come again, and you will again win. Afterward, you must strip my clothes from me, put me in the ground, and take away all the weeds. Then you must bury me there. Don't let any weeds grow there, but come from time to time to see if I have returned to you. And then you will have your wish."

In the morning, Wunzh's father did come with food, and the youth said he would wait till sundown to eat it. When the visitor came again, Wunzh was surprised by how strong he felt, and he seized the figure, threw him down on the ground, and stripped off his yellow-and-green clothes. The figure was dead, and Wunzh buried him as instructed, and went back to his father's lodge to eat. In the days that followed, Wunzh would go off unannounced to the spot where he had buried his friend and clear the place of weeds. Toward summer's end, he came to the spot and noticed that his old lodge had disappeared. In its place grew a tall graceful plant with clusters of yellow on its side, and long green leaves, and a graceful plume of gold nodding from the top.

"It's my friend," Wunzh said to himself, and suddenly he knew his friend's name—Mondawmin. He ran to fetch his father and told him that this was what he had dreamed for in his fast. If everyone cared for Mondawmin the way Wunzh had been instructed, they would no longer have to rely only on the hunt. He showed his father how to strip off the yellow clusters just as he had stripped off the spirit's clothes earlier that year, and he showed him how to hold the ears to the fire to turn them brown. The entire family gathered for a feast on this new presence in their lives, and expressed their lasting thanks to Mondawmin, the spirit, the beautiful visitor, who had given it to them.

And so corn came into the world.

CHAPTER THREE

HIGH SOCIETY

When Europeans first encountered the more monumental ruins that littered several areas of North America, they were quite convinced that the Indians simply could not have been responsible for them. Other races must have been present—cleverer people with a great knowledge of engineering principles and architectural aesthetics, people who were more *organized,* even perhaps *civilized.* And then, after abiding amid the splendor for a while, these other races (who have ranged from Welshmen to a lost tribe of Israel to escapees from the inundation of Atlantis) packed up and left the scene; their mysterious vanishings matched their mysterious comings.

By now, most people have gotten over this condescending myth of the white man (though the myth is equally strong and equally condescending among those silly cultists who persist in believing that visitors from elsewhere in the universe built such sophisticated structures as the pyramids of Egypt and etched the enormous figures called the Nazca Lines on the desert coast of South America). Today, we have a far better notion of when these monumental structures and complex schemes came into being, as well as how, why, and who was responsible. We also have a far more realistic notion of the possible reasons why they were left behind as people moved on to other places and other ways of life. None of them arose in a sudden, unprecedented, revolutionary explosion. They all developed—just as did the American, French, and Bolshevik Revolutions—in response to ideas and pressures that had been present for a long, long time. Knowing this may remove some of the romance that has swirled around them for so long, but it renders them no less remarkable for all that.

The Mound Builders

The serpent has a tightly furled tail, a spiral, and its body undulates across the ground like the oxbows of a river. Jaws wide, it holds in its mouth an egg-shaped object. This snake is nearly a quarter of a mile long (1254 feet, to be exact) and it consists of earth piled up along a low ridge. The oval object in the snake's mouth is a large burial mound. This, the Great Serpent Mound in Ohio, is one of the most celebrated earthworks, but it was evidently built much later than the first efflorescence of mound building in the Ohio Valley—called Hopewellian—which took place from about 200 to 400 A.D. Near the Ohio town of Chillicothe, the site named Hopewell contains thirty-eight mounds within an earthen rectangle covering

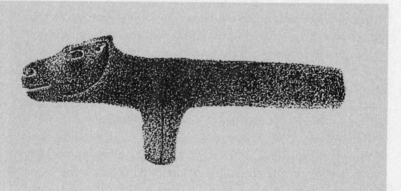

Adena pipe (dog)

more than a hundred acres. Numerous such sites occur in the Ohio Valley, and the Hopewell customs spread widely from there. The mounds, of course, contain burials, but these burials are on a new and unprecedented scale—at least among the elite.

Most Hopewellian people lived among their family members in small hamlets (one to three households) spaced out more or less equidistantly along the tributaries of major rivers. In the more resource-rich main river valleys, the density of hamlets increased, and what might be thought of as villages are found. About every ten miles, larger mound areas presided over the area in one way or another. The mounds came in many shapes and sizes—circles, octagons, rectangles—and many seem to have been built according to some standard unit of measurement.

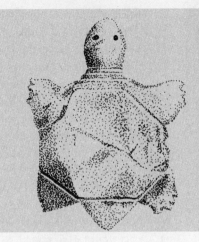

Adena turtle effigy

These were evidently sacred areas, marking the boundary between the sacred and the secular, the corporate ceremonial and the domestic, and death and life. Most people in these societies were simply cremated, but the elite were buried intact in the mounds after a great deal of preparation.

Typically, a large if simple structure of large poles and a thatched roof was erected and the individual was placed in a log-lined tomb inside the shelter. Phenomenal amounts of grave goods accompanied the dead in the tomb—thousands of freshwater pearls, for example, and copper ornaments of all sorts, as well as objects made of mica, silver, and tortoiseshell—mostly exotic objects made of exotic materials. Figurines and carved pipes were relatively common and showed a similarity in design throughout the regions where such burials became the fashion—notably, the Ohio Valley, Illinois, and throughout the Southeast. Around the houses, called charnel houses, animal-bone scatters suggest that a considerable amount of feasting took place—while the corpse was there—probably feeding the great numbers of people (most likely relatives) who arrived for this extended funeral service, which ended with the charnel house and its contents being set afire and a mound subsequently built over it.

From the proliferation of ever more exotic grave goods, the assumption is that trade networks expanded and intensified in this period—but then suddenly the phenomenon ebbed. The reasons are probably many. Long-distance trade in exotic materials and products was probably an important feature of the rise of powerful political figures in Hopewellian societies—men who could organize the mutual gift giving between disparate people as a way of ensuring themselves against bad times locally. But as agriculture took hold and became an important component of nutrition, each local area would have had much the same food resources available to it: gift giving might have become less needed. At the same time, given the possibility of losing harvests to bad weather, the Hopewellian peoples developed more elaborate storage arrangements. With maize agriculture, then, long-distance trade might have become less necessary, and along with it the personal prestige of powerful individuals would have waned.

From 400 A.D., for the next three or four hundred years, maize spread rapidly throughout the East, becoming the dominant but not the only crop in many places by 900 A.D. Native plants continued to be cultivated as well. Daily life was not much different for most people, except that burial practices (and whatever they represented of a social and political nature) were simpler. Then, around 1000 A.D., in the Southeast along the Gulf coast and north into the Mississippi Valley, larger centers reappeared, most of them near lakes, river oxbows, and swamps. In such places, seasonal flooding from rivers brought rich new soil to add to the seasonal visitors' riches of fish and migratory birds. The large communities were often fortified and typically organized around central plazas—relatively large open spaces where feasts and great ceremonies, perhaps tied to planting and harvest cycles, were carried out along with funeral rites. Each such center probably was home to a major figure, a chief, along with his particular lineage of nobles, all of whom would be buried with increasingly great fanfare in what can be thought of as the family (or clan or lineage) mound. The elite were

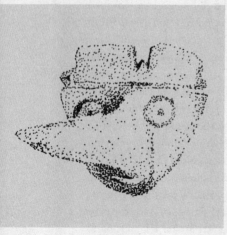

Long-nose god, shell, Tennessee

buried with great quantities of riches, from shell beads to elaborately made icons—snakes, raptorial birds, and costumed dancers being among the most frequent, along with trophy heads.

Weeden Island duck effigy

Indeed, from different arrays of grave goods, it appears that there were usually three political offices to be filled by members of what could be thought of as the noble clans or lineages. One such office was sacred, responsible for spiritual mediation between this and the spirit world, in order to maintain a proper balance and salubrious conditions; this included the proper care of the dead. These spiritual leaders, or priests, carried out their tasks and probably lived on the center's flat-topped mounds. The proper celebration of the dead was geared to maintaining public appreciation for the lineage from which sprang the chief (the second office), whose roles included initiating such corporate projects as mound building and food sharing, and diplomatic or warlike relations with neighboring chieftainships. The third office was that of war leader.

Around the centers, spreading out into the countryside, were smaller centers—villages, each with its own mounds, and numerous hamlets, where households were the primary unit of production, small families tending fields and gathering resources from nearby. It is only in recent decades that archaeologists have turned their attention to these smaller, basic units of society, glimpsing more of the components of daily life. In the hamlets, five to ten people of a family might live in two houses (one of them more substantially built and used in the cold of winter). Around these houses were specialized areas for cooking, storage, the making of craft objects. Each such settlement was permanent, year-round, and used usually for some ten years before the family moved on. Life was generally good: except for such relatively minor health problems as dental caries (from eating so much corn), the commoners were generally in as good health as the elite. They gainsay the adage that with the coming of agriculture, people tend to grow smaller in stature.

In times of food crisis or hostilities, these households would be knit together in larger cooperative efforts, presumably under the management of the nobles, who paid ultimate obeisance to the chief. This stage of cultural affairs is referred to as Mississippian, and extended throughout the South and well into the Midwest, even casting its influence on some of the farmers of the eastern Plains and the northeast woodlands. One way to imagine this is to think of a presentation made with an overhead projector. The cultural and political system of the Mississippian was rather like an overlay of a single color, lying atop a multicolored mosaic, each color representing a local adaptation and style. Each local style or mini culture had its own integrity, but all were colored (some more than others) by the overlying style of the Mississippian.

Some of the Mississippian centers were immense, none more so than the place called Cahokia (now East Saint Louis), located in a wondrously rich and naturally diverse plot of floodplain on the Mississippi River called the American Bottom. Most likely, more people lived at Cahokia than in any other single place north of Mexico—some estimates reaching as high as thirty thousand.

Mississippian gorget, Tennessee

Between 1050 and 1250 A.D. Cahokia extended over five square miles, the site of numerous open plazas, each ringed by mounds of various sizes and shapes—in all about a hundred mounds—the entire landscape dominated by one vast central edifice we call Monks Mound. This monumental structure rose high above all others, in all a hundred feet above the ground, in four terraces surmounted by a large building that was almost certainly the sacred home of the ultimate chief, a personage who almost surely was akin to a deity. Several other giant mounds existed with Monks Mound within a palisaded enclosure of some two hundred, acres. Here, then, in Cahokia, it was thought, was an actual city.

On the other hand, modern archaeologists doubt that the population at any given time was anywhere near the estimate of thirty thousand. More than likely some five hundred people lived in the central enclosure, with perhaps another four or five thousand in single-family houses sprinkled around the floodplain in the manner of neighborhoods, many with their own, lesser mounds. These farmsteads, some with their own sweat lodges, probably represented many more or less socially equal and politically independent groups, all

Mississippian southern cult shell head

of which looked to the grand center of Cahokia for ultimate leadership. Burials in Cahokia could be astonishingly elaborate. In one, a man was buried on a bed of twenty thousand beads of shell. Nearby three people were buried at the same time along with eight hundred arrowheads and a host of other objects. These were probably close relatives, sacrificed at the death of the great man. Also nearby, more than fifty women between the ages of eighteen and twenty-three were interred, evidently strangled as part of the funeral ceremony.

Once it was understood that the mound builders were, in fact, American Indians and not some alien race, many scholars assumed that all their monumental achievements and their agricultural feats were a result of direct contact with people from Mexico. Indeed, some of the Mississippian artifacts bear a resemblance to Mexican motifs. But modern archaeologists have satisfied themselves that the Mississippian phenomenon was homegrown, a natural enough extension of practices and cultural norms that had arisen long before and independently, just as the people of this region developed their own agricultural practices with local plants long before the introduction of maize.

By the time Europeans came across Cahokia, it had long been abandoned. Chieftainships were evidently unstable arrangements. And once abandoned, Cahokia was not repopulated, even by small farmers. This was the fate of numerous other Mississippian centers throughout much of the South and Midwest. Particularly along the southern tier of the region, and especially along the Gulf coast, the Mississippian style persisted, and was present to greet Spanish explorers who arrived in the sixteenth century—with results that were swift, unpredicted, and catastrophic.

Elsewhere in North America quite different societies flowered, with elaborate engineering and architectural works and with what may have been quite elaborate social engineering as well; but unlike the Mississippian mound builders, they were all gone—moved on to new lives—before the Europeans arrived.

The Hohokam: Master Hydrologists

About twenty-three hundred years ago, a group of people probably one hundred strong made their way through the northerly reaches of the Sonoran Desert, with its treelike saguaro cacti standing sentinel over a flat valley that stretched miles away, east and west, to blue, saw-toothed mountains on the distant horizon. It was a place of mesquite bushes and numerous lower-growing cacti and the long and wayward fronds of ocotillo that sway in the slightest breeze. The group was familiar with this kind of place; they knew that the saguaros, the other cacti, and the mesquite would provide them food in season. Though large animal prey was sparse, they could trap a mouse or a lizard and swallow it whole if they felt the need for meat. In baskets they brought various useful items such as shells and the seeds of corn and beans.

In due course, they came to a place along a free-flowing river, its banks shaded by cottonwood trees and willows in which small birds chittered. The riverbanks were low, with flatland on either side; about five hundred yards north, the land rose slightly. Making some calculations of a sort we no longer understand, they found this place perfect, or at least better in some way than other, similar places along the river. Here, on the rise, they began to build a village, with houses dug into the ground a foot or so, with walls and a roof of branches and mud. The houses were set well apart from one another in a style that would later come to be called *ranchería*. Just inside the entrance to each house, they built a hearth.

Then the major work began. Able-bodied men and women, probably fifty in all, spent most of the next hundred days digging a broad, shallow canal from a few miles upriver to let the river's water irrigate

Hohokam *Glycymeris* shell bracelet

the flatlands along the shore below their village. During this time they lived on saguaro fruits and mesquite seeds, and when the canal was done, they planted the seeds they had brought with them. That they knew just what they were doing in engineering this canal is suggested by the fact that it would be in use, largely unchanged, for almost one thousand years. These land- and water-wise people were the pioneers of what is one of the longest-running, most stable irrigation cultures in the history of the planet. They would come to be called Hohokam by archaeologists—the word, in the language of the Pimas (or Akimel O'odham) who inherited this region much later, means "all used up."

The "perfect place" that the group of one hundred came upon is located on the Salt River, about twenty-five miles south of Phoenix, and it came to be called Snaketown by archaeologists. In modern times, at any rate, there were a lot of snakes living there, and the original inhabitants seem to have been fascinated with them, carving serpents as well as frogs and horned toads on various objects that they made from stone. During Snaketown's thousand-year existence, its population reached as much as five hundred souls. Meanwhile, other villages of comparable size grew up throughout the region, along with outlying hamlets, each located to take advantage of a growing array of major and minor canals and transecting canals—a vast network that stretched across the landscape like the multiple branches of a tree with two trunks, the Salt and Gila Rivers. These arise in the highlands far to the east and, after meeting in the desert lands, empty into the Colorado River, which flows southward to empty into the Gulf of California.

There is no reason to imagine these Hohokam people were unaware of this geography. They came in the first place with seashells, many of them *Glycymeris* shells from the northern Gulf of California. From these and some twenty other shell species they fashioned jewelry. Grinding away the center of such a shell leaves a delicate circle, a fine bracelet, and if it breaks, one need only drill two small holes on each side of the break and stitch it all together with strips of yucca—prehistoric jewelry repair. Before long, the Hohokam learned (on their own, evidently) the art of etching designs into shell bracelets. A wine was distilled from the fruit of the saguaro and evidently used for ceremonial purposes. If it was left to turn acidic, the vinegary product was used for etching away parts of shell not protected with pitch. They also made turquoise earrings and amulets, and used pitch to glue small, tilelike fragments of turquoise (and pink shell for contrast) onto other shells in the form of mosaics that could be hung around one's neck. The closest source of turquoise was a mine in California several hundred miles away. No doubt some Hohokam made the long treks for such materials; surely traders from the south came bearing shell, copper bells, and the feathers of macaws and parrots. Some of the people in Snaketown, indeed, had their own macaws, imported from the tropical south, and perhaps locally bred in captivity. One can imagine the sounds of daily life in such a place—the oceanic silence of the landscape punctuated with the insane squawking of parrots, the shrieks of little children playing, mothers tut-tutting, while birds like vermilion flycatchers sang in the riverside willow trees. Nights would

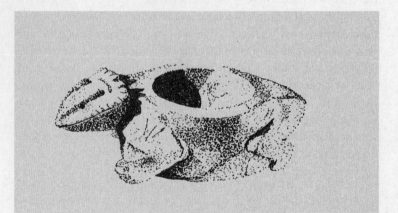

Hohokam horned lizard censer

mean stories told around hearth fires, the yipping of distant coyotes in the dark, and the barking of local semiferal dogs playing their universal role of alarmist.

Fanatically neat, the people of Snaketown regularly swept the dirt yards clean and took their trash some distance away to be dumped into elongated pits, which were also latrines, where no doubt the village's dogs argued over scraps. Eventually a pit filled in and the people continued dumping their trash there, creating a mound. Periodically they would cover a trash mound with clay or adobe (mud brick), perhaps for sanitary reasons. Some of the mounds reached twelve feet in height and were of sufficient extent to perform a second role. Flattened and surfaced with brick, they became places for ceremonies, perhaps placing celebrants that much closer to the spirits they needed to commune with. What sort of rites took place there is unknown today but they involved the burning of incense in specially carved censers. Some may have accompanied the cremation of the dead, whose bodies were burned along with all of their precious possessions. Some ceremonies almost surely were an important kind of spiritual engineering, complementing that of the grand waterworks and tied to the agricultural cycle, which included two plantings a year. Despite all the control provided by the extensive use of canals, this was an errant climate, often subject to drought periods, during which, if the irrigation ditches failed in spite of every effort, the people could survive well enough on wild foods gathered and hunted in the surround. They were ensured water to drink: wells dug some ten feet deep in the village tapped into the slower, wider subterranean river flow in times of need.

For a long time, life in places like Snaketown changed but gradually, almost imperceptibly. Pottery came into use in about 300 A.D., no doubt from Mexico, spreading north and east to other peoples beyond the Hohokam realm. Over the centuries, pottery designs changed and evolved, as did various other material things, including corn, which became more productive. Several kinds of corn came into use, including some that could grow in drier country such as dry washes; needing only a few timely sprinkles of water, it sent roots deep down to where some moisture persisted in the ground. This technique, called dry farming, was used alongside the irrigated fields. The Hohokam also learned to make canals narrower and deeper, lessening leakage and evaporation.

After about 700 A.D., a major feature of public architecture in many

Hohokam settlements was a large ball court, not unlike those in Mexico, where teams played a relatively violent ball game of one sort or another for high stakes—the losing team, it is said, was sacrificed. We know of no such activity in the Hohokam ball courts, which were usually dug down a ways into the ground and about half the size of a football field. Almost surely deriving from Mexico, they were usually built some ways outside the large villages, surrounded with land left otherwise unused, which no doubt served as campgrounds when people from the outlying hamlets arrived to participate or observe what were most likely religious as well as athletic events. Most likely the ball courts provided widespread groups of people with a sense of unity and community of purpose (not unlike a large-scale outdoor musical festival of today). Such a sense is necessary in a place dependent on the flow of rivers and canals, for there is nothing like water use to start an argument, and those who live upstream often have the best of it if some larger community spirit or system is not present. Surely, the digging and maintaining of canals was a major and frequent community endeavor. When a canal's sides

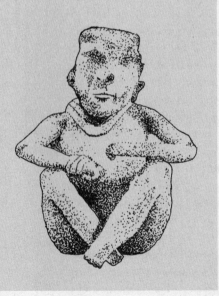

Hohokam figurine, Santa Cruz phase

were breached, the break was patched over with thick and water-resistant clay. In the ground disturbed by canal work, such opportunistic plants as amaranth colonized, providing yet other wild food for forage in times of need. Generally speaking, the Hohokam people had desert life figured out.

After 700 A.D., Hohokam culture spread well beyond the Salt and Gila river basins, as far north as Flagstaff, Arizona, and in a territory as large as South Carolina. Throughout this area, people were making the characteristic red-on-buff Hohokam-style pottery. People along the Verde River to the north were practicing Hohokam-style irrigation. On higher ground, people instead used small catchments to trap runoff from the melting snows of winter. Life was simpler, settlements smaller in these provincial areas, but still recognizably Hohokam in style.

Other peoples now noticeably surrounded the Hohokam territory, some who lived to the west being mostly hunters and gatherers still, eking out an existence along riverbanks and streams, mostly in the western highlands. Others to the north and east were also now adept at farming. At any such frontier, there is always a certain amount of cultural, if not physical, pushing and shoving, and from some people that archaeologists call the Salados, Hohokam people evidently took up building houses of adobe brick entirely above ground. Such buildings also appeared on the increasing numbers of ceremonial mounds, perhaps as temples, perhaps as granaries for distribution in lean times—probably both. Around the end of the eleventh century A.D., moisture in the region generally declined for a time, then increased, each change evidently followed by a change in population size.

By 1150 A.D., the world was changing more rapidly. At about this time, fewer ball courts were being built, and more mounds—now erected expressly for ceremonial (and perhaps administrative) purposes, often located equidistant between towns. Some people began living full-time in the buildings on mounds. It is possible that the need for coordinating the communal activities of growing populations in an expanding territory called for the rise of a priestly class, a form of governance that went beyond a more egalitarian system in which the canals may well have been managed by certain old heads who could produce consensus merely by virtue of their obvious wisdom and persuasiveness. People stopped making elaborately carved ritual items like censers and ceased etching and otherwise decorating their shell jewelry. Population continued to grow. Some settlements still consisted of houses built in pits, but more and more were built of contiguous adobe rooms, some of these as walled compounds, some multistoried, some on platforms. Great houses appeared with massively thick walls of clay.

In the southern core of Hohokam culture, the canal system reached its greatest complexity. Then, around 1275 A.D., the climate turned drier again. The Hohokam culture began to recede from its frontiers as provincial areas with marginal conditions for growing crops were abandoned. But the climate underwent yet another oscillation beginning in about 1325 A.D., evidently the product of a temperature change in the highlands that brought about a change in the patterns of snowmelt, which led to large-scale and highly destructive flooding of the canals. After more than a thousand years during which they had managed a successful life in a harsh land and had mastered their country's wayward fluctuations, the Hohokam lost control over (or some might say balance with) their world. A host of reasons in addition to the changes in climate have suggested themselves, ranging from disease to factional disputes to a similar decline in the cultures to the south in Mexico (from which much cultural energy had always derived), to the arrival of hostile nomadic tribes (the Apaches, for example). In any event, even villages in the old core area began to be abandoned. In some cases, old-style pit houses were built over masonry structures. By 1450, the last traces of Hohokam culture seem to disappear from the archaeological record.

About two centuries later, when Spanish missionaries arrived in this region, they found a not very large population of people they called Pimas living in *ranchería*-style settlements along the Salt and Gila Rivers. The Pimas lived in houses made of poles and brush and mud, and planted two crops a year of corn and squash and other foodstuffs, using a simple irrigation system. Many scholars now assume that these Pimas (including the Papagos south of the Salt and Gila Rivers) were the direct descendants of the Hohokam, now living a far simpler and more dispersed life. When the Pimas would pass by some of the old mounds, now covered with desert scrub, or the signs of the earlier canal system, they called it *hohokam*—"all used up."

Mimbres design

Mogollons and Anasazis: Master Builders

During the same long period in which Hohokam culture flourished, people were making a life in the more mountainous regions to the east—the great jumble of mountains and high valleys of the Arizona highlands stretching east into the Gila Mountain area of New Mexico. This large region experiences a good deal of precipitation, chiefly as snow, and a short growing season; it came to be known as the seat of the Mogollon culture. Here, when the pioneer Hohokam canal builders were getting to work in the Sonoran Desert, extended families were living in hamlets in pit houses, usually located on higher ground. These were hunters and gatherers who, over the centuries, gradually took to such imported Mexican innovations as pottery and maize. It would not be until about 200 A.D. that they—or at least some of them— switched to a preponderance of domestically grown food and the more sedentary lifestyle that agriculture calls for. Indeed, there may have been a certain amount of regional hostility between the agriculturalists, who tended to settle in the valleys near water sources, and the hunters and gatherers, who remained in the higher areas.

Rabbit, from Mimbres funeral pot

This region is the sort of place to tantalize and frustrate archaeologists, a place of numerous local styles in everything from pit house design to settlement design to pottery design. In fact, it appears to have been a continuing melting pot of shifting ethnic traditions, people arriving from time to time from the Hohokam region, Mexico, and the North. There are signs, for example, of families from several different ethnic groups inhabiting the same town. Most of these settlements had, in addition to the residential structures, variously shaped underground rooms that were larger than the typical pit house, probably rooms where certain ceremonial affairs took place, judging by the nontool items found in them: bone flutes, body painting materials, quartz crystals, pipes of stone, and effigies of one sort or another. (We call such underground ceremonial chambers *kivas*.) From 600 to 1000 A.D. little changed, but the population grew. By about 1000 A.D., most pit house settlements had been replaced by buildings of contiguous rooms made of masonry; they ranged from four to six rooms to far larger structures—some of five hundred rooms ranged around a central plaza. Kivas were now, for the most part, larger and rectangular, with masonry walls. Agriculture was widely practiced, and masonry storerooms with stone slab floors provided a hedge against hard times and a barrier against rodents and the damp. There appears to have been a fairly active trade with cultures to the south in Mexico, and for some four hundred years beginning in 900 A.D., a spectacularly original form of pottery came into being, called Mimbres Classic Black-on-White. While black-on-white geometric shapes on pottery were common among the people who lived to the north on the Colorado Plateau (the Anasazis), the Mimbres people produced not only elaborate geometric designs but naturalistic ones showing fish, humans, lizards, insects, and composite creatures, an exuberant bestiary of great imagination and unrivaled draftsmanship, what one scholar called "an expression of the sheer ecstasy of living."

By about 1400 A.D., however, the joy of life in the highlands appears to have ended. A process of abandonment of Mogollon settlements ended then, with a number of towns burned. Ethnic differences may have flared into hostilities, but no one knows. The inhabitants simply left, minimal evidence suggesting that they (or at least some of them) migrated northward to join the Pueblo people of northern Arizona and the upper Rio Grande, who were by then flourishing. Wherever they fetched up, it seems most likely that they gave up the farming life in the mountains, with their wayward weather and short growing season, as a bad job—not worth the effort, given whatever other troubles they had to cope with.

By the time the last Mogollon kiva stood empty, void of prayer and ceremony forever, what are generally considered the grandest examples of prehistoric architecture north of Mexico stood equally mute, abandoned even earlier. These were the astonishing "stone cities" (as people have called them, with considerable exaggeration) of the Anasazis, the people who dwelled in the vast region of the Colorado Plateau. This is essentially a huge flat table of land that was raised up intact from the surround long ago in geological history and immediately underwent the continuing process of erosion. Rivers and flash floods and windblown dust carved the land into uncounted canyons (including Grand Canyon) and sculpted rock into a phantasmagoria of shapes—natural bridges, high buttes and pinnacles, and caverns scoured out of cliffs. Here, for a time, people lived in multistory dwellings exquisitely constructed from rock, stunning structures that, in their elaboration, were unlike anything seen elsewhere on the continent.

The word *anasazi* is Navajo and means approximately "old enemies" or "the enemies of the old ones." The irony is that the Navajos seem to have arrived in the Southwest *after* the great Anasazi structures had been abandoned. Most of the great Anasazi ruins have been given national monument status, most notably Mesa Verde in southeast Colorado and Chaco Canyon in northwestern New Mexico.

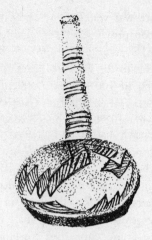

Chaco-style ladle, Utah, 950–1150

Recent investigations of some of these ruins have turned up amazing feats of engineering beyond the astonishingly high craftsmanship involved in building such high, straight walls and such aesthetically pleasing archways. A crescent-shaped array of formerly multistory buildings in Chaco Canyon, for example—a place called Pueblo Bonito—was found recently to have been one of the cleverest bits of passive solar architecture anywhere. Engineers have measured the ruin's efficiency in admitting the heat of the sun into its various parts. At winter solstice, the efficiency curve of solar heating is at its highest, and it remains high throughout the day, allowing the sandstone walls to store heat for the extremely cold nights. At summer solstice, the efficiency curve is properly at its lowest, but it is higher in the cooler hours of morning and lower in the afternoon, when the ambient temperature is at its hottest. In other words, this structure was designed (and built over time) to take maximum advantage of the sun and the shade in both winter and summer.

Pipe from kiva, Pueblo Bonito

Elsewhere in Chaco Canyon, located partway up a pinnacle of rock called Fajada Butte, modern investigators found what they have taken to be a sophisticated astronomical observatory. There, some enormous slabs are arranged in such a way as to cast a shadow on a cliff face on which is inscribed a spiral petroglyph. The arrangement of the slabs is such that a dagger of sunlight descends through the shadows and at exactly noon on the summer solstice bisects the spiral. Even without knowing of such achievements, the early European discoverers of these ruins believed they had to have been constructed by an extraordinary race of people long since disappeared without a trace—in the same manner as the mound builders of the Mississippi and Ohio River Valleys. It is now, however, generally agreed that the descendants of the Anasazis are present and mostly accounted for elsewhere in the Indian lands of the Southwest. For example, the Hopi word for those we call the Anasazis is *hisatsinam,* meaning "ancestors." In Hopi history, the various clans that make up the tribe originally came from many directions, fetching up, by virtue of the careful following of an ancient prophecy, at their current home in northeastern Arizona. Many of the clans speak of stopping off temporarily along the way, such as the Eagle clan, which spent about a generation in a wind cave in a canyon north of Hopi, a place with the ruins of an extended family's residence called Betatakin, part of today's Navajo National Monument. Archaeology bears out these stories, and today the National Park Service, among others, uses the Hopi name for the inhabitants of such old places.

The people called Anasazis started out, like virtually everyone else in the Archaic Southwest, living in pit houses, which were dug a few feet in the ground, with several posts holding up a roof that might be made of mud, and walls that might be made of branches laced together. They used a rudimentary set of tools to hunt game and gather and process wild seeds and fruit, following the seasonal patterns and generational variations of climate. They lived in small groups, probably family groups, gradually, conservatively taking on new ways—a bit of corn farming, pottery, the bow and arrow (as opposed to the atlatl, or spear-throwing stick), hedging their bets in an arid place subject to violent and changeable weather, extremes of temperature, drought, and flash flood. As elsewhere in the region, pottery—learned from the south in about 300 B.C.—brought with it better storage of grains and seeds, and storage pits came into being as well. By about this time, improved corn along with squash and beans (and cotton) had begun to bring about a more settled existence, with domestic plants forming an increasingly important part of the diet. As the population grew, which it did slowly, people began to dispossess large mammals—deer, prong-horn—and this process may well have compelled each step toward the farmer's life, however poorly suited the area was to such pursuits.

It was, over the centuries, a hard life. We know from burials that a man of forty-five would be worn down, old; and average life expectancy was less than that. We know that childbearing women suffered more severely from malnutrition than their men (and tended to die earlier), and children more than their mothers. Not infrequently, people died from diseases arising from what we now know to be poor sanitation. Drought came and went, with wet periods allowing people to spread out into the landscape but also, occasionally, flooding out small patches devoted to horticulture and turning shallow streambeds into almost useless deep arroyos.

By as late as 1050 A.D. a typical Anasazi settlement was no grand hotel of stone, complete with local artisans and astronomical establish-ments, but instead a rudimentary hamlet consisting of a line of masonry-walled rooms used for storage and entered via ladders through a low roof. The storage rooms had two connected wings with walls of sticks and mud, called jacales, all this forming a wide *U*. In the jacal wings, which one entered through ground-level doorways, were hearths. These were the living areas. Just outside the wings of the *U* was an underground room, the kiva, for ceremonial affairs, and beyond that a trash heap. (The idea for kivas most likely came from the Mogol-lon people to the south, where they predate anything similar found in Anasazi territory.) There might, as well, be an underground room or two within the arms of the *U* for grinding seeds and corn on flattened stones, called metates, just as earlier Desert Archaic people did. Such a hamlet was typically located near a river bottom or wash where small agricultural plots could be watered, at least seasonally, by small-scale irrigation. Such a settlement probably housed an extended family, and this mother village might have daughter villages farther up in the higher ground, places configured the same but without a kiva. The people here no doubt returned to their mother village for ceremonial (and probably merely social) occasions. More than likely these were matrilineal groups, with husbands coming to live in their wives' places, as is common in the pueblos of today. Beyond the daughter vil-lages, which were probably year-round dwellings given to dry farming and a good deal of hunting and gathering, were simple, impermanent camps where the people went in season for major hunts or to gather plentiful piñon nuts and other wild staples.

While remote, though less so as the overall population expanded over time, these hamlets were surely in touch with one another and presumably were visited by traders bringing various items such as shell, turquoise, and copper bells, and other trade goods from far and wide, exchanging them for food or hides. One can imagine the excitement caused in a quiet hamlet when one of these wayfarers arrived, laden with interesting things and perhaps with astounding stories to tell of the world beyond. In this period, the traders were also surely headed for the larger aggregations of people, the bigger markets, places like Chaco Canyon, where people had been building large structures as early as about 800 A.D. It was here too that the provincial people no doubt went on pilgrimages to attend special ceremonial occasions. In Chaco Canyon, from about 800 A.D. to 1150 A.D., a vast religious, social, and economic network existed, its influence reaching for miles across the unpromising landscape of the San Juan River basin. In Chaco Canyon, along an east-west running stream, were several (eventually nine) major structures, or pueblos, including Pueblo Bonito.

In all, the rooms in these great buildings were sufficient to house five thousand or more people, though it has been estimated that no more than two thousand ever lived there at any given time, and generally less than that. Most of the rooms were, in fact, given over to storage, and the rest may well have served as accommodations for visiting pilgrims coming into town for ceremonial festivals, where markets would have flourished and where young people underwent the wonderful rush of infatuation.

No one knows exactly what events led to the rise of this center. Its early buildings had a primary role as storage sites for food grown around the Chaco drainage and shared in bad times with the people from the surround. Even then, turquoise was plentiful, ground into beads and pendants, perhaps by full-time lapidaries. The nearest turquoise mine (and the source of most of it found at Chaco) was about a hundred miles to the east, across the Rio Grande in Cerillos. Near the mines at that time were Chaco-style masonry buildings, suggesting that the Chacoans controlled those mines and the route between. Jewelry items made from turquoise no doubt played a significant ceremonial role—it is still considered a powerful talisman and to some it embodies the sky—but it was also evidently used in the exchange of other items, such as homegrown food or trade goods like parrot feathers and copper bells from far to the south. In other words, turquoise may have been a rudimentary kind of money, linking places thousands of miles apart.

In due course, roads began to push out of Chaco, roads of an unnecessary, even fanatical straightness, leading up from the canyon via carefully excised steps and far off into the hinterlands hundreds of miles. Typically some thirty feet wide and raised slightly above the ground or at least lined with rocks, they appear to have linked Chaco to other settlements large and small. It is also possible that they were not roads

Mesa Verde mug, 1150–1300

in the sense that we think of roads, but symbolic structures, serving purposes more complex than mere transportation. In any event, building them was an arduous and labor-intensive task and it presumably called for a considerable amount of administrative oversight. Building the great houses of Chaco themselves called for community labor as well—not just the masonry but hauling the great logs needed for the ceilings and roofs from as far as a hundred miles away. It is not unreasonable to assume that among the permanent residents in Chaco was a class of priest-administrators who organized the work of building and maintaining this amazing center and performed another kind of engineering on behalf of the people—rituals that controlled the climate, that brought rain to a society now almost totally dependent on agriculture in a place where it was a dangerous game at best. If so, it worked. For most of the tenth and eleventh centuries, moisture in this region was either average or well above average.

Around 1100 A.D. a period of intense drought began in the San Juan basin. Within fifty years the Chaco system collapsed. The great centers in Chaco Canyon were abandoned—not in a sudden catastrophe but in an orderly departure, people taking with them whatever useful goods they could carry. Whatever was left of an administrative system may have moved to the north—to Aztec, probably, nearer to the San Juan River. The rains had ceased, the system did not work anymore, the ceremonies had failed. Throughout the region, much the same thing was occurring. Mesa Verde, north of the San Juan River in Colorado, also fell. In the hinterlands, people abandoned each area as it became more marginal, and sought more reliable sites.

West of Chaco, in the middle of what is now the Navajo Reservation, lies a huge geological feature called Black Mesa, the scene of provincial Anasazi life over centuries. North of Black Mesa, in a steep-walled canyon, is the cliff dwelling called Betatakin. It is a collection of sandstone houses built under a wind-carved overhang in the red rock. About a hundred feet or so below the dwellings, a stream flowed at least seasonally, and the canyon floor is still filled with cottonwoods, willows, and other riparian species. It is a secluded place, highly defensible. It contained 135 rooms at its height, and archaeologists have determined (by tree-ring dating some 298 wooden posts used in its construction) that the nucleus of this village was begun in the year 1267. It consisted of three clusters of dwellings and storage chambers, mealing rooms, and fire pits. A fourth such cluster was built the following year. Most likely a previously united group, perhaps an extended family, moved in during these first two years to make a new life for itself. Slow growth thereafter suggests that the population grew from within, continuing until the mid 1280s, when some 125 people lived there. By 1300, Betatakin too abandoned. All through the region, people were moving on.

In the eastern parts of the Anasazi cultural area, some people sojourned awhile in a great urban-style dwelling carved into the lava ash cliffs in today's Bandelier National Monument. They apparently spoke a language derived from Chaco and Mesa Verde, called Keresan today. Eventually they moved on from this place, which they called White House, to settle in villages along the upper Rio Grande—today known as Zia, Santa Ana, San Felipe, San Domingo, and Cochiti. Yet other people found their way to places downriver or to the west. About a thousand years ago, give or take a few decades, some people expatriated from Anasazi country founded a village on top of a four-hundred-foot high butte and called it Acoma. Acoma now vies with two others (the Hopi village of Oraibi and Taos Pueblo) for the right to call itself the oldest continuously inhabited spot in North America. Just west of Acoma lay the lands of the Zunis, a group of people whose language has resisted identification with any other in the Southwest or elsewhere. Where they came from remains anyone's guess; most likely they amalgamated from a variety of people on the move from the south and the north. The decades and even centuries after the collapse of Chaco were a period of regionwide disruption and reorganization.

On the Verde River south of Flagstaff, Arizona, another salubrious place of many rooms, now called Tuzigoot, was also suddenly abandoned, as was a similar town, now called Wupatki, in the shadow of the San Francisco Peaks, the remnants of a great volcano perched atop the Colorado Plateau at Flagstaff. These places and others like them were inhabited by people the archaeologists call the Sinaguas, an Anasazilike culture that flourished for a century or so in the environs of Flagstaff, on the Colorado Plateau, and south.

By about 1400 some people began painting pictures on the walls of their kivas of figures called *katsinas* by the Hopis. (In Utah one finds rock art figures that look very much like katsinas, dating back to the time of the Fremont culture.) These are benevolent spirits of nature in a more or less human form, and they intercede in behalf of the people with those deities responsible for rain. That is, they bring the blessings of life. Katsinas became an important part of life for the people who were spreading out into the territories of today's pueblos. They are more publicly known in the western ones, Hopi and Zuni, and are almost entirely private in the Rio Grande pueblos. Their impersonators come in season to the village plazas, where they are given the opportunity to perform dances and are fed spirit food (cornmeal). In return for these pleasures, they are told that the people have been leading proper lives and that the katsinas are obliged to tell the deities that they should allow the rains to come. These ceremonies are not prayers in the sense of pleas—instead they bespeak a reciprocal arrangement, a sacred deal between people and spirits. The performances

Katsina from Awatovi, mural in kiva

still take place in plazas, with lines of katsinas adorned with foxtails, sashes, kilts, and brightly colored paint dancing to and fro to the rhythm of a drum, turtle shells on their legs clattering, bells chinking, back and forth, over and over under the hot sun. As the day wears on, clouds materialize in the overarching cathedral of the sky and the wind kicks up; little dust swirls come and go in the plaza. Observing these ceremonies over the years, Yale University art historian Vincent Scully pronounced them to be the most profound work of art on the North American continent. They have been taking place for some six hundred years now, beginning probably as a response to the great period of disruption.

Throughout the Southwest, cultures had fallen apart—Hohokam, Mogollon, and Anasazi. People were leaving ancient sites, and presumably leaving behind many old ways, and amalgamating in a form of social polymerization into new peoples. Archaeologists have documented much of this movement and have puzzled over its exact causes, and other questions as well. Were these old societies, like that at Chaco Canyon, more egalitarian than one might infer, or less so? Did the elaboration of structure and society come about as a response to hard times, or did it arise in a time of abundance, when there was leisure time to invent new building techniques, new ceremonies? Archaeologists, by the very nature of the evidence available to them, tend to see causes of a material nature. Indian people, looking backward, are inclined to see things from a more metaphysical viewpoint.

The period of climate-caused disruption in the Southwest documented by archaeologists, and the subsequent migrations and rearrangements of people, have an analogue in the tribal history of the Hopis. Having emerged into this, their Fourth World, the people who would become Hopis ventured forth in all directions, eventually to return in a migratory implosion called the Gathering of the Clans. For example, the Bear and Bluebird clans tell of how they onetime lived at Tuzigoot, on the Verde River, but left, driven by the original prophecies to keep going until they came to their destined final place in this world. Similarly, the Eagle clan arrived from the North, having sojourned for a generation or two in a deep canyon where they built a small village in a cliff. They left because the prophecies commanded it. Today, Hopi priests still make regular pilgrimages to this place—called Betatakin on a map but Ky westima by the Hopis, one of several sacred shrines that are the standards, like flags planted in the ground, denoting the extent of the ancestral Hopi territories.

There is a darker side as well to these migrations, based on a well-honed understanding of human nature. Throughout the Hopis' history of migration, when a group was settled into a particular place, trouble would eventually start. In one such place, called Palatkwapi, men began after a time to pay less attention to their fields, gambling instead. There was a good deal of adultery. Humility was lost. It became the duty of a few Hopis there who understood the right path, the Hopi way, to call in the deities to help. In this case, a great plumed serpent called Balolokong arrived and brought about a flood that destroyed Palatkwapi. Only a few righteous Hopis survived to move on, as the prophecies required.

In many of these accounts, trouble starts, perhaps because of witches in the people's midst, and often takes the form of too great an elaboration of things—some people become arrogant, too fancy—and society needs to be purified and return to a simpler, more humble existence. Looking back at a place like Chaco, for example, a Hopi would say that there is really no need to create so elaborate and precise a device for marking the summer solstice as that at Fajada Butte. All one needs to do is to observe the annual passage of the sun and take note of when it reaches its most northerly point on the horizon at sunrise. In fact, a day or two this way or that really does not make all that much practical difference. The sun dagger phenomenon at Chaco would have been a greater benefit to priests than to farmers.

One compelling way to look at the collapse of the Chaco system is to note the drastic change in the climate and guess that it discredited the ceremonial-economic system of the priests and administrators, and forced a disillusioned people to move. Another way to look at it is that the ceremonies grew too fancy, too far off the mark, serving the priests more than the people, speaking of matters the spirit world was not interested in. Arrogance, unfairness, and a host of other sins were rife. People were not living up to their part of the bargain with the spirit world. No wonder, then, that the climate (which is the business of the spirits) did not cooperate.

Coda: The Athapaskans

Well before the great cultural upheavals in the American Southwest, people speaking a language called Athapaskan had settled in Alaska and northwestern Canada. At a point in time unknown and for reasons unknown, some of them headed south. Being accustomed by then to a subarctic climate, they may have stuck close to the Rocky Mountains as they migrated, though archaeologists have not been able to pin down their route or routes. Inevitably they would have bumped into other people already established along the way, and what they may have picked up from these people depends, to a degree, on which side of the mountains they spilled out on during their southward trek. One guess is that different groups of these Athapaskans journeyed on different sides of the great cordillera, each group picking up somewhat different approaches to things. Some of them, for example (those who would much later come to be called the Navajos), arrived in the Southwest practicing some horticulture as well as hunting and gathering. On the other hand, some (particularly those who would become the southern Apache groups, like the Chiricahuas) relied almost entirely on hunting and gathering and, at least later, explained that grubbing in the ground was beneath them. Agriculture was little known and practiced by the people of the Great Basin, west of the mountains, especially after the demise of the Fremont cultures.

They had all begun moving south as small bands. They built conical dwellings, used sinew-backed bows and single-shafted arrows, made flat coiled baskets, and used dogs for hauling their worldly goods. Their religion was almost certainly centered around the divining and healing practices of shamans. Along the way, it is presumed, they learned a little pottery making and perhaps how to weave. Thus they arrived in Anasazi country, but when exactly is not known. Estimates vary from 1000 to 1500 A.D., and most scholars seem to split the difference, suggesting that these bands began to appear around 1300 A.D., just as the great Anasazi experiment was coming to an end. That these new arrivals had anything to do with the Anasazi (and other) departures is not especially likely. In any event, with the old Anasazi lands largely depopulated, the Athapaskans were on hand to move right in (otherwise, it is reasoned, other established tribes such as the Utes might have moved in).

As noted, these people lived in bands, probably of extended families, and more than likely did not identify themselves in any tribal manner that we recognize today. They had nothing like chiefs, but followed the advice of leaders who earned respect by their own charisma.

At least later, several bands would hook up for special purposes such as retaliation on some neighboring malefactors. With apparent enthusiasm, they took over the empty lands of the Southwest. Those whom we call the Western Apaches today (who include several different bands, or groups, such as the Tonto Apaches) settled in the mountainous areas of eastern Arizona—onetime Mogollon country. In Arizona's southeast and across the border in Mexico and north into the Gila Mountain area, also once Mogollon country, the Chiricahua bands roamed. Both groups would move in around the Pimas and Papagos living in old Hohokam territory (and both Pima and Apache legends suggest that in early times at least, when the Apaches fought the Pimas, the Apaches more often than not lost heavily). To the east, chiefly on the eastern side of the Rio Grande, other bands took over the land—later to be called the Mescalero Apaches. Several Athapaskan groups wound up out on the Plains to the east—Kiowa Apaches, Lipans—where they adopted much of the culture of that region, roaming as far south as Texas and beyond. Between them and the Pueblos of the northern Rio Grande, a group that came to be called the Jicarilla Apaches came to lead a part Plains, part Apache, part Pueblo life in northeastern New Mexico. In the northwestern part of New Mexico, in the land that had been dominated by the Chaco Canyon system earlier, other groups of Apaches took up residence, hunting, gathering, and farming: these were the people who would eventually be called the Navajos.

At that time, in their earliest days in the Southwest, and for a long time afterward, these Apachean groups would not be very numerous, but they would come to dominate these recently emptied lands with a potency far greater than their numbers would have suggested. In due course, they both traded with and raided the more sedentary people in their midst and probably engaged in small wars with other, less settled tribes, such as the Utes and Paiutes to their north. Moving often within their chosen lands, traveling light as nomads must, following the game in its seasonal movements up and down the mountains or along rivers, they left little behind by way of footprints for modern archaeologists to track. No doubt their existence in these precincts was noted with the caution and even the dismay most outsiders are greeted with. It would not be until well after the first Spanish conquistadors ventured into this region that the profound influence of these relatively few Athapaskans would be felt.

October 11, 1492

The day before Christopher Columbus sighted land in the New World, a far more complex world existed in this hemisphere than most of us have been led to believe, and it had been here longer than most people could imagine until recently. Perhaps the most lasting misperception of the American Indians is that, in their pristine, pre-Columbian state, they were mostly hunters and gatherers. Part of this picture is also that, as hunters and gatherers, they lived gently on the land in a kind of benign ecological mutuality and in relative peace, until their lifeways were skewed by the coming of the Europeans.

In fact, most people in North America were not chiefly hunters or gatherers but agriculturalists. Most of them by far lived in villages, small and large. They had made significant changes in the nature of the American landscape, clearing plots of land, diverting streams, creating irrigation channels, building huge mounds, burning large areas to encourage new vegetative growth and the presence of such animals as deer. Fire was used as well as a herding device. The Indians were, to the degree they were capable, engineers of the landscape. Even the buffalo hunters of the Plains had long been constructing clever arrangements of the land in which to trap their prey, and some evidence suggests that they were not always above wantonly killing more than they needed.

They were an enormously polyglot people with a nearly incalculable number of cultural ways of living in their world—which is to say, as tribal groupings of one sort or another. They were people of complex ethnic distinctions, probably not having seen one another as one people for ten millennia or more, if ever. Adapting to the continuously changing nature of the places where they found themselves, they had invented new tools, new talents, new habits, new meanings, new gods, all to suit their circumstances. They had changed shape many times. There may well have been—in most regions—too many of them for the land to sustain without not only overuse of resources but jealousies and territorial squabbles, leading to a more or less continuous state of ethnic warfare. Signs of warfare and hostility increase in the archaeological record from about 2000 B.C. to 1000 B.C., depending on the area. California and the Great Basin, with their numerous small bands, seem to have been the only places where such warfare was not a constant—more an accident of geography, perhaps, than a special kind of psychology—for when crowded, the Californian Indian groups did fight, while the Great Basin people did not at all, so far as can be told. (That what may have been the most peaceable kingdom was in what is one of the most parsimonious of landscapes might well reorganize some thinking about human nature.)

On their own, which is to say without the help of the civilizations of Mexico and Central America, American Indians had invented numerous forms of agriculture, numerous indigenous crops, and their own needed variations on such imports as maize. They had experimented with highly complex societies replete with caste systems, with wholly egalitarian ways, and with many social forms in between. Like people everywhere on earth prior to the Industrial Revolution and the birth of modern science, they had discovered, perhaps by trial and mortal error, how to use the plants of their regions as medicines. They were immensely practical people, but also ideologues, true believers, artists, thinkers, dreamers, athletes, traditionalists slow to change, and pragmatists capable of quick response to catastrophe. They were just as smart as people today—and no smarter. They simply had other things (as Smithsonian archaeologist Dennis Stanford has said) to be smart about. And there was no way on earth that these people could have been prepared for what was to come.

PART TWO

Contact and Response

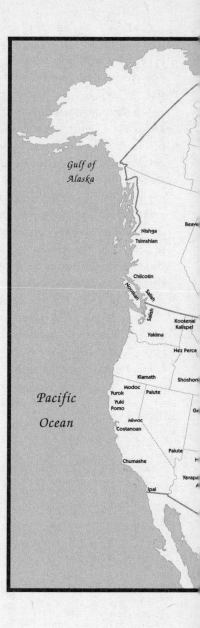

Gulf of
Alaska

Nishga
Tsimshian

Beave

Chilcotin

Nootkan

Salish

Salish

Kootenai
Kalispel

Yakima

Nez Perce

Klamath

Shoshoni

Modoc

Yurok
Paiute

Yuki
Pomo

Miwoc

Costanoan

Ge

Palute

Chumashe

H

Yavapa

Ipai

Pacific

Ocean

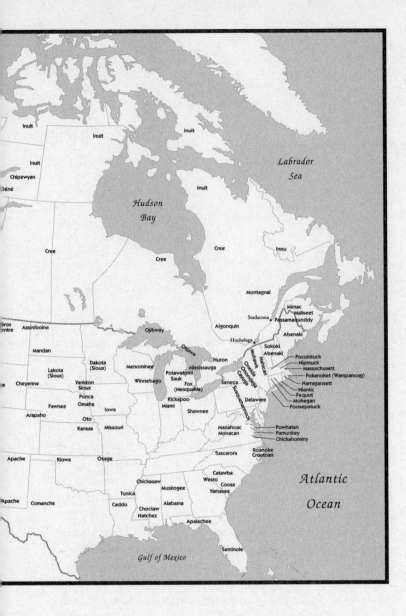

CHAPTER FOUR

MYSTERIES

Prophets

Plumed serpent. God of the wind. The master craftsman of life. The civilizer, Creator, patron of all the known arts. This was Quetzalcoatl, the Aztec god and founding king. He lived in a house of jade and the plumes of the quetzal bird, and presided over the golden age before the evil ones came, the necromancers bent on destruction. One of these was Tezcatlipoca, who one day entered the city and danced with bells on his ankles and sang, and the people lost their heads, congregating in revelry on a bridge. But the bridge collapsed and the people perished in the water below, and Tezcatlipoca entered the palace of the god Quetzalcoatl, holding a mirror.

The god saw himself in the necromancer's false mirror. He saw a bearded being with a long, homely face. If my people see me, he reasoned, they will be frightened, so he decided he would have to leave. For four days he lay in a stone box, and finally feeling ill, he rose up and sang a long, sad song, promising one day to return from the east. So he left, accompanied by bright-colored birds. Once on a shore in the east, he set fire to himself and rose up, along with the birds of many hues, into the eastern sky. So he became known also as the Lord of the Dawn. From then on, he rose each day enthroned in the morning sky as a star.

In the absence of Quetzalcoatl, the people kept a watch for him on the easternmost shore of their land, remembering his promise to return. One day the sentries saw someone coming across the sea, glittering and shining, and ran to their emperor, Montezuma, announcing that Quetzalcoatl had returned. Montezuma sent presents, including a snake mask adorned with turquoise and the plumes of the quetzal.

Of course it was not Quetzalcoatl, but the Spaniard Cortés, who within a year destroyed the great city, burning it and even setting fire to the aviaries that graced each home with color and song. The songs of the birds were silenced and the story was over, but the people who remain wonder still if Quetzalcoatl will make good on his promise and return.

The Hopis say that after people emerged into this, the Fourth World, the mockingbird (named Yaapa) sorted everyone out and into tribes and gave them their language. So there were Hopis, Navajos, Utes, Apaches, Comanches, Pimas, Zunis, and the white men (*pahanas*), all with their different languages. The next day, the people left, going off in the directions Yaapa had assigned them. The last to go were the Hopis and the white men, and a witch girl who had snuck through the passage to this world called the *sipapuni.* The leader of the *pahanas* said that since the witch girl had great knowledge, she could join them. With that, they left, heading east (some say south), and the Hopi leader warned his people that the *pahanas* would learn good as well as evil, so the people should listen very carefully if they encountered white people again. But, the leader added, one day a particular white man, the Pahana, the White Brother, would return and bring harmony and kindness and peace.

In 1955 at a congressional hearing in Washington, D.C., an eighty-year-old Hopi named Dan Katchongva explained these things. He said it "was known that the White Man is an intelligent person, an inventor of many words, a man who knows how to influence people because of his sweet way of talking and that he will use many of these things upon us when he comes." Katchongva went on to say that these prophecies had come true, that the Hopis could see "how many new and selfish ideas and plans are being put before us." The Hopis still await the White Brother, or at least hope he has not come yet.

■　■　■

Throughout the land, Indian people prophesied that the white man would come. A great Sauk leader named Black Hawk told how his great-grandfather, Nanamakee (his name means "thunder"), had a dream that in four years he would see a white man. Nanamakee blackened his face and fasted, eating but once a day. This was at a time when the Sauks lived in Canada. After three years of this, the Great Spirit told him the white man would arrive in a year and would be a father to him. Seven days before the anticipated arrival, Nanamakee set out to the northeast with his two brothers, directing them to listen for any unusual noise. They returned the next day, saying they had heard a noise and set a marker to point in its direction. Going there alone, Nanamakee found a tent. A white man emerged from the tent, took Nanamakee by the hand, and welcomed him inside. He said he was the son of the king France and that the Great Spirit had told him to come to this place, where he would meet people like Nanamakee who had never seen a white man. These people would be his children and he their father.

The Kwakiutls of the northwest coast tell how a beautiful young woman fell in love with a man from another tribe who was subsequently killed. He returned to her nevertheless and took her off in his canoe, but then abandoned her, leaving her floating in the water, from which she could see no land, nothing but water. She drifted about for years until, one night, she saw some foam in the water, which she scooped into the canoe. When day broke she discovered it was not foam but calico and thread. Though still lost, she was happy to have clothing. Then, before long, the canoe ran aground and she unloaded all the calico and thread, and sewed herself a house on the beach.

Two men soon appeared at her doorway and she invited them in. They were white men and she asked why their clothes were so ragged and poor. She offered to give them some better clothes, and they accepted. Once they were dressed, she asked if they were the only two of their people, and they said no, their village was not far off. She told them to go to their chief and ask him to come carry all the rest of her clothing. So the chief came in his boat and they filled it with clothing and the woman sailed off with them to their village and became their queen.

■ ■ ■

In the latter part of the twentieth century, a Brulé Sioux named Leonard Crow Dog told how the trickster Iktome forecast the arrival of the white man, and he let the story be tape-recorded by researcher Richard Erdoes. Iktome went from tribe to tribe—the Sioux, Arapahos, Crows, Shoshones—heralding the ominous arrival of a dangerous new nation of people, a new man who was pitiless, a liar, who would take everything. Though warned, the people all forgot and went back to their normal ways. But then one day two Sioux women who were out gathering food saw a pale bearded creature with a black hat arrive mounted on an animal big as a moose. The creature, a man, carried a cross and a fire stick, and from his black coat he took a glittering object that contained clear white water. "He offered it to the women to drink, and when they tried it, the strange water burned their throats and made their heads swim. The man was covered with an evil sickness, and this sickness jumped on the women's skin . . . and left them dying."

Not long ago, a southwestern Indian elder approached the Dalai Lama and spoke of his tribe's prophecies, of how the end of the world had been forecast long ago and only the few righteous people would escape this new Armageddon. The Dalai Lama is reported to have said, "But aren't all prophecies about the past?" One does not need to be an overzealous skeptic to imagine that the more specific such a prophecy is, the more possible it is that events that already have taken place informed it. On the other hand, it is all too easy for skeptics or people from other religious traditions to be comfortably rational and dismissive about such matters as prophecies (particularly other peoples' prophecies). And there is some reason why at least some of the native people on this continent would have noted the existence (or the imminent arrival) of a white man long before Columbus reached these shores. That is because white men indisputably reached these shores about a thousand years ago, half a millennium before Columbus.

In 1001 A.D., the Hohokam culture of the Southwest was reaching its grandest level, and the Hopewellian mound builders in the Ohio Valley had already packed up and left their great earthen monuments behind. In that year, a contingent of Norsemen led by Leif Eriksson made a landfall on North America, probably on the northern tip of Newfoundland, which they called Vinland, and found it a "choice" country. There, on a rise overlooking a bay in a place now called L'Anse aux Meadows, they built at least eight Viking-type houses of sod, a forge, and some boathouses, and there they overwintered at least once, perhaps remaining a few years altogether. In due course, the Norse met the natives, probably an Algonquian-speaking group, perhaps ancestral to the Beothuk Indians of Newfoundland. Whoever they were, the Norse sagas refer to them as Skraelings. The two groups no doubt took each other's measure, apparently traded a few items, and also apparently fought, the Norse getting the worst of it and leaving. But Norse hopes for a foothold in this choice land were evidently long in dying. A Norse coin minted in the eleventh century was found in Maine, where it apparently was taken and dropped in the thirteenth century. However many such contacts there were, they were all, in the grand sweep of things, completely inconsequential—*except* for the possibility that the Algonquian-speaking people on Newfoundland might have passed along stories of these (ineffectual) white invaders to other Algonquian speakers, who could have passed them on. And the Norse could well have become fiercer in the telling. How far could such stories have traveled? No one knows. There was, it is becoming clear, a great deal of interchange between the far-flung peoples of Turtle Island, but it is hard to imagine that the Skraelings' tales of the Norse could have evolved into a myth about the Aztec god Quetzalcoatl. It all remains speculation, which is not, after all, entirely unrelated to prophecy.

Population and the Pox

A far more mysterious and far more serious question arises, however, from the comparison between these early contacts and later ones. How is it that a band or so of Indian hunters and gatherers could have turned away the Norse, who had already established a reputation in much of Europe as ferocious raiders, when, five hundred years later, a relative handful of Spaniards could enslave an empire of millions in a trice?

To be sure, the Spanish burst upon the Aztec civilization with fire sticks—clumsy protorifles called harquebuses—and metal armor, mounted on huge beasts with surging power in their haunches and death to the unwary in their hooves. And they probably seemed god-like, perhaps representing Quetzalcoatl himself. In the spring of 1520, after six months in the city of Tenochtitlán, seat of the Aztec empire,

Hernando Cortés left to fight a battle elsewhere, leaving a few hundred troops behind. These were set upon in May by the Aztecs and almost destroyed. Cortés quickly returned with 1,250 Spaniards and perhaps eight thousand friendly native warriors, only to be driven away after two-thirds of his Spanish soldiers and innumerable native warriors were killed. A year later, in 1521, he returned and conquered the Aztec state. This time he won handily because of what, back in Europe, was considered a childhood disease: smallpox. By the time Cortés returned, smallpox had taken the Aztec leaders and uncounted numbers of people. The Spanish siege was merely the coup de grâce.

Smallpox thrives in close quarters and does poorly in extreme cold weather. It is probable that smallpox was not much present among the Norse, and had it been, it probably would not have spread very far among relatively isolated bands of hunters in their own boreal lands. But teeming, subtropical Tenochtitlán—with a population of two hundred thousand, and over a million more living in the city's shadow—was a pathogen's paradise, as were the native populations of the Western Hemisphere to whom it was introduced. They possessed no immunity to this kind of invader. Nor had they ever before suffered, so far as anyone knows, anything of a pandemic nature. The infectious diseases of their hemisphere could create chronic ailments but were rarely fatal. Nothing in the extensive pharmacopoeia of herbal remedies or the techniques of the shaman could cure the unprecedented scourges that struck in the sixteenth century and afterward. This viral and bacterial innocence may well be the most historically important element in the initial conditions of the American Indian.

In historic times, beginning in the Caribbean, Peru, and Mexico, smallpox and a host of other introduced diseases—measles, influenza, plague, and others—would repeatedly devastate Indian populations, up till the very end of the nineteenth century, erasing some altogether from the world.

(Two possible exceptions to this general picture are syphilis and tuberculosis. Shortly after Columbus's return to Europe, an epidemic of venereal syphilis broke out there, and a common retort in some circles is that if Europeans gave the Indians smallpox, the Indians gave Europeans syphilis. In fact, there is evidence of syphilitic disease on both sides of the Atlantic before Columbus, and the new and venereal version was probably a result of genetic mutation of the disease organism, which also causes yaws, pinta, and nonvenereal syphilis. Similarly, tubercular lesions have been found among pre-Columbian Europeans and Indians. Whether tuberculosis arose separately in the two hemispheres or was present in some form when the first Americans crossed Beringia is in dispute—the bacterium can survive in the cold and among small populations. In either case, both populations had evolved at least limited immunity to the older strains.)

It may be no exaggeration that European-borne disease killed more American Indians in those first few decades than were born in the next four hundred years. To ask how many Indians died of these causes is also to ask how many were living here before Columbus. This is both a concern laden with high emotion and a question for which we may never have a precise answer, in spite of many attempts to reach one. But first, nearer to hand is an answer to a related question—why the lack of immunity to pandemic diseases? Why this particular innocence?

The answer lies mainly in timing. Whenever exactly it was that the first Asian emigrants made their way eastward across the sparse, cold grasslands of Beringia or down the coast in hide boats, it was well before 11,500 years ago. At that time, virtually the entire human population of the earth consisted of hunters and gatherers living, at least most of the year, in relatively small bands. The exception was beginning to be seen in the region of Mesopotamia, where

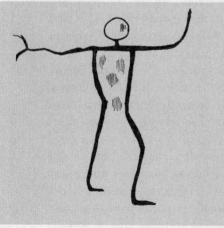

Dakota smallpox

people had just begun to settle down to practice a more sedentary, agricultural life. By the time another thousand years had gone by, they had also domesticated a number of animals—cattle, sheep, pigs, and goats. Here, then, was a more reliable way of life, it must have seemed, and one that could support ever-growing numbers of people (although life expectancy declined at first). Here also was a new and unprecedented witch's brew, for large numbers of people were living in close and daily association with the same animals, the same soil, the same water, and this new broth also gave comfort to a new kind of pathogen. Smallpox evidently evolved from cowpox (indeed, much later, when an observant Englishman named Edward Jenner noticed that milkmaids who caught cowpox did not get smallpox, the door was opened to vaccination). Influenza arose from pig diseases, measles possibly from canine distemper. Close quarters and the increasing presence of wastes of all kinds provided a new ecological theater for the evolution of pathogens and their vectors—rats, mosquitoes, worms, and so forth—and for people. Agriculturalists evolved along with these lethal new diseases, gradually developing a certain amount of resistance or immunity, until they could coexist in an uneasy relationship in which children were most likely to succumb. (If a parasite is too virulent, after all, and eliminates its host species, it too is eliminated.)

When people came to North America, they crossed a region too cold for most vectors of these human pandemic diseases—if in fact any existed at the time. Any small band so afflicted would have vanished in any case, probably without passing it on, since people were so few and so mobile. They were greeted here by an astounding array of large mammals, which might well have harbored the sort of pathogens that could have evolved into human pathogens, but soon most of these species were extinct, and in any event, the hunters' contact with them was hardly constant or in crowded conditions. Once they were gone, there were few species to choose to domesticate. A potential domesticate needs, among other traits, to be social, with some dominant and some submissive personalities, and without an immediate flight response. None of this applied to the remaining large mammal fauna of this hemisphere—moose, elk, deer, musk ox, mountain goats, and pronghorn antelopes (which are in fact closer to goats than to African antelopes). Only the few remaining camel relatives—like llamas, in the high mountains of South America—guinea pigs, and turkeys wound up as domesticated animals in this hemisphere—and of course, dogs. (Canid-based pathogens in the New World simply did not evolve into the sort that could jump over to humans, as evidently occurred in the Old World.) Bison are not unlike cattle, but why domesticate them if they are already so plentiful and if you already know how to pick off whatever you need? Furthermore, any such experiment with bison would have proved what Ted Turner and other bison ranchers have learned to the alarm of their cowboys: bison are a lot more unruly than cows.

While Indians throughout the hemisphere came to rely heavily on domesticated plants and many took to a relatively sedentary life, they were without the other ingredient (domesticated animals) of the broth that cooks up most epidemic disease. The pathogens simply were not here—and it is ironic, as archaeologist David Meltzer has pointed out, that the early European colonists flourished in this relatively disease-free and, at first, uncrowded world, their life expectancy rising into the seventies.

Introducing epidemics into the New World that make the biblical plagues seem like mere inconveniences was clearly not part of the policy of the first Europeans on these shores, though some would quite happily take advantage of the results. Various scholars have long argued over how devastating these results actually were, which is to say, how many people inhabited North America before contact, when they were exterminated by disease, and how many.

The debate is an old one and estimates of the pre-Columbian population vary widely—from about a million in the United States to 18 million and even more. In the 1930s, ethnographers, and in particular A. L. Kroeber of the University of California, were of the belief that Indian cultures had not changed a great deal over the ages until the European colonists and settlers began to actively interfere with their land base (which is a mild way of saying took their land) and with their cultures (by introducing new technologies, beliefs, and so forth) or, of course, simply killed them. Kroeber and his associates sought to reconstruct the pre-Columbian state of Indian cultures by sorting out the ancient from the recent, chiefly through the technique of interviewing living people, called informants. Having determined this pristine state—what they called the *ethnographic present*—they then looked at historical records (censuses and the like) to measure the effect of such things as epidemics on populations since the ethnographic present.

This brought them to the low figure of some 1 million American Indians present at contact.

Later, in midcentury, archaeologists and other ethnographers began to perceive that change rather than stability had long characterized the world of the American Indian, and by the 1980s an entirely different scenario was being debated—the work of Henry Dobyns at the University of Oklahoma and others. Taking the Spanish estimates of the population of Mexico when Cortés first arrived and those a century later, it was determined that for every survivor there were twenty who had died—chiefly of smallpox—which is to say, about 95 percent of the population of Mexico. Given that the main strain of smallpox can cause total mortality among people with no immunity, this figure is not unreasonable. Dobyns looked at the record, seeing that some forty smallpox and measles epidemics alone struck the American Indians from the middle of the sixteenth century to just before the twentieth (1898 being the last outbreak of smallpox). Using the ratio of twenty to one, Dobyns applied it (and census data) to the American Indian and concluded that there were some 18 million in 1492—and overall, throughout the hemisphere, 112 million, the vast proportion of whom were in Mexico and Central America.

Dobyns's figure, larger by orders of magnitude than previous estimates, came in for criticism, much of it based on the incompleteness of knowledge of how many epidemics did actually strike and of what diseases. A physical anthropologist from the Smithsonian Institution, Douglas Ubelaker, used other methods—combining what seemed the most reliable tribe-by-tribe censuses with what evidence was available from such things as human remains—and came up with an estimate of just under 2 million, which Ubelaker himself thought might well be low.

By the early part of the twentieth century, there were only some 250,000 American Indians alive, their lowest ebb since millennia ago. Their population had been reduced in the four hundred years of recorded history by as much as 95 percent (Dobyns) or as "little" as 75 percent (Ubelaker)—in either case a terrible catastrophe, but the less conservative estimate seemed all the worse, being on the same scale as some twentieth-century holocausts, like that of the Jews by the Nazis and other Europeans, or Russians by Stalin, or Cambodians by the followers of Pol Pot. What was clear was that an enormous die-off occurred between the time Europeans first probed the shores of the New World and the time they began to make even unreliable censuses of the native populations.

Ann Ramenofsky, then an archaeologist at the University of Louisiana, essayed an even more synoptic approach, taking whatever could be determined from the archaeological record and considering that as an independent measure to hold up to the ethnographic and historical evidence. She reasoned that epidemics in virgin territory can bring about mortality ranging from 30 to 100 percent, enough to alter the structure of a population in one or two generations. If, then, the archaeological record points to such large changes after initial contact—such as with Cortés, in 1519, or with de Soto, whose 1540 expedition took him through much of the American Southeast—but *before* any sustained or prolonged European presence in a region, then disease is the only probable cause. (Ramenofsky has pointed out that pigs left behind by de Soto might well have helped spread smallpox throughout the Southeast after the expedition was over.) If, on the other hand, the major losses followed sustained European presence, then other factors could have been at work as well—warfare, chiefly.

Archaeology is a tricky arena. The archaeologist can count grave sites, for example, but burying the dead is not the only way to dispose of them, and not all such sites either remain or are found. Another approach is to look at the remains of living quarters through time in known settlements and make estimates of how many people lived where for how long—again a matter fraught with ambiguity. What, for example, is the average size of a prehistoric family living in a pit house with one hearth?

With such caveats in mind, Ramenofsky analyzed the record in three regions where archaeological evidence extended from precontact times well into the period of a permanent European presence—the lower Mississippi River Valley, central New York State, and the middle Missouri River Valley. The record shows that huge population losses were suffered in the lower Mississippi Valley after de Soto and before the onset of French colonial efforts in the region more than a century later. These people lived in agricultural villages, as we have seen, often a large central village surrounded by smaller outlying hamlets. After de Soto's expedition, a great many villages were abruptly abandoned, and other (but far fewer) villages of hybrid cultural traits sprang up.

After the initial devastating losses, a slight upward trend in population occurred, followed by a downturn after the French arrival.

In central New York, the picture is somewhat different. European trade goods appeared in this region between 1500 and 1550, presumably traded by European fishing crews who began plying the rich fishing grounds off the American northeast coast at this time. Sustained colonization in Iroquois country did not begin until several decades into the next century, when Dutch traders established a fort in Albany. In the years prior to that, the archaeological record suggests a slight population *increase* among the Iroquoian tribes of central New York. But an epidemic in 1535 had nearly eliminated an Iroquoian group that lived along the Saint Lawrence River, to the north, and the survivors probably joined their southern cousins, which accounts for a population bulge but also for a spread of disease (surely smallpox) among the central New York tribes, leading to a catastrophic population collapse. This can be read, up to a point at least, in changing village sites, village size, and even changing housing structures (from large longhouses to smaller cabins spread farther apart).

In the middle Missouri Valley, athwart the North and South Dakota border, the first Europeans did not appear until the 1730s, and a sustained European presence began only in the early 1800s. Yet it appears that the local populations of Mandans, Hidatsas, and Arikaras began to suffer enormous losses beginning in about 1700, long before European trade goods showed up in their midst. Villages, even entire areas, were abandoned. But by then one of the most important of Spanish introductions had arrived in the Plains region—the horse—and it could well have been newly mounted Plains Indians who brought smallpox even to such a remote section.

The archaeological record, then, seems to support the Dobyns position—that catastrophic epidemics spread throughout some if not many parts of the continent before the people in particular regions actually saw their first European. Depending upon region and timing, there was a period quite different from either prehistory or history, a gray region of time that extended for differing lengths of time in different places, when sudden and drastic change was wreaking havoc on the populations and cultures of the American Indian. This murky time has been called *protohistory*—the period between the earliest arrivals of Europeans on these shores and the time when Europeans and Indians came face-to-face in different regions. Protohistory brought anything from disruption through catastrophe to extinction, depending on population density among other things. When Europeans did encounter many of the American Indian tribes, the latter were the few survivors—either still reeling from the unimaginable turmoil of the worst catastrophes ever to befall them or in the process of recovering, creating new societies, new traditions, new norms, and possibly new faiths out of the wreckage of the old.

Perceptions

One of the Europeans' earliest representations of the people they found in North America is an engraving that appeared on a French map of 1613 showing a *"sauvage"* couple of the New England coast (see illustration in photo section). Among other distinctly European features, they both have wavy blond hair and European facial features, and he a blond beard to boot. This was a time, as well, when European artists painted small children as if they were simply tiny adults, not noticing, for example, that real children's heads and eyes are disproportionately large. Europeans simply had a very difficult time *seeing* the people of North America, and once seen, the Indians were hard to fit into the categories available to the European mind.

Indeed, for many the question arose: were these really human beings, with souls? There was no accounting for them in the Judeo-Christian annals or in classical works, except perhaps as the lost tribes of Israel. Clearly they were heathen, not Christian. And surely they were barbarians, not civilized (which is to say, they were not literate and lacked a proper form of government and social administration, not to mention European social graces). The church argued strenuously that these were humans with souls and deserved better treatment than many of the lay adventurers and colonists were willing to provide. Before too long, it was generally accepted in theological circles that the Indians were human beings and that they ranged along a continuum of barbarism—from just a bit less civilized than Europeans to forest-dwelling savages. But further trouble lay ahead: an Indian who followed the missionaries and converted became a Christian barbarian, and therefore something of a philosophical embarassment. Eventually, but not until a century and a half had passed, Europeans generally accepted that non-Christian people could be rational and that there were various levels of society, from high-grade civilization to low-grade savagery. These perceived levels, and the parlance associated with them, would remain in the Western mind as late as the early years of the twentieth century. Even in academic circles of the day, it was not uncommon to hear Indian people catalogued as *civilized* (meaning Christian and literate); *barbarian* (meaning settled into an agricultural village life, like that of most of the Pueblos of the Southwest); and *savage* (people whose tradition was that of the mobile, free-ranging hunter and gatherer). The fact that *most* American Indians by far were, at the time Columbus arrived, agricultural villagers who supplemented their crops with wild or semidomesticated food never really sank in until recently.

Mental pigeonholes aside, the Europeans had a practical problem on their hands once they came across the native populations of the Western Hemisphere. The king of Spain pondered the question of how to deal with the people who lived in the lands the Spanish had just "discovered." An unwritten rule had governed much of human history: those who came upon and conquered other lands had the right of possession—of the land and its riches. The conquered people could go somewhere else, be assimilated into the conquering population, or go extinct—it mattered little, except for the Spanish duty, delegated by the pope, to convert the heathen.

On the ground, such duties led to a good deal of violence, as well as absurdities. Upon arriving at some new piece of territory, Spanish explorers read—out loud and to the winds, or in some instances to a handful of bewildered Indians who were present—the Requirement, a long and pompous statement about the identity and power of the pope and the Spanish court, and other examples of European superiority, which went on to require the native population to accept the Spanish as their rulers or be enslaved, protesting further that "the deaths and losses which shall accrue from this are your fault and not that of Their Highnesses, or ours, nor of those cavaliers who come with us." This screed often was read to an empty wilderness, a situation comical enough to get a laugh even from some Spaniards, and one can imagine the befuddlement of any Indian people who happened to be present at such an incomprehensible reading.

For several generations after Columbus, Spanish theologians squabbled in refined terms about the nature of these newly discovered people, some explaining (along with Aristotle) that there were, after all, people who were just made to be enslaved, and that the Indians were of that sort. Others objected in terms we might today find more familiar. It was also clear that the Bible commanded believers to go forth and bring the true word of God to all peoples of all countries—no Spaniard doubted this—but the questions arose about what to do if some Indians refused to listen, as some certainly did. Should they be left to their own beliefs, or punished and forced to accept Christ?

The Spanish monarch, however, was an utterly devout Catholic and earnestly wished that his country follow policies in its empire building that accorded with the dictates of the church. He asked a leading theologian, Francisco de Vitoria, to ponder what rights the Spanish could claim in these new lands. Vitoria decided that the Indians truly owned the land and, merely discovering it themselves, the Spanish could not claim ownership. Ownership by discovery, he concluded, was only legitimate if the land was already unowned. Instead, the Indians could *voluntarily* agree to cede land to the new arrivals—unless, of course, a just war took place, and such a war could not be simply a matter of whim. Justification for a war would arise only if the Indians did not allow the newcomers to "sojourn" there, to live there, to travel, and to trade.

This became the philosophical basis, generally accepted by the other European nations as well who were nosing around the continent at the time, for dealing with Indians of at least the Northern Hemisphere. It would, of course, often be ignored by conquistadors and others on the ground thousands of miles from the enlightened courts of Europe. But in this age of rapid European expansion into other parts of the world, this position did recognize the Indian peoples as legitimate entities that should be dealt with by means of treaties, agreements, and other mutual arrangements. There were good practical reasons to abide by this, particularly in the early years, when Europeans were very few and Indians very many, but as often as not what seemed practical reasons for starting a "just war" arose as well. Rejection of Christ's message was often seen as a good reason for hostilities. Yet behind all of the clashes—physical and cultural—that would ensue in the centuries following, this principle did exist, however tenuously, as a guideline: the Indian tribes (whatever that meant) were to be taken as something akin to nations with certain (extremely limited) rights.

At the same time, underlying all of the rationalizations and justifications for the Europeans' presence was the belief that as Christians they and they alone had the truth. This had justified the astonishing excesses of the Crusades against infidel Islam, centuries of anti-semitism, and with the discovery of native populations on other conti-nents, a missionizing zeal that justified any kind of violence seen to be needed, since by definition such people were mentally and culturally below par, not being Christian—the colonial version of a Catch-22. This underlying attitude about Christianity infused and justified all other actions in the New World, and would do so well into the twenti-eth century. After the ravages of European-borne diseases, the religion of the Europeans was the single most dangerous force the Indians across the entire hemisphere would ever face. As historian Wilcomb E. Washburn summarized the matter:

> In the first centuries after the birth of Christ, the Christian message spoke for the weak and oppressed. Its message was one of peace and love. The New Testament message might have been understood and honored by the Indians of America had it been preached as it was on the shores of Galilee. But by the time the American Indian came face to face with the doctrine of Christ it had hardened into a mold of bigotry, intolerance, militancy and greed which made it the mortal enemy of the American Indian. . . . The new look of Christianity reflected the changed status of the sect: from that of persecuted minority to domi-nant majority.

The Question of Cannibalism

From the very outset of contact, the Europeans' view of the native pop-ulations of the Americas was colored by dark talk of cannibalism. Columbus arrived in this hemisphere at a time when the local people of the Lesser Antilles, the Arawaks, a society of village agriculturalists with complex social ranking, had been preyed upon and largely driven out by people from the mainland of South America—the Caribs. These were a loosely organized society of hunters and seafaring warriors who raided the Arawaks for women and food. The Arawaks' name for the Caribs gave us the word "cannibal." That the Carib warriors were reputed by their victims to be cannibals helped justify the subsequent Spanish enslavement and extermination of Caribs in the islands of that sea to which they also had their name attached. No reliable evidence exists that the Caribs were in fact cannibals, but it was common in much of the world for one group of people to explain to European explorers and conquerors that the next tribe over was of sufficiently low character as to eat people. This apparently roused the moral ire of the conquerors to the point that the enemy tribe might suffer most at their hands. Apparently more than half of the tribes of California, for example, told stories of cannibalism on the part of others, but again, evidence is lacking. Lesser forms of such bad-mouthing—or at least indirection—are also common. After the Spaniard Coronado reached and brutalized the Zuni in his great *entrada* into the present United States seeking the seven fabled cities of gold, the Zuni with wonderful disingenuousness sent the Spanish on to the Hopi villages far to the west.

European reports of cannibalism among various groups of American Indians would accompany virtually all of the movements of Europeans into Indian territory, and the subject is (as can be imagined) one of the most emotionally laden in Indian history and, of course, one of the most painful to discuss in any context.

For many Indian people today, such accusations smack of colonialist put-downs motivated, at the very best unconsciously, by racist attitudes that the European-American mind simply cannot get over even now, whether dealing with the native peoples of the Americas, Fiji, New Guinea, or Africa. Anthropologists have been roundly chastised even from within their own ranks for uncritically accepting ethnographic accounts of cannibalism as true; as early as 1937, Ashley Montagu said flatly, "In fact, cannibalism is a pure traveler's myth." And in 1979, William Arens, an anthropologist at the State University of New York, decried his profession's uncritical support of "the collective representations and thinly disguised prejudices of western culture about others." Having reviewed the worldwide literature on cannibalism and having found the evidence at best merely anecdotal, or what could be called hearsay, Arens said, "The idea of 'others' as cannibals, rather than the act, is the universal phenomenon."

Many Indian people today are not overly fond of anthropologists, and anthropology, to boot, is among those disciplines most given to internecine squabbles, but controversy is heard equally in the realm of ethnohistory, which is essentially the study of the earliest (European) records of the nature of Indian life, a subdiscipline lying athwart the frontier of history and ethnography in the odd compartmentalization of the scholarly world.

Reports of cannibalism were not infrequent among what came to be called *captivity stories,* accounts by Europeans who were captured by and lived with Indians for various periods of time. Captivity tales, indeed, would become a highly popular literary genre both here and abroad for three hundred years as the frontier moved westward, and many were not unlike the titillating and at best exaggerated material regularly sold to today's tabloids. Seen as such, captivity tales have tended to be dismissed as highly untrustworthy, given their source, almost surely riddled with the perfervid inventions of someone looking to make a name (and some money) for himself, and also blinded by cultural pre-conceptions. But here, it is useful to be careful. To say that every reporter tends to see another culture through the lens of his own is by now a truism, and not an especially useful one, given the fact that it is universally applicable. But to claim that all observers from an alien culture are incapable of reporting facts and events about another is to commit, in historian James Axtell's words, a "genetic fallacy." More precisely put, it is racist.

Many who wrote of their experiences as captives of Indians wrote long after the fact, and in the relatively straightforward voice of some-one not seeking to embellish events for sensational effect. One of these was Alexander Henry, a British trader on the Michigan frontier in the 1760s who found himself witness to an attack by the Chippewas on an English-held fort at the height of a widespread revolt led by the great Ottawa leader Pontiac, and in the midst of the nearly continuous war-fare between the French and English, with whom the tribes variously aligned themselves, depending on what they saw as their interests. The Chippewas entered the fort by feigning to play a game of baggataway (the forerunner of lacrosse), chasing an errant ball into the confines of the walls and then setting upon the British there. Henry witnessed the killing of numerous countrymen, noting that "from the bodies of some, ripped open, their butchers were drinking the blood, scooped up in the hollow of joined hands, and quaffed amid shouts of rage and vic-tory." This is an example of *ritual* cannibalism, often based on taking into oneself the courage or other desirable attributes of the victim. Henry himself avoided death by the intervention of a Chippewa named Wawatam, who took the Englishman in, less as a captive than as a member of his family. At one point, after some white prisoners were killed, Henry evidently observed the Indians cut the bodies of "the fat-test" apart and put them into kettles hung over fires.

> A message came to our lodge for Wawatam to take part in the feast. . . .
> Wawatam obeyed the summons, taking with him his dish and spoon.
> After about an hour he returned, bringing in his dish a human hand and
> a large piece of flesh. He did not appear to relish the repast, but told me
> it always had been the custom, among all the Indian nations when
> returning from war, to make a war feast from among the slain. This, he
> said, inspired the warriors with courage in attack.

For about a year, Henry lived with this family, hunting, fishing, and otherwise involved in its normal affairs, they taking on the responsibility of keeping him out of the hands of Indians hostile to the English. At one point, as part of a hunting party, Henry shot a female bear.

> All, but particularly my old mother (as I used to call her), took the ani-mal's head in their hands and stroked and kissed it several times, calling
> her their relation and grandmother. They begged a thousand pardons of
> the bear for taking away her life. . . . The pipes were now lit and
> Wawatam blew tobacco smoke into the nostrils of the bear, telling me
> to do the same and thus appease the anger of the bear on account of my
> having killed her. . . . At length the feast was ready. Wawatam com-menced a speech [in which] he deplored the necessity of men to kill
> their *friends* thus. He represented, however, that the misfortune was
> unavoidable, since without doing so they could not live.

In due course, Henry had the chance to leave safely and the family agreed he should go.

> I did not leave the lodge without the most grateful sense of the many
> acts of goodness I had experienced in it, nor without the sincere respect
> for the virtues of its members. All the family accompanied me to the
> beach, and the canoe had no sooner put off than Wawatam commenced
> an address to the Great Spirit, beseeching him to take care of me, his
> brother, till we should next meet.

These hardly seem the words of a totally culture-bound racist bent on sensationalism. Even so, such stories—regardless of their accumulated number—are by their nature unconfirmable and hardly the sort of thing likely to be accepted as unarguable evidence in a court of inquiry. At the same time, however, forensic evidence is harder to dismiss, and the archaeologist often addresses his or her workplace in much the same manner as forensic specialists address a crime scene. Except for extraordinary cases of desperation, such as the plane wreck survivors in the Andes some years ago, cannibalism is not likely to occur in any society anymore. So aside from such accounts as that of Henry, this leaves the matter, most agree, in the hands of the archaeologists.

Reports of cannibalism, as noted, abound from all quarters of North America as well as elsewhere in the world, some of them based on early if questionable archaeological work. What is not questionable is that interpersonal violence—without cannibalism—is known to have occurred often in most parts of the continent. The region in North America that has been most intensively dug and studied is the Southwest, and most particularly the lands inhabited by the Anasazis. Their predecessor cultures in the region, known as Basketmakers and dated as far back as 500 B.C., were given to taking scalps and trophy heads. What are taken as signs of cannibalism do not occur until much later. As early as the turn of the twentieth century, archaeologists thought they had found evidence of cannibalism in some old Anasazi ruins, and it is here that many recent investigations have been carried out as well.

The question immediately arises: what exactly is meant by cannibalism? It is reported to come in many forms, often ambiguous, from drinking diluted ashes of a relative by way of reverence to partaking of some part, such as the inner organs or flesh or blood, of a slain enemy, as in Henry's observation (a matter of gaining power), to the symbolic rite of Christian communion, to the actual quest for nutrition—either in rare instances of extremes or as a more or less routine part of the diet—to an act of terrorism. Motive is not a matter, either, that archaeologists can address with any great certainty, so their investigations are limited mainly to the question: does a particular site show physical signs that people were butchered and eaten in order to gain nutritionally? In other words, what is the unmistakable signature of cannibalism in an archaeological site? This means, of course, analyzing human remains, a task not everyone would find pleasant to engage in. Indian people specifically resent such investigations, seeing them as unthinkably sacrilegious, and recent federal law requires the repatriation of remains of Indian people now residing in museums and other collections to the tribes that are thought to be the descendants. This will presumably bring such studies to a close in North America, resolving what has always been a painful clash of cultures in favor of the Indians. In the meantime, however, evidence is evidence, and as one physical anthropologist and osteologist, Tim D. White of the University of California at Berkeley, has said: "Our effectiveness as scientists is grounded in our ability to recognize [cultural] bias and avoid it in our research. We must study the material evidence for cannibalism as we would study that left by any other human activity."

White's chief professional interest is in early hominid and human evolution, and in order to settle the question of whether the early progenitors of mankind were cannibals (as they are from time to time accused of being), White set out to establish precise criteria for making such judgments from the archaeological record. To this end, he studied the vast literature on cannibalism worldwide (most of it unconvincing) and focused primarily on the remains found in an Anasazi site in southwestern Colorado not far from Mesa Verde, on the reservation of the Ute Mountain tribe. The site had been researched and documented with great care by Larry Nordby and Paul Nickens in the 1970s, and the tribe turned the material over to White in the 1980s for his analysis, the result of which was a book of nearly five hundred pages, filled with hundreds of photographs, tables, and charts, entitled *Prehistoric Cannibalism at Mancos 5MTUMR-2346*. The site with the elaborate identification number is in Mancos Canyon, one of many Anasazi habitations in the canyon over the centuries, and it consisted of a pueblo of some twelve rooms plus a kiva built about 1100 A.D., home for an estimated thirty-three people. It was abandoned shortly thereafter, with a new pueblo of some five rooms (plus the old kiva and a new one) built on the still extant older pueblo's crumbling walls, and it served as a home for perhaps fourteen people.

Nothing much distinguished this settlement from others of the era and place—the usual formal burials of individuals were uncovered, and the reuse of the old kiva was not uncommon. In short, it was a fairly typical settlement—except for some concentrated arrays of bones that lay over the fallen roof and detritus of several rooms of the old pueblo, where they had apparently been tossed. In these scattered beds were the bones of rabbit, turkey, and artiodactyls (pronghorn and deer), and also humans. The human bones showed no sign of purposeful burial, but instead were in well-preserved fragments. In all, more than two thousand fragments of human bone were recovered and, having been painstakingly conjoined or reassembled by White, were later found to represent twenty-nine individuals—seventeen adults and twelve children. White found nothing by way of physical characteristics to distinguish these people from others who lived in the region and nothing in the state of the bone beds to suggest that the disposal of the bones was an erratic occurrence in time, separated by long intervals. It appeared to be a fairly continuous, if not simultaneous, process.

Nothing in the way the bones were scattered resembled the patterns of bones left by predators (which have been carefully mapped for various carnivores, including dogs), and the patterns were unquestionably not the result of any known mortuary practice, such as cremation or reburial. Nothing about them suggested magico-religious practices of any sort (though of course prayer leaves few physical marks). They showed signs of fire, but not of being burnt where they lay. The smaller bones were usually found intact, while large, long bones such as femurs were broken into pieces. Skulls were consistently broken open. Under the microscope, the bones showed unmistakable signs of having been chopped, sawed, and otherwise butchered by humans, but none of the marks associated with the teeth of carnivores. Many showed an odd polish on the ends, which White determined experimentally was (or at least could best be explained as) the result of rattling around inside a pot as they boiled.

The treatment of the human bones was, in fact, basically identical to that of the bones of the large mammals—in the manner of defleshing, segmentation, fracturing, cooking, and discarding. Defleshed bones, for example, do not turn the same color as bones left in the ground with the flesh on them, and such thoroughly processed bones would not attract carnivores such as wolves or domestic dogs. The unavoidable implication is that these twenty-nine people, once dead, were butchered, their flesh (including brains) cooked and eaten, the larger bones broken to get at the marrow, and the bones rendered for grease, the remains being tossed aside into nearby trash heaps. Besides differences in purely anatomical butchering requirements between the human and animal remains, the only other major (if subtle) difference was that no tools such as needles or awls were found to have been made from the human bones, though the splintered ends would have lent themselves to such use as a practical matter, as did the bones of deer that were consumed.

The remains at Mancos Canyon were without doubt the most thoroughly analyzed of any such remains in North America, and indeed, White's book is as much a textbook and how-to manual for other investigators as it is a report about this single instance and its context in the rest of the region and the world. In it, he reviews similar reports and evidence from nineteen other sites in the Four Corners area, most in southwestern Colorado. Some of these are more ambiguous, others less so. Since the publication of White's book in 1992, archaeologists have claimed that some forty or more southwestern sites all told show signs similar to those at Mancos, though differences abound as well, particularly in the number of victims, the lowest number being one. In one instance, in a Colorado site, archaeologists found a human coprolite (a fossil stool) of the Anasazi era that contained unmistakable molecular evidence of digested human muscle protein. Many of the occurrences, though not all, are in the period when particularly great stress was experienced by the Anasazis—the fifty years after 1150 A.D., which were a period of a rapidly occurring and long-lasting drought, marked also by the arrival in their midst of people from elsewhere, notably the Mogollon and Hohokam regions, and quite possibly people from the north.

While White is unwilling to speculate about what was going on beyond describing the physical evidence of cannibalism, others have been less reticent. Christy Turner (he of the teeth) believes the practice was widespread and suggests that the Anasazis were terrorized by Mexican gangs who chose cannibalism as the surest way to strike horror into their victims' hearts.

These were not, as White points out, "amiable times" in this region. Plenty of human remains in the region show signs of violent death, including some of those suspected of having been cannibalized. But the original excavator of the Mancos site, Nordby, found lacking the scenario in which some people attacked the Mancos pueblo and ate the inhabitants, the chief reason being that more people were disposed of in this manner than probably lived in the place. Another scenario is that the Mancos inhabitants raided another pueblo and brought most of the bodies home (among missing parts in these bone beds were most pelvises). A more humanly logical explanation is that the sudden change in the climate at this period brought about famine in sizable areas and cannibalism was the last, cruel resource for starving people whose options, even in the best of times, were limited. Localized famine was probably not at all rare in the centuries preceding this period, as well, when other occurrences of cannibalism appear to have been found. The people of the Mesa Verde area, for example, had a diet over the centuries that was as much as 80 percent maize. Local drought could reduce available food at such times to nearly zero. Gatherable and huntable food was always comparatively sparse in this entire region, and especially when the population had increased to what may have been the countryside's maximum carrying capacity. On a local level, there could have been some element of vengeance or interethnic rivalry involved as well. On the other hand, if actual starvation was involved at Mancos, for example, one might expect the human skeletal remains to show signs of even more intensive processing than occurred.

Some important facts—such as who was eating whom—and the motives will almost surely prove ever elusive. The evidence, however widespread it may turn out to be, will be believed by some and rejected by others.

An alternative explanation for such bone assemblages—or at least some of them—has been suggested: witchcraft executions. Witchcraft, known to be present in most tribal societies, surely was common long before Europeans arrived in North America with their own versions. Witchcraft is still widely recognized in many traditional Indian societies, and one way of ridding a community of a witch, once discovered, is to execute the person and his or her immediate family (witchcraft is often taken to be inherited), violently breaking the bodies up into pieces to ensure that the witches cannot reconstitute themselves. It still happens, at least among some southwestern tribes. This too is a phenomenon many Indian people would prefer not be memorialized, but it is more in keeping with cultural norms than cannibalism, which surely existed as well, though probably in limited instances and only in extremis. Perhaps some comfort can be taken in this quarter, however, from the fact that modern archaeologists have been quite catholic in their inquiries: some compelling archaeological evidence for cannibalism elsewhere in the world has been found in England, France, and Spain.

What the Indians Made of Europeans

Indians' perception of Europeans varied widely. When Francis Drake reached the coast of California in 1579 on his globe-circling voyage, he was received by the local population with a good deal of festivity. Drake assumed he was taken to be a deity. Probably not, but there is evidence (in the form of early European accounts, of course) that some Indians took the white man to be a fairly powerful shaman type, since he was immune to the diseases that had suddenly struck so many Indians. In the earliest contacts, the locals tended to welcome the white man with at least a show of curiosity, and as often as not with generous displays of gift giving (though there were plenty of exceptions). In the East, it was fairly common for Indian people to greet visitors with elaborate patting and rubbing. From the early reports of the Europeans, the Indians typically patted them where they were especially hairy—arms, chest, and chins. It seems that the Indians were less surprised by the whiteness of European skin than its hairiness, but many Indians evidently looked upon the hirsute newcomers as not quite human.

In Florida, as we will see in the next chapter, word seems to have spread from the Caribbean about the Spanish: most early forays onto the Florida peninsula were met with violence. Many southern chieftains would react to the Spanish in kind, seeing nothing godly about them. The early French explorers tended to marry in, as did many Spanish settlers in later decades. For nearly a century before the British, the Dutch, and the Swedes established a presence in the Northeast, thousands, even tens of thousands of European fishermen had plied the northern coast—particularly off Canada's maritime provinces. There they took up temporary (seasonal) residence on land to process their fish and learned to bring various goods as gifts or for trade. There was already a lively and far-flung trade among Indians for fancy furs; these and soon the more common beaver pelts brought them glass beads, copper implements like kettles, and iron tools. From archaeological records, it appears that the Indian people generally were most eager to obtain items like beads and copper kettles, rather than tools, since these fit into their traditional category of sacred items. Kettles, for example, were chopped up to make gorgets and other religious items, passing from Indian to Indian and reaching well inland. In fact, the arrival of such trade goods seems to have kindled a revival in some of the Mississippian burial practices in places where they had lapsed before the coming of the Europeans. Only later did European iron tools replace the traditional ones.

The Swedes recounted that on their first visit among the Delawares, they handed out a number of tools such as axes. Returning a year later, they found the Indians wearing such things as axe blades around their necks like gorgets. When they demonstrated the intended use of axe blades, the Indians apparently laughed themselves silly over their mistake.

The question of what to take on from the white man—and what to try to avoid—would become a burning question for virtually every group of Indians and is one that is still asked to this day. And wherever (and as long as) choice was possible, the responses would be as varied as the people. Meanwhile, after a period in North America, some Europeans would find that they were indeed a new kind of people themselves, not merely because they had reached a place of vast distances and unprecedented riches but because they perforce would absorb important features from Indian life—if only in an unconscious process of osmosis.

CHAPTER FIVE

THE SPANISH

In the dawning decades of the sixteenth century, imperial Spain established firm colonial footholds in the Caribbean, notably in Hispaniola and Cuba, and in New Spain (Mexico and Central America), across the Gulf of Mexico. The native populations in those two areas were being variously exterminated, enslaved, or Christianized, and Spanish adventurers were beginning to explore more northerly realms, as well as heading south into Peru. For a half century, these expeditions were typically financed and outfitted by what we would call private money, though often bearing authorization in the form of royal patents from the Spanish crown. The conquistadors were, in a sense, venture explorers whose backers expected a return on their investments.

From New Spain, the Spanish would probe the American Southwest and California; from Caribbean bases they would pierce the American Southeast, from the Florida peninsula north as far as Virginia and west across the Mississippi River into Arkansas. They came to call this huge and salubrious region La Florida, the place of flowers. Taken by most standards of the time, including the standards they set for themselves, most early Spanish efforts in La Florida were disastrous bungles. For the Indians living there, the Spanish efforts were catastrophic.

La Florida: Place of Flowers

The earliest recorded probe of the lands to the north was led by Juan Ponce de León, a member of Columbus's first colony who, until recently, was credited in schoolbooks with the much romanticized discovery of the Florida peninsula while in search of the fountain of youth. He may well have been the first European to land on the Florida peninsula and he may have believed in the idea of the fountain of youth—but he had more specific business. In 1513, he set forth with a royal patent to settle new lands and to enslave the native inhabitants and distribute them among settlers. However arduous a voyage it was, given the experience of the Cuban and Haitian boat people in recent times, this discovery can hardly be called a miracle of navigation and endurance—the distance was a hundred miles or so. Ponce de León sailed up and down the coasts of what he thought to be an island and eventually landed in the area of today's Fort Myers, only to be driven off by hostile Calusa Indians.

Not a great deal is known about most of the Indian peoples present on the southern peninsula at the time besides their names—Tocobagas, Ais, Calusas, Tekestas, for example—and that they were primarily nonagricultural chiefdoms, mostly dependent on the fruits of the sea. By the late eighteenth century, these tribes were no more, and gone with them was any knowledge of exactly what languages they spoke. We know, chiefly from archaeological studies, that the Calusas were a highly developed society with an estimated four thousand (and possibly ten thousand) people at the time of European contact. This is unusual for any society without an agricultural base, but the Calusas inhabited one of the most biologically productive places imaginable— a vast flat realm where freshwater flowed in a stately and eternal sheet across the land through cypress groves and endless stands of saw grass, to mix with the tidal salt water from the sea, the edge of which was marked by wide ribbons of mangroves with leggy roots penetrating into the rich muck. In canoes that could carry up to forty people, Calusa fishermen plied the estuaries and open water of the western Everglades for its abundant fish and shellfish. Seafood proliferated in these warm brackish waters and inland, where, also, one had to be wary of the likes of alligators and water moccasins (the serpents of this particular Garden of Eden). In the absence of much by way of natural stone, they made tools from bone and wood and the omnipresent whelk shell, and used the salt-loving mangroves for firewood. They built long canals, some thirty feet wide and one of them extending seven miles, linking natural waterways, and on one island erected a mound of some thousand square feet, where the chief received tribute from his people as well as food, adornments, and slaves brought in by a small army of especially skilled and locally feared warriors, who would hardly have been intimidated by the arrival of Ponce de León and his small Spanish force. In archaeological and anthropological retrospect, the Calusas were probably, at the time of contact, one of the most advanced fishing societies ever known. After the arrival of the Spanish in the Caribbean, they became adept, as did other Florida coastal groups, in diving down to wrecked Spanish ships and recovering valuables, which they traded, in some cases back to the Spanish.

Given the Indian reaction to Ponce de León's thrusts, it is not unreasonable to speculate that the peninsular tribes had received an earlier Spanish visit or perhaps escapees from the Spanish pogroms in the West Indies (evidently there had long been some trade between the two areas). In any event, they evidently knew these newcomers spelled trouble as soon as their sails appeared on the horizon. When Ponce de León returned to Calusa country six years later, in 1521, with another colonizing expedition, he was

Key Marco, Florida

promptly set upon and personally wounded, dying soon back in Cuba.

Several Spanish forays preceded and followed Ponce de León's second, fatal one—explorers, would-be colonizers, and slave hunters—and by as early as 1525 they had visited points along much of the east and southern coasts of today's United States. In 1528, a man named Pánfilo de Narváez brought four hundred colonists to the area of Tampa Bay. Seeing the Spanish sails, the Indians abandoned their villages, but returned the next day to demand that the newcomers leave. One hundred did, turning back with the expedition's ships, but de Narváez and the rest plunged on to the north, to be relentlessly harassed, presumably by the Tocobaga and Timucua people. Before long the beleaguered Spaniards killed their horses, made rude boats from the hides, and set off to sea, only to be wrecked near Galveston Bay in Texas. We will pick up their tracks as they made their way west and south in the next part of this chapter.

Time after time, hopeful little colonies foundered. In most cases the Indians were cautiously friendly, but typically the colonists would offend the Indians, capturing some, and the Indians would then do their best to make life difficult. In one instance, at least, a colony was founded too late in the year to grow any food and the starving colonists tried to go home, many perishing on the way. Another difficulty was the weather: Spanish ships were often blown off course or wrecked in storms and hurricanes. What impelled these exploits? For one, the Spaniards sought mythical kingdoms of wealth. They heard stories of a place called Coosa, a supposedly fabulously wealthy province in northwestern Georgia—in fact, a principal settlement of the people who would come to be called the Creeks, but of course no city of gold. They heard of a country rich in pearls on the South Carolina coast (and indeed there was a richness of freshwater pearls), and of land just north of the Florida peninsula that was a new Andalusia. This latter notion arose from an exaggerated description by an Indian. Besides the quest for riches (and slaves), they sought as well a waterway to the Pacific, which would have been the crown jewel of North American exploration, making travel to the Orient all the easier. Spanish prestige, too, was on the line in a time when other European nations were also looking to expand their reach on this new continent—notably the Dutch, French, and British. And the Spanish soon developed an almost unimaginably devout zeal to missionize the Indians of North America and thus save their souls for the church, in opposition to the apostate

Protestantism growing in Europe like dangerous weeds. As for expanding the geographical knowledge of the New World, they did so perhaps beyond their fondest hopes, but the entrepreneurial Spanish explorers of the Southeast rarely made their routes public, being jealous not only of one another but also of other European nationals. As a result, a number of places such as Pensacola Bay were discovered, then lost, and had to be rediscovered in a matter of only decades.

Probably the best known of the Spanish explorers of the American Southeast was Hernando de Soto, who, as Francisco Pizarro's right-hand man, had made a small fortune from the sack of the Inca empire in Peru. Named governor of Cuba, de Soto staged a relatively massive *entrada* into the interior of the Southeast, landing first near Tampa Bay in 1539 with some seven hundred followers, including smiths to make chains for slaves and attack dogs to make meals of troublemakers. He proceeded north and west through the country of the people who would become the Creeks, Cherokees, Choctaws, Chickasaws, and Qapaws. His journey took him through Georgia into North Carolina, west through Alabama and Tennessee, across the Mississippi, and finally down into Louisiana. Earlier, we noted the probable effect of his expedition (and previous probes) from the surely unintentional introduction of European diseases, but de Soto's actual intentions were by no means benign, however conventional to the imperially ambitious in those days. Usually upon encountering an Indian village, he and his men would sack it, killing whoever resisted, enslaving the rest, and making them lead him on to the next stop. One method of executing Indian malefactors was simply to throw them to the war dogs. Early on they happened upon Juan Ortiz, a member of the Narváez expedition who had been captured by the Calusas, among whom he had lived for more than a decade. De Soto considered the meeting with Ortiz a sign that God had blessed the expedition, and indeed, it might well have gone nowhere without Ortiz's ability to translate the languages of most of the Indian people of the South. From Ortiz, de Soto also learned another tactic: playing one chiefdom off against another when he learned of rivalries or hostilities between them.

In one Indian temple town in South Carolina, a female noble (and probably the chief) explained that because her people had lost so many to a recent pestilence, she could not offer to feed de Soto's party. Instead, she took him into the temple and offered him a quantity of freshwater pearls (which he managed to send back to Havana as proof that he was on the track of riches to rival those of Peru). In return, he captured the noblewoman, among others, and hauled her along in shackles on his way west. She subsequently escaped. One can only imagine the terror with which each group of Indians saw these potently armed and armored people arrive astride their huge brutish horses, with livestock bawling, the war dogs slobbering eagerly, and other Indian people in chain gangs serving as beasts of burden—an enormous congregation of alien beings arrived from nowhere.

Nonetheless, at various places along the way the chieftains were not about to bow down to the newcomers or show any fear of them: Indians severely harassed de Soto's party. In one instance, the Indians methodically picked off some fourteen men, who were beheaded and whose bodies were dismembered and hung from trees as an (unsuccessful) object lesson. Near Mobile Bay, in Alabama, in 1541, de Soto met the strongest resistance up to that time by far when a chieftain named Tuskaloosa unleashed hundreds of warriors on the invaders—an Indian army drawn from several surrounding chiefdoms. Almost overrun, the Spanish were able to rally, burning the palisaded town and killing the inhabitants as they fled the flames. De Soto lost numerous men in this engagement, along with horses and other livestock and supplies.

In the spring of 1542, camped on the west bank of the Mississippi, de Soto fell ill. He sent word to the Indians on the other side of the river demanding that inasmuch as he, de Soto, was the Son of the Sun and all obeyed him, they should help him cross the mighty river. Evidently the chief refused, saying that any true son of the sun should be able to make the river run dry. In response, the weakened de Soto ordered his men to sack a nearby village, which was done. Shortly after that, de Soto died and his men "buried" him in the Mississippi River, lest Indians find his corpse. The logistics of maintaining slaves proving arduous, the remaining Spaniards freed most of them and wandered a bit aimlessly for about a year through parts of Arkansas, Louisiana, and east Texas, then back to the Mississippi. From there, under continuing attack from a confederacy of chiefdoms, they made their way downriver to the Gulf, eventually reaching New Spain, where they vied among themselves to explain what a grand success the expedition had been.

Along the way, de Soto evidently sent a map of his route back to the colonial viceroy—it is long since lost, and de Soto's exact route is still unknown in most details—which made public few details of this new geography, while describing it promisingly as a big country with many of the natural amenities of Spain. Spending four years crossing so much uncharted territory inhabited by hostile people was no mean feat, of course, but by any other measure this grand and much storied expedition was a failure, and one that the crown was no doubt relieved had not been funded by the Spanish treasury. As the last of the de Soto expedition straggled off to sea, the Indian people may well have thought, and certainly hoped, they had put an end to such intrusions by Spaniards. After all, some three quarters of the original seven hundred were now dead. But the net result for the Indian societies of the region was far more cataclysmic, for the Spanish had brought their diseases, such as smallpox, to the urban societies of the Southeast.

And of course, the Spanish kept coming, even as their reports tended to be less glowing. The fabled new Andalusia on the east coast kept being moved northward, as far as Cape Hatteras, finally to vanish altogether from the Spanish imagination. In 1557, the Spanish crown ordered that a settlement be established on the northern coast of the Gulf of Mexico, and a Franciscan missionary was sent along to establish missions as well. These efforts stumbled, and by the 1560s another royally mandated and financed expedition concluded that no lands on either coast of La Florida were suitable for colonization, no native people suitable for conversion, no gold and no silver there for the taking. The days of boosterism were over, though the Spanish (and the other European explorers) remained certain they could find that elusive water passage through to the Orient. Even so, the Spanish might well have given up but for the fact that the French looked ready to settle these same areas, posing an unconscionable threat to the Spanish colonies in the Indies.

As early as 1555, the French had settled some Huguenot (Protestant) countrymen in Brazil, and throughout the 1560s a privateer named Jean Ribaut sought to place more of them along the Gulf coast of North America. A few small French settlements did result, along with a French fort, but the Spanish rooted them out, dispatching the French defenders. Frenchmen finally gave the area up as a bad job in 1572, but their initiatives and the lurking presence of British privateers like the royally sanctioned pirate Francis Drake had provided Spain with ample reason to continue its efforts in La Florida.

The man responsible for ridding the region of the French—and for a number of other achievements—is far less celebrated than de Soto or Ponce de León. This was Pedro Menéndez de Avilés, who, as captain general of the Spanish Indies fleet as early as 1554, developed the idea of annual fleets between Spain and the Caribbean. Eleven years later, King Philip II contracted with Menéndez to recolonize La Florida and convert the natives as a buffer against the French. Menéndez left that year from Cádiz with some fifteen hundred persons, and on September 8, 1565, founded San Agustín on the Florida peninsula's northeast coast, the first permanent European colony in the United States, now Saint Augustine, Florida. (Within a few decades, Indian women and Spanish men had intermarried in San Agustín, and what is called a *criollo*—or mixed—culture existed there, something quite new in North America.) A year after San Agustín was founded, another colony, called Santa Elena, was founded on South Carolina's Parris Island. Next Menéndez captured a French fort a bit to the north, founded San Mateo, and went on to trounce the French when they attacked under the command of the privateer Ribaut, cutting all their throats. After founding the two colonies Menéndez pushed on to Chesapeake Bay, finding it no Andalusia but a sandy place where the Spanish would have a hard time making a living. Over time he sent forth various other expeditions, which showed conclusively that Florida was not an island, and sought but did not find an overland passage from La Florida to the rich silver mines in New Spain. All of this added to the Spanish understanding of the region's geography (and its increasingly lackluster possibilities).

Something of an idealist at the outset, Menéndez thought that Indians and Spanish could coexist comfortably in La Florida; to this end, he married the sister of the leading Calusa chief, a man whose name comes down to us as Carlos. Menéndez initiated a pledge of peace between himself and various Indian leaders, and exchanged valuables with them, a proper form of courtesy. He established, as well, a regional government and brought Jesuit priests to convert and minister to the native populations. But in his frequent absences, disputes between the military, ecclesiastics, and lay Spaniards led to friction with the Indians, and the result was skirmishes, killings, the rejection of priests, and other "rebellious" acts. Franciscans soon replaced the Jesuits, but to little avail; no missionary effort in La Florida would succeed for very long until after the beginning of the seventeenth century.

West of the colony of San Agustín, stretching across the upper peninsula of Florida and north into Georgia, lived some two hundred thousand Timucua Indians, a people who lived in small to medium-sized villages and grew corn, beans, and squash in surrounding fields. One or several villages were presided over by a chief (a hereditary position), who dealt with other chiefs and administered his (or sometimes her) people's affairs, calling for labor and tribute. The early presence of San Agustín in their midst proved deadly, leading to an ongoing series of epidemics that severely reduced the eastern Timucua population—those living in proximity to the Spanish colony.

Far fewer aboriginally than the Timucuas, a group called the Guales lived north of San Agustín, along the Georgian coast in the salt marshes and on barrier islands. They lived in small villages (perhaps two hundred people to a village) and supplemented shellfish and the other riches of the coastal waters with agriculture, under the command of hereditary chiefs. It was among the Guales and the western and northern Timucuas that the missionary system took hold.

The Franciscans made the most of the role—and vanity—of the local chiefs, supplying them with valuable gifts, such as fancy clothes and contact with a very great chief, the Spanish governor in San Agustín. Since they seemed immune to the ravages of the diseases that had already struck with such horrifying force, the friars appeared to be powerful shamans, and it made sense to many of the chiefs to accept Christianity from them. At the chief's bidding, his people would help the Franciscans build missions (mostly impermanent and relatively simple buildings of mud-and-wattle walls and thatched roofs) and then pitch in to supply them with food. And soon the Timucuas and the Guales found themselves working a good deal of the time growing food for the Franciscans in residence, but also for the ever-struggling colony of San Agustín, and hauling it there as well. The missions were strung out to the west among the Timucuas and north among the Guales, a day's march from each other along royal roads (*caminos reales*), which were, of course, maintained by forced Indian labor. Soon enough the exhausting labor added to continuing outbreaks of disease reduced the Timucua and Guale population to remnants. Seeing the handwriting on the wall, Spanish leaders in San Agustín pressed the missionaries farther west into the country of the Apalachees, beginning in 1633. Located in the vicinity of Talahassee, the Apalachees were among the easternmost of the major Mississippian cultures. They were more centralized than the neighboring tribes to the east, and their land was better suited to agriculture. Soon the Apalachee chiefs and the Spanish were prospering, sending large amounts of food to San Agustín on the backs of conscripted Indians—and by boat to Cuba as well, avoiding San Agustín taxes. When a handful of Spaniards took up ranching in that territory, matters began to fray. On February 19, 1647, some non-Christian Apalachees and members of another tribe attacked a number of Spanish, including friars—the beginning of a rebellion that resulted in, among other things, the arrival among the Apalachees of Spanish troops and heavy loss of life on both sides.

The rebellion was soon put down, the leaders handed over to the Spaniards and, for the most part, executed. Animosity continued between the Spaniards and the Indians, and between the friars and the military. Yet from the Spanish point of view, this was a time of great success, considered by some the golden age of Spanish missionary work in La Florida. Generation after generation of Indians of the three tribes were brought up Christian; the elaborate Mississippian burials of chiefs halted, and Indians were buried, clutching rosaries or crosses, under the mission floors or outside in a cemetery nearby.

Towns now had both a mission and a traditional council house, often across from each other on a plaza surrounded by small round dwellings—all made of wooden posts and palm thatch. The council houses were used for village business and for visitors; all the old ways were widely questioned. As one historian put it, thanks to the missions, those Indians who remained "embraced a new faith, iron tools, the Spanish language, monogamy, and peaches."

But the deck was now almost completely stacked against them. Most were malnourished, weakened by the forced labor (osteoarthritis became a common ailment), and always fighting off epidemics and secondary diseases. The epidemics were, evidently, local in nature, apparently too lethal to spread very far. The rigors of life, plus the fact that males now spent much of their time away from home, created a lower birthrate, and the populations of Guales, Timucuas, and Apalachees continued to plummet. Towns were fewer and smaller in size. By mid-century, only ten thousand Apalachees lived, compared to the fifty thousand at the time of Ponce de León's *entrada* in 1513, some forty years earlier. Twenty-five thousand Timucuas were left by 1600; fifty years later there were but twenty-five hundred. Perhaps fifteen hundred Guales survived to midcentury.

In 1656, the few remaining Timucuas—mostly in Georgia—rebelled, not against the friars (the Timucuas were all good Catholics) but against the Spanish military, who were accused of mistreating the chiefs and the Indians. This rebellion was soon put down and the Timucuas devastated, their leaders executed or jailed. The Spanish undertook to relocate the northern Timucuas southward; meanwhile more northerly groups, like the ancestors of the Creeks, began raiding southward as well, looking for slaves to take north and sell to the British settlers, who were now, in 1670, as far south as Charles Town (Charleston, South Carolina). The French were also well established, from Mobile to the Mississippi. Desperately, the Spanish sought to colonize Indians west of the Apalachees, but this put the missions too far from San Agustín. They thought about importing Mexican labor but never did it. They sent some friars into Calusa country and those pious gentlemen were ridiculed, mooned, and sent fleeing south to Cuba in a small boat.

Earlier, by the mid-1660s, Indians of various tribes—those whom the Spanish called Chichimecos—were raiding constantly, often arriving from as far away as Virginia. Other tribes, now polymerized into a group called the Yamasees, were fleeing south to avoid the raiders, fetching up in Guale country and providing the Spanish with a temporary boost in the labor force. Demographic and ethnic chaos were loose in La Florida. By the eighteenth century, matters only grew worse. Carolinian British joined in the fighting, and the Indian groups that would become known, corporately, as Creeks descended in force, wreaking havoc on the Spanish and the remnants of their allies among the Apalachees, Timucuas, and Guales. By the end of 1706, the Spanish had abandoned northern Florida and southern Georgia. The Indians who had lived there originally were gone—killed or moved away to assume new tribal identities if they could.

Thanks to the arcane affairs of the nations of Europe, Spain would begin its withdrawal from La Florida in 1763, taking a tatterdemalion remnant of, in all, eighty-nine Apalachees from San Agustín to resettle in Cuba. During all this period, the Spanish presence was widely felt elsewhere beyond Florida and Georgia. Many native societies throughout the Southeast virtually hit bottom and had to reconstitute themselves. Throughout the region before contact, the chiefs had not been merely political leaders. They, the priests, and the noble families from which they arose were spiritual leaders as well, using ceremonies to maintain direct contact with deities and other spiritual entities that made the land productive. But suddenly, when the people began to die in untold numbers, disfigured by the eruption of multiple sores on their bodies, fields went untended for lack of labor, adding starvation to the scourge. The sores of smallpox arrive about four days after high fever and vomiting begin. For those who survive, the sores dry up after a week or so, the scabs eventually falling off to leave pockmarks. Some are blinded by the disease. Before long, and often before the arrival of aliens in their midst, virtually every native person in the region either had died or intimately knew someone who was dead from this scourge. All this *before* contact; next came the chaos of warfare and enslavement. Mound building came to an abrupt halt, mass burials were common, and in some places bodies were simply stacked up, producing yet further health hazards. Many remaining central towns and even outlying villages were abandoned; others struggled on in postapocalyptic tatters. Those nobles and chiefs who did not succumb to disease had been scarred in another, irreparable way: they had lost their powers to keep the spirit world looking benignly on the people. The keepers of lineages, oral history, and religious rites were dead or discredited. The bonds of society after society were broken. No one at the time knew how such diseases as smallpox were transmitted. In the face of such a mystery, the Indians surely would have fallen back on witchcraft as an explanation. (Witchcraft—typically the use of charms and incantations of one sort or another to harm other people—is common in most preliterate societies and is not, as some suggest, a European invention. It has always been a part of traditional life in most American Indian tribes and is rampant among the Navajos and other southwestern tribes, for example. Many Navajo healing ceremonies are explicitly designed to undo the effects of being witched.)

One can only guess at the virulence of witchcraft claims that would, as they usually do, have set even close relatives against one another. We have little direct historical evidence of the events that took place among the people of La Florida when these catastrophes struck, but history provides a somewhat analogous situation: the devastation wrought on late medieval Europe by the arrival of the Black Death— bubonic plague—in the fourteenth century. The plague arrived from Asia on shipboard at Mediterranean ports, then spread rapidly throughout the continent, striking urban populations first and hardest. It came in two forms: one bacillus spread to humans via rats and fleas, the other (once a person was infected) spread directly between humans by breath or sputum. In all, during two major outbreaks in the century, something like 50 percent of Europeans perished. From numerous accounts, one can get some sense of the effects of such a bewildering and sudden scourge on the human psyche in a society dominated by belief in an all-pervading religion—in this case, Roman Catholicism.

Before long, wherever it struck, the dead bodies had outrun the capacity to bury them; mass graves were soon overwhelmed and bodies just rotted where they fell. Traditional medicine had no remedy, no idea of the cause, no idea for prevention (except to flee to safer ground, as did the lords and ladies in Boccaccio's *Decameron*). Parents abandoned children who were struck, and vice versa. People did not band together in mutual distress—quite the opposite. As historian Barbara Tuchman pointed out, "The sense of a vanishing future created a kind of dementia and despair." Fields and livestock went unattended, which led to subsequent severe food shortages, local famines, and widespread economic chaos. Bands of flagellants roamed the streets, challenging the discredited priesthood: they, the flagellants, would now intercede between man and God. Scapegoats were sought, and soon enough, accusing eyes fell on the Jews, who in many cities were rounded up and put to death. In Europe, most of the noble families and most of the church hierarchy survived, being happily isolated in palaces. There was an eerie tendency, after the devastation was past, not to talk about it very much.

One can only imagine what would have happened to the course of European history if most of the leaders of church and state had perished along with 90 percent of the population, not merely half. For that is evidently what happened throughout the region the Spanish called the Place of Flowers. In the stories of creation from this region that were taken down centuries later—old tales about the origin of things—one finds few if any traces of either the original killing pandemics or the god-chiefs and their noble assistants, or their grand temples and the days of mound building. About all this there is mostly an eerie silence.

When asked by the British about the mound their village was built upon, some Cherokees simply shrugged. They did not, they said, know how the mound had come about. In one of the very few stories that refer to prehistory in this region, the anthropologist Alice Marriot retold the tale of a group of people led by twin brothers, Chatah (Choctaw) and Chikasah (Chickasaw), in search of a new place to live. Eventually they found a good place but there was not enough room for everyone, so Chikasah led half the people off to find yet another place.

But before they split up, the people agreed to bury the bones of their ancestors (which they had brought with them on the journey) in a large bluff nearby, "in this sacred mound of earth, as a symbol that we will always be brothers." Called the Fruitful Mound, or Nanih Waya, it is located in Mississippi.

"Where today," Tecumseh, the great Shawnee leader, would ask in the late eighteenth century, "are the Pequot? Where are the Narragansett, the Mohican, the Pokanoket, and many other once powerful tribes of our people?" He might also have asked where in his day were the Ochesees, Cowetas, Yamasees, Coosas, Abihkas, Yuchis, Apalachees, Guales, or Oconees. These were among the remnants of the numerous chieftainships or tribes that had thrived during the flowering of the Mississippian culture that was so rapidly brought to its knees by European epidemic diseases. We do know that some of these groups maintained their ethnic identities for many decades, and with them their old snobberies. Most of them spoke one or another version of Muskogean, a branch of the overall Algonquian language, but there were many versions of Muskogean, most of them mutually unintelligible. In brief, after the Spanish arrival in the sixteenth century, the ensuing years for the tribes of the Southeast were a major experiment in what would later, in the United States, be called the melting pot. And among the southeast Indians, as later in the United States, it would be more a stew pot than a melting pot, with each ingredient taking on a bit of flavor from the others but each maintaining its own identity.

By Tecumseh's time, most of these southernmost peoples, however aware of their differences, would be referring to themselves as Creeks and Seminoles—as opposed to the other major (and more northerly) tribes of the region, the Choctaws and Chickasaws, who also spoke Muskogean tongues, and the Cherokees, whose language was more closely related to that of the Iroquois. Some Europeans, noting the continuing diversity among them, would also know them as the Creek Confederacy, though it was nothing at all like the Iroquois League (or Confederation) and nothing like Powhatan's Confederacy, having little by way of political cohesiveness. "Creek" was not just an ignorant and arbitrary label assigned to these polyglot folk by Europeans: it goes back to the original groups, who spoke Hitchiti, and later-arriving groups, who spoke Muskogee. The Hitchitis called the Muskogees by the name Ochesees, and some of these lived on Ochesee Creek, coming to be called by that name, and later simply Creeks. The name then spread (among the late-arriving British), finally coming into use by the Indians themselves.

Similarly, the group called Oconees would move from Georgia down into Florida in the early part of the eighteenth century, and (to the British) called themselves "Cimallons,"—their pronunciation of the Spanish word *cimarrón*, which means wild and untamed, a word used by the Spanish for any nonwhite whom they had trouble containing. "Cimallons" then became "Seminoles," a Creeklike amalgamation of groups that still spoke Hitchiti dialects, not Muskogee. And so it went. Yuchis, Shawnees, and others would also move into the abandoned lands of Florida and be called Seminoles. Like the so-called Creek Confederacy, the Seminoles were a confederation of differing groups, some of which were mini confederations themselves, eventually to mix with Africans.

At the end of the seventeenth century, French missionaries made their way into the country of the Natchez people, in present-day Mississippi, and encountered a recent amalgamation of various tribes. The Natchez had, in earlier times, been a far more extensive culture, with its own language (called an isolate, being so different from other Algonquian languages), but disease and other disruptions had shrunk them to a single medium-sized village. Survivors of various other chieftainships, fleeing the pandemics, had joined the Natchez, who, when the French first came, in about 1700, were still ruled by a god-chief and his family, along with a noble class, all of whom dwelled or performed on a high mound surmounted with a temple, as in the olden times. This was in fact the last dwindling holdout of the old ways of the mound builders. When a French missionary visited the Natchez early on, he was horrified to witness the funeral of the chief at which his widow and extended family and a number of maidens were all ritually strangled to join the fallen god in the afterlife.

Those refugees from other tribes made up a lower class of citizen, called, in the local dialect, "stinkards," and this was a term that came to be used in many pure Muskogee Creek towns to characterize other non-Muskogee-speakers (like the Seminoles), as well as slaves or enemies. Later, after being attacked by the French, the Natchez would move east into South Carolina and become yet another fragment of the Creeks.

In the Southeast, almost everything was characterized by movement, upheaval. Decision-making in the new Indian towns that arose tended to be democratic, based on consensus. Burials were simpler—no mounds were involved; instead the body was laid on the ground or in a cabin or dugout canoe and was burned. Old tribes, grievously reduced in numbers, were losing coherence, being replaced by new groups and new ethnic rivalries and class distinctions. People were moving north and south, east and west in what could be seen as either a grudging polymerization or cultural agility. Creeks would soon include virtually everyone in the Southeast who was not Choctaw, Chickasaw, or Cherokee.

As polyglot and fractious and egalitarian as this confederacy was, it was overlaid (as had been the many Mississippian cultures before) by certain common traditions and traits presumably derived, at least in part, from the mound-building times. The clan system persisted: one was born into one's mother's clan and got one's primary identity from the clan. Marriages were outside the clan, and in some cases outside what anthropologists call a *phratry,* a grouping of related clans. Belief systems were relatively similar. Most of the people who would be called Creeks and Seminoles believed in the notion of a tripartite universe—earth, air, and water—and the need to maintain a proper balance between the three realms. The supreme god, equated with the sun, was the Master of Breath, a sky god, and birds like the eagle could soar into contact with the sky gods. Fire, also thought of as the breath maker and the means by which the gods taught men, was of the sky and should never be extinguished with water. The color white represented, among other things, peace as well as the east and the importance of the sun, of maize, and of the sacred fire; red was war, and black was death. Throughout the Southeast, the tribes told very similar, almost interchangeable stories of origins, of the trickster Rabbit, and of the other animals.

In earlier Mississippian times, it is assumed (by extrapolating backward from ethnographic information), most tribes had been split into halves, or moieties: white and red. This created what were exogamous marital groups—whites married reds and vice versa—one of the ways such societies avoided inbreeding, another being the clan system. This red-white dichotomy tended to break down after the arrival of Europeans (and perhaps because of European plagues), to be replaced with those who were pure, or original, Muskogee and those who were not—often within the same village.

A major holdover from earlier times was the busk, or green corn ceremony, which took place at the full moon in July or August and ushered in the new year. Corn continued to be the most important crop, both in terms of nutrition and symbolism; the second most important was tobacco. The busk ceremony, often lasting for as many as eight days and nights, took place on an elevated spot, often an old platform mound, in the presence of a new fire made from four logs laid on white sand. It involved various rituals such as purging oneself and abstaining from sex. Old fires were put out and embers from the new fire distributed, green corn was roasted, and everyone joined in a great feast and dancing.

Soon enough, in the eighteenth century, all the southeastern tribes would come to thrive on, and at the same time suffer from, an unshakable addiction to the white man's trade goods. This dependency would change their culture and its economic emphasis almost completely—yet again.

Seven Cities of Gold: Nuevo México

By a series of events improbable enough to make a grand adventure movie, the first non-Indian to be encountered by the Indians of the Southwest was not someone they would come to call a white man. Instead, he was black, a slave variously called in the records Esteban or Estevanico. He was one of the five final survivors of the ill-fated de Narváez expedition, the remnants of which had fetched up near Galveston Bay in horsehide boats. These five included the man who had served the original expedition as treasurer, Alvar Núñez Cabeza de Vaca, evidently a kindly and devout man. For six years they remained in quasi captivity among the Texas coast Indians, who one day explained to the Spanish that they were extraordinary men and therefore should be able to heal those Indians that had fallen ill to the pestilence—otherwise they would not be allowed to eat. Cabeza de Vaca evidently combined the gestures of the Indian shamans he had seen with Christian prayer, and miraculously, the sick did recover (as some victims of smallpox do).

Eventually Cabeza de Vaca and three of his companions, including Esteban, escaped (the fifth choosing to remain among his captors) and visited another Indian tribe, where Cabeza de Vaca healed another sick Indian. They remained among these grateful folk for nearly a year and

Zuni deer

then set out westward, their reputation as healers ensuring them warm welcomes along the way. Soon enough, Esteban was proclaiming himself a healer too and swaggering about, shaking a rattle festooned with feathers, while Cabeza de Vaca remained more humble about his achievements. In their travels they crossed the Rio Grande, probably south of El Paso, and by 1536 made their way to Mexico City, having discovered, however inadvertently, the overland passage Menéndez had sought from La Florida to New Spain. Once there, Cabeza de Vaca and the other trekkers repeated (and presumably exaggerated) tales they had heard en route about big towns to the north, full of people who wore fine cotton clothes and bedecked themselves with turquoise. The big towns ballooned into grand cities, and to fine clothes and jewelry was added an abundance of gold—the element that burned so bright in the Spanish imagination. Thus bloomed on American soil the compelling European myth of the seven cities of gold.

Cabeza de Vaca himself returned to Spain, seeking the governorship of Florida (which had just been awarded to Hernando de Soto), the other two Spaniards essentially retired, and Esteban, the gaudy slave, managed to insinuate himself into a scouting expedition that preceded the great *entrada* being organized in 1539 by Francisco Vásquez de Coronado, a young and successful military leader in New Spain. The reconnaissance mission was entrusted to a Franciscan named Fray Marcos, who in turn sent Esteban and some friendly Mexican Indian auxiliaries ahead from northern New Spain. Esteban was the first of generations of shameless boosters of the glories of the American West; along the way he sent runners back to Fray Marcos with further tales of riches and gold awaiting the Spanish in places called Cíbola and Quivira. In truth, Esteban encountered an outlying Zuni town in the arid mesa country of western New Mexico, a place called Hawikuh, one of six Zuni villages. Accounts vary on the details of this encounter, but Esteban must have been disappointed. Hawikuh consisted of one large, six-story building, each story reached by wooden ladders, the entire structure being surrounded by a wall of stone. Outside of town, Esteban encountered a number of Zunis standing on their side of a line of cornmeal that had been sprinkled across the path to welcome home some Zunis who were at the time off on a pilgrimage to sacred outlying shrines. Almost surely, the Zunis had an inkling of what they were seeing with this arrival, since trade in such items as turquoise from elsewhere in New Mexico and macaw feathers from the Mexican tropics had long flourished, and tales of the Spanish would have penetrated the north along the trade routes.

Not only did Esteban bluster across the pilgrims' sacred line of cornmeal, but he demanded tribute in the form of food, turquoise, and women (the latter to be added to what apparently was a sizable harem of Mexican Indian groupies). The Zunis considered this—some accounts say for three days—before responding. By way of an answer, they fell upon the intruder and killed him. Thus was first contact in the Southwest made by more of a con artist than a conquistador. Hearing of Esteban's fate, Fray Marcos beat a hasty retreat to New Spain, not only with Esteban's personal bad news but with his buoying reports of glittering riches as well, telling of a city "larger than the city of Mexico." The rumors of riches in the north would, in due course, cause far more harm than the murder of Esteban.

Coronado arrived, presumably dismayed, in the environs of Hawikuh in July 1540. He had crossed nearly a thousand miles with a vast caravan of three hundred splendidly mounted Spanish officers and Spanish foot soldiers, along with eight hundred Mexican Indian warriors, plus Fray Marcos and a few other friars, and fifteen hundred head of horses, sheep, cattle, and swine, though these provisions were largely exhausted and hunger had plagued the expedition as it made its way through the desert lands and the rugged highlands of eastern Arizona.

It is well nigh unimaginable that Coronado's progress through these lands was not observed by Apaches, but they did not show themselves to the invaders.

For several decades, the Spanish crown had received petitions, particularly from a scholarly friar named Bartolomé de Las Casas, the first priest ordained in the New World, that the colonists of the New World treat the native populations with kindness rather than hostilities. Coronado's orders were to explore and take possession of the lands to the north, but specifically not to harm the Indians. He was met at Hawikuh by an assemblage of some two hundred Zuni warriors, who refused his demand for food and drew lines of cornmeal on the ground with dire warnings about crossing them. Coronado ordered a charge and in the ensuing melee he himself was severely wounded, but within an hour it was all over. Arrows and stones that the Zunis shot and rolled down from the terraced building were no match for the Spanish arms, and the surviving Zuni warriors fled, joining their women and children, who earlier had been secreted in the mountains.

So much, then, for priestly petitions. Coronado's army remained at Hawikuh for five months, feeding on the pueblo's stores of corn and other vegetables and on its domesticated turkeys, and managed to make an uneasy peace with the Zunis. Questioned about the cities of gold, the Zuni referred Coronado to the Hopi villages to the northwest, calling them Moquis, a name that stuck for centuries and that the Hopis never cared for, the word being close to the Hopi word for "dead." Coronado's lieutenant, a man named Cárdenas, visited the Hopis, met with resistance that he immediately overcame, and went on from there to be the first European to gaze upon Grand Canyon.

For reasons that are obscure, a delegation from the easternmost pueblo, Pecos, visited Coronado in Hawikuh, telling of a great river to the east (the Rio Grande) and of many villages along it. Coronado sent a detail to explore. Traveling upriver as far as Taos through neatly farmed fields along a river bordered with greenery, this Spanish force was met with hospitable overtures. Coronado then moved his headquarters to a region just north of Albuquerque, where a dozen Tiwa-speaking villages were clustered around the river—an area the Spanish dubbed Tiguex. Hospitality by the Indians was soon replaced by resentment of the overtaxing Spanish, however, and hostilities broke out. Pueblo after pueblo was sacked, with hundreds of surviving warriors burned at the stake. In all, ten villages were abandoned.

Even so, the Spanish were impressed by what they saw: well-planned houses of mud brick with whitewashed interior walls, excellent pottery, household flocks of turkeys, and industrious people with neatly tended fields of corn, squash, and melons. But no riches. Disillusioned, Coronado made a last stab, looking for fabled Quivira out in the Plains to the east, impelled by stories he was told by some of the people at Pecos, who no doubt hoped to send the invaders off elsewhere. Coronado reached the central Plains of Kansas, noting the hamlets of people—probably the Wichitas—who farmed and hunted the shaggy dark "cattle" that roamed the Plains in astonishing multitudes, comparable only to fish in the sea, as one Spaniard put it. At the easternmost point of his journey, Coronado was camped only some three or four hundred miles from de Soto's expedition, though neither side was aware of the other. Then what has to be one of the more bizarre events of this period in American Indian history occurred. A Plains Indian woman who had been captured earlier by the Pueblos was brought along by Coronado, and at this point she escaped. She headed east, only to run into de Soto's expedition, and was recaptured. What happened to her thereafter no one knows.

Disappointed still further, Coronado executed the Indian guide who had lied about Quivira, returned to Pueblo country, and in April 1542 headed south for the last time, needing to be carried home because of a head injury inflicted by the hooves of one of his horses. Back in New Spain, his mission a colossal failure except from the standpoint of cartography, he was later indicted for his misbehavior in the north, but not convicted. In the north, meanwhile, resentment and fear and recrimination smoldered among people who have always had long memories.

In New Spain, dreams of northern gold fizzled, but the embers did not go completely out. Other adventurers and explorers marched north over the next half century, in one case leaving behind among the southern Pueblos a pair of Franciscans whose missionary efforts ended abruptly with their execution. In the 1580s, a Spanish seeker of treasure named Antonio de Espejo became the first European to encounter some Apachean people who would later come to be known as the Navajos. The encounter took place beneath Mount Taylor (in New Mexico, near Grants), one of the four sacred mountains that delineate the spiritual home of the Navajos to this day. The place was littered with lava from the old volcano that is considered to be the congealed blood of monsters who had to be dispatched by two Navajo hero twins before the world could be safe for their descendants. Espejo and the Navajos he met were friendly enough, but then the Navajos asked that some of their people (who had been captured by the Hopis and whom Espejo had just taken from the Hopis) be turned loose. The Spanish refused and fighting broke out, a pattern already familiar to the Pueblo people.

In 1595, interest in the northern country swelled yet again and the crown authorized Don Juan de Oñate, the scion of a prominent New Spain mining family and an able soldier, to effect a conquest and found a colony. His orders bore the caveat that the Indian populace meet with "peace, friendship, and good treatment" by the Spanish so that they might become willing Christians and loyal subjects of Spain. To this end, Oñate was commanded to take sufficient provisions so that no troublesome burden be placed on the natives.

After many delays, during which men who had signed on signed off, Oñate set out on February 7, 1598, with some four hundred men, including seven friars and two lay brothers, more than a hundred women and children, and livestock and supplies hauled in heavy carts. They forded the Rio Grande near El Paso on the last day in April. There Oñate took possession of this promised land at the outer edge of the then-known world, claiming it in the name of the Spanish crown, the holy pontiff, and Jesus Christ. These would-be colonists were devout people who saw Spain as the most important power acting in behalf of the pontiff in Rome. Oñate's standard, borne high in the crystalline air, was topped by a cross; on its front was the Virgin of Remedies, patroness of New Spain, and on the back the gold castles of Castile on red, with red lions on white. For these people it was another crossing of the river Jordan, and there was holy work to be done. Whatever hardships were ahead were to be borne with penitential reverence.

From the start, the *entrada* was propitious enough. North of El Paso, the Spanish caravan needed to cross badlands that came to be called La Jornada del Muerto, a parched and sun-blasted land of white sands and congealed black lava flows, with saw-toothed mountains in the distance on either side. At one point a little dog—probably a stray from an Apache hunting party—approached them, tail wagging, and led them to a spring. Later on, nearing the Rio Grande above the badlands, they came upon two Piro-speaking pueblos that offered them large quantities of corn. Oñate named the place Socorro for the succor received. They proceeded north along the river, seeing green fields and trim villages, at thirty-four of which the residents came out and happily made homage to the Spanish crown, though it is difficult to imagine what they understood by that. But clearly these Pueblo people had concluded that it was senseless to oppose people who, like the ones fifty years earlier but well within living memory, had been so destructive.

Later in the year, Oñate established his capital in a Tewa village called Okeh Oweenge (now San Juan Pueblo) and established seven missionary districts from Hopi to Pecos and from Taos to El Paso— what amounted to eighty-seven thousand square miles of largely unexplored land. For each of these districts he appointed a civilian leader, an *alcalde*. The order of the day was twofold: the settlers should establish their own farms and herds apart from the pueblos, while the Christianizing and civilizing of the native populations was to be left to the Franciscans. But before the end of 1598, another, more ominous prong of Spanish policy emerged. The trouble occurred at Acoma, an ancient pueblo to the east of the Zunis, built on a four-hundred-foot-high redoubt of a mesa, accessible only by a few precarious foot trails. People had lived in this village for about half a millennium already. Passing by Acoma, a small expedition led by Oñate's nephew, a man named Zaldívar, asked for provisions. Receiving what he considered an insulting offering, he and fourteen men stormed the rock fortress to make their own collection. The people of Acoma fell upon them, slaughtering Zaldívar and all but two of his men. Oñate, learning of this, reasoned that if the act went unpunished the few Spanish would have no hope of maintaining rule over what they estimated to be sixty thousand Indians in the province. He dispatched Zaldívar's younger brother to administer punishment. In the slaughter that followed, some eight hundred people of Acoma were killed, the remainder being taken to San Juan, where they were all sentenced to servitude—and every man over age twenty-five suffered having the Spanish cut one foot off before going into bondage. So military terror became the third prong of Spanish policy in Nuevo México, and this three-pronged scheme continued to spread calamity.

Four hundred years later, in 1998, a large bronze equestrian statue of Oñate erected near the town of Espanola, New Mexico, was vandalized, the conquistador's bronze foot cut off in defiance of a statewide celebration of the arrival of the Franciscans four centuries earlier. At the same time a distinguished pueblo historian, Joe Sando, suggested that the Pueblo tribes join the celebration, saying that the Franciscans had come to be "understanding and tolerant," and had introduced improved farming methods, including an extended irrigation system, and such new crops as wheat, apples, peaches, and Mission grapes. "Throughout the Spanish colonial period," Sando wrote, "the Franciscans were occasionally exhibited as defenders of the Pueblo Indians."

Some seventy new settlers arrived from Mexico the following year, but in 1601 the colonists were in despair. The land available beyond the pueblos was poor, mineral wealth nonexistent. The winters were freezing, Indian tribute minimal, and the missionary program was stalled. Risking the death penalty for desertion, two-thirds of the Spanish colonists fled. Soon it was clear in Madrid that maintaining this remote colony would always be a drain on the treasury, not the reverse, but it was also made clear that were the Spanish to give up on Nuevo México, the few hundred Indians who had accepted Christ would be murdered. In 1609, Oñate was fired for the false claims by which he had enticed colonists north, a new governor was appointed, and again friars, soldiers, and settlers began to flow northward. The new governor moved the capital from San Juan south to Santa Fe in 1610—it is the United States' oldest continuously used capital city—but the continuation of Oñate's three-part policies threw all three Spanish groups into increasingly harsh competition—chiefly over Indian labor and tribute.

The settlers wanted nothing more than to be *hidalgos,* noble landowners free of taxation and feudal snobbery, left to develop their own herds of sheep and cattle, for which the nonpueblo lands were well-suited. They were required to pay for Indian labor. The Franciscans were free to use Indian labor (without pay) to build missions and serve their other needs as the Indians, hopefully, converted to the cross. The governor, the military, and other officials expected not just free labor but tribute from both Indians and settlers. They had little intention of staying as colonists but meant instead to accumulate what wealth they could before returning to Mexico, if not Spain. While all this put multiple heavy duties on the shoulders of the Indians, matters were made far worse when the Franciscans took as part of the conversion process the task of stamping out the native religions, seeing devil worship and immorality in Indian practices, notably the katsina dances carried on in smoke-filled underground kivas that the Spanish called *estufas,* or stoves. Religious leaders were whipped or worse as sorcerers, and religious paraphernalia such as masks and altar pieces were destroyed. Governors complained to the viceroys and tribunals in New Spain of this maltreatment of the Indians, while friars complained of the secular leaders' abuse of Indian labor and their blatant profiteering. It was not long before the Indians learned to play the factions off against each other—for example, offering help to the governors in return for official encouragement to flout the friars' strictures against the practice of pagan rites. In all, for a half century, the Indian response was, variously, to accede, to resist openly, and to go underground. Different pueblos had different strategies, which could change over time, and this further increased suspicion (both external and internal) among these typically fractious tribes.

Added to the tinderbox was the fuel of raids by the more nomadic tribes in the surround, soon more efficiently carried out with the use of stolen Spanish horses, and all the more attractive given the herds of livestock in the region. The triennial pack trains that brought supplies fifteen hundred miles from Mexico were compelling targets, as were both Spanish and Pueblo herds and food stores. The relations between Pueblos and nomads were marked by raiding, interspersed with inexplicable (to the Spanish) periods of peace and trading—of food, fur, and slaves. The slave trade, long a tradition among the Indians of this area, increased markedly with the arrival of the Spanish, who provided an excellent market for Indian slaves from both the Pueblos and the Plains for resale in Mexico, where they became house servants or mine workers.

Meanwhile, society in New Mexico had steadily grown more complex. How many Pueblo people were Christianized is hard to say, but there were many of them. Oñate's original notion of keeping Spanish settlers and Indians separate soon went by the wayside. There was so much intermarriage and miscegenation that visiting Spanish inquisitors complained that even many high secular offices were held not by Spaniards but mestizos (Hispanic-Pueblo mixes). There were complaints also that many of the Hispanic colonists were making use of Indian healers and herbal medicine, along with the associated pagan rites of the shamans, hardly surprising in light of the fact that there were no doctors in the colony, only Franciscans who were poorly trained in medicine and spread thin on the land. Hispanics, using the accumulated botanical wisdom of the native population, developed their own somewhat shamanistic healing methods, many becoming noted *curanderos* themselves. In addition a new ethnic group had come into being. Called *genizaros,* these were Indians from non-Pueblo tribes who were captured, raised in Spanish households as slaves, and then set free. As Indians (from various tribes, mostly from the Plains) who were thoroughly imbued with Spanish ways, they were pariahs.

At the same time, the Pueblo Indian population was in a steady decline that harked back to the 1540s, when, it was estimated, some 110 or more pueblos existed. By the 1580s, this number had dropped to about sixty, with probably 130,000 inhabitants. Oñate estimated that some sixty thousand Pueblo Indians were present at the time of colonization, but forty years later, in 1638, the population was down to forty thousand. In another forty years, the count was seventeen thousand people living in forty-six separate pueblos. Presumably wave after wave of smallpox, influenza, and other European introductions took their toll, and epidemics struck again, in 1640 and in 1671, the latter perhaps an outbreak of anthrax. But more than disease was doing the grim work. Famines occurred with sorry regularity, the result of periodic droughts exacerbated by increasing use of the land by the Spanish settlers for livestock, causing overgrazing and erosion. Nor was there any letup in demand for tribute by the Spanish overlords. This mostly took the form of food, and the demands were raised even as the population of farmers dwindled and the best farmlands were given over to cattle. Raids also took their toll as the outlying tribes went almost totally unchecked by the small Spanish force, which was rarely more than a hundred men. Protection from the raiders was a paramount reason for the loyalty of some Pueblo people to the Spanish, and as defense efforts grew feeble, loyalty too dwindled.

Over the years, several aborted rebellions took place, typically involving a few pueblos and typically betrayed by Indians loyal to the Spaniards or the church. These resulted in numerous mass executions but also an increasing sense of isolation among the still greatly outnumbered Spanish. In the 1660s, a major uprising by the Piro pueblos, clustered south of Albuquerque, was narrowly avoided when the authorities got word of it and hanged the leader and others only just in time.

In the late 1660s and early 1670s, the region suffered a period of drought so severe that people were forced to eat the leather tack of the livestock, boiling it and mixing it with corn mush. To this was added the epidemic of 1671, along with increasingly bold raids on the weakened populace by Apache bands. Matters were so bad that the Spanish officials and the friars began a period of at least grudging cooperation. Meanwhile Indian anger seethed, reaching a new heat when, in 1675, the Spanish authorities joined the friars in publicly whipping forty-seven Pueblo religious leaders for encouraging idiolatry and fomenting discontent. Four were killed and the rest were imprisoned, but freed after a strong Indian protest to the governor. This, evidently, was the spark that lit the single most successful Indian rebellion in the history of the continent. While it took place more than a century beyond what could be considered the contact period, it was the paramount Pueblo response to this contact, long in coming perhaps but typical of the measured manner in which these people, in their highly developed traditional conservatism, confront such arrivals in their world.

The Pueblo Revolt of 1680

In every period of history, people perceive the world in the terms with which their minds and senses are familiar. Early on, the Spanish referred to the Pueblo kivas as mosques, before they came up with a more apt disparaging term, since it was not all that long since Isabella and Ferdinand had ejected the Muslims from Spain, the necessary military success that permitted them to pull the Iberian peninsula's separate fiefdoms into a nation and set forth to explore and to conquer the rest of the world in the name of glory, gold, and the cross. We today look at the world through senses and understandings honed by a different and, we tend to find, superior set of values than could have occurred to most Europeans at the time they undertook the conquest of the New World. But it should be kept in mind by those who might be called "presentist" that the twentieth century has produced more mayhem, and on a grander scale, than any other era in all of human existence on the planet. In this light, perhaps, one can understand how driven the Franciscans were to exterminate the Indian practices that were clearly the works of Satan. For Satan was a palpable daily threat to even the most devout. He was the personal engine of evil. Both the Spanish and the Indian people they conquered understood the idea perfectly.

After the Spanish authorities—secular and religious—had humiliated the forty-seven Pueblo medicine men in Santa Fe in the name of a deity who was brutally nailed up to a wooden cross by his own people, it was obvious to the Indians that evil was in control in the land and survival was at stake. One of the forty-seven was a man from San Juan Pueblo named Popé, who left with fire in his eyes and in his soul a fierce determination to rid his homelands of the embodiment of evil, the Spanish yoke. He went into hiding, eventually finding refuge in a Taos kiva, where he carefully played the complex instrument of Pueblo politics and persuasion, and plotted something unheard of—a unified Pueblo response. In this, he was aided by Po-Se-Ye-Mo, a deity who resided in the north and was revered by most of the Pueblo Indians, especially the Tewa-speaking villages of the upper Rio Grande. Popé not only invoked this deity but, it became clear, consulted with him regularly. Po-Se-Ye-Mo called for vindication, and for the primacy of the Pueblo gods and the rituals devoted to them.

Popé found allies among many Pueblo leaders, and from many pueblos with different languages, different traditions, and even histories of mutual distrust and hostilities. These polyglot men and others met in secret, sometimes coming together under cover of the bustling crowds at Pueblo feast days, to lay their plans, mindful of earlier uprisings that were betrayed from within. As if to underline the need for total secrecy, Popé, it is said, executed his own son-in-law when he found out the man knew of the plans and might well betray them, having been appointed a secular leader at San Juan by the Spanish.

The conspirators chose August 12 to act, and sent forth runners with this word embodied in knotted strings. Upon receiving the knotted string, the revolutionary leader in each pueblo was to untie one knot each day. When the last knot was untied, it was time to strike. Nevertheless rumors of the imminent revolt were in the air and reached Don Antonio de Otermín, the recently installed governor, in his headquarters in Santa Fe.

On August 9, Otermín received word from loyal leaders of the easternmost pueblos (Pecos, Galisteo, and two others) that two young runners, Omtua and Catua, were spreading word of the uprising. The two runners were promptly captured, grilled, and then executed, but not before they had informed Otermín that the revolt was planned for August 12. This gave the Spanish, Otermín reckoned, time to prepare. Aware their plans were now known, the rebel leaders sent out new runners with an earlier date.

August 10 dawned with a Franciscan, Fray Juan Pío, accompanied by a Spanish soldier named Hidalgo, riding from Santa Fe to his mission in the pueblo of Tesuque, some ten miles north of the capital. In an arroyo outside the village, he saw a mass of armed Indians, their faces red with paint. Pío approached, calling out: "What is this, children, are you mad? Do not disturb yourselves; I will die a thousand deaths for you." He descended into the arroyo. Hidalgo next saw an Indian referred to as El Obi emerge with the padre's shield and another, Nicolas, spattered with blood. Hidalgo took off for Santa Fe as the Indians charged him and tried to pull him from his mount. He managed to outrun them and reach Otermín with the first news of that day's violence.

Throughout the morning, the Pueblo people struck again and again, overrunning hacienda after lonely hacienda in the north, killing every man, woman, and child, taking horses and whatever weapons they could find. In mission after mission, Indian bands fell on the priests and slaughtered them, vandalizing the images, smearing altars and crosses with feces, and setting the churches on fire in terrible retribution for the stolen masks and the other depredations the friars had wrought on their ceremonial ways. The world was on fire.

Otermín ordered all the settlers in and around Santa Fe to congregate in the walled plaza of the city for safety, the chief building there being the governor's large, low adobe palace (which still stands). By noon, the plaza was jammed with about a thousand settlers and a number of livestock. From today's Albuquerque all the way north to Taos, virtually every Spaniard was either dead or had joined the swelling crowd in the Santa Fe plaza. Vengeful Indians now began to make their way to Santa Fe to lay siege to the Spanish capital. There, among the throng in the plaza, were Indians who were thought loyal to the Spanish but who began spreading the tale that every Spaniard in the south had also been killed. Otermín could not count on help from any quarter.

In fact, to the south, in the pueblo of Isleta (near Albuquerque), Indians sympathetic to the Spanish and settlers alike gathered under the command of Lieutenant Governor García. A standing Spanish order forbade anyone, even the lieutenant governor, to leave the province without the express permission of the governor. Believing it now useless to try and aid the people in the capital, and believing that the governor was dead—while at the same time the situation in Isleta was rapidly growing untenable—García made a short reconnaissance north, discovered a land devastated, and hastened back to Isleta, his worst fears confirmed. Later, he ordered everyone to head south in the hopes, perhaps, of meeting up with the triennial pack train and some welcome reinforcements.

Over the next two days in Santa Fe, there was some light skirmishing, with some Indians raining shot and arrows down into the plaza from above, adding to the panic that was rapidly growing there as food supplies ran out. Fires set by the Indians grew closer and closer to the plaza, and evidently the Indians deflected the flow of the river that ran through the plaza, cutting off even the water supply. Conditions in the plaza had gone from frightful to utterly desperate. Every Spanish soldier bore at least one wound, and Otermín had been hit three times himself. In an act of both despair and courage, he decided the best hope was to break out with as great a show of force as possible. The Spaniards managed to take the Indians by surprise, killing a number of them and capturing others, who, along with supplies of water, were brought back into the plaza, where they were questioned and then executed.

Still, the situation appeared hopeless for the Spanish on August 21. They said a mass and, carrying their standards high, filed out of the plaza, mostly on foot and carrying on their backs whatever they could, expecting death but hoping however wanly that some of them might survive long enough to meet up with the pack train from Mexico.

No attack came. Instead, some two thousand Pueblo warriors simply watched as the primary goal of their entire uprising was clearly taking place. The hated Spaniard was leaving—leaving the province. All along the dreary road south, the one thousand Spanish soldiers and settlers were met only with jeers and insults hurled from the surrounding high ground. Days later they reached El Paso, where García and some fifteen hundred others had already arrived, a number of them being Indians from Isleta who remained loyal to the Spanish and also feared violent retribution from the revolt's leaders if they chose to stay in their homeland. There, in what are now the slums of Juárez, these few Indians and the former masters of the fate of New Mexico would settle uncomfortably, some for good, wondering if the entire enterprise of New Mexico had been a long nightmare that now, however humiliatingly, was over. Thirteen years later, in 1693, after a few earlier forays north, the Spanish would return—considerably though not totally chastened—and they would find a New Mexico that was markedly different from the one they left. Today there is no dispute that this uprising, so well planned and executed, is the chief reason why the Pueblo Indian cultures remain among the most viable and most intact in the nation.

Also at this time, the Spanish made their first serious foray into what is now southern Arizona, an area the Spanish called Pimeria Alta. This is the northernmost part of the Sonoran Desert, a subtropical landscape dominated by the giant saguaro cactus and its smaller but equally bizarre cousins. Near Tucson, this is called the green desert, where two short rainy seasons encourage an undesertlike profusion of plant life; farther west, toward Yuma on the Arizona-California border, is one of the nation's most discouraging badlands, the still primitive road through it known even today as the Devil's Highway. The Indian people in this region called themselves O'odham, meaning essentially "we, the people." In villages along the Salt and Gila Rivers, they lived in year-round villages, farming the land with the help of irrigation. These were the Pimas until recent times, when they have been called, as they prefer, the Akimel O'odham, which means "river people." It is they who gave the name Hohokam to the people who came before them and were probably their direct ancestors. They and the other O'odham (until recently known as the Papagos) speak a Uto-Aztecan language, as do the Hopis and the Shoshoneans of the Great Basin, along with people from Mexico.

At the time the Spanish came across the Papagos (now Tohono O'odham, meaning "desert people"), some were thought of as two-village people, who moved seasonally between two loosely organized villages to take advantage of the availability of food in low and high ground and the runoff from the mountains to cultivate gardens and fields. West of these villagers were the no-village people, also known as the Sand Papagos. They lived in small bands that were ever on the move, collecting whatever food they could from a harsh country dominated by great heat and at best a handful of permanent water holes. Their shelter consisted mainly of rings of stone, sleeping circles that acted mainly as windbreaks. They made few tools and no pottery, exchanging shells and the like from the Gulf of California with people to the north. The Pimas were called one-village people, having permanent, year-round residences along the rivers.

There is virtually no means by which we can know how many of these Piman and Papago people were struck down by epidemic disease prior to the first Spanish arrivals in their midst, but it is impossible to believe that they escaped the ravages of smallpox and other scourges brought to them by traders and people from the south fleeing disease or fleeing the Spanish. It remains a possibility that the great culture of the Hohokam continued in some attenuated form beyond the date of 1450, when it is supposed to have disappeared.

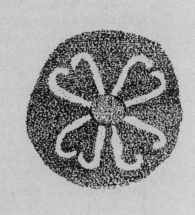

Papago shield

The first European to reach the O'odham was an ebullient, indefatigable man named Father Eusebio Kino, who arrived in 1687. Kino was an Italian and a Jesuit who, along with others of his order, had been missionizing the tribes south of Arizona and had developed a technique that was, in important ways, markedly different from that of the Franciscans. The Jesuits tended to arrive among a new group of Indians bringing cattle and other livestock as an immediate and tangible benefit, as well as seeds of new crops such as wheat. Handing out these gifts, they would immediately begin to tell exciting biblical stories and demonstrate fascinating new ceremonies. The strategy was to establish a simple mission building and to encourage villages to form around the missions, converting these free-ranging people to an orderly life in service to the missionary, the church, and the crown. In other words, they attempted to turn people whose only real allegiance was to extended family living in a particular neighborhood into *citizens* of towns, and thus of New Spain, and thus, however remotely, of distant Spain itself. A crucial part of the Jesuit strategy was based on the chastening experience of earlier efforts, where competition between missionaries and settlers had led to an array of troubles. Father Kino arrived in the Pimeria Alta carrying an order from the viceroy of New Spain that disallowed any forced Indian labor by settlers and exempted Indians from any tribute so long as the missionary program was under way.

The Jesuits tended to make a greater effort than the Franciscans to learn the local language, and Father Kino seemed to take a delight in sitting around for days and nights, listening to the Indian elders talk before talking himself. Kino was unique in other ways: he was something of a supersalesman. Instead of establishing a mission and staying on, Kino traveled extensively among the O'odham, from the relatively lush region of the San Pedro River all the way west to the Colorado. Generally he was well received, the Indians often erecting a cross to welcome his arrival. He would soon send word back to New Spain that such and such a group greatly desired a missionary in their midst, and then move on to another. He was as much an explorer as a missionary, and one of his side ventures demonstrated that California was not, as was then believed, an island. The erection of new missions and the arrival of new missionaries never did catch up with Kino's one-man sales department, however. In the 1690s, he established a large cattle herd among the Indians in a place called Bac, south of Tucson, along with a great hunger for a missionary. He began to erect a rudimentary church, named for his patron saint Francis Xavier, before moving on, but by 1711, when Father Kino died, the Indians at Bac still had an incomplete mission and no regularly visiting missionary.

Except for a few exploratory forays, one of which would reach as far north as Paiute country in Utah, the Spanish did not penetrate farther north into Arizona than Tucson, which they established as one of several defensive presidios. Elsewhere in this region, they were blocked largely by the presence of a relatively small but extremely talented people, called Apaches, who in essence dictated the rules for the next two hundred years. And one thing or another would prevent much further exploration or settlement in such places as Texas and California until the following century (the 1700s). Throughout the 1600s, Spain basically had enough to handle in New Spain, La Florida, and its other New World outposts. La Florida did not amount to much at all, and New Mexico was an albatross around the royal neck, a continuing drain on the treasury and of little other value to the crown. The Pacific coast of North America was at this time one of the least known coastlines in the world for all the would-be European hegemons interested in it. There, the winds blew mostly from the west and northwest, making Spanish passage up the coast difficult enough, even had the Spanish empire not been going through financial difficulties. In Texas, the only particular Spanish interest was among the religious, ever eager to convert souls; but except for a few exploratory trips into the heart of Texas and the establishment of a temporary mission, the native people of Texas would be spared until later, as would those of California. Only when the Spanish saw themselves being directly threatened in this vast region by the other imperial powers—French, British, and Russian— would they take Texas and California seriously.

The Spanish presence among the O'odham, even given the well-meaning nature of Father Kino's efforts, was devastating. The Akimel O'odham (Pimas) tell a sad story about it.

First Man, the great hero of the Akimel O'odham, grew arrogant and insisted that he was more powerful than the Great Spirit. Demanding labor from the people, First Man also made it impossible for the people to understand the language of the animals and of other tribes. Evil settled into the world and the Great Spirit was sad. But he decided to vanquish those who had rebelled and sent locusts to the East to summon some new people from far away. These new people arrived on great ships from the East, their faces and bodies covered with hair, carrying metal weapons, sticks that could spit fire. And they took away First Man's power, so he left to live in the underworld and never came back.

CHAPTER SIX

THE FRENCH AND THE ENGLISH

Virginia

Wahunsunacock was what they called him—his own people, that is—even though he was a demigod. Wahunsunacock was what might be thought of as a familiar name, not the official or royal name he gave the English: Powhatan. By the time Englishmen arrived to establish Jamestown, in 1607, on the banks of one of the several rivers debouching into the greatest bay on the east coast south of the Arctic, Wahunsunacock had noted the brief appearance of the Spanish in nearby waters, and no doubt had heard of the English's failed attempts to start colonies such as the one on Roanoke Island—the so-called Lost Colony. And so, when Captain John Smith and a handful of others came ashore with a certain hopeful swagger, Wahunsunacock was probably not terribly surprised. They would, he decided, become just another of his vassal groups.

For by this time, Powhatan (whose reigning name was taken from his original village, near the fall line of the James River) ruled what has since been called the Powhatan Confederacy, an array of thirty Algonquian-speaking groups that lived on both sides of the bay, mostly in what is now the state of Virginia, in rich countryside that included the coastal plains and the Piedmont (the foothills of the Appalachians to the west). There would have been thirty-*one* such groups, but the Chesapeakes (who lived near today's Norfolk, at the mouth of the bay that ironically bears their name) had been unwilling to join up with Powhatan, so he saw to it that they were totally exterminated. It was, in fact, no confederacy at all, the word implying a form of consent. Powhatan was what we call a paramount chief, ruling over some thirty other chiefs (in essence, district commanders), who each ruled over the several chiefs of different hamlets in their districts; and Powhatan had established himself thus out of military might as well as persuasion. This was a new arrangement. Powhatan, clearly a man of foresight, had early seen the value of large numbers of people working as one in defense of a large and welcoming homeland against the depradations of other Indian people, like the Iroquoian Eries from the north and the Monacans from the immediate west, not to mention the hairy, light-skinned men of Spain and England. Powhatan was the architect and first ruler of the alliance, which, culturally, lay somewhere in between the great Mississippian-style chiefdoms to the south and the more egalitarian peoples of the Northeast.

Among the people of Powhatan's empire, only he, his priests, and the lesser chiefs could expect to enjoy an afterlife once they died. They would proceed, it was believed, to a place of plenty where they would dance and feast and go on satisfying hunts. But they would age in this good place until they reached an age where they again died, to be reborn as new human beings.

By the time John Smith arrived, there were some fourteen thousand people under Powhatan's sway, living in small villages usually of thirty or fewer houses, located amid several acres of agricultural fields and never much more than a mile or two from the next town or hamlet. That the population had once been far greater, and many towns far larger, is likely. Powhatan's imperial scheme may have emerged in response to the mystery and horror of epidemics. In any event, a new political system was being invented. Except for the chiefs, called *weroances,* and priests (who supported and were supported by the weroances), there was little social stratification—nothing like a group of aristocrats between royalty and the common people. When not engaged in affairs of state or ceremony, Powhatan and the chiefs did the normal chores that all men of this region did, hunting, making weapons, and so forth. While the chiefs and particularly Powhatan (the *mamanatowick,* or paramount chief) had power over their people's lives—since they were also judges and executioners—they could not act outside the box of cultural tradition without losing support from those they ruled over.

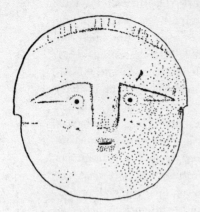

Patawomeke shell ornament

Well before any trade with Europeans in such goods as deer skins for metal knives, axes, and other trade goods, the people of this Tidewater region had put a great deal of pressure on the local deer population, a pressure that apparently went back as far as late Archaic times. Here, it seems, there was an exploitative attitude to such resources, rather than what we think of as a conservationist's ethic enforced by fear of retribution from the animal spirits. Deer were hunted typically in the late fall, and the annual food quest depended on the seasonal availability of such things as berries, nuts, fish, oysters, crabs, wild potato roots, snakes, and rattlesnakes. The leanest period was evidently in late spring and early summer, when the corn harvested in the previous fall was gone and the berries had yet to ripen. People grew noticeably thin at such times.

The overexploitation of deer, sending the hunters farther west, into the Appalachians, where enemy tribes used the same hunting grounds, was probably lessened by depopulation from epidemics but then almost immediately exacerbated by the tribute that Powhatan and, to a lesser degree, the lesser chiefs now demanded. For every deer a hunter might kill and use for his own purposes, he would need to kill several others for payment to chiefs, some English colonists' reports saying as many as four extra. In addition, Powhatan claimed some (uncertain) amount of corn and other produce from his subjects, as well as bits and pieces of copper and other valuables that found their way into his realm, which he would then judiciously bestow upon those who served him well as chiefs or warriors. The food paid him in tribute does not appear to have been for redistribution to the people in hard times, but simply for himself and his entourage, which included bodyguards, an array of priests who manned longhouse-type temples around the territory in his name, and his wives. By the time Jamestown was shakily established and Powhatan was in his sixties, it is said that he had already enjoyed a hundred wives or more. Part Solomon and part Stalin, Powhatan had built a personal kingdom by both persuasion and force.

In fact, he (and to a lesser extent the district commanders) practiced a kind of serial polygyny. Powhatan had a dozen wives or so at any given moment, selected from time to time from among the most attractive women in his subject districts. (Men attracted wives based largely on their ability as hunters and warriors and the favoritism they enjoyed among chiefs.) Once Powhatan's wives gave birth to a child of his, they were usually dismissed and sent home, where they could remarry, the child being sent to Powhatan's seat of government to be raised. Thus all of Powhatan's children were half siblings to all the rest, but there was no question of their inheriting his mantle. Such positions were to be passed on from the mother's side in this traditionally matrilineal society. Powhatan's brothers and then sisters, and only then *a sister's* children, stood in line to inherit the paramount chieftainship.

Without what appeared to be straightforward generosity on the part of Powhatan's people, the ill-equipped and, it seems, malingering Jamestown colonists would almost surely have perished before their first year in Virginia was out. They were wracked by disease and especially hunger in this period they called "the starving time." Smith later would write of several instances of cannibalism: "So great was our famine that . . . one among the rest did kill his wife, powdered [salted] her, and had eaten part of her before it was known; for which he was executed, as he well deserved. Now whether she was better roasted, boiled, or carbonadoed, I know not; but of such a dish as powdered wife I never heard." The colonists readily accepted gifts of food from the Indians' largesse and indeed went about asking for more rather than doing their own planting. No doubt such behavior by the colonists was confusing, if not absurd, to the Indians, just as the colonists never understood the actual plan Powhatan had for *them*.

Pipe from Wythe County, Virginia

For Jamestown was slated to be the thirty-first of the Powhatan district chieftainships, and John Smith, who was clearly the Englishman in charge, would be the chief. In 1607, Smith was captured when he blundered into a large hunting party, and for a year he remained with the Indians.

In the meantime, one of Powhatan's myriad daughters, Pocahontas (her name means "mischievous one"), had from the start been a frequent visitor to the English fort and showed a great interest in, even fascination with, the English ways. Prepubescent girls in this area went about in warm weather without clothes, and evidently Pocahontas captivated the colonists by turning cartwheels in the nude, as well as by her wit and outgoing personality. She was, Smith wrote in 1608, "the only Nonpareil" in Virginia. By then, of course, she had flung herself upon his supine body, which awaited a sure death by beating, successfully pleading with her stern father for his life—or so John Smith thought. In fact, this was probably an act carefully planned and part of a larger ceremony in which Powhatan was essentially adopting Smith so that he would be one of his district chiefs. For in Powhatan's world, someone who was the chief of a group he wished to incorporate into his empire was far too valuable to kill. He could either be kept on as a chief, if he was loyal to Powhatan, or taken away and made to do women's work, a humiliation so great that his former followers would give up and join Powhatan. Smith's interpretation of these events, however, is the one that endured in history, making Pocahontas probably the best known and most romanticized American Indian personage of all time. (In recent years, Disney's Barbie doll version summoned forth a good deal of indignation from Indians, though several younger Indians were quoted as saying words to the effect that "she's pretty cute.")

In fact, Pocahontas would better be remembered for her continuing role as a go-between who constantly sought mutual understanding and peace between the Europeans and her own people. She interceded with her father for the release of English captives and arranged the return of Indian captives of the English, carried diplomatic messages back and forth, and according to Smith, risked her life to reveal "trecheries" and save the colony. For of course, fracases occurred: no chief was sufficiently powerful to deny an Indian warrior revenge, and the English were not about to put up with trouble from what they considered devil-worshiping savages. By 1610, another four hundred English

colonists had arrived, and English effrontery, coercion, and land grabbing had become intolerable, and well beyond the ability of Pocahontas or anyone else to mediate. Powhatan's complaint to the English
colonists is now emblematic of Indian-colonial relations:

> What will it avail you to take that perforce [which] you may quietly
> have with love or to destroy them that provide you [with] food? What
> can you get by war, when we can hide our provision and fly into the
> woods, whereby you must famish, by wronging us, your friends?

For the most part, the English were never able to bring themselves
to believe that Indian generosity was sincere. It *had* to conceal some
treachery: generosity must precede extortion. Given the requirement
in most Indian cultures for revenge for a wrong, the English suspicion
of Indian aid became a self-fulfilling prophecy. The first Anglo-
Powhatan War lasted until 1614, a five-year exchange of atrocities.
Meanwhile Pocahontas, it was believed, married an obscure warrior
and no longer came to the English settlement. In 1613, however, she
was captured near the headwaters of the Potomac River and taken to
live among the English in what seems to have been a relatively comfortable year as a hostage. During that time, she converted to Angli-
canism, was baptized "the Lady Rebecca," and then married the
widower John Rolfe in a diplomatic union that brought the war to an
end (both sides had apparently been hoping for a way out of the ever-
expanding gyre of violence) and prevented any further outbreaks for as
long as she lived.

By way of drumming up support back home for the still fragile
colony at Jamestown, the sponsoring London Company arranged an
English tour for Rolfe, his new wife, and their son, Thomas. Lady
Rebecca, *"la belle sauvage,"* charmed the English, including King James
I. She was not merely an exotic oddity; she comported herself with
style, being the daughter, after all, of a king herself. But she soon fell
ill from England's cold, bad air, and foreign diseases, and died on
March 21, 1617, to be buried thousands of miles from home at
Gravesend, Kent. She had become so potent a symbol of mutual tolerance between the two peoples that her death—particularly at so young
an age, her early twenties—dashed any hopes of continuing cooperation in Virginia.

Meantime, the colonists were doing a bad job of establishing themselves as a viable community, but soon they discovered the way not merely to self-sufficiency but to wealth. They began to grow tobacco, which had found a devoted market in England. (Pocahontas's son, Thomas, would return to Virginia in the 1640s and take up as a tobacco farmer.) The result of this lucrative business was more colonists arriving, and more land taken by the English from the Powhatan people—or bought from them, a concept they found bewildering since land was not something, in their lights, that one could own like an arrow or a hat. With increasingly widespread cultivation, wild game habitat was diminished, and English livestock was overrunning what remained of the Indians' fields. By now, Powhatan himself having died in 1618, his brother Opechancanough was paramount chief and, like some younger brothers, rather more of a hothead. Almost immediately, he began planning an uprising. On March 22, 1622, Indians began drifting innocently into the English settlements. Suddenly striking, they slaughtered 347 of the twelve-hundred-odd colonists and wiped out entire English settlements sprinkled here and there along other rivers. Jamestown, alerted by a converted Indian, survived the attack and mounted its own in response, devastating Indian fields, villages, crops, canoes—everything in their path. The Indians, they thought, were thoroughly subdued.

One English plan that died in this uprising was the intention of building a school and university some fifty miles up the James River where Indian youth—specifically, boys and men—could be educated as part of their conversion to Christianity. Already the English had been encouraged by people of a missionary bent back home to kidnap Indian boys to "bring them true Knowledge and Worship of God." But with the outbreak of 1622, the plans for the school and university foundered on the ill will of the colonists toward anything Indian. The thought was rekindled some seventy years later with the founding of the College of William and Mary, one purpose of which was to provide teaching to Indians. But this goal faded thanks to lack of interest by the Indians. (It is, however, a happy circumstance if not an outcome of these earlier dreams that James Axtell, one of the preeminent and wisest historians of American Indian life, teaches at William and Mary.)

After 1622, the English population and territory continued to grow, the colony thrived, and the problems of old grew more severe. In 1644, with Opechancanough still paramount chief and about a century old, the Powhatans struck again, this time with even less likelihood of accomplishing much against the now far vaster and better organized English population. Two years later, Opechancanough was captured and executed, his people totally subdued, and a treaty signed. Powhatan's creation of a paramount chieftainship ended forever in 1649. Hereditary chieftainships were on the way out, and so was the language of the people, now living in diminishingly small communities and pushed (or bought) out of virtually all their ancestral lands. Their religion would disappear with their priests, and most of the Indians would later become Baptists. But for now, the treaty and subsequent ones accorded the Powhatan groups that remained provided them certain civil rights in the commonwealth of Virginia and a handful of small reservations in the colony. Their traditional culture, which had evolved over an unknown period of centuries and had put forth its last, elaborately inventive (and ephemeral) flower under Powhatan, was thoroughly uprooted and essentially no more.

The Northeast

In a time of constant feuding, warfare, and dissension between those who dwelt among the long thin lakes, everyone felt the pain of loved ones being killed. No one suffered more deeply than the man called Hiawatha, all of whose daughters were slain one after the other. (Longfellow's Hiawatha, hailing from Minnesota, was a fictional character, though the poet believed he was basing his Indian hero on the real thing.) So great was Hiawatha's grief and rage that he lost all reason and wandered off into the forest. Eventually, he encountered a figure called Deganawidah, the peacemaker, who had been born of a virgin. He gave Hiawatha several strings of shell beads, called wampum, and uttered a litany of Words of Condolence that in turn dried Hiawatha's eyes, opened his ears, then his throat, and so forth, until Hiawatha's grief was assuaged. Deganawidah explained that

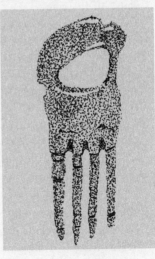

Precontact Iroquois comb

true power came from being at peace with others, thinking good thoughts about those who might otherwise be enemies. He sent Hiawatha back to teach this gospel of condolence, peace, and power to his own people and the others.

Hiawatha returned and gathered disciples from among the Mohawks, Oneidas, Cayugas, and Senecas, but the chief of the Onondagas would hear none of it. This was Tadadaho, a hater of all mankind, a sorcerer so full of anger he had gone insane. His hair had become a tangle of snakes. Hiawatha ("he who combs") smoothed out the tangle of snakes into hair and cured Tadadaho's mind with this grooming and with the Words of Condolence.

The old sorcerer joined the others in creating the Great League of Peace and Power, with the Onondagas appointed as *fire keepers,* those who would host the annual council of fifty sachems (chiefs) drawn from the Five Nations. No one knows exactly when the league was established—possibly a century or so before the first Europeans showed up, perhaps only upon their first shadowy appearances—but it knit together these five tribes into what would come to be called the Iroquois Confederation. They thought of themselves in the image of a longhouse, running east and west. The Senecas were the keepers of the western door, the Mohawks the keepers of the eastern door. In the center, the Onondagas kept the council fire. Between them and the Senecas to the west were the Cayugas, and between them and the Mohawks to the east were the Oneidas. Among all the many Indian peoples of the vast region of the American Northeast, it was the Iroquois Confederation that would play a major role in the outcome of French and English efforts to colonize and control the Northeast.

Partly, this was an accident of geography. The Iroquois inhabited western New York State athwart all the major trade routes of the region, a place with direct access to rivers leading north to Lake Ontario, south to what is today New York City, and to the Susquehanna River, leading yet farther south into Chesapeake Bay. At the same time, they were far enough from the centers of early colonization efforts to be able to adapt to new ways *before* being done in by epidemics and Europeans swarming into their land. Furthermore, the Iroquois found themselves located in between the competing interests of the French along the Saint Lawrence River and the Dutch (and then the English) on the Hudson River, not to mention the English in New England. Quickly they learned to play the imperial competitors off against one another.

Like most of their neighbors, the Iroquois were agriculturalists, living in densely populated and heavily palisaded villages surrounded by their fields of corn, beans, and squash. The fields were tended by women and children; the men supplemented these stores by hunting and fishing, often in far distant hunting grounds. In all, at the time of contact, there were at least ten Iroquois villages of size and a greater number of outlying hamlets with a population, overall, of about twenty thousand, perhaps more. Theirs were matrilineal societies, with women playing important political roles in tribal affairs, such as appointing new sachems (chiefs) and counseling them. Women owned the longhouses and the crops they tended.

It appears that the Iroquois were whipped by as often as they whipped other tribes in the years before European contact, but by the time they appear in historical accounts, the Iroquois warriors were known and feared in a vast area stretching through the Northeast to the Great Lakes and south to the edges of the Mississippian cultures. Like their neighbors, Iroquois warriors engaged in a ritualized form of combat and took captives, either adopting them as full-fledged members of the tribe or torturing them to death. No other Indians in the region were more efficient at this, or more terrifying. Either alternative—torture and adoption or torture and death—was the means by which the Iroquois gained the captives' power. The captive—once dead—would often be dismembered by the women and cooked for a village-wide feast—a *ritual* practice that some scholars believe went back for hundreds of years before Columbus. On the other hand, by adopting a captive, a family not only derived the benefit of his (or her) power but also replaced some family member who had been lost to war or, later, to epidemic disease. The raids that produced these captives were *mourning wars:* the women of a family grieving over a lost family member would get revenge or consolation by demanding that warriors go forth and bring back replacements—a highly rational system under the circumstances.

Reaching an Iroquois village, captives were greeted by an unearthly howling, a gauntlet to run through, a day or so of intermittent torture, and then a formal adoption into a family who would then—by a method unknown—decide whether a given captive was a keeper or was to be executed. If the latter, the captive was further tortured with burning sticks, knives, and so forth by men, women, and children, eventually scalped, and then dispatched by knife or tomahawk. Ideally, through the entire horror, the captives were supposed to remain silent, stoic, thus teaching the youth of their captors how to behave when and if it became their turn in the endless gyre of feuding. If adopted and kept, the replacement would take on the role of the one he replaced, and could even rise in tribal respect to the office of sachem.

"Iroquois" is evidently a French version of an Algonquian word—*irinakhoiw*—that means "real adders." The derivation of "Mohawk" is also Algonquian: "eater of human flesh." Algonquian was the root language of most of the Indian tribes of New England and down the Atlantic coast into Virginia; Iroquoian was a root language shared by the Five Nations and many of their neighbors, including the tribes that made up the Huron Confederacy, to the north and west; the Susquehannocks and Tuscaroras and Cherokees, to the south; and the Eries and a group known as the Black Minquas, along with some (now) little known people referred to only as Saint Lawrence Iroquois. In their own language, the Iroquois referred to themselves as *haudenosaunee,* "people of the longhouse."

A longhouse typically housed several related families, with two families living on opposite sides of a single fire, a physical sign of

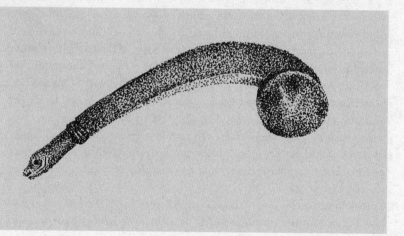

Iroquois war club

the need for sharing. A major component of their culture was the reciprocal giving of gifts between families, clans, and other nations. The giving of a gift lent power and credence to one's words. Another fundamental component of the Iroquois worldview was that one's dreams were powerful guides and one should follow their guidance without restraint. With the arrival of European alcohol in their midst (as with so many other tribes), the acting out of drunken visions or just plain drunken stupidity came to be regarded as similar to the acting out of one's dreams, and therefore tolerated—particularly by the drunks.

It may seem paradoxical for the Iroquois to consider themselves as bound together by a league of peace when they were, at the same time, so warlike that they would be thought of as the "Romans of the Western world." But the league of peace involved peace only between the five Iroquois tribes; the councils of fifty sachems that met annually, or whenever one of the fifty died and needed to be replaced, did not engage in what we think of as secular politics. Instead, their role was a spiritual one, to assuage grief with the Words of Consolation and to knit any raveling of intertribal cooperation. If unanimity could not be reached on some topic, it would be deferred until another meeting. These councils, however, took on an additional, political role as well once the Europeans arrived on the scene.

The Saint Lawrence Iroquois were among the first of the Iroquois to feel the brunt of the European presence: sometime after 1550, their villages were abandoned. More than likely, their fate was sealed by one or more epidemic diseases from contact with the French explorer Jacques Cartier in the early 1530s, perhaps exacerbated by famine from a cold spell and attacks by their neighbors. There is reason to believe that some of them, voluntarily or otherwise, may have swelled the population of the Five Nations.

By the 1550s also, thousands of fishing and whaling boats from Europe—Portuguese, Basque, English, and French—had been plying the waters off Newfoundland and Labrador and the Gulf of Saint Lawrence, the crews coming ashore to process their catches and perhaps clandestinely trading such items as copper kettles, wool blankets, hatchets, knives, and glass beads in exchange for beaver and other pelts from the coastal peoples. Some estimates suggest that as many as twenty thousand Europeans had set foot on the east coast of North America by the 1580s—forty years before the Pilgrims blundered into

Plymouth. Soon enough, many native people were making traditional use of these new trade goods—the kettles, for example, could be cut up to make arrowheads or adornments that found their way into graves. The people of the longhouse, farthest upstream from the points of European contact, noticed that their downstream neighbors had a great deal more of these goods. By the 1610s, Iroquois mourning wars fulfilled a double purpose—the original one of replacing a lost relative, combined with a desire to ambush Hurons and Algonquins laden with trade goods purchased at the French settlement of Quebec, founded by Samuel de Champlain in 1608. (Jamestown was only a year old, and there already was a French colony on Nova Scotia.) More and more, the native people came to depend on these European trade goods, to the point where some older crafts atrophied and died out. From metal, for example, the Iroquois could fashion more elaborately decorated combs with finer (and more) teeth—what might be thought of as progress, but a sign also that the Iroquois, like other Indians, were already becoming dependent on materials and objects the source of which lay beyond their control. Soon enough, the world of the Iroquois would change even more profoundly.

In 1613, two Dutchmen sailed up the Hudson River to present-day Albany, where they expected to establish a trading post to take advantage of what promised to be a valuable fur trade. Four years earlier, Henry Hudson and his Dutch crew had been given pelts by the local tribe, the Mahicans, who were Algonquian-speaking agriculturalists who lived on both sides of the Hudson River. The Dutch traders soon discovered that their two nearest tribal customers, the Mohawks and the Mahicans, were mutually hostile. The Dutchmen proceeded to organize a treaty between the two tribes and themselves, the first treaty between American Indians and Europeans. But the Mahicans sought tribute from Mohawks passing through their land to the river, the Mohawks objected violently, and the resulting skirmishes sent the Dutch packing in 1617. Then, in 1624, a group of Walloons founded Fort Orange (again, at present-day Albany) and the Iroquois again had a nearer, more convenient place to obtain trade goods.

All that stood in their way was—still—the Mahicans. So the Mohawks called off their warring with the Indians to the north and with the French; they concentrated on the Mahicans, soon driving them permanently to the other, eastern side of the Hudson River, leaving free passage for the Mohawks to Fort Orange. The Dutch traders, then, became the Iroquois' main source for trade goods. The Mohawks and the other four tribes of the league found themselves lacking in beaver to trade, their streams having been quickly trapped out. The best pelts came from farther north, above the Great Lakes. Hijacking raids in the north began again, targets this time being canoes headed for Quebec loaded with furs, rather than those headed home with trade goods. As firearms became available from Dutch traders, there was an even more urgent requirement for pelts to trade. It was a spiral of new needs and commerce. Soon enough there was an added motive for Iroquois raids, and they intensified and grew all the more deadly.

In 1633, a massive outbreak of smallpox swept through the Mohawks (and probably others of the Five Nations). By the early 1640s, the population of the Iroquois was cut in half, down to ten thousand, and the epidemics continued, erupting every few years with devastating effect, striking hardest at those in the prime of life. As adults succumbed, there would be little care for sick children and little food harvested, leading to further deaths. Many headmen succumbed, which led to a loss of control over angry young warriors egged on by grieving women. Mourning wars exploded beginning in 1634. Iroquois attacks on their old enemies the Hurons turned from raids into nearly continuous warfare, with heavy casualties on both sides. In one battle, the Senecas captured more than a hundred Hurons. By 1647 it appeared to some observers that the Iroquois intended to destroy the Hurons altogether, absorbing half into their own tribes and killing the rest. Other Iroquoian-speaking tribes to the west, such as the Eries, who provided refuge for escaping Hurons, were ruthlessly attacked as well; many escapees from these attacks banded together to form a Great Lakes tribe called the Wyandots. The Iroquois were soon at war with virtually every surrounding tribe, fighting as far from home as the upper Mississippi River and Virginia. No Words of Consolation could satisfy the grief and rage of the Iroquois—or their need for population numbers. By the 1660s, about two-thirds of people in some Iroquois villages were adopted from other tribes—and still the overall population remained at ten thousand. With all their apparent success, they were merely holding their own.

In 1664, at the mouth of the Hudson River, far away from the Iroquois lands, the town of New Amsterdam became New York. While many Hollanders remained in place under the English flag—especially in Fort Orange (soon renamed Albany)—Dutch power in the New

World was gone. For the most part, the Dutch had been content to set up their trading posts and leave it at that. They were mostly merchants, with little ambition for extensive land grabbing, though in the vicinity of New Amsterdam and out onto Long Island they were as brutal as any of the other European invaders, taking land over, evicting native people, and reacting with outraged brutality when anyone stood up to them. Unlike most other European arrivals, however, they seemed to have no heavily armed theology, no designs on the souls of the Indians.

Generally speaking (and from hindsight, of course), of all the Europeans who set out to colonize this new continent, the Spanish and the English would prove to be the most arrogant and insensitive about the native populations, the most intense interferers in Indian religion and behavior, and the greatest bunglers. Yet the English and the Spanish prevailed, at least for a few centuries, while those Europeans whose policies were most benign and wrought the least havoc on the Indian populations lost out: in particular, the French.

When Samuel de Champlain and his handful of colonists arrived on the Saint Lawrence, it was perfectly clear to them that if they were to obtain what they wanted—enough furs to make New France a viable colony—they needed the full cooperation of the Indian people, who not only knew the terrain, knew the use of the canoe, and knew the rivers and streams that were the only real highways in this wilderness, but also outnumbered them vastly. The French ingratiated themselves among the Indians by various means, including going native, many marrying into Indian societies. The king of France even fancied that the intermarriage of French and Indians would create a splendid new race, and later on, in the early 1600s, a royal decree ordered that all Indians converted to the Catholic faith would be considered as natural-born Frenchmen, with all the privileges available to French citizens. No other colonizers of the New World began with so open and benign an idea. By happy circumstance, their first three colonial installations—Quebec, Montreal, and Trois Rivières—were in the territory that had been abandoned by the Saint Lawrence Iroquois and thus encroached on no tribe's land.

Occasionally, the few French settlers also made themselves militarily useful to the Indians, such as the Hurons and other northern tribes. On one occasion Champlain accompanied a group of warriors who were seeking a battle with the hated Mohawks. As they confronted each other, Champlain marched to the front, aimed his harquebus (an early and cumbersome flintlock weapon), and shot two Mohawk leaders. The Mohawks fled in panic and despair after this, their first experience with firearms—and the French were, from that moment, roundly detested by the Iroquois nations.

Soon after the establishment of Quebec, the Jesuits—the Black Robes—came to New France, and it was clear to the French that a symbiotic relationship was needed between priests and the other colonists. In civilizing and converting the Indians, the priests would be making economic life for the colonists more reliable, and the Jesuits saw that once the Indians were hooked on European trade goods, they would be more easily converted. As those Indian tribes associated with the French suffered repeated outbreaks of epidemic disease, they noted that the priests and other French were not affected. This made the priests powerful shamans in their eyes, possessors of *manitou,* in Algon-quian parlance—power. Taking advantage of this, and using other capabilities such as predicting eclipses, along with ridiculing native shamans, the priests began systematically to replace the shamans and bring about conversions. But as historian James Axtell has pointed out with not a little humor, the Jesuit priests had a lot to overcome in the eyes of the Indians they sought to convert.

First of all, most of the Jesuits wore neatly trimmed beards, as in the pictures of saints in stained-glass windows at home. To the Indians, close-cropped hair anywhere on a person was utterly revolting. The Jesuits' robes seemed effeminate as well as totally impractical in the woods or in a canoe. And they took no sexual interest in women, an unimaginable attitude even for warriors who were sworn to abstinence before and during a military operation. Also, Jesuits forswore the carrying or use of weapons of any sort, an inexplicable failing that, among other things, made it necessary for Indians to defend these helpless, effeminate priests from hostile Indians. Nonetheless, many of the Jesuits plunged off bravely and alone into the hinterlands, away from the more urbanized settlements, and tried to make themselves useful to the remote bands and tribes.

Another obstacle the priests faced was their own countrymen. The Jesuits preached a lifestyle based on Christian principles, holding this up as superior to the ways of the Indians. But the Indians not only felt themselves to be superior in all ways; they could point to the French voyageurs and traders in their midst—drunken, uncouth, profane—

and ask the priests why their own countrymen didn't get the Jesuit message. Slowly, nonetheless, the Jesuits succeeded in making converts.

Over the decades, New France remained small—at least in Frenchmen. By 1640, only 356 French people were in Canada; in 1663, only some three thousand. Part of the slow growth was attributable to harassment by the Iroquois, particularly the Mohawks, who detested the Indian allies of the French colonists, particularly their greatest trading partners, the Hurons. By 1663, a Mohawk chief could boast that they were so effective that the French were not able to "go over a door to pisse." Even so, by this time too, the warriors of the Five Nations were stretched pretty thin. They had been decimated by smallpox and other diseases during outbreaks in the 1630s and 1640s, but so had the other tribes of the region. The Hurons were estimated to have been cut in half, from some twenty thousand souls. Soon the Iroquois were warring not only with the Hurons and the French but with the Susquehannocks (another Iroquoian-speaking group) to the south on the Delaware River, and also with tribes as far off to their west as Michigan, in order to maintain their control of the trade in beaver skins, which brought them needed trade goods and, now of great importance, guns and ammunition. The entire northeastern quadrant of the continent was feeling the repercussions of the Iroquois' ambitions and their attempts to maintain a dominant role among the other tribes as well as a role that was at least equal to the Europeans'. In New England, the Iroquois, in particular the Mohawks, had long been deeply involved in the grand disruption of the tribal people there.

One of the major trade goods of the time was wampum, beads manufactured in great quantity by coastal New England tribes, particularly the Pequots in eastern Connecticut and the Narragansetts in Rhode Island, and traded to the Mohawks in return for various favors. Wampum (the word derives from a longer Algonquian word meaning a string of white shell beads) was in use in the Northeast as far back as four thousand years ago. Upon arriving in North America, Dutch and others saw great benefit in producing wampum beads, and numerous cottage-type factories sprang up to fill the expanding demand. According to George Hamell of the New York State Museum, the last such factory—the Campbell Factory in New Jersey—closed when northern quahog shell became unavailable. Commonly seen as an Indian version of money (which it was), its most important role was for belts and strings affirming kinship ties and in rituals of condolence for people who died or were killed. By the seventeenth century, other colors, particularly red and purple (a purple bead being worth two white ones), had come into use, and wampum belts were also used as mnemonic devices for recalling past events of importance, such as battles or treaties. In due course silver beads were in use, signifying relations between the Iroquois and the British colonists.

When the British colony of Connecticut was established in 1636, the Pequots tried to retain control of the wampum trade on the lower Connecticut River—control that had already alienated them from neighboring tribes. Soon enough, Puritan colonists from both Massachusetts and Connecticut, along with two other New England tribes, the Narragansetts and the Mohegans, launched a surprise attack on the Pequots' villages. Some four hundred Pequots—men, women and children—were killed on the spot in such a slaughter that some of the colonists' Indian allies refused to participate and went home. Most of those Pequots remaining alive were hunted down and enslaved. A handful escaped and sought help from the Mohawks, who promptly killed them. The few remaining Pequots eventually retreated into two separate enclaves in Connecticut, virtually disappearing from sight for three centuries.

These were brutish times. Christians and Indians alike were accustomed to blood, to butchering meat, to close-in killing; and human lives—that is, the lives of *other* peoples—were measured differently than we like to think they are today. As often as not, on all sides (and still to an extent today), the measuring of an enemy's life simply and conveniently excluded him from full personhood. Not surprisingly, two fundamentally different notions of war clashed in colonial times, just as so many other aspects of culture clashed.

To the extent that the English colonists were schooled in warfare, it was the sort of war where militia laid siege to a fortress and both sides fought on with heroism and high losses until one or the other prevailed. On the other hand, the English colonists were not, as long supposed, always the sort of warriors who, once a fortress or village was taken, acted the gentlemen and were honor bound to leave children and women and other noncombatants alone. Part of their tradition was the relentless search-and-destroy missions carried out against the Irish and Scots, where the rule was to take no prisoners.

Of course, the English thought that Indian warfare was utterly uncivilized—a style characterized by "skulking." It consisted of ambush, sneak attacks, and the taking and torturing of captives. Indians rarely put themselves too plainly in harm's way and skedaddled whenever it looked as if there would be too much hell to pay, gaining the reputation of unreliability when allied with the English against other tribes. Rather than slaughter enemies on the spot, they (the Iroquois and Algonquian peoples at least) preferred to take captives home for one fate or another. Worse, once Indian warriors got their hands on firearms, they soon made themselves what military historian Armstrong Starkey has called "the most formidable marksmen in the seventeenth and eighteenth century world." So when expert Indian marksmen picked off English soldiers or militiamen from cover, exerting a moving fire on the colonists and surrounding them in a horseshoe formation while remaining mostly hidden, the English considered it unfair and barbarian. And of course, it was terrifying being stalked by these unseen shooters.

Shortly before the Pilgrims arrived in 1620, epidemics derived perhaps from French traders or visiting fishing and whaling ships eliminated an estimated 90 percent of many of the coastal New England tribes, including the Wampanoags. (From an estimated 144,000 native people in New England in 1600, this epidemic left some 15,000 just two decades later—an unimaginable loss.) The Wampanoags were left easy prey for the Narragansetts and Pequots to their south. So a Wampanoag leader named Massasoit welcomed the little band of English colonists and saved their lives by feeding them through their first winter. In return, they offered him and his people the protection of their arms and themselves. But other nearby tribes, the Nausets and the Massachusetts (who had formerly numbered some twenty-four thousand and were now down to less than a thousand), were not interested in English offers of protection and had to be forced to accept it. This was, one might say, the first European example of the protection racket in America. Before long, the Puritans had subdued most of the neighboring Indians, and by 1646 some fifty thousand colonists lived in New England, a wholly different situation from that in New France, where the French colonists were always vastly outnumbered by the native population.

Instead of an active missionizing policy, the Puritans at first simply and smugly assumed that the Indians would be persuaded to seek out the means to a Christian way of life merely because of the superior example laid before them by the Puritans themselves. This has been called a policy of *passive seduction.* It became clear fairly soon that none of the Indian people were seduced. Indeed, it was more likely to work the other way around, with at least a few white settlers running off to join Indian society, or white captives preferring to remain with their captors. (The reverse was rarely true: Indians brought into white society usually went home as soon as they could—an embarrassing situation for the English and their claims to a superior lifestyle.)

A more active policy for saving Indian souls came into being: persuading them to stop worshiping false gods and to resettle in special villages established for them, where they were converted to Protestant Christianity and came to be called *praying Indians.* This worked tolerably well: the clergy got a following among the Indians, and those who converted and went to the praying towns were no doubt fulfilled by their new beliefs. It was not, however, all a benevolent matter of free will. Medicine men specializing in herbal remedies were discouraged from their (usually quite effective) practice because they accompanied their herbal remedies with "diabolical spells and mutterings." Thus did some 170 drugs, now approved in the *United States Pharmacopeia,* fall out of use. The English explained that disease, including the continuing outbreaks of epidemics, struck at the Indian population because they were not acting in the manner approved by the Christian God.

The ministers in the colony made occasional forays in behalf of this effort but never went too far afield, being tied to their own congregations. Nevertheless, by the end of the century, there were some thirty Indian congregations in New England, served for the most part by Indian preachers. By the end of the century, there were only a reported two pagans among the two thousand Indians living on Martha's Vineyard. One major effect of this missionary effort was that many Indian people were moved from their traditional agricultural lands and pursuits into the praying villages, with the former lands being taken over by the growing tide of English settlers. Also, the English supported traders who claimed land in return for Indian debts—the fur and wampum trade was falling off—and Indians found guilty of English crimes had their land seized. The widespread presence of alcohol exacerbated all this: getting sozzled was seen as akin to ritually entering an inspired altered state and met with little initial cultural resistance. Soon enough, here as everywhere on the continent, alcohol addiction became destructive of Indian life—perhaps more destructive than any other European influence besides epidemic disease.

Beginning in 1675, however, several of the tribes—including the Wampanoags and the Narragansetts—refused to be overwhelmed by these social upheavals and undertook violent opposition to the English. Surprise raids on English settlements were at first successful, and it looked for a time as if the Indians might well drive the English into the sea in spite of the support the colonists received from a few other tribes, including the Masssachusetts. This was King Philip's War, so called for the name the English gave to the man they believed to be the war's leader, a Pokanoket headman named Metacom. In fact, there were numerous leaders from various tribes involved in the uprising, and some evidence exists that Metacom in fact lost control of his tribe's efforts to younger and more hotheaded warriors.

The turning point of the war came early in 1676 when some Mohawks, armed by the English in New York, ran Metacom and his followers back into New England, where disease, hunger, continuing Mohawk attacks, and a reinvigorated English military effort finally put an end to the war. Metacom himself was killed, and his wife and children along with many others on the losing side were deported as slaves.

While the Iroquois were playing empires off against one another, the settlers did the same thing with local tribes. In 1663, seeing that the colony of New France, still the creature of a private consortium without much by way of funds, might be doomed, the French king had taken it under his royal wing. An early initiative was to reinforce the French colonists with additional troops. Meanwhile, some eight hundred Senecas, Cayugas, and Onondagas had set out to attack the main village of the Susquehannocks in the south, and the Susquehannocks beat the attack back, showing that the Iroquois were no longer so invincible. (The Susquehannocks had the use of a Swedish cannon, apparently the first use of artillery by American Indians.) The next year, 1664, the Mohawks had suffered a major defeat as well. By 1667, after continued pummeling by the French, first the western Iroquois, then the Mohawks had sued for peace with New France and its Indian allies.

By this time, a few intrepid Jesuits had established fragile missions among some of the Iroquois, converting some, and this produced a new kind of internal dissension among the people of the longhouse. The converted tended to be pro-French, as did some of the unconverted; others were pro-Dutch (and then pro-English). The Black Robes had the greatest success among those who had been captured by the Iroquois and adopted into the tribes: even forced melting pots don't melt perfectly. Many of the converts went to live in towns the French established in Canada for them. Through the decades, people would go back and forth, joining relatives in Canada or vice versa—all of which complicated Iroquois diplomatic efforts. Three factions arose, pro-French, pro-British, and traditionalists, or neutrals. Soon, with peace on their northern frontier with the French, the Mohawks were raiding New England tribes, who in turn soon asked the English in New York to arrange peace. The Mohawks thus became allies of the English, helping to quash the uprising led by Metacom against the English.

With peace on their eastern flank, the Iroquois again turned their attention to the west and the coveted fur trade, but by this time their unprecedented weakness had begun to tell, and the good beaver grounds were yet farther west now. By the 1690s, the Iroquois had resumed hostilities with the French, were being cheated (they felt) of weapons and ammunition by the British, and began to lose in large numbers to the western tribes that were ganging up to fight them. This—and the century or so preceding it—was a time of great fluidity among populations of the Northeast, with what were often mutually hostile groups finding themselves allied as adversaries of the overweening Iroquois Confederation. Even the Montreal Iroquois—their relatives!—were fighting them. The chief weakness involved in the Indian use of firearms (which they could maintain and repair over long periods of time) was the need to rely on Europeans for gunpowder.

Many Iroquois villages were destroyed. Disease, famine, capture, and death in combat all combined to reduce a population of some eighty-six hundred to six thousand or fewer. In 1701, at their lowest ebb since they had formed their confederation, the Iroquois again sued for peace. Exhausted, depleted, soundly defeated, the Iroquois nonetheless would manage to pull off at least one more shrewd diplomatic coup, in a sense pulling the wool over the eyes of both the French and the English—a diplomatic coup that would reinstall them as players in the continuing competition between European nations for imperial control of the northeastern woodlands.

The Upper Country—Great Lakes

By about 1650 the *pays en haut* was a nightmarish land of refugee groups that had hated one another, warred against one another, massacred one another, and were now forced to live together—even in the intimacy of small polyglot towns. The refugee towns were centered in several places, including what is now Green Bay, in a strip running from the Great Lakes to the Mississippi. To their east and south was an enormous tract of land stretching from the lakes to the Ohio River, a region emptied of its former inhabitants, who were fleeing west to avoid the repeated onslaughts of the Iroquois. They could flee only so far; to their west were the Sioux and other groups, some as implacable as the Iroquois. Caught in between, the refugees simply had to mix and meld like molecules becoming a new substance. They were Hurons (Iroquoian speakers) and Winnebagos (Siouan speakers), but mostly they were Algonquians—Miamis,

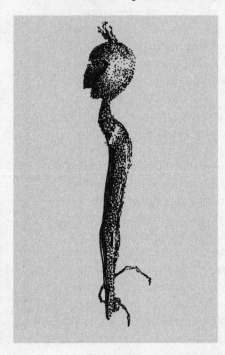

Ojibway effigy

Illinois, Sauks, Fox, Ottawas, Ojibways, Shawnees, Potawatomis, and others. By the 1670s, some twenty thousand refugees lived in small settlements on Green Bay or within a couple of days' hike from it—a territory they had had to wrest from the earlier arrivals there, Menominees and Winnebagos, who had simply had to let them come, so great were their numbers.

Uprooted, now in new lands, the refugees found themselves not only plagued by outbreaks of pandemic diseases but threatened with extreme hunger if not famine in a world that ran on somewhat different seasonal cycles than they were familiar with. Crowded together in new country, they soon overtaxed many wild food resources—such as deer and bison—and came to rely mostly on corn and fish from the Great Lakes and their tributaries.

These otherwise unremarkable cores (from which blades could be struck) date back as far as sixteen thousand years ago, making them some of the oldest artifacts known on the North American continent. They, and other artifacts of similar age, have come from the Meadowcroft Rockshelter and environs in western Pennsylvania. The rock shelter, enclosed and well lighted, was excavated chiefly in the 1970s and pushed the date of human arrival in the New World back some five or six thousand years. *Mercyhurst Archaeological Institute, Erie, Pennsylvania.*

At its peak a thousand years ago, Cahokia (now East Saint Louis) covered some 5 square miles. Monk's Mound rises 100 feet on the far side of the giant plaza (shown here in an artist's reconstruction). *Cahokia Mounds State Historical Site.*

The Great Serpent Mound in Ohio (left) is almost a quarter mile long, a celebrated example of Hopewell earthworks and perhaps a burial site of an important lineage. *Ohio Historical Society.*

Below: One of the most important of all Anasazi structures, Pueblo Bonito was a major center of the Chaco Canyon phenomena in New Mexico. *Photograph by John Running.*

A decoration on Champlain's 1612 map of the New World shows an Indian couple looking like northern Europeans. *The Newberry Library, Chicago.*

A 1735 drawing by Alexandre de Batz, *Drawing of the Savages of Several Nations, New Orleans,* suggests that Europeans still had a hard time actually seeing Indians. *Peabody Museum of Archaeology and Ethnology, Harvard University.*

An 1852 drawing by Henry B. Brown of Wintu men gambling in a subterranean lodge near Mount Shasta in northern California. *John Carter Brown Library, Brown University.*

The twin whirls of hair designate this Hopi girl as a maiden. Some Hopi ancestors lived in Chaco Canyon, and such traditions as this are probably very ancient. *National Anthropological Archives, Smithsonian Institution.*

Ute woman Tannah, photographed in 1899 in a Denver studio in traditional face paint and dress (except for the button saying "souvenir"). *Denver Public Library.*

Above: Young woman of California's Upper Salish people, with baskets and a dress of bark. *National Anthropological Archives.*

Left: A transvestite male shaman and headman of a Tolowa village in coastal northern California was photographed in 1910. The bone noseplug and beads denote wealth. *National Anthropological Archives.*

Photographed in 1859 in Nebraska by painter Albert Bierstadt, an Eastern Shoshone rider has bow, quiver, and blanket but no saddle, how it must have been when horses first reached the Plains a century and a half earlier. *Kansas State Historical Society.*

An etching of a Carl Bodmer painting of a Mandan lodge with family at fire, domestic and hunting implements here and there, and dogs and even horses present. *National Anthropological Archives.*

The murder of Jane McCrae, which may or may not have happened, incited American revolutionary ardor. John Vanderlyn's melodramatic and deliberately sensuous rendition of 1803–1804 emphasized the Indian as savage. *Wadsworth Atheneum Museum of Art, Hartford, Connecticut.*

Joseph Thayendaneken, also known as Joseph Brant, was a talented Mohawk leader who led many Iroquois and other Indians in frontier actions against the American rebels. *National Anthropological Archives.*

Seneca Ely S. Parker penned the terms of Lee's surrender to Grant, who later made Parker the first Indian to hold the post of Commissioner of Indian Affairs. *National Anthropological Archives.*

Civil War hero and Grand Canyon explorer John Wesley Powell, shown here with Paiute friend Tau-gu, led the Bureau of American Ethnology's efforts to record Indian ways, the first federal recognition that tribal cultures were both distinct and worthy. *National Anthropological Archives.*

The ardent and often fatal resistance by Plains tribes and the Apaches is legendary. Two of the men shown here were among the resistance's most implacable leaders; two others were important transitional leaders. *All from National Anthropological Archives.* Upper left: Sitting Bull, a warrior and holy man of the Hunkpapa Sioux, fought at Custer's Last Stand and died resisting religious repression in 1890. Lower left: Oglala Sioux Red Cloud led the effort that forced the United States to abandon the Bozeman Trail to Montana, but later became a peacemaker, explaining Indian ways to easterners.

Above: Comanche warrior and mixed blood Quanah Parker led his people into a new lifeway when removed to the Indian territory after 1875. He is credited with bringing the beginnings of the Native American Church to the Comanches and the other Plains tribes. Below: The Chiricahua Apache called Geronimo led the last significant free-ranging band of about fifty Indians to hand themselves over to the United States, in 1886, but only after one quarter of the American army had pursued him for almost a year.

Indian Police on Drill
Pine Ridge Age S. D.

One of the earliest Indian police forces was organized in 1879 on the Pine Ridge Reservation in the Dakota territory. Here the force, with Chief of Police George Sword at left, was photographed in 1890. *National Anthropological Archives.*

A Kiowa delegation to Washington led by Lone Wolf, seated at left, sought help from the Supreme Court to uphold earlier treaty rights, and lost in 1907, the Court giving Congress the right to overturn any treaty as it saw fit. *National Anthropological Archives.*

Northern Paiute Wovoka, shown here posed with a B-movie western actor, Tim McCoy, was the inventor of the Ghost Dance that swept the Plains in the 1890s particularly among the Sioux, leading to the Wounded Knee massacre. *National Anthropological Archives.*

On a state reservation in South Carolina with much Mormon influence and use of the English language, Catawba Ben Percy Harris and the other members of the tribe have long clung to old tribal ways. *National Anthropological Archives.*

In a traditional house called a *chickee,* a Miccosukee woman sews the brilliantly colorful clothing of rickrack, which had its origins when the Seminole people in Florida were hounded by the army and had to make clothes by sewing rags together. *Photograph by Susanne Page.*

Photographed in Wisconsin about 1907, Winnebago women play a gambling game with bone dice. The woman at left hid her face from the photographer. *National Anthropological Archives.*

Dennis Banks, an eloquent and charismatic founder of the American Indian Movement, helped to bring the real plight of both urban and reservation Indians to public attention in the 1970s. Below: Banks (second from left), Oren Lyons, Iroquois leader (far right), and young AIM members brought the message to a Congregational church in Connecticut. *Photographs by Susanne Page.*

Many urban Indian youths, as this one above, seek roots in Pan-Indian gatherings far from their familiar city streets. The future for most tribes is in the hands of those who can maintain old traditions and those who make the most of educational opportunities, like these young Navajo high school graduates on their way to higher education. *Photographs by Susanne Page.*

Green Bay, with a growing season of only 160 days, was at the northern limit of corn growing, and the crops often failed. Fisheries, though rich enough to support large concentrations of people, were seasonal, and winter hunts for sparse game were typically desperate affairs, with starvation and death by exposure always a threat and often occurring.

It was a world, as well, full of squabbles, plots, murders, accusations of witchcraft, and revenge among people who had already suffered the ravages of epidemics that struck and continued to strike throughout the remainder of the century. The different groups ranged from hunting bands, like the Ojibways, to near chiefdoms, like the Miamis. Some were matrilineal, like the Hurons; a few had no clans, like the Ottawas; but most had clans and were patrilineal. Virtually no one in this region lived on original homeland. For these people, the world had been splintered, like an exploding mirror.

Against these centrifugal forces, scattering old lifeways into chaos, some centripetal force was needed, something to create order from the chaos. The world needed to be rebuilt, just as the distant ancestors of all these different peoples had somehow managed to create some form of orderly world out of the primordial chaos of mythical time. For this, they could fall back on but three tools. First was the giving of gifts, a reciprocity they had all known and practiced *among themselves.* The giving of gifts would create a mutual reliance between peoples, as did the second tool: intermarriage and adoption, with the attendant rules of familial obligations. They could also fall back on the ceremony of the calumet—the long-stemmed pipe of peace that had evidently been invented by the Pawnees to the west, taken up by the Sioux, then the Great Lakes peoples, and then even the Iroquois. The calumet, usually with a bowl made of a hard stone called catlinite and the stem highly decorated with carving and feathers, was a sacred object that, when brought forth at a time of potential hostilities, called for an immediate truce, negotiations, and a symbolic and at least temporary kinship between the smokers. This worked especially well among the refugee peoples, but they in turn often breached the traditional etiquette when dealing with Iroquois or Sioux enemies. In any event, these measures—gift giving, intermarriage, and the calumet—began to counterbalance the natural and age-old ethnic rivalries of the refugee peoples of the upper country. A largely social alliance was beginning to form—usually local, even only village-wide, and often fragile enough to hold together only when outside forces like the Iroquois threatened.

Other tribal alliances, as we have seen, came to little. King Philip's military alliance in New England and that of the Powhatan chieftainship in Virginia foundered against the sharp-edged military might of the land-hungry and vengeful English colonists. They were simply overpowered. But what was a fragile, almost reluctant merger of rival factions in villages in the upper country would become a region-wide political alliance of considerable effectiveness—thanks to the intercession of those other imperialists in the northeastern quarter of the continent: the French.

Like moths to flames, French traders and Jesuit missionaries began to show up in the refugee towns. Here the traders promised French protection for any Indians who went forth and trapped beaver. As historian Richard White has pointed out, the Jesuits claimed many converts to Christ, but in the meantime they allowed Christ to become the manitou, what might be called an Indian version of himself. It was he who brought the spring migration of fishes, for example. But if the fish did not show up for some reason, it was Christ, the new manitou, who had failed. Even so, here (White suggests) was the beginning of a new society involving practical and even theological accommodation and the creation of new institutions—a middle ground.

The French themselves had a good deal of fractious internal hostilities to overcome as well. The Jesuits, out to save souls, often enough found themselves at odds with the traders, particularly the illicit ones, called *coureurs de bois,* who in turn often sent the refugee Indian groups beaver trapping, thus diverting them from what the French governor in Quebec wanted them to do—attack the Iroquois. Both the French and the Indians of the upper country had time to sort out their differences, since in the 1660s, the Iroquois and the French enjoyed more than a decade of truce, if not real peace. The Iroquois were engaged in warring to their south, among the Susquehannocks. But then the Iroquois turned west again, attacking the Illinois and threatening to turn the entire upper country into a war zone. The French intensified their efforts to create unity among the refugee Indians by becoming mediators between rival refugee groups. Some of the Indian groups, particularly the Ottawas and the Hurons, were suspicious of the French, assuming that these Europeans would betray them whenever it was convenient, and the Iroquois played on this suspicion, promising them better trade goods at lower prices with the British if they would abandon the French.

In due course, however, and by the strategic bestowing of gifts and actual displays of protective military might, the French wound up as the leaders of a fairly grand alliance of Great Lakes Indians against the Iroquois. The actual head of the alliance was Onontio—the Iroquoian word means "great mountain"—as the French governor of Canada was called. Onontio and the French he commanded were not perceived as conquerors—they were allies who bestowed gifts and received gifts in return. A new class of chiefs emerged among the Indians of the alliance. They were not civil leaders who by clanship or some other kin essence became leaders, nor were they the war leaders who were appointed from among warriors. They were called *alliance chiefs,* and were a kind of ad hoc chief. These men (and sometimes women) represented each group to the outside world, just as oftentimes the French interests in the alliance were represented in an ad hoc manner by clergy and traders as well as by officers and distant bureaucrats in Quebec and Montreal. The more success such people had as intermediaries, the greater became their influence, which in turn increased their success. A new world, neither all-Indian nor all-French, was emerging in the *pays en haut.* Together the French and the western tribes hammered the Iroquois at the end of the seventeenth century, sending the previously invincible-seeming Five Nations begging for peace in 1701.

Century's End

Purely by chance, the year 1700 forms a useful political boundary line. The Iroquois were newly weakened, and the balance of power in the Indian Northeast was shifting. The change would have significant effects in the century to come, with its final resolution of the English-French competition and the birth of the United States, the result for the various Indian tribes being a cascade of catastrophes. The very nature of warfare was about to change in the colonies, particularly in the Northeast.

For both the French and the English were ever more busily building forts around this time—so much so that military historian John Keegan could write that by the time of the French and Indian War in the 1760s, "North America was one of the most fortified regions of the world." And nowhere was any piece of territory more fortified than the ground along the Hudson River north to the tributaries of the Saint Lawrence. Against these fortifications—erected at portages, landing places, narrows, mountain passes, harbors, towns—the skulking form of Indian warfare that the English so deplored as inappropriate and uncivilized was of little use. As the eighteenth century dawned, warfare in North America was becoming Europeanized. Sieges of stationary installations, better done with cannon than guerrilla tactics, were becoming the way to win. Indian allies of both sides in the Northeast would find themselves playing a diminishing military role.

By the turn of the century, the Powhatan tribes were fragmented, no longer a political force, and many had been forced off their land by rapidly increasing numbers of colonists from England plowing larger and larger portions of Virginia under for the successful growing and marketing of tobacco. (The same, of course, was the fate of parts of Maryland and most of the Delmarva Peninsula. The Delawares, known to themselves as the Lenni Lenapes, had sought new lands in western Pennsylvania, and there they would continue as a force to be reckoned with in the next century.) In New England, the story was much the same. Except for the Abenakis of Maine, the New England tribes had all entered a long period of almost complete obscurity. Most of the survivors lived here and there in obscure villages, often intermarrying with those other pariahs, free blacks. In the Southeast, British traders from today's Charleston, South Carolina, were stealing a march on the Spanish proprietors of the region. They were fomenting wars and creating huge markets for deer skins—a trade that would soon become a near addiction for the Indian tribes reconstituting themselves from the wreckage of the Mississippian cultures.

In 1699, the French built a post called Fort Maurepas on the sandy shore of Biloxi Bay, the culmination of a few earlier attempts to establish themselves between the Spanish colonial realms of La Florida and New Spain. By 1700, European contact was also reverberating into the Great Plains, where western Indian groups had long relied chiefly on hunting while eastern groups had relied chiefly on horticulture, the two sides sometimes trading and sometimes warring in an uneasy, interlocking native world. In the western Plains, tribal territories had long been shifting as new arrivals appeared. Apaches had shown up to the east of the Puebloan cultures as early as 1525, and probably a good deal earlier. Being among the first to run off with Spanish horses, and using leather armor, they rapidly expanded their territory, even as far north as South Dakota and as far south and east as west Texas by the end of the seventeenth century. To the Apaches' north and west were

Shoshones, who had spilled out onto the Plains from the Great Basin as early as 1400, reaching as far north as Montana and the Canadian border. Other Shoshonean speakers—Utes and Comanches—were also beginning to move eastward from their Great Basin lands across the Rockies by century's end. (The Utes in the Rocky Mountains of southern Colorado were among the earliest to use stolen Spanish horses. By about 1640, they used them in addition to dogs to drag their possessions on an apparatus made of two poles call a travois, taking up riding only in the next century.)

On the plains in Canada, the Blackfeet and, to their east, the Assiniboines held sway, linking up to fight the Dakotas (whom we also think of as the Sioux), who were still forest people living in northern Minnesota. Among all these larger territories were smaller groups or tribes—the Gros Ventres and Arapahos, who had split apart well before the seventeenth century, and the Crows, who had originally been part of the horticultural Hidatsas on the Missouri River. In South Dakota, the Kiowas would eventually move south and combine with some of the plains Apaches to become the Kiowa Apaches.

As yet, some of the fiercest and best remembered tribes had not made their appearance on the Plains—the Comanches from the Great Basin and the Rockies and, from the woodlands, the Cheyennes and several subdivisions of the Sioux. (The name "Comanche" derives from a Ute word, *komantica,* which means "enemy"; "Sioux" is an abbreviated form of an Algonquian word, *nadouessioux,* again "enemy.") Also yet to come to the Plains by 1700, with the few exceptions noted above, were the horse, firearms, and smallpox. Spanish horses—in this case geldings, which were all the conquistadors brought with them, thinking their treks were too harsh for mares and other breeding stock—had early made their way out into the Plains. These were stolen horses, of course, and prepared the nearby Plains Indians—particularly the Apaches by about 1650—for the care and feeding of these animals. With Spanish colonization in 1598 came breeding stock, which the Spanish guarded with fanatic zeal, horses being the key to any military success they might have against the far more numerous Indians. But the Pueblo Revolt of 1680 led among many other things to great numbers of breeding stock escaping into the grasslands to be captured, stolen, or traded. Except for the expansionary (and now horse-breeding) Apaches, the tribes that were barging into the northern Plains by 1700, such as the Shoshones, were evidently doing so on foot. It would not be until decades into the next century that the horse would almost totally transform the cultures of the Plains and the non-Puebloan Southwest, producing some of the finest light cavalry ever known on earth.

Firearms would soon begin to leak into the Plains, chiefly from French traders via the northerly Crees and Assiniboines beginning in 1670. On the Plains, as a tribe gained either firearms or horses—and later, both—its territory would expand at the expense of others that were less endowed. The Plains Apaches were among the last to obtain much by way of firearms, thanks to the Spanish policy of not arming Indians, whether barbarians or savages, with the result that soon in the next century, armed and mounted Comanches would send most of the Plains Apaches packing into the southernmost part of their territory— Texas.

So far as can be known, it wasn't until well after 1700 that epidemics broke out among the tribes of the Plains, even the village dwellers of the eastern Plains. It is not unlikely that some small groups—hunting bands or villagers—were infected and largely wiped out without spreading the disease on to others, or spreading it only minimally, a function that would theoretically have been speeded up by the adoption of the horse. The first European on the northern high Plains was a French trapper who arrived in 1691; the Spanish had made forays into the southern Plains since Coronado ran into some Caddoan people, probably ancestors of the Wichitas, in 1541. Permanent European settlements in this region, however, did not occur until the late eighteenth century, which is the first time we know for certain that smallpox reached epidemic proportions, at least among Hidatsa and Mandan villagers of the middle Missouri region.

Elsewhere—on the Pacific coast and inland in the Great Basin—no significant contact by Europeans was to occur until well into the eighteenth century, and in the most remote stretches, not until the nineteenth century. Hundreds of Californian tribes, speaking hundreds of languages and dialects, and rarely greater than five hundred members, lived in relatively close proximity with one another, occasional squabbles breaking out into larger-scale hostilities. For the most part, however, the California tribes were relatively isolated from one another in their own valleys. Only a few, most likely, were even aware of the appearance on the Californian shores of Spanish and then English explorers. By 1700, the entire Pacific coast had been declared both

Spanish and English by right of discovery, and it was thereafter largely ignored by Europeans of any kind until well into the next century, when the Spanish would establish a colonial foothold in California, seeking land and souls, and in the north, the Russians would come across the strait navigated by Vitus Bering, seeking furs. But for now, and for nearly another century, the Indians of California and the Pacific Northwest and some of the tribes of the Great Basin would continue to exist much as they had all along. Their lives would be largely untouched except by the forces they had always dealt with—the weather, the tides, the seasons and the migrations of salmon, marine mammals, the acorn crop, the occasional squabble with a neighboring group, and of course Raven, the trickster, who always had something unexpected in store.

PART THREE

The Reinvention of Indian America

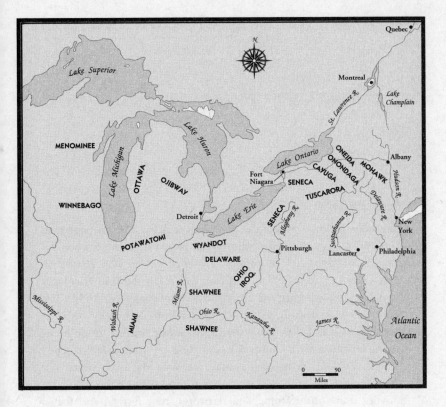

CHAPTER SEVEN

THE FRENCH CONNECTION

Winnebago Destiny

Sometime near the turn of the twentieth century, a Winnebago man told anthropologist Paul Radin of the period long gone when his people saw their first European, a French trader who arrived in Green Bay in Lake Michigan. In fact, this might be Jean Nicolet, a French trader who arrived among the Winnebagos in 1634. The Winnebagos had migrated much earlier from Kentucky into the area of the Great Lakes. They were a ferociously warlike group numbering in the tens of thousands, and their reputation had reached French ears well before any contact between the two. When not attacking their neighbors (Ottawas and Illinois, and Foxes who were moving north into Winnebago territory), they farmed and fished along the shores of Lake Superior, moving on to Green Bay later. They spoke a Siouan tongue, and referred to themselves as *ho-chunk,* "people of the real (or original) voice." But raids, food shortages, and especially smallpox brought them to the edge of extinction. By the time another French agent arrived in their midst in the late 1660s, they had been reduced to six hundred souls or less, with a mere 150 warriors.

According to Radin's storyteller, when the first Frenchmen hove into sight on the lake, the Winnebagos gathered on the shore to greet the new arrivals with offerings of tobacco and deer skins.

Before coming ashore, the French in turn fired off guns as a salute, and the awed Winnebagos decided they were thunderbirds. Once ashore, the French stuck out their hands (to shake hands), and the Indians put tobacco in them. The French didn't know what to do with the tobacco, having never seen it, and suddenly one of the newcomers saw an old Winnebago man smoking and poured water on him. The French then taught the Winnebagos to use an axe and a gun, but the Indians thought both were holy and "remained aloof for a long time through fear. . . . After a while they got more accustomed to one another."

One day, the leader of the Frenchmen took a liking to the daughter of the Winnebago chief and asked to marry her, gaining the consent of her brothers, who had the say in such matters. The Frenchman, a man known to history only as Decora, "lived there and worked for the Indians and stayed with them many years and he taught them the use of many tools." In due course, the couple had one and then a second son, and once the first son was old enough, Decora thought to take him to live among the French, where it was safer. The Indians agreed, and Decora left, leaving his wife to rear their second son.

But the oldest son, though lavished with affection and gifts, never got over being homesick, and would not eat. So his father brought him back to the Winnebagos and said, "My sons are men and they can remain here and grow up among you. You are to bring them up in your own way and they are to live just as you do."

Eventually, the eldest of the two sons went off into the wilderness. "After a full month the boy came home and brought with him a circle of wood [that is, a drum]. He told the people that this is what he had received in a dream, and that it was not to be used in war; that it was something with which to obtain life." The son became a leader:

> They called him the Frenchman, his younger brother being called *Tca-posgaga,* Whitethroat. And as they said, so it has always been. A person with the French blood has always been the chief. Only they could accomplish anything among the whites. . . . His descendants are the most intelligent of all the people and they are becoming more intelligent all the time. What they did was the best that could be done. The ways of the white man are best. That is the way they were brought up.

Radin's informant compressed the time of these two events. Decora was apparently a French officer at Green Bay in the eighteenth century, and his Winnebago wife was Glory of the Morning, a head chief's daughter in one of the Winnebago towns. As often as not, French-Winnebago progeny did have leadership positions over the next century or so, probably as alliance chiefs, those who represented their people to outsiders, as opposed to those chiefs who looked after the internal affairs of the people. Neither kind of chief enjoyed the power of command but instead acted as mediator, needing the consent of their councils. Even Frenchmen who became alliance chiefs in Indian towns or tribes lost whatever role they might have previously had as commanders.

By the beginning of the eighteenth century, the Winnebagos, like most of the other tribes that had moved more recently into the region of the Great Lakes, were amalgams, remnants, groups characterized by a great deal of tribal intermarriage, adoption, and the absorbing of one another's cultural traits. For example, the Winnebagos had originally been matrilineal, as so many primarily agricultural peoples tend to be, but as the fur trade came to dominate their economy, they began to take on attributes, including patrilineity, from the surrounding Algonquian-speaking people, who already were deeply involved in the economy of peltry. By this time, Winnebagos would later explain, there were no full-blooded Winneba-

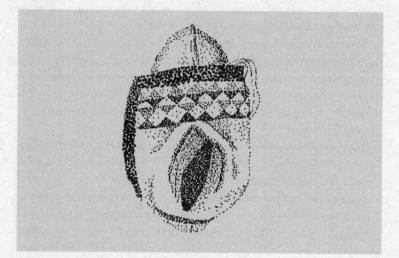

Winnebago moccasin

gos. Still productive agriculturalists, however, they sniffed at their neighbors like the Ojibways who depended almost entirely on gathering wild rice and hunting and were thus more prone to famines. But in the 1700s, the Winnebagos themselves began to split up into smaller towns and more mobile arrangements to permit them to participate more fully in the fur trade.

Distinctions between previously separate peoples became more remembered than apparent: loyalties were as much to one's locale (which might include people of several tribes) as to one's nominal tribe, whose members were now apt to be spread fairly far and wide over the landscape. And this left plenty of space for intratribal factions to arise, as they did among the Winnebagos as well as many of the refugee tribes in the region. In 1687, the Winnebagos allied themselves with the French in hostilities against the Iroquois, and then, when the Iroquois made peace with the French in 1701, the Winnebagos fought alongside their former enemies, the Foxes, against the French over control of the fur trade in their area. In 1728, in the midst of these hostilities, the Winnebago council elected Hopoe-Kaw, their first woman chief, who desired peace with the French. Part of the tribe sided with her, another part fought on, but both factions joined together again in 1755, aiding the French in what came to be called (by the ultimately victorious British) the French and Indian War. The imperial peace of 1763 removed the Winnebagos' European ally—and the overarching father of the French and many Indians of the region, Onontio—from the scene as a political, economic, and diplomatic force. A little more than a decade later they found themselves allied with the British against the upstart American colonists, whose expansionary intents were seen as a far greater threat than British rule. Once again, the Winnebagos were on the losing side. In pantribal unity with their neighbors, they would rise up twice again in desperate rebellion, only to lose twice more. Their fortunes were on a downward slide that would last well into the second half of the twentieth century, when their name was recognized by most people in North America not as a once self-sufficient group of people but as a gas-guzzling house on wheels found in great herds in the campgrounds and parking lots of America.

Yet, for a brief period, the Winnebagos and the numerous other tribes of the region the French called *le pays en haut* were—however reluctantly—part of a grand experiment in cross-cultural and interracial living and learning. This was historian Richard White's middle ground, and one side of it is clearly, if poignantly, reflected in the twentieth-century Winnebago man's account of the founding of the Decora lineage. What is poignant in his account is not so much the felt need for European blood in Winnebago veins in order to deal with a new, partly European world, but that there seems to be so little memory of, or yearning for, how things were before the (semicomical) meeting of the two peoples. There was a New World at hand, however, and for the most part the Indians—so many of them refugees or invaders from elsewhere now thrown together—were practical people.

Pressures from the East

The New World at hand extended north into Canada, south to the Gulf of Mexico, west across the Appalachians to the Mississippi and beyond. For approximately the first half of the eighteenth century, during which Indians far outnumbered the colonists, something akin to the middle ground in *le pays en haut* existed throughout much of this large region, where the main colonial presence was French. At the same time the greatest pressure arose from the East, from the English, who had come in what could be thought of as three flavors (with a fourth on its way). In New England, Puritan and other Protestant religionists mostly from southeastern England were the norm, people with a tendency to theocracy and intolerance of native ways, not to mention a detestation not far from utter horror of the Catholicism of the hated French. In New York and the rest of what we now call the mid-Atlantic states—New Jersey, Pennsylvania, Delaware—a more polyglot colonial presence existed, the Delaware Valley being dominated by William Penn's Quakers, who in turn welcomed other extremely low-church folk from various nations, such as Germany. But these more tolerant folk were also land hungry, and the net effect of their gathering presence was to shove such Indian people as the Delawares westward into new habitats in western Pennsylvania. Here they ran into the scrambling of tribal people already brought on largely by Iroquois expansionism and diplomatic influence.

In Virginia and settlements to the south, reaching as far as present-day Charleston, South Carolina, the dominant colonial force was English cavaliers and indentured servants—given more to the established Anglican Church (which was just a few steps away from Roman

Catholicism in many regards) and a stratified social world. They were not given to peacemaking and happily used any Indian uprising as a justification for all-out war, just as did the New Englanders. Eliminating the Powhatan tribes as a major presence, they kept up their relations with certain other tribes, like the Nanticokes, which could act as buffers against tribes such as the Iroquoian Tuscaroras.

By the turn of the century, English traders from Virginia south were openly defying the Spanish presence in Florida and the French to the west. To the north, the Iroquois had made peace in 1701 with both the French and the English, promising a form of loyalty to both, and continued their mastery of the game of playing one off against the other, a game that virtually all the tribes east of the Mississippi were soon playing. The world, then, was a grand kaleidoscope of Indian people, many reconstituting themselves as new groups or tribes, new cultures, and at the same time continuing old intertribal hostilities or inventing new ones. All of the Indian groups east of the Mississippi were to one degree or another becoming dependent on European trade goods, and they were always ready to shift allegiances to different traders among them, depending on the quality of goods, the price, and in particular the simple generosity that Indian cultures all demanded from trading partners. By this time, the Spanish in La Florida were a diminishing presence, found almost exclusively in San Agustín. The English (except for the traders in the South) had largely eliminated most Indians from their midst, or at least from their daily ken. Never particularly good at understanding the reciprocal nature of Indian cultures, the English were inclined to move in, by force if necessary, and hope that the Indians would go away—or see to it that they did.

A few decades into the new century, a new breed of English-speaking people would show up in the eastern ports. These were what have been called Scots-Irish, or border people (many of them coming from the English-Scottish borderlands). Most were Scots who had been forced to move to northern Ireland in a kind of seventeenth-century ethnic cleansing campaign. The English colonists already present looked askance at these new arrivals: they were raw, hardy, not especially well educated people with a defiant independence of spirit and a pride that belied their humble origins. They were clannish and quick to anger (and to fight), which made them poor neighbors. Their countrymen in America saw them, in short, as the dangerous dregs of British society and not all that different from the vengeful, unpredictable, and egalitarian Indians in the forests. Happily for the east coast English, whose settlements now extended to the Piedmont (the foothills of the Appalachians), these rude and raw-boned interlopers headed west into the mountains to hack small farms and small communities out of the valleys and hollows and to press farther west into the Ohio Valley as well as transmontane points south.

Throughout the seventeenth and continuing into the eighteenth century, many eastern tribes had entered into arrangements with the colonists whereby they ceded lands to the Europeans. These land cessions were done by treaty, by sale, by possession in return for unpaid debts, and by force. At various times, the Europeans drew lines somewhere to the west of their current positions, promising that European expansion would go no farther than that. Probably the most elaborate but not the first such agreement was the Treaty of Fort Stanwix in 1768, wherein the English left everything west of the Appalachians as open lands for the various Indians. All such lines turned out to be wishful thinking: the Europeans shoved west largely at will.

West lay the Ohio Valley, which had been essentially depopulated by seventeenth-century Iroquoian wars with the original inhabitants, which left a large, rich, and mostly empty area defined by the Ohio River drainage and its tributaries, most notably the Monongahela and the Allegheny, which meet in today's Pittsburgh to form the Ohio. Into this large area, numerous tribes migrated—those dispossessed from the East and some who moved north. Here were Iroquoian remnants who had formed the Wyandots. Here too came the Shawnees, a much-traveled tribe that may have originated in the Carolinas, who had moved north to the Ohio Valley, thence eastward into Pennsylvania, and in this period, pressured by Iroquois and British, westward again into the Ohio Valley. Many of these groups, like those to their west in *le pays en haut,* formed multiethnic villages called *republican,* a pejorative term among the French colonial administrators, who wished that people would obey their authoritarian edicts instead of deciding things on their own. Such polyglot arrangements provided a certain amount of safety. Who would attack a mixed village that numbered among its members one's own relatives?

Into this milieu came the Scots-Irish, paying no regard to such lines as had been drawn by treaties, colliding with the refugee tribes, with whom they soon developed a deep and implacable mutual hatred backed by some of the worst violence in the history of Indian-white relations. Ironically, it was these difficult people, European refugees themselves, who toward the end of the eighteenth century would become the true sons of liberty. It was they who would in a real sense kick off the American Revolution, before the Boston Tea Party, Paul Revere, and all that, by going after tyrannical Britishers on the frontier.

Meanwhile, nearly from the earliest arrival, Frenchmen tended to be comfortable among Indian people, and to rely on them to the point, as noted, that a new, part-Indian and part-European culture began to emerge. But the French colonies tended to be relatively weak compared to the English ones in population numbers, mercantile economics, and overall strength of arms. For example, in 1717 the French established Fort Toulouse near New Orleans, the better to anchor the southern extent of their territory (which extended up the Mississippi to the Great Lakes region and east into present-day Maine) against both Spanish and English pressure. A colony was soon established in today's Louisiana, which, it was hoped, would become an exporter of food and raw materials to the homeland, but this didn't happen for a century. Instead, from the outset, the settlers were poorly and irregularly supplied from France and the settlements remained small and dependent on locals for much of their sustenance. Not only were such settlements far away from direct control by policies set by royal bureaucrats in France; local authorities—both secular and ecclesiastic—found it impossible to exert much control over the day-to-day affairs of the settlers, who found themselves essentially freelancing new lives face-to-face with local and very real Indians, while back home philosophers were in the process of ballooning Indians into grand abstractions such as Rousseau's noble savage. In the middle grounds of the New World, destiny bobbed on the tides of empires; but those middle grounds were also local worlds where the basic matters of daily life were most pressingly in need of resolution.

Sex, Murder, and Food

Among most of the Indian tribes in *le pays en haut,* married women might meet with severe punishment, even disfigurement or death, if caught in adultery. Such punishments seemed extreme to many of the French, including the Jesuits, who made everyone's sexual life their business, but it was at least understandable to men in a male-dominated society like that of France, where a woman achieved her identity from her husband. On the other hand, the Jesuits frowned on the frequent practice of polygamy among the Algonquians, and frowned yet further on the fact that unmarried women were, as the French put it, mistresses of their own bodies and gave them free exercise. Often elders of the tribes also frowned on the sexual freedom of youth, blaming on it such scourges as smallpox. To the unmarried woman, however, the only real risk from promiscuity was conception (a baby by the wrong sire might preclude a successful, upwardly mobile marriage), but the Indians had their own herbal and other means of abortion.

In this period too there were considerable demographic imbalances. Internecine warfare eliminated many warriors, leaving a surplus of Indian women (which explains the utility of polygamy as well as of adopting captives into one's tribes), and the French colonists were almost exclusively male, with the exception of a relative handful of nuns typically sequestered in the main colonial population centers. This left a great many Frenchmen loose among the tribes, where there were also many women who chose not to get married, some of them presumably not interested in being one among an Indian man's several wives. In any event, a woman's status and identity had a great deal more to do with her own family—siblings, parents, aunts, and uncles—than with a husband. Many Indian women were happy to accompany the French traders and *coureurs de bois* on their journeys into the wilds, providing for them the normal wifely services in return for a stipend. To the Jesuits, this was clearly prostitution and they railed against it. Among the women, there was no such concept as prostitution. If such a liaison resulted in the Frenchman marrying the Indian woman, this was acceptable to the church, but only if the woman converted to Catholicism. The Jesuit categories of women—virginal and single; married and loyal; sinful adulterers or, worse, prostitutes—had little correspondence to native customs, and those Frenchmen who lived among Indians and depended on them almost always adopted the native customs.

No matter how the Jesuits complained about all this sexual activity, it flourished. The result was that a great many Indian women and their relatives came to know a great deal about the French, and vice versa, and a great many mixed-blood children grew up with a foot more or less comfortably in each world. Traders—and their part-Indian offspring, called Métis (meaning mixed-bloods)—often found themselves as alliance chiefs, those who did the negotiating between the two worlds, like the Decora lineage of the Winnebagos. Put another, perhaps more accurate way, the alliance chiefs were those men responsible for maintaining the middle ground where the two worlds overlapped.

But the middle ground was by no means all wine and roses.

Murder and war, for example, meant different things to the French and to the Algonquian and Iroquoian peoples with whom they were most closely associated in the *pays en haut*. For the French, a murder called for the identification of the murderer and then, by the authority invested in the state, his or her execution: a death for a death. On the other hand, when an Indian was murdered, his relatives or clan were the ones empowered to deal with it. Their goal was to deal with the murderer's relatives or clan. This could be done in many ways, ranging from blood revenge to extracting a payment from them. The payment could take the form of "restoring the dead," by supplying a slave to take the place of the victim, or payment in some assets that were deemed the equivalent, thereby "covering the dead." A family or clan that failed to make such reparations was no longer an ally but an enemy, and the resulting clan revenge could escalate into a series of retaliatory deaths.

To the French, war was a straightforward business of two hostile sides fighting. Killing a member of your enemy did not constitute murder, and therefore the end of hostilities did not bring about a huge series of murder trials. For the Indians, on the other hand, if an enemy killed one of your people, it was an act demanding an eye for an eye— a death. And in this logic, if a family failed to make reparations for a murder, it became the enemy, and the family of the murder victim was obliged to seek a death from the other side. The Indians thought the French way was most strange—killing an *ally* in the case of murder, and sparing an *enemy* in the case of war. For the Indians, war often became an ongoing personal feud.

In the case of murders of French by Indians, or vice versa, both sides had to learn how to negotiate the situation so that the two separate cultural views were somehow observed. In one instance cited by historian Richard White, the French need for blood revenge (execution) was served finally by killing two of four Indians implicated in the murder of a Frenchman, and in turn, the giving of appropriate gifts by the French to the families of the two men executed, thus "covering" the dead. Much of this social improvisation took place without the knowledge, and certainly without the approval, of the colonial authorities back in Montreal. Sadly they and their British counterparts, in responding to imperial duties in the mid-1700s, would soon destroy the fragile and shifting arrangements of life and society in *le pays en haut*.

Far to the south, down the Mississippi River, similar social improvisation between French and Indians was taking place. As early as the 1680s, the Frenchman La Salle had sought to establish a colony that would extend French imperial influence over trade by commanding the Gulf coast near the Mississippi. It was a misbegotten venture from the start. La Salle was assassinated by his own men, and his colony dwindled and failed. But in 1699 Pierre Le Moyne d'Iberville jump-started the original plan at Biloxi and soon built a series of forts and settlements that included Biloxi and New Orleans in the realm La Salle had called Louisiana. Aside from imperial designs, the plan for this area was largely commercial—to supply France with furs, minerals, or crops. With this in mind, the French began by enslaving Indians from the surround, at the same time working with the tribes who helped capture the slaves. Except for the Natchez, whose villages were a ways upriver, and the Choctaws, Chickasaws, and Upper Creeks to the east and farther north, the tribes located on or near the delta were small, most of them having suffered large population losses as a result of diseases. (The larger tribes in the region were almost entirely the result of amalgams of previously separate tribes—the mound-builder cultures that had been brought to almost a complete end, chiefly by European diseases, beginning with de Soto's *entrada*.) The smaller groups near the French settlements were such as the Atakapas, Houmas, Biloxis, Tunicas, and Opelousas. They tended to see the French presence as an opportunity for selling their crop surpluses, in some cases moving closer to the French settlements to facilitate the trade.

To the disgust of the French authorities, the few settlers—only a few hundred at first—found that they could get along fine on this trade with the surrounding Indians, and so they did not take up the life of the plantation and produce quantities of grain such as wheat that could be shipped back to the mother country. Worse, the Indians who were captured and put to work as slaves were totally unreliable, often simply disappearing back into the wilderness. As a remedy, West African slaves were soon being imported. At the same time, only a handful of Frenchwomen were among the settlers, and soon enough the French were living with Indian or African women either as concubines or as common-law wives. The African slaves did their work for the settlers but also tended small plots of vegetables and herbs, which they sold in marketplaces that emerged here and there like weeds. This was where the three separate cultures met and traded and sold, and of course shared one another's worlds. There arose an on-the-ground way of life that had little to do with the original French plans for the region: a genetic and (particularly) cultural mix that is present in Louisiana to this day. It is called Creole, and it is most apparent in Creole cuisine, which came about in the early eighteenth century in the colony so unpromisingly established by d'Iberville.

Both settlers and slaves were quick to adopt Indian maize and the forty-odd local ways of preparing it. A common Choctaw corn dish called *tanfula*, for example, included a high-alkaline lye from wood ashes, which, it was thought, added color, flavor, and bulk, but which we now know enhanced corn protein to the extent that it kept a heavily corn-based diet from bringing on pellagra. Indians also brought local fruits and nuts as well as bear oil to the table. Meanwhile the Africans, who already knew about corn, it having been introduced to West Africa by the Portuguese, cultivated rice planted before the rivers overflowed, making it a good hedge against the vagaries of growing corn, which had to wait for the rivers to calm down. From all this, plus European domestic fowl and mutton, along with local fish, venison and other game, Indian beans, African okra (the common ingredient in all gumbos), and sassafras powder, came a diet common to the polyglot peoples of the region. Along with other traded items, this sustained the three groups of people in a kind of economic if not social parity.

As the decades passed, however, the French authorities got their way: a plantation system did arise, and the colony became an exporter of goods. With this development, the Indians declined in influence as they came to be outnumbered (locally) by non-Indians, who numbered about seventy-five hundred in all by the 1760s, more than half of them African slaves. Meanwhile, tribes in the hinterlands had gained a certain amount of immunity from European diseases and began to grow at a rapid rate, the Upper Creeks reaching some nine thousand by this period. But among the towns and farms that made up the colony, the Indian presence was gradually reduced in numbers and in influence. The markets such as the one at New Orleans became formalized, and watched over by colonial authorities, and with supervision it became another institution by which racial and ethnic differences were emphasized and even magnified.

From the beginning, the French had known that making gifts of food was one of the most important elements by which Indians maintained alliances and friendships, and the French in Louisiana were assiduous in using food (and other gifts such as firearms) to cultivate the loyal friendship of the Choctaws, the largest local group of Indians, and to encourage them to fight the Chickasaws, who were allied with the British traders from the Carolinas. Indeed, the French colony survived largely through the sufferance of the Choctaws. But the Louisiana colony was low on the list of priorities for the government in Paris, which never provided the colony with sufficient wealth to keep up with the generosity of the British, and even this diminished over the years and decades. Before long, with stingier gifts of food by government officials, the bonds between Indians and the French (and their slaves) began to break down. Indians who had once moved close by to provision the French settlers now began to rob their fields and livestock. Even so, small-scale peddling on the fringes of society continued.

Even with the changing imperial tides that would soon sweep Louisiana into the hands of the Spanish, back to the French, and finally into the hands of the new nation, the United States—and even as the larger tribes (Choctaws, Creeks, and Chickasaws) were later removed to Oklahoma—the local Indians and the slaves would continue to peddle food and other items. In 1819, architect Benjamin Latrobe, British-born but considered the first professional architect in the United States, visited New Orleans to supervise a waterworks project and took note of the astonishing variety at the New Orleans food market:

> White men and women, and of all hues of brown, and of all classes of faces, from round Yankees, to grisly and lean Spaniards, black negros and negresses, filthy Indians half-naked, mulattoes, curly and straight-haired, quarteroons of all shades. . . . Their wares consisted of as many kinds as their faces. Innumerable wild ducks, oysters, poultry of all kinds, fish, bananas, piles of oranges, sugar cane, sweet and Irish potatoes. Corn in the Ear and husked, apples, carrots and all sorts of other roots, eggs, trinkets, tin ware, day goods, . . . wretched beef and other butchers meat. . . .

Latrobe, who appears to have held his nose at least figuratively as he looked upon this remarkable culinary and human scene, contracted yellow fever in New Orleans and died there the following year. By the time of Latrobe's visit, the influence of the Indians in these affairs, as well as that of the slaves, had been significantly marginalized in terms of supplying the area with food. But as historian Daniel H. Usner Jr. has pointed out, "the most persistent remnant of eighteenth-century food marketing rests in the food itself, from the ubiquitous ingredients of corn and rice to the delicate uses of sassafras and okra." The point is that in the matter of food and many other realms, and with or without the approval of the authorities on either side, a frontier was rarely a one-way street. Typically it was an arena of creativity and social innovation on the ground, much of it violent and tragic, but some of it relatively benign. In the nature of things, however, once the frontier moved away and beyond, usually to the west, so did this vernacular creativity.

CHAPTER EIGHT

INVADING THE PLAINS

The Three Worlds of the Cheyennes

The Cheyennes tell a wonderful story about how it came to be that people eat buffalo, rather than vice versa. The matter was resolved in myth time, when all the animals including the humans could talk to one another, and they agreed to settle this question with a great race. In some versions of the story, the race included all the split-hoofed animals like buffalo and elk on one side, and the humans and birds on the other. In this fairly straightforward version, the hawk wins the race, making him the greatest of all birds and making the buffalo and all the other split-hoofs prey of the people. In another version, the winner is the fast-flying magpie rather than the hawk. But perhaps the most appealing of the several versions holds that the magpie (a relative of the crow and the raven, both notorious tricksters) wins for the two-legged side, but by means of a clever trick. Instead of wearing himself out flying the entire course, which extended all across the Plains to the Teton Mountains, he rode on the buffalo's shoulder and, just before the end, leapt into the air and swooped across the finish line ahead of the now flagging buffalo.

And thus, it might be said, began the Second World of the Cheyennes, the time of their signal prominence in the affairs of the Indians of the central Plains, a prominence eclipsed only by their like-minded fellow invaders of the Plains, the Sioux.

Cheyenne bison on pipe

By the turn of the eighteenth century, only some twenty years after the initial uprising of the Pueblos in 1680, the two items of trade (and theft) that historians agree were the most transforming of life on the Plains were on their way into this vast grassy world—though from opposite directions. In the north, tribes like the Plains Crees in Canada and the Assiniboines in North Dakota were obtaining guns—in this case, muskets—from the French and, before long, from British traders, neither of whom saw much reason not to arm tribes who were generally hostile to one another. The Spanish, on the other hand, were fastidious about trying to keep guns (and horses) out of the hands of the Indians—Pueblos and wild tribes alike—but by the time they reestablished themselves in New Mexico in the 1690s, the horses had already escaped and it did little good to close that barn door. By the turn of the century the Apaches had been making horse-borne (but musketless) raids for a decade or so on the Plains tribes to their east and north, such as the mostly agricultural village-dwelling Pawnees and Otos in Nebraska. To the north of the Apaches, other people were arriving on the Plains, like the Shoshones and Nez Perces from the northern plateau region, drifting across the Rockies into the grasslands. Among the Shoshones were a subgroup who came to be called Comanches. Before long, armed with guns from the north and seated on horses that they would master as perhaps no other light cavalry ever on earth, they would run the Plains Apaches southward and become the scourge of the Pueblo people and the Spanish and, indeed, anyone else who got in their way.

A complex geopolitical pushing and shoving was well under way throughout the Plains. Semisedentary people like the Mandans and Arikaras in the north and the Caddoan people in the south were about to see their world change for good. These groups had long lived mostly from agriculture and gathering plants along the verdant riverbanks that drain the Plains, with some hunting of bison and other game animals of the grasslands. The hunting of bison on foot was presumably done in the ancient manner—chasing them over cliffs or into cul-de-sacs of one kind or another. Such hunts were probably infrequent, and surely they were as wasteful as always, there being no way to transport that much meat any distance. The arrival of the horse would change all that, but not overnight. For example, in 1719, visitors to two Pawnee villages along the Arkansas River noted some three hundred horses, less than one horse per man. By 1800, any Pawnee village had thousands of horses. It took time to breed up huge herds, or to create huge herds through raids, and it took time as well to learn how to use them and care for them.

By 1700, too, the beaver trade was still an important economic factor in the North (or what the British colonists called the Northwest), and here huge pressures from the East had long been scrambling tribes and inexorably shoving them westward away from the now over-trapped Ohio Valley and the Great Lakes toward the Plains. The pressure would only intensify as the French were replaced by the land-hungry British, who were, in short order, replaced by a far more land-hungry and fierce group, the citizens of the brand new nation called the United States of America. But even as early as 1680, a group of agricultural people from Minnesota were beginning to look westward: the Cheyennes.

In the course of a little more than a century, the Cheyenne people would deliberately transform themselves and their entire way of life and purpose so thoroughly that they would take on a new name for themselves. Their story and that of those other Minnesotans who followed them onto the Plains, the Sioux, provide a clear window on the immensely rich opportunities American Indians found in the Plains once the horse and, to a lesser degree, the gun became available. For these two tribes above all others would become emblematic American Indians in the minds of most of the world—superbly equestrian, elab-

orately feathered, warlike, daring to the nth degree, artistic, courageous, given to dying for honor, finally fighting the onslaught of the
white man against all the obvious odds and zealously to the death. The
statement "It is a good day to die" would come to symbolize the spectacular heroism of the macho Plains warrior.

The Cheyennes had no such notion in their minds as they moved out
of the now overhunted and increasingly overcrowded world of Minnesota and onto the easternmost edges of the Plains starting in about
1680. By the 1770s they lived in three villages in the upper Missouri
Valley in central North Dakota. They had continued the agricultural
life but also found plenty of bison to hunt, the eastern herds being
somewhat depleted by now. They adapted quickly to this more western
style of life, learning to use the bison for numerous purposes: as Elliot
West of the University of Arkansas has pointed out, various portions of
the bison "were eaten, worn, fought with, slept on, traded, played
with, and worshiped." By this time the Cheyennes had given up the
wigwam and took up the earthen houses like those of the Chippewas,
Hidatsas, and Mandans, who were now their not entirely welcoming
neighbors. This period was what the Cheyennes think of as their Second World.

In 1780, the nearby Chippewas devastated one Cheyenne village in
a raid, and soon an epidemic of what was probably smallpox hit all
three. The tribe again moved—away from the river and south onto the
Plains, thus entering what they refer to now as a Third World. By this
time as well, the entire Plains from Canada to southern Texas was a
scene of geopolitical pushing and shoving among tribes, each seeking
some sort of new life, the destiny of each depending in large part on its
access to and expertise with both horses and guns. Both of these trade
items, as West has pointed out, brought explosive new forms of energy
that could be harnessed, energy far beyond what had ever been possible. The gun made raiding a village practically casualty-proof: one
could, for example, kill the enemy from a great distance when they
went out to work their fields or tend their animals. The horse made it
possible to roam far and wide for game and for needed plants (both
wild food and medicine plants). It created a wholly new, astoundingly
efficient way to kill buffalo, the horseman leaning in at close range
with shorter bows and arrows than previously used (muskets were too
heavy and unwieldy for this activity). And with the horse, one could
haul a great deal more buffalo meat back to the band's camp. Indeed,

one could haul plenty of meat and pelts to feed and clothe one's family and band, and at the same time have plenty left over to trade either for Indian corn, beans, and squash or for European goods such as kettles, metal knives, gunpowder, guns, and shot.

Bison, Sun Dances, and the Plains Ecosystem

The horsing of the Plains would bring about major social revolutions among the tribes. New mythologies would come about to explain their existence and that of the horse, and no wonder. The sheer physical exhilaration of riding a horse—being high above the ground and feeling the explosive and enduring power of the thousand-pound animal doing your bidding beneath you—would call for stories to match the grandeur of this thrilling new sense of mastery over space and time, a sense not to be exceeded until the invention of the airplane. New ceremonies as well were called for to celebrate and ensure the continuity of this new life: central to most of the new Plains cultures was the sun dance, a ceremony that several tribes claim to have invented and that may have grown, at least in certain important aspects, out of a Mandan agricultural ceremony.

Typically, a sun dance took four days, usually in late spring, the time of nature's welcome renewal. Prior to the ceremony, a particular tree would be located, brought down, and erected in the form of a sacred pole in the center of the ceremonial grounds. In the first two or three days, feasting and socializing and storytelling were carried on while the participants in the final day of the ceremony—the dancers—fasted and otherwise readied themselves. Then, with ropes of grass running from the top of the pole through the skin of their chests or arms or backs, and attached to pegs, the dancers performed, straining all the while against their tethers. In due course, the skin would break and the dancers, fainting in pain and hunger, were tended by their families, having taken on the pain and suffering of the tribe in the hope of a good year to come, with plenty of bison to hunt and other blessings. (The obvious similarity to the role of Christ on the cross did not go unnoticed by the Americans who would eventually wind up in charge of the Sioux, and they, finding the sun dance little more than a pagan mockery of Christ's sacrifice, banned it. In addition, whites found the associated frenzy and disordered mental states disturbing and believed that the sun dance inevitably led to violence.)

Ceremonies like the sun dance, held when the people congregated in the beginning of the bison season or other times in the summer, served to keep tribal members psychologically together even though they were, at other times of the year, spread out in smaller groups. This appears to be much the same pattern archaeologists have perceived for earlier hunting societies on the Plains, not a matter of cultural continuity by ethnic groups but a more or less natural human response to a particular ecosystem.

Bison, which became the single most important resource in Plains life, took on a profound spiritual significance as well, in many cases becoming the deity who made the people what they are. Such was White Buffalo Woman, who appeared to a starving band of the Sioux and brought them, among other rites and sacred objects, the sacred stone pipe that is so central to the ceremonial life of virtually all the Plains tribes. When she left (someday perhaps to return), the Plains filled up with buffalo herds for the people to make proper use of as food, clothes, housing, and tools.

Sun dances and other ceremonies of these new cultures on the Plains could and often did include people from various tribes, as did trading and other activities. People from differing tribes and backgrounds were, after all, far more mobile now thanks to the horse, far more likely to encounter one another on the vast treeless reaches of the Plains. As one result, the various tribes, regardless of their origins in the East or West, North or South, regardless of their differences in language and other ancient customs, came to share numerous fundamental similarities. Just as navies from various nations have their own languages both verbal and symbolic, but also share certain naval conventions and means of signaling one another, so the Plains Indians developed signs, signals, and symbols that could be read and understood by all. The placement of feathers in a headdress, for example, had meaning (essentially bespeaking the wearer's acts of bravery). Buffalo skins came to bear the drawings of special events and were understandable accounts to all and sundry. Sign language became a lingua franca of the Plains.

An important side effect of the horse was that it would soon diminish the social role of women in certain ways. Bison hunting was replacing the agricultural life, in which women typically owned the fields and the produce, and therefore had a major stake in the tribe's economy and a major say in its destiny. Soon, on the Plains, married women would be little more than indentured servants subservient to the goals and needs of the male warrior-hunters. A highly successful hunter needed more than one wife to deal with all the buffalo skins he brought home. Society changed in other significant ways. If you made a tepee from five buffalo hides, it could be pulled from place to place by a dog harnessed to a travois made of poles—but a horse could pull *twenty* buffalo hides. Tepees grew larger. Possessions of many kinds proliferated, no longer avoided because of the exigencies of a nomadic lifestyle. The more horses a family had, the more things it could own and carry with it. Horses, which became intensely desired as signs of wealth and prestige, were the private property of men. Soon the largely communitarian style of the agricultural villager gave way to a new kind of social and gender stratification, and a nascent individualism (and vanity) that drew unprecedented celebrity to the hunter and warrior, his achievements and property. Men's societies proliferated as secretive groups of warriors and of males performing other functions. The richer in resources and the more socially organized the tribe, the greater the elaboration of men's societies. (The Cheyenne Dog Soldiers was such a men's society.) A wife's prestige now derived from the success of her husband rather than the social value placed on her own parents and brothers and siblings. This was profoundly new.

These sorts of changes were not something that the Cheyennes could have predicted for themselves when they made the transition into their Third World and began to refer to themselves as the Called Out People. They report that the transformation occurred at a place today called Bear Butte. This rounded hill stands alone on the eastern edge of the Black Hills of South Dakota—a site sacred to many of the Plains tribes today, and also a state park. The Cheyennes called this steep-sided hill Noaha-vose. On their trek to the Plains (probably around the turn of the nineteenth century), a religious leader of the tribe was taken inside the hill for four years, visiting there in what was the lodge of Maheo, their supreme deity, who gave the Cheyennes four arrows signifying their power over the region around Noaha-vose—and their new identity.

Before long, the Cheyennes would become one of the quintessential Plains tribes, horse-borne masters of their portion of the central Plains. Controlling the bison hunting in their territory, they became the major trading group there as well, trading more and more, as time went by, directly with the white traders themselves—people like the beaver-seeking mountain men, who would realize by the end of the 1840s that beaver hats were out of style and bison pelts were in. The more the Cheyennes thrived, the more they became dependent upon their ever larger herds of horses.

Today we do not think much about horses in connection with the ecosystem around us, but the simple ecological requirements of large herds of horses had a profound effect on how the Cheyennes and other new Plains Indian societies structured themselves. The arrival of the horse suddenly released all of the energy stored up in the grasses and put it in the hands of humans in a new, direct way. But grass has its own dialectic, directly shackled to climate and the annual cycle of the seasons. The coming cold in late autumn drove the tribes and their herds from the high plains into lowland areas, canyons, and creek and river beds, where they would be sheltered from the frigid winter snows and winds, and where the riverine woodlands provided some forage and firewood and, for truly horrendous winters when horse forage ran out, the edible shoots of saplings. Even so, large numbers of horses perished every winter, the die-off greater the farther north on the Plains. With spring, new grass in these lowland enclaves would put meat on the survivors' skeletonic bodies, and before long they could head up into the highlands.

The cycle of seasons and the needs of the horses put pressure on the Cheyennes to break up, at least in the colder seasons, into smaller bands. When the summers came, people might congregate for the great bison hunts and ceremonies like the sun dance, but for much of the year, individual Cheyennes were isolated from the larger tribal group. Not only that, they moved south on the Plains, driving others like the Kiowas before them—who in turn pushed the Comanches farther south. In the process, the Cheyennes split into two separate halves—the Northern and Southern Cheyennes—that exist to this day; and both found themselves well to the south of Noaha-vose, Bear Butte, which was still the spiritual if no longer the geographical center of their universe. By the 1830s, the northern bands of the Cheyennes were located in northeastern Wyoming, the southern bands some five hundred miles away in southeastern Colorado. The two groups were separated by the lands of the Arapahos, yet another group originally from Minnesota who had arrived on the Plains sometime before the Cheyennes.

While becoming potent warriors, superb bison hunters, and preeminent traders—in short, a dominant human factor in the kaleidoscopic geopolitical world of the central Plains in their glory days—the Cheyennes were also strung out ever closer to the breaking point in their new social, economic, and spiritual Third World. Their niche only grew more precarious as they became increasingly dependent on a single resource, bison, and a marketplace over which they had no real control (that of the whites). This tenuous hold on their world was hardly apparent in the years of hard-riding glory and bloody triumph. It would be brought to a premature end by the westward advance of Americans in the nineteenth century, but it could not have lasted much longer anyway.

Surely, though, the Cheyennes would have stayed longer in the vicinity of Bear Butte and managed the frightful winters if left to their own devices. They were not. They were followed onto the Plains by those other Minnesotans, the Sioux, for the same reasons that had drawn the Cheyennes into these new lands—tumult to the east, overuse of the resources of their homelands, and chiefly the promise of a richer life to the west.

Counting Coup and Open Warfare

One custom that spread rapidly among tribes on the Plains, at least those in the northern and central Plains, was *counting coup*. This was a system wherein one gained points by achieving proximity to an enemy, in particular touching him with a lance or bow or by hand, and escaping unharmed. In a given scrap, to be the first to touch a particular enemy earned more than being the second to do so, and so forth. This kind of bravado was practiced particularly on raids when the purpose was to run off with another tribal group's horses or other assets without getting killed or wounded. It was a kind of game, though often enough a lethal one. The levels of expertise achieved in these contests would be reflected in one's garb—for example, a feather worn erect in the headdress might indicate you were the first to touch an enemy on a particular raid, while a feather worn at an angle might indicate you were the second to do so.

Over the years fascination with this practice has led many commentators—both Indian and non-Indian—to suggest that this ritualized mayhem was about as far as the Plains tribes took hostilities among themselves. There arose a wonderful, nearly jovial picture of boys being boys, hunting in ecstatic bursts of horsepower, joining clubs and secret societies, and playing what amounts to a huge, Plains-wide, endless game something like Indian lacrosse (what the Cherokees called "the little brother of war")—a sporting, even glamorous period brought to a bloody and heroic and tragic end only by the invasion of the Plains by European-Americans, who, among other things, did not play fair but instead engaged in actual *war*. Until recently, many historians and anthropologists held this view, even though they all tended to agree that it was horses *and guns* that impelled the great cultural transformations on the Plains—and they knew that guns were not particularly useful in hunting bison until well into the nineteenth century. That view, however, has now been largely abandoned.

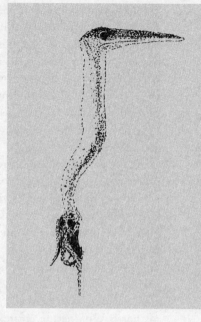

Sioux war club (elk horn)

What were the guns for? Why were they so valuable, if not for hunting bison? Chiefly, and not all that surprisingly, they were weapons of war, well designed for moving other people out of your way or gaining enough control over them so they would do work you had no inclination to perform. Few Plains Indians excelled at this more than the various bands that made up the Sioux, otherwise known as the Lakotas.

The Coming of the Sioux

In the late 1600s, Siouan groups that would come to be called the Tetons, Yanktons, and Yanktonais began to move westward from their Minnesota homelands to the edge of the Plains. The Sioux emerged into the world of the Plains early in the 1700s, lured there by the availability of beaver pelts for trade and bison for sustenance. They were well armed, trading with the French for guns, and they shoved other tribes, including the recently arrived Cheyennes, ahead of them, soon becoming the preeminent trappers east of the Missouri River. They also began trading for horses, and by 1770 the

Tetons were more or less in charge of the lower Missouri River drainage south of the agricultural villages of the Arikaras and Mandans and north of the Omahas. By now, all these tribes were armed and well horsed—in fact, the Sioux groups, being farther from the source of horses, were typically not as well mounted as those to their south. By the end of the eighteenth century, the Tetons and Yanktonais had significantly overhunted the bison and beaver in their territory, and at least one band, the Oglalas, opted briefly to become agriculturalists and part-time hunters.

As the century ended, European traders were in the region (among other things, competing directly with the Sioux for bison pelts), and with them came epidemics that struck hardest at those who lived in large villages, such as the Arikaras, who were reduced from some thirty villages to two. Living in small bands that were usually on the move, the Sioux were far less affected. The village tribes that had blocked Sioux expansion to the north were severely weakened, and Sioux war parties of up to two thousand warriors, banded together for the occasion, began to systematically shove the Arikaras, Mandans, and Hidatsas north, eliminating entire villages. Eventually, the Arikaras would move back south among the Sioux, who allowed them to live in villages growing crops for the Sioux and otherwise filling "the economic role of women," as Richard Wright puts it.

By the turn of the century, Sioux warriors had also reduced the tribes to their south, such as the Omahas and Poncas, to mere shadows of their former selves and were contesting the central Plains with the Cheyennes, Arapahos, Kiowas, the Crows. The Sioux never had much success fighting the tribes to their east, such as the Sauks and the Foxes, who were also being pushed toward the Plains, as had the Cheyennes and Sioux before them. In any event, when Lewis and Clark reached Sioux country in 1803–4, sent forth by Thomas Jefferson to reconnoiter the new American lands to the west, they were quick to notice that the Sioux were by far the dominant force they had encountered—vile miscreants, they called them, "the pirates of the Missouri." On the other hand, to the Sioux, the whites seemed just another (relatively weak) addition to the tribes in the region who had to be dominated.

CHAPTER NINE

WORLD WAR
AND A NEW NATION

An event with a shattering effect on Indian history in the eighteenth century was what amounted to the first world war. In the early decades of the century France and Great Britain were often at peace in the New World—but often not. Hostilities would break out in response to European wars over succession in one monarchy or another. An ultimate struggle between France and Great Britain, however, was clearly in the cards, and when it broke out it was fought in Europe and the New World and as far off as the Philippines. With it would come nothing but confusion for the Indian people caught up in its gales and riptides. Of course, *two* wars were on their way in Indian country. The first, variously called the French and Indian War (by the British) and the Seven Years War, would in 1763 shift Canada to the British, along with the formerly French possessions to the south. Fought in other parts of the globe that few Indians even knew existed, this war would exhaust both the French and the British. The second war, following hardly more than a decade later, is known to most as the American Revolution, the war that wrenched the American colonies from British rule and set the United States into motion as a free and independent nation. Most Americans today see these two wars as quite separate events, one between imperialists and one against imperialism, but that was not how it appeared to the Indians.

Instead, the two wars were basically the same: they merely settled which group of imperialists the tribes would have to deal with. (Indeed, the two wars were more closely connected than most histories of the Revolution generally admit.) Worse, the two wars soon made it impossible for the tribes to employ one of their long-running survival strategies: playing one group off against the other—France against Britain, say, or, Virginia against the Carolinas. By doing this, at least some Indian tribes had managed to retain a certain independence. The Five Nations of the Iroquois (soon to become six nations with the addition of the Tuscaroras) had made treaties with both the French and the English in what is called the Grand Settlement of 1701, which provided them with a certain form of independent neutrality. They were thereby free from wars with the Indians of *le pays en haut;* they could freely hunt to the west, and concentrate their traditional mourning wars on peoples to the south; they could trade with Indians passing through their traditional lands; and they were finally free of involvement in European squabbles and wars. Also, they felt free to extend their influence into the Ohio Valley, claiming hegemony over the refugee tribes like the Shawnees and Delawares. This, however, was an illusory claim. The real powers in the Ohio Valley were now the land speculators from Virginia and Pennsylvania and the French, and it was here that the clashes would come in the mid-1750s that would ignite what has been called the first true world war. And in this clash the Great League of the Iroquois, which had dealt with the imperial powers as an equal for more than a century, would become largely irrelevant.

The Case of the Catawbas

Throughout the land from the Atlantic to the Mississippi, most of the Indian entities—bands, villages, or tribes—had passed through much the same gauntlet by the time the two great imperialist powers England and France settled their claims to this part of the New World. From the beginning, the forces set in motion by the arrival of the Europeans were much the same in every region and came in the same order. First was the devastation by European disease; second, the desire, almost to the point of being an addiction, for European goods, from copper kettles and beads to muskets and metal tools to alcohol, traded from afar through tribal intermediaries or by a few white traders in the ever-moving frontier areas. Third was the actual presence of white settlers in their midst, first as a minority but soon enough an overwhelming majority. In each instance, with each successive wave of this rising tide, those Indians who could not flee (and none would be able to flee far enough in the long run) needed to reinvent their world. Then, having gone through this process, they would all have to cope with a quite distinct, largely implacable fourth wave, indeed what would sweep over the continent like a tsunami—the United States of America.

This dolorous process is nowhere clearer than among those people who came to be called the Catawbas, people of the Carolina Piedmont whose passage through these upheavals has been carefully chronicled by James Merrell of Vassar College. Who, for example, recalls the Saponis, Saxaphaws, Enos, Sewees, and Shutarees? These and several other village-dwelling, largely horticultural tribes living in the foothills of the Appalachians and east of the Cherokees were devastated by disease before they saw their first European, populations of their villages plummeting below the point that they could continue to be self-sufficient. While they shared what might be thought of as a fairly uniform adaptation to the ecological circumstances in which they found themselves, they were separate in many other cultural particulars, such as language and ceremony. But dispossessed by the magical onslaught of bacteria and viruses, they had to bury their differences and find refuge and some sort of peace among one another's remnants.

While some of the Piedmont people moved as far north as Iroquois country, or west over the mountains, most migrated into the country of the Catawbas, in the high foothills of the Appalachians and far from the coastal region. On the coast by 1700, Englishmen had settled in places like Charleston and inside Pamlico Sound, the bay formed by North Carolina's Outer Banks, not to mention throughout the far larger Chesapeake Bay area, to the north, where Powhatan had already seen to the process of tribal amalgamation before the English arrived.

Most Indian people in the eastern Carolinas became Catawbas. In 1743, a visitor to Catawba country heard more than twenty languages in the tribe's six villages. But intermarriage, time, and the exigencies of this new, reduced life erased the differences in a matter of generations. Linguistic differences disappeared, as did numerous ceremonies and stories, as these many different peoples had to evacuate familiar places, leave the graves of their ancestors, and move on to form new aggregations large enough to survive, and new cultures.

The process of amalgamation, or what might be called reinvention, was not aided by the white traders and government officials, who would ply the Indians with distilled liquor to confuse the tribes before negotiations over land or trade took place. In 1743, a Catawba elder whom the English called King Haglar complained to the colonial authorities: "You sell it to our young men . . . they get very drunk with it . . . and commit those crimes that is offensive to you and us and all through the effect of that drink. It is also very bad for our people, for it rots their guts and causes our men to get very sick and many of our people has lately died by the effects of that strong drink. . . ."

An old multiethnic world had disappeared. At the same time, a new technological world had emerged. The Catawbas were no less appreciative of European trade goods than other Indians around the continent. To obtain them they entered into trade, supplying what the traders in turn desired of them—chiefly deer skins and Indian captives to be sold into slavery. This tended to pit Catawbas against other tribes with what appears to have become a greater and more regular violence in the region than had been the case earlier. Eventually deer to hunt and other people to capture became depleted, leaving the Catawbas without the means to obtain the goods they now needed not as luxuries but as necessities, except by further overhunting and also by running down and returning escaped African slaves. In other words, as the eighteenth century began, the Catawbas were almost wholly dependent on European traders and economics, and were the first to admit it. What may not have been so clear to them is that their own destiny was no longer in their own hands, even though at the time they outnumbered the English considerably. (This too would soon change.)

Meanwhile, with their 1701 treaties with the French and English in place, the Iroquois turned their attention to the south and began raiding the Catawbas in straightforward, old-fashioned mourning wars, bringing home captives for the usual treatment of torture and adoption or torture and death. These expeditions kept the Iroquois population on an even demographic keel, if not slightly growing. The English authorities in New York and the southern colonies seemed utterly baffled by these Iroquois-Catawba battles, seeing no useful reason for them (and not being equipped to do much about them anyway), while the French took appropriate pleasure in the consternation they caused the English. But for the Catawbas, who evidently gave as good as they got in these intertribal hostilities, this was yet another strain.

Worse, perhaps, by the 1730s and 1740s British settlers had begun moving in on their territories in significant numbers, farming and hunting in direct competition with the Indians. Most of these settlers were the fiercely independent and typically unruly Scots-Irish, and troubles between them and the Indians were constantly breaking out. Catawba leaders often found themselves appealing to the colonial authorities for help in stemming these depredations on their land, largely to no avail. On the other hand, they had learned to play the authorities in Virginia and the Carolinas off against one another to get some of the trade goods they needed. In 1763, after allying themselves with the British in the French and Indian War, the Catawbas sued for a kind of local peace, successfully petitioning that a reservation be set aside for them exclusively. By then a new Catawba strategy was in place, a strategy that James Merrell says was accomplished not as any large-scale plan but by the individual decisions of hundreds of Indians. They ceased hunting. They had long since ceased raiding the Scots-Irish farms; now they rented lands from the settlers, and rented some of their reservation lands to settlers. They took up exhibiting their skill with bows and arrows for money and sold pottery, all the while keeping their (new/old) ceremonial life, their language, and other intimate parts of their culture to themselves. They survived.

When, later, the American colonists rose up against the British, the Catawbas sided with the revolutionaries. Few Tories, after all, lived up in the hills and hollows of the Carolinas where the Indians had become neighborly with these earlier tormentors, the Scots-Irish. As a result, and despite the fact that they actually did very little for the revolutionary cause except provide a few warriors, the Catawbas would be remembered fondly after the Revolution as allies and spared the fate of the

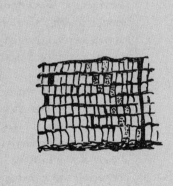

Detail of Iroquois wampum belt

Cherokees and other tribes, whom a youthful and greedy nation would uproot in the 1830s in a wholly unjustifiable, even criminal action and force off their lands. But even so the Catawbas' tribulations were by no means over. Even by the outbreak of the Seven Years War in 1756, it was clear that the Catawbas, like virtually all the tribes east of the Appalachians, were at best of marginal importance in the great currents of continental history.

The Seven Years War

Some historians enjoy specifying the exact event that triggers a major war. Many, for example, mark the beginning of the American Revolution with the passage by the British of the onerous Stamp Act, which sent the colonies into a spiraling series of rebellions that soon turned into revolution. But the Stamp Act was largely a direct response of the British government to the exhaustion of the British treasury brought about by the expensive waging of the Seven Years War. In turn, it is quite possible that the triggering event of that globe-spanning war was, as suggested by Fred Anderson of the University of Colorado, the moment in May 1754 when an Iroquois leader named Tanaghrisson, who was acting as a scout for a small detachment of Virginians led by the young George Washington, buried his hatchet in the head of a young French officer in the eastern portion of the Ohio Valley.

Evidently, Washington's group of some forty troops, guided by the Iroquois and his warriors, snuck up on a small group of French troops led by an ensign named Jumonville. This meeting was part of the previously freelance pushing and shoving the French and the British colonies of Virginia and Pennsylvania were engaged in over the lands of the Ohio Valley, where the so-called republican Indian villages had sprouted. The French saw that by controlling these lands they could complete an arc of French influence that would hem in the British all the way from Pennsylvania and New York to Louisiana. The British saw expansion into the Ohio Valley as a logical next move and a necessity, given the growing population east of the Appalachians. The so-called Ohio Indians (mostly Delawares and Shawnees) merely wanted to retain control over their own destinies.

On this morning in May 1754, the French were soon defeated, a wounded Jumonville announcing their surrender. Under the rules pertaining to such things, the French should have been allowed to collect their wounded and head for home with a promise of not engaging in hostilities for some agreed upon period of time. Everyone present understood such gentlemanly protocols, but the Iroquois proceeded to slaughter the wounded French soldiers, including Jumonville, much to the astonishment of George Washington, who stood passively by until he came to, as it were, and surrounded the remaining French prisoners and bundled them off to safety.

Before he was dispatched by Tanaghrisson, the French officer explained that he bore a letter from the French colonial authorities requesting that the Virginians and other British colonists abandon their outposts in the Ohio Valley. Given the increasing tension between empires, it is no surprise that this outbreak of violence soon led to others and thence to the world war.

Tanaghrisson, by the way, was a Seneca by adoption, formerly a Catawba, and was considered by the British as a "half king," a man who spoke for the local tribes. If his act did indeed trigger the Seven Years War, it was one of the more significant moments for the Indians in the oncoming military campaigns that would sweep through eastern North America for the next several years. Contrary to much common understanding today, the finally victorious British—like the victorious American colonists years later—largely waged war without much Indian help or even much by way of Indian tactics. At the outset of the Seven Years War, this decision led to what many consider one of the most humiliating defeats in all of British history. In the end, however, it also further marginalized the Indians in the eyes of the ultimate winners of the war.

George Washington's venture into the Ohio Valley failed completely, in spite of Tanaghrisson's help, and the British soon determined to send a louder message to the French, putting Major General Edward Braddock in charge of all North American forces, with the task of mounting a multipronged attack on the French at Fort Duquesne (later to be called Fort Pitt, and now Pittsburgh), Fort Niagara, and in the area of Lake George and Lake Champlain.

By now, east of the Great Lakes, the French were relying upon numerous forts strung loosely around the perimeter between the two imperial territories. Equally, the British had built forts throughout their domains. Taking a fort, of course, calls for an entirely different kind of warfare than the skulking sort of hit-and-run forest ambushes that Indians tended to practice and that the British tended to look askance at. Instead, it calls for large numbers of attackers using heavy firepower, including artillery, as often as not for a long-running siege. In any event, what the planners in London and Braddock overlooked was that for him to take Fort Duquesne he needed to lead an army of twenty-two hundred along what appeared on the maps to be a road, but what was in fact the forest trail that George Washington had taken from western Virginia in the direction of Fort Duquesne. Braddock was, it has been said, no dummy, but he was accustomed to following plans to the nth degree, so even when he discovered how arduous his path was going to be from Virginia to the French fort, he simply persevered, even though the route through Pennsylvania would have been shorter and less onerous.

By May 1755, Braddock's army was on its way, followed by hundreds of wagons and packhorses and a variety of heavy artillery, with less than ten Indians brought along as guides. Braddock neither feared nor admired Indian warriors, but simply considered them troublemaking exotics. Before setting out toward the West, he had turned down the help of a multitribal horde offered to him by the assembled chiefs of the Ohio Indians—mainly Delawares, Shawnees, and a few Senecas. These Indians were unaligned, having maintained a delicate but consistent neutrality. The assembled leaders had wanted to know what Braddock had in mind for the Ohio Valley once he defeated the French: would the Ohio Indians continue to have control of the region? Braddock replied that "No Savage Should Inherit the Land." He did not need their help, he affirmed; the Ohio Valley would be settled exclusively by the British. The enraged Indians left and enlisted to help the French.

Marching through forest pathways (at best) and widening them into roads to accommodate all the heavy equipment was tedious, painful, and slow. The terrain was hilly, even mountainous, with steep gorges to cross. By July, making a mere handful of miles a day, Braddock's main force (what he called the flying column) was tens of miles ahead of the troops bringing up the materiel. All his troops were exhausted from the weeks of hard trekking and hauling, and many of them were sick with such afflictions as dysentery. Young Colonel George Washington, who had volunteered to lead some Virginia provincials, had both dysentery and hemorrhoids, which made riding his horse a nightmare.

When the Indians and some French troops began attacking from the woods, the leading force of Braddock's flying column was about ten miles from Fort Duquesne near the Monongahela River. The British soldiers tried to form up as they were accustomed, while the French and Indians picked them to pieces from the cover of the trees. The advance force of British retreated just as Braddock ordered the main force forward: the two collided, mixed, and lost track of their officers. Chaos ensued. It was no contest. The Indians took huge numbers of captives (which is what they always wanted from such engagements) and the remaining British fled, fearing they would be massacred. Braddock himself was shot and died on the way back to Virginia, to be buried in the middle of the road. Two-thirds of the officers and men of the flying column were dead or wounded. The rearguard officers meanwhile had ordered all the wagons and supplies destroyed, and the remaining troops (about thirteen hundred in all) went home with their tails between their legs. Ironically, once the Indians had dispatched the dying and had taken their captives and other trophies (clothes, weapons, scalps), they too went home, satisfied, leaving Fort Duquesne in the hands of some two hundred French troops. Had the British regrouped and attacked they might well have taken the fort.

Meanwhile, other British officers concluded they at least needed some way of protecting such columns and supply trains from ambush, and began to develop the notion of special divisions of rangers who could skulk in the forest, providing cover and intelligence from behind enemy lines. The most famous of these—Rogers' Rangers—were already being formed and would play an important role in the ensuing campaign on Lake Champlain. Washington, who had ridden close beside Braddock throughout and was a great Anglophile, took umbrage at the Indians, finding them unreliable allies, as did most British officers. Furthermore, the Indians stood in the way of the land sales Washington and other speculators had in mind for the Ohio Valley. In any event, Washington continued to be a firm champion of the European style of warfare, believing that even the likes of rangers were too unruly.

In the first years of the Seven Years War, the British fared extremely poorly. Another major battle they lost was on Lake George, in New York, a lake whose waters run northward into Lake Champlain, which drains northward into the Saint Lawrence River at approximately the site of the important French settlement of Montreal, all of which made this north-south corridor of the utmost strategic importance. The major British loss was the battle in 1757 for Fort William Henry, their northernmost outpost in the region, located on the southern shore of Lake George. Only some thirty-five miles north, at the northern end of Lake George, was the French installation Fort Carillon (later to be named Fort Ticonderoga).

About two thousand Indians, including such far-off warriors as the Ojibways from Lake Superior and such nearby ones as the Abenakis from what today we call Maine, met at Fort Carillon in the summer of 1757 and there joined nearly six thousand Canadian militiamen and French regulars under the command of the marquis de Montcalm. Montcalm found himself with warriors from, in all, thirty-three tribes, and he knew that he could accomplish little in the woods without them, but at the same time he could not control them. Montcalm was very popular among the western Indians thanks to the French policy of ransoming captives the Indians took in such engagements. Meanwhile, only some eleven hundred men fit for battle, including provincials (always thought inferior by the British regulars), were on hand at Fort William Henry.

In August, men watching from the ramparts of the fort saw some 150 war canoes and almost twice as many French bateaux emerging from the predawn gloom, many of which were carrying cannon. The main French force was on its way by land. The assault began on August 3; four days later the British offered to surrender. The terms were that the British would be given safe passage to the south and refrain from joining any hostilities for eighteen months. Once this surrender had been signed, Montcalm called in the Indian war leaders and explained that they could not harm the British or take their arms or other materiel. This made no sense to the Indians. The massacre of Fort William Henry ensued, the Indians attacking the unarmed British troops massed for the march south. The French did their best to contain the violence but nearly two hundred British soldiers and camp followers were killed and as many as five hundred taken captive. Satisfied, the Indians left with their captives, but the western Indians felt betrayed by Montcalm and thereafter in this war did not materially aid the French cause. Worse from their point of view, some of the people at Fort William Henry were carrying smallpox and the Indians brought back to *le pays en haut* the makings of an epidemic that devastated their homelands.

In due course the British rallied, less by superior military brains than by sheer manpower, and eventually drove the French from their most important forts. Finally, in 1763, the war was concluded by the Treaty of Paris, which ceded Canada and other French lands in North America to Great Britain. While the British use of rangers continued—especially for obtaining intelligence from behind enemy lines—the war by its end was almost wholly Europeanized, the military role of Indians largely marginalized. Especially in the Ohio Valley, the Indians had been torn over whom to support, and in their discussions they began to forge the beginning of an ethnic unity in the face of European expansion of any kind. Also, Indians were becoming less and less willing to fight Indians aligned with the opposite side. Such pan-Indianism was something quite new, and it would erupt into violence only three months after the two European imperial powers had signed their treaty in 1763.

Pontiac's Rebellion

When the British forces in the Seven Years War began to gather a head of steam in 1760, a revived Fort William Henry was in the hands of one of the least attractive British soldiers of the time, Sir Jeffrey Amherst. A competent soldier but one (like others) with no appreciation or understanding of Indian allies, Amherst presided over the fall of Canada and the subsequent peace. He overlooked the fact that while the French regulars would simply go home, the Indians remained. And none of them thought that the French had enjoyed the right to turn their homelands over to the British, or anyone else for that matter. After all, no one had conquered the Ohio Indians or those of the Great Lakes. They looked with total suspicion at the policies Amherst was putting into effect. For one, he continued to occupy the forts the British had taken from the French, and even worse, he cut back on gifts to the tribes and villages—those crucial symbols of understanding and friendship. British settlers began again to pour into the Ohio Valley (reaching an overwhelming fifty thousand by the year 1776).

By 1760 the Indians of the region had begun to hear from several self-styled prophets. Things had gone from bad to worse for the tribes in the Ohio Valley, and the prophets saw this as retribution from a spirit world angered by the degeneration of Indian traditions and the acceptance of European ways, goods, and even attitudes. The most influential of the nativist prophets was a Delaware named Neolin, who was deeply influenced by Christian theology, seeing the Indians burning in hell unless they returned to the old ways (many of which were, sadly, forgotten by now), giving up their reliance on European clothes, tools, and so forth. His message was heard far and wide west of the Appalachians and it reached the ears of an Ottawa war chief named Pontiac. Neolin's message, and particularly his anti-British stance—he predicted the British would be sent packing in seven years—became an important arrow in Pontiac's quiver. Pontiac used this message to help lead the uprising on May 7, 1763, in which Indians attacked the British at Detroit. Detroit was relatively well manned by the British, but it was connected to the rest of the British world by a fragile necklace of small forts manned by young and inexperienced officers and few troops.

At about the same time that Pontiac began a siege of Detroit, other groups of Indians attacked the other, smaller forts and overwhelmed them. Pontiac's own siege failed when the fort was reinforced by British troops, but for nearly a year the British were back on their heels, fighting a widely decentralized foe. Pontiac had not, it turned out, been the leader of the areawide uprising anymore than the so-called King Philip had masterminded the uprising in New England in 1695. The uprising was fought by different Indians for different reasons. Pontiac and the Great Lakes tribes desired to get rid of the British so that the French would return. Life with Onontio, the French father, had been fine. The Ohio Indians, on the other hand, wanted the British out of their country so that they could resume their wholly neutral, wholly independent, and wholly Indian ways.

Amherst only belatedly understood what was taking place in his western domain. He could barely comprehend it, so great was his contempt for the "savages," an attitude made clear when he wrote to one of his officers, "You will Do well to try to Inoculate the *Indians* [with smallpox] by means of Blankets, as well as to Try Every other Method, that can serve to Extirpate this Execrable Race." The officer agreed to try this first known bit of bioterrorism, and wished as well that they had the means to accomplish the goal the Spanish way as well—with war dogs.

There is no record that this particular suggestion for germ warfare was ever actually carried out, but in 1763 a William Trent noted in his journal that when two Delawares came into Fort Pitt for negotiations, "we gave them two Blankets and an Handkerchief out of the Smallpox Hospital." Soon, smallpox broke out among many of the Indian towns.

Even without that, the Indians surely never had the warriors—or even the stomach—to perpetuate a long, multitargeted war against such superior numbers and implacable foes. The rebellion ended in a stand-down, the Indians unconquered but unable to stem the tide of British settlers, and the British policy for the Indians (that is, Amherst's) totally discredited. Neolin faded into the mists of obscurity, his prophecy having failed. The settlers who arrived, more Scots-Irish among them, had an utter disdain for the rules and regulations of the British empire and a profound hatred for Indians. Peaceful relations were not possible, and the region would be characterized (on both sides) by what we would today call outright terrorism.

Through all this mayhem, the British fastened upon Pontiac as a great statesman and diplomat. He became lionized by his previous British enemies as a pan-Indian wise man who could broker peace among the tribes: they referred to him as the emperor Pontiac. He evidently began to believe in his publicity, and thereby earned the growing disrespect of the Indian tribes of the region for overstepping his authority by far. Eventually even his own tribe lost faith in him, and he was assassinated by a cousin. Even so, he was made into an epic hero in a popular drama called *Ponteach,* purportedly written by none other than Robert Rogers of Rogers' Rangers, a man who—to the extent that he was literate—had been self-taught in the New Hampshire backwoods and probably was incapable of even the deadly prose in which the drama was cast. Pontiac became, among Europeans, the most famous Indian of the century, but recently his rebellion has been renamed by historians: it is now called the Western Indians' Defensive War.

As inconclusive as that war was, and as obscure as Neolin soon became, in both lay the seeds of far greater movements in the near future. These would take place at the urging of another prophet and his brother, a remarkable leader named Tecumseh, as well as of another prophet, who came to be known as Handsome Lake. But these great revivals of the Indian spirit were decades off. They would take place at a time when the world of the Indians east of the Mississippi River had changed hands yet again.

The Americans Take Charge

It goes without saying that for most Americans, the American Revolution is the defining moment in the nation's history, our very birth.

Most of us, without much thought, measure our real history from July 4, 1776, the date of the Declaration of Independence, and we measure the wisdom, courage, and character of our leaders against what we know of the great heroes of that period: Washington, Jefferson, Adams, John Hancock, Patrick Henry, Betsy Ross, the minutemen, the Founding Fathers. These people took on mythic proportions quite early, and their luster still shines.

But for the Indians, the American Revolution was an unmitigated catastrophe of incalculable proportion. By July 1776, the handwriting was not just on the wall; it was inscribed clearly in that most quoted American document, the Declaration of Independence. There, in enumerating the sins of the British in the person of King George III, the document points to the tyrant's effort "to bring on the inhabitants of our frontiers, the merciless savages, whose known rule of warfare is an undistinguished destruction of all ages, sexes, and conditions." This clause is rarely quoted these days at Fourth of July celebrations. It seems to have been included by Thomas Jefferson at the last minute as a result of mostly unsubstantiated rumors that the British were inciting both the southern tribes and the black slaves to rise up against the rebellious American colonials. It signals a larger truth, that one of the main roles the Indians would play in the Revolution was that of propaganda pawns, with each side rallying its energies and forces by accusing the other side of colluding with merciless savages.

The most egregious example among many is the tragic legend of Jane McCrae. Jane McCrae was a young and evidently virginal woman, a loyalist, who with Indian guides was on her way to meet her fiancé, a loyalist as well and an officer in the British army led by Major General John Burgoyne. On July 27, 1777, the poor woman was savagely murdered by her Indian guides near Glens Falls, New York—so goes the story. And so outraged at this barbarous act were the yeomen of New York and New England that they poured forth from their homesteads, rallied the flagging spirits of the regular army, and roundly defeated Burgoyne at Saratoga. Indeed, any country (meaning Great Britain) that would instigate such a bloody and uncalled for act had lost any legitimacy. This, of course, was heralded as the turning point of the war.

In reality, it is not at all clear who killed poor Jane: it might have been Catholic Abenakis, or this might have been a case of collateral damage from American frontiersmen pursuing Burgoyne. In fact, it is not even clear that she was killed. But spin is spin, and this was a masterful bit of spin: a loyalist woman engaged to an officer in the British army is murdered by Indians and it is used as an example of *British* nefariousness. Later, in one of the first major paintings made in the new nation of the United States, John Vanderlyn would paint the dreadful scene: In the gloom of the forest, a terrified Jane is on one knee, desperately trying to ward off a tomahawk blow from one naked savage, his face a mask of cruelty, while another pulls her head back by the hair. Jane's right breast is about to burst from her bodice. The painting became a popular image and, as Dartmouth historian Colin G. Calloway has pointed out, helped to keep Americans filled with sexual and racial fears of the Indians, a fear (and titillation) that would persist throughout the next century.

Each side in the Revolutionary War tried to tar its adversary with the brush of inciting the Indians to terrorist acts, and both sides did make some use of Indian allies, but not very much. The war was finally decided in the eastern theater by the ultimate success of Washington's Continental Army—a force and strategy based on the European model of proper warfare. Washington, as we have seen, distrusted Indians as soldiers, avoided their use, and carried this distrust even to the notion of colonial rangers using Indianlike skills and tactics.

In the eastern theater (if such it can be called) as on the frontier, the Indians made their choices based on what they perceived to be their best interests. The Catawbas, as noted, found themselves among white settlers who were anti-British, and their choice to support the Revolution was easy. To the west, the Cherokees split along generational lines. Before the outbreak of hostilities, the "beloved elders" of the tribe had already ceded considerable Cherokee lands to the British colonists in order to obtain necessary trade goods, and a disgruntled younger generation of Cherokees went off on their own, attempting to clear newly arrived settlers from their lands. This led to colonial forces marching among them, destroying villages, crops, and fields, and leaving the tribe destitute. Farther to the west, the southern tribes like Creeks and Chickasaws maneuvered to retain whatever independence they still commanded, facing the French west of the Mississippi and the Spanish in Florida, as well as the British crowding in from the East.

Elsewhere, British landholders had been buying up all the lands around—and even within—the praying villages in Massachusetts and Connecticut, usually obtaining land in return for forgiveness of debt.

Some praying villages such as Stonington, Connecticut, were now essentially white. Stockbridge, Massachusetts, was now half white and half Indian—mostly remnants of the Mahicans, who were now living good Christian lives in frame houses with European accoutrements, but still determinedly Indian. It was from Stockbridge that Robert Rogers had recruited most of his Indian rangers to fight for the British against the French and the dreaded Catholic Abenakis to the north. Now the Stockbridge Indians took up the revolutionary cause— though perhaps less out of patriotism for a yet-to-become American nation than because they hoped to see the British landholders in their midst disappear. Elsewhere, Delaware and Shawnee elders sided with the American revolutionaries in the hope that this might finally get them out from under the intrusive and unappreciated thumb of the Iroquois, but soon enough they were discredited by younger members of the tribes who sought a connection with the British.

For the Iroquois, the Revolution spelled the end of the centuries of unity of the Six Nations. Many of the Mohawks decided simply to leave their ancestral home and go north to Canada (where they remain to this day). The rest, along with the Onondagas, Cayugas, and Senecas, sided with the British, while the Oneidas and the Tuscaroras sided with the Americans. A Mohawk leader, Joseph Brant, who was the brother-in-law of the British agent to the Iroquois, became a much-feared leader of raiders on the frontier, and it was on the frontier—as opposed to the populous East—that Indian warriors had the greatest impact. For on the frontier, tribes like those of the Great Lakes and the Ohio Valley had long since been threatened by the arrival of settlers, who simply ignored the treaties tribes had made about how far west the colonists could go. Indian raids on these frontiersmen, many of them sufficiently independent to be neutral, drove them into the American camp, and the frontier was characterized by raid and counterraid throughout the entire period of the war and afterward.

The war eventually was decided when Cornwallis surrendered to Washington at Yorktown in 1781; in the frontier lands, it was neither won nor lost. There was instead merely a momentary standoff, with continued skirmishing for the next several years. In the end, it made little difference which side, if any, the Indians had chosen to favor. The new nation's Indian policy would not be shaped by whatever the real interests of the Indians might have been. What mattered was, first, that the nation was utterly broke, and second, that many of its citizens were headed west into the Northwest Territory. If the entire territory were declared federal land, it could be sold to the settlers who were going there anyway.

The new nation simply adopted the conquered-nation policy, whereby Britain had ceded all claim to the lands north of Florida (still part of Spain), east of the Mississippi, and south of the Great Lakes. Whatever treaties the British might have made with the Indians were null and void, especially since so many of the western Indians had fought with the British. In short, not only were the Indians landless, they could be thrown out of the country. With that sword hanging over their collective heads, the tribes in Ohio country created the Grand Council, making formal the on-again, off-again alliance that had begun with the French. It met first in 1783, and for the next several years protested any cessions of land by individual tribal leaders to the United States, since they had not been negotiated with the council. The council insisted that lands north of the Ohio River were Indian lands. The United States countered with the notion that the land cession treaties were valid, but the United States should make payment for such lands. The Grand Council (which was, by the way, promised various kinds of support by the British in Canada that never materialized) refused this offer.

In reaffirming the notion of treaties and of payment for lands ceded, the Americans were essentially giving up on the ruthless conquered-nation doctrine. Instead, they affirmed the treaty process as the appropriate means for dealing with the Indians, and the underlying meanings of this affirmation had immediate and long-term effects. First of all, the Constitution forbade any of the states from making treaties. The federal government would be the sole arbiter (and executor) of Indian policy. Second, only sovereign nations can enter into treaties with one another, so the notion of Indian tribal sovereignty was institutionalized, however murkily. Making treaties with the tribes would continue for another century; the notion of sovereignty—how far it reached, and into which political and behavioral realms—would persist, to be debated to this day, and no doubt well into the future.

Meanwhile, the Indian policy favored by George Washington was that of Henry Knox, his secretary of war. Knox called for making treaties with the tribes that would result in opening the lands of the Northwest to settlers, but the treaties were to be made fairly and squarely—"honorably," to use the contemporary word. Expansion with honor. This can be made to sound utterly cynical, especially since Washington himself had been a considerable speculator in the lands in question. It was championed by Thomas Jefferson, also in Washington's cabinet, who wrote both the line about merciless savages in the Declaration and, later, that "I believe the Indian to be in body and mind equal to the white man." These evidently irreconcilable views were shared by most of the Founding Fathers and they were reconciled through the concept held by many at the time that so long as Indians remained "hunters" they could not coexist with yeomen farmers. Even this seems cynical, or at least deliberately disingenuous, given the well-known fact (in those days) that virtually all the Indians east of the Mississippi River (and many to the west of it) were villagers engaged in farming. But one's way of life was categorized by what the men did, not women. Indian women did the farming. Men hunted (or fought). Until men settled down to till the earth on normal-sized plots of ground, they were still hunters—savages, uncivilized. Washington, Jefferson, and the others had every confidence that Indian men could be civilized, turned into yeomen, and then they would simply not need so much territory and would happily cede it to the United States.

Each year, in this regard, Congress authorized a total of $10,000 for "civilization." This meant, chiefly, making farm tools and spinning wheels available to those who asked for them, with the rest of the civilizing effort given over to those Protestant missionaries who volunteered for the duty. However, as historian Michael Green has pointed out, forcing Indian men to be tillers of the soil was not merely a humiliation of proud men whose culture called on them to hunt and make war; it went against the entire spiritual plan of the universe. It was women who were in tune with the spiritual world of plants, not men. Changing these gender roles was an outright defiance of the spirit world and a recipe for catastrophe. Not surprisingly, few tribes bought into the new scheme.

In 1787, Congress passed the Northwest Ordinance to fulfill the goal of selling off the millions of fertile acres in that region, as well as ensuring that with time and increased population, the territories would become states with the same status as the original thirteen. In the Indiana territory, the Shawnees and others erupted occasionally into attacks on settlers encroaching from Kentucky and other directions, while the Grand Council was holding firm in its insistence that none of the treaties already made were valid.

To put a stop to all this, in 1790, Washington sent General Joseph Harmar and some enthusiastic recruits from Kentucky and western Pennsylvania to the Wabash River settlements, where most of the violence was fomented. The Shawnees and their allied Miamis and Delawares abandoned their villages (which Harmar burned), and then ambushed the Americans, slaughtering 250 of them. Harmar beat a hasty retreat. The next year, Washington sent Arthur St. Clair, governor of the Northwest Territory, on the same mission, and he too walked into an ambush that saw 630 of his men dead, the most costly battle any army of the United States ever suffered at the hands of Indians.

Finally in 1794 General Anthony Wayne, armed with a large congressional appropriation, raised and trained a proper army, and set forth to engage the two thousand warriors of the alliance near the British Fort Miami, at a place called Fallen Timbers in Canada. The Indians were promised the assistance of the British, but when the battle was under way, the British perfidiously denied the promised support and barred the fort's gates. Neither side suffered very many casualties, but Wayne burned a host of Indian towns in the area, and the Indian alliance—so badly cracked that it fell into a disarray that would last more than a decade—would never again be so cohesive.

It may be difficult for someone living today to understand just how powerless the federal government of the new United States of America was in those early days. Abroad, there was plenty of reason to think that the new nation might not last at all, that sooner rather than later its revolutionary experiment would fail and it would return to the British fold. Not until it defeated the British once again in the War of 1812 would that matter be settled once and for all. In the meantime, vis-à-vis the separate thirteen states, the Constitution reserved various powers to the federal government, but it had neither the money nor other means to employ those powers.

Indeed, perhaps the most delicate job of the delegates to the Constitutional Convention had been to strike a balance between federal powers and those of the several states. In recognition of the squabbles that had taken place between the colonies over Indian lands, the framers reserved to the federal government the chief power over Indians. Picking up a principle spelled out first in the Articles of Confederation in 1781, the Congress, in one of its first acts, passed the Trade and Intercourse Act of 1790, which was soon succeeded by four similar acts known as the Indian Non-Intercourse Acts. These acts stated that any transaction between a tribe and a state or private citizen that conveyed Indian land was invalid unless a representative of the federal government had participated in the negotiations.

Meanwhile the federal government rewarded the Oneidas with treaties signed between 1784 and 1794 guaranteeing that the United States would not interfere with the tribe's possession of its lands, which comprised some 6 million acres. Raids on Iroquois country during the war by both British and American forces had destroyed most of the villages and fine agricultural lands of all the Six Nations. Of thirty Iroquois villages, only two remained after the war. The Mohawks and many Cayugas and Onondagas would simply have to remain in Canada. The world of the Iroquois had to start over.

(It is widely held today that the framers of the Constitution owed the Iroquois a debt of gratitude for pointing the way to the assembling of the colonies, ever fractious, into a single federal unit. No less than Ben Franklin is supposed to have taken the idea from the Iroquois Confederation. This is more legend than fact: the kernel of the legend dates back to the 1750s, when Franklin was already urging a union of the colonies. At that time he wrote, not so much in admiration but in the tone of a man trying to embarrass his colleagues into paying attention: "It would be a very strange Thing if six Nations of ignorant savages should be capable of forming a Scheme for such a Union, and be able to execute it in such a Manner, as that it has subsisted Ages, and appears indissoluble, and yet that a like Union should be impracticable for ten or a Dozen English Colonies, to whom it is more necessary, and must be more advantageous: and who cannot be supposed to want an equal Understanding of their interests.")

Even as the new nation saw fit to reward the Oneidas with promises to leave them alone, New Yorkers developed amnesia over the role the Oneidas had played in American independence. The state began pressuring the tribe, still reeling from the exigencies of war, into ceding large parcels of their land. A member of the federal cabinet reminded New York governor John Jay of the Indian Non-Intercourse Act but he simply ignored it. This and subsequent lands cessions, which by 1848 reduced Oneida land holdings to 1 million acres, would come back to haunt the state in a later century.

Another state bent on ignoring whatever control the federal government might exercise over the Indians was Georgia. Unlike Virginia, which had given up its claim on the Ohio country, making it a federal domain, Georgia continued to claim the country to its west, extending through Alabama and into Mississippi. Much of this was Creek country. Compared to the Ohio Valley, little of it was in demand at the time for settlement. The Creeks, who had suffered a good deal of disruption during the American Revolutionary War, were led by Andrew McGillivray, the son of a Creek woman and a Scottish trader (Creek society was matrilineal, so McGillivray was as much a Creek as any full-blood.) He was well educated in both worlds and had fought with the British. After the war, he joined leaders of the Choctaws and Cherokees to protest any claim the Americans might make on their lands simply because they had defeated the British. After all, the tribes said, they had never ceded any rights over their lands to the British king. But in 1783, Georgia demanded the cession of 3 million acres of Creek land as compensation for damages Creeks had done during the war. Several local Creek chiefs went along with the cession in hopes of restoring the flow of trade goods.

McGillivray sought to play the Spanish off against the Americans, seeking guarantees of Creek independence, but nothing was going to stop the influx into Creek country of westering Georgians. Inevitably, war broke out, with the Creeks using Spanish arms and becoming so successful that the Spanish themselves worried about too much Creek power and cut them off. But in 1788, the Constitution was sent to the states for ratification and McGillivray realized that if he continued a war with the Georgians he would incur yet greater hostilities from the federal government. Summoned to New York to discuss matters with Washington's administration, he eventually agreed to the Treaty of New York, whereby the two *nations* made peace, McGillivray agreeing to cede a large part of the lands Georgia had taken, and the United States agreeing to guarantee the borders of the remaining Creek territory. It was, for both sides, a win. The Creeks could now resume trade and other normal aspects of life safe within their lands, and the United States would not have two wars on its hands and thus was free to concentrate on "expansion with honor" in the Northwest, even if that were to call for hostilities (which of course it did).

All in all, for Indians and others such as blacks (slave or free), the new world of freedom and independence created by the American Revolution and the brave new Constitution of the United States was instead a world of exclusion. The British, and of course the French before them, had imagined a New World that included Indians living among the colonists. The young United States, as historian Calloway has written, "looked forward to a future without Indians." The next century would come very close to bringing their vision about.

The West Coast

Even at the time of the American Revolution, huge stretches of the continent were still Indian country, largely untrammeled by people from other lands. The passion play of contact and destruction had yet to begin on the west coast of the continent.

The Chinooks of coastal Washington State tell a story about their first sighting of *wasichu*, the white man. It is a story that is both a bit funny and a bit eerie, and essentially accurate.

> In a village near the mouth of Big River, an old woman grieved for a son who had died. For a whole year she wept. One day, trying to think of happier days, she took a walk along the beach. She walked a long way south along the strand, making her way among the great rocks and driftwood on the shore. Finally, feeling better, she turned around and headed for home. It was then that she saw something strange out on the water—maybe a whale.
>
> But as she drew closer, she saw it had two spruce trees standing erect on its back.
>
> It must be a monster, she thought.
>
> Coming closer, she saw this strange creature had copper on its sides and ropes up to the spruce trees. She saw a bear appear from inside it—a bear with a human face.
>
> She ran back to her village crying, and her people came out, thinking she had been attacked. She explained that there was a monster in the water near the shore to the south, and everyone ran down the beach with their bows and arrows. When they got there, they saw two bearlike creatures standing on the monster. They seemed to be asking for water to drink.
>
> One of the people climbed up on the monster and looked inside. He saw boxes in there and other things. He also saw that the monster had caught on fire, so he jumped off, and the two bearlike creatures followed him. The people took the two creatures to their village, and soon

people from all around came to see them. The people of the village had noticed that everything on the monster had burned up except the copper and other metal, so they traded the metal for deer skins and necklaces, slaves, and other useful things. The people of the village grew rich, trading and selling metals that no one else had ever seen before, and the two bearlike creatures were kept in separate villages.

By the middle of the eighteenth century, the longest coastline still uncharted by European explorers—besides the Arctic and Antarctica—was the Pacific coast of North America. This would soon change, with *four* major powers nosing around from Alaska south to San Diego, all variously looking for souls for the church, imperial expansion, or the advantage in a lucrative trade with the native inhabitants. By 1741, the Russians had made their first landing on this continent when the second Bering expedition reached Kayak Island and made two more brief landfalls, the last of which was on Bering Island, where Vitus Bering, the Danish

Southern Coast Salish spirit canoe figure

explorer who had navigated a northeast passage for Russia, died. The Russians began almost immediately to take advantage of the fur trade, particularly the pelts of sea otters, and in this endeavor brutalized and enslaved the Aleuts on the Aleutian Islands and those natives they ran into on the coast of Alaska.

Much earlier, in 1542, a Spanish expedition of one ship under the leadership of Juan Rodríguez Cabrillo had sailed northward up the coast from New Spain, reaching as far as the Channel Islands off Santa Barbara, and claimed the entire region for the king of Spain. But so pressing were Spanish affairs elsewhere on the continent that they did not return to what they came to call Alta California for another 167 years. In 1774, a couple of Spanish expeditions headed up the coast, one of them reaching as far as the Queen Charlotte Islands, but neither accomplished much besides a discouraging skirmish with some Indians. They were impelled as much by the suspected presence of Russians on the coast to the north as by any other motive, but it would be a long time before they returned.

To make matters worse, the adventuresome master navigator Francis Drake, on his third and last voyage, fetched up on the coast of today's Marin County in the summer of 1579 and interrupted his raiding to spend a month among the Miwok Indians, believing that their standard welcoming ceremonies were, instead, the rites by which they deified him. He too claimed the coast—in his case for the queen of England—and then he and his men left, having discovered the stunning beauty of the sea otter pelt, and having left behind a host of venereal diseases such as gonorrhea that would plague the native population thereafter. Two European powers had learned of the sea otter, and American maritime traders were not far behind. (The Spanish, meanwhile, drew in their horns, concentrating what they had of available resources on the coast of southern California.)

Coast Miwok split stick wand

From the outset, of course, when the Spanish expedition arrived in 1774, smallpox spread like wildfire via the normal trading routes throughout the relatively dense villages and towns of the northwest coast. The best estimate is that those populations dropped by a third from 1775 to 1801. As a result some smaller tribes amalgamated with others, but so far as can be told, the cultures of the region remained surprisingly intact. Indeed, the remaining

Indian peoples of the region entered a time of what appears to be cultural growth and enrichment, not shattering and degradation, as a result of the flourishing trade with Europeans—just as the Chinook tale suggests.

The northwest tribes had all the leverage in these early days when the European presence was almost wholly maritime, ships arriving laden with trade goods. First off, the traders were a long way from anywhere else and had to trade the goods they carried because the cost of returning home with them was prohibitive. So the Indians could bargain them down in price, or even refuse to trade if the Europeans brought the wrong things. The goods most in demand early on were iron for tools and copper for decoration, along with cloth, beads, muskets, and shot. In return the Europeans got fresh food and pelts, especially sea otter pelts, for which there was a voracious demand in China, their next port of call. There they would trade for spices and go home. Soon the coast was flooded with iron (which the Indians soon learned to smelt) and copper, but muskets and ammunition remained popular. Some traders brought adornments such as iron neck pieces, but they soon learned that such things would go out of fashion in a year or so, and the traders would have to respond with new decorative baubles. The Indians drove increasingly hard bargains, the rate of exchange for a sea otter pelt inflating enormously over a couple of decades. They were confident, astute, quick to play one nationality of European off against the others. If anyone was exploited in this trade it was the Europeans. By the end of the century, most of the maritime traders were American, chiefly Bostonians, engaged in the China trade, and Europeans began to find their way overland to the Pacific Northwest and establish permanent posts. The good times for those Indian tribes would soon be over.

To the south, in what would become California, the Spanish *entrada*—geared chiefly to create a presence that would keep other European powers away from New Spain—proved to be one of the most destructive of Spanish imperial ventures in the New World. Nevertheless, its spiritual leader, Father Junípero Serra, would be beatified in 1988 and is a candidate for canonization by the Roman Catholic Church for bringing Christianity to the California Indians. Resources back in New Spain were strained at this time, so the expedition to Alta California was a stripped-down version, expected to

Tipai-Ipai effigy

become self-sustaining by virtue of Indian labor. As they had in much of northern Mexico and among the Piman tribes in southern Arizona (but not in New Mexico, where they encountered preexisting villages), the Spanish intended to establish missions that would be the focus of Indians brought in from their scattered villages to live in central mission towns. Indian labor would produce enough by way of surplus grain, meat, cloth, and other necessities to supply the military garrisons, called presidios, established to keep the peace. A handful of colonists came as well when the Spanish made their move, founding the mission of San Diego in July 1769, the first of twenty-one that by 1823 would extend along a narrow strip of coast as far north as Miwok country.

In effect, the mission plan was designed to reorganize the California Indians economically, tribally, and of course, in terms of religion. Most California tribes gathered, hunted, and fished—agricultural labor, indeed sustained labor, was something new. They lived in small groups that anthropologists refer to by the diminutive word "tribelets," and in the mission towns ethnic distinctions were supposed to disappear. In only one aspect did the Franciscans' mission plan coincide with local cultural practice, and that was the hierarchical nature of most California tribes, which were led by high-status, wealthy men and women, holding social positions that were typically inherited. The Spanish appointed Indian officials they called alcaldes to enforce the regulations by which the Indian converts (called neophytes) were to be organized and controlled. This was perhaps the only aspect of life in the mission towns that was not altogether strange to the Indians.

Resistance to this new presence in their midst was almost immediate. The local Tipais attacked the San Diego mission before a month had passed. They were almost immediately subdued by Spanish guns, swords, and armor, and an uneasy peace ensued. It would be a long time before the Indians would band together to resist, instead of an individual tribelet waging an easily overcome, small revolt.

In the early years, some of the Indians were attracted to the missions out of curiosity or perhaps because they knew them to have a steady, reliable food supply. But it did not take long for the word to get out about conditions in the mission centers, and soon the only Indians in the system were those rounded up and brought in by the military. In the first place, once inside the mission system, Indians were not free to leave. Unmarried Indians were segregated by gender, girls and single women living in barracks in order to halt what the friars saw as rampant promiscuity. The barracks tended to be dank, airless places without any arrangements for sanitation, and this led to outbreaks of dysentery and other diseases among the women and children. Quite commonly, it seems, Indian women in the system were raped by the Spanish soldiers, who would sometimes go forth into the fields and lasso the women who ran from them. If a husband intervened, as likely as not he would be shot. Rape disgusted the women, so that most would secretly strangle and bury any white child they bore. Soon enough, at least one of the friars got wise to this and decided that any miscarriage was for the same reason. The punishment typically doled out to a woman for miscarrying was having her head shaved and being flogged daily for fifteen days, as well as having to walk with her feet shackled for three months carrying around a hideous doll in her arms.

Strict daily work schedules were imposed, and punishment for malingering was whipping by barbed lash, solitary confinement, branding, mutilation, or even execution—these punishments typically being carried out by the Indian alcaldes. The barracks and other structures of the mission towns were built, of course, by Indian labor. The Franciscans also would rent out Indian laborers to both the military and the colonists. Malnutrition was common—for people who had enjoyed a basically balanced and nutritious diet plucked from the bounty of the land and the sea, mission food, which consisted of little but gruel made from grain, was devastating, making the neophytes all the more susceptible to the diseases that arose from overcrowding, poor sanitation, and alien bacteria introduced into their midst. Indian children born in the missions rarely survived to adulthood, while the children of soldiers and colonists usually did.

The mission populations never became in any way self-sustaining. Mortality was sufficiently high that before long increased military raids on outlying, inland groups became the only way to maintain the needed pools of labor. Indeed, so onerous was the task of managing these huge holdings that by the end of the eighteenth century the friars had become more managers than preachers. The saving of souls for the church was a secondary task that often went overlooked.

Many commentators, including Scottish and Russian visitors, described these conditions and some remarked on what appears to have been clinical depression among the Indians in the missions. "At first surprise and astonishment filled their minds; a strange lethargy and inaction predominated afterwards. All they did was hide themselves as best they could from the oppressor." (One can only imagine how widespread this still often overlooked malady was among Indians who were dispossessed across the continent, or who lost families or even whole villages to disease or to unequal battles with technologically or numerically superior imperial forces.)

Not everyone in the missions remained passive, however. Resistance was common, the simplest form being to continue, however secretly, one's ceremonies and other religious practices while paying lip service to the cross. At least one secret cult existed in many of the missions for years. It appears that many of the mission Indians took this route, and the Franciscans never were able to stamp out all the old ways among the neophytes. Another straightforward form of resistance was simply to flee to villages elsewhere. Most flight was by individuals or families, but in 1795, for example, 280 converts fled the San Francisco mission, and another two hundred vanished the following year. After a time, unmissionized Indian people became leery of accepting fugitives into their midst because they might be followed by a vengeful military contingent, or they might bring new and lethal disease with them. Fugitive bands (often derived from several tribes) sprang up, a kind of reinvention of culture on the fringes. Before long the friars were seeing to it that barracks were built for single men as well as for the women, in (vain) hopes of making flight impossible.

In a few instances, significant numbers of neophytes, sometimes led by turncoat alcaldes, offered armed resistance, having stolen guns and even horses, but these revolts were usually put down promptly and with relative ease. Another form of resistance was murder—several friars were martyred over the years. One friar, whose knowledge of human nature may have been the dimmest among all his Franciscan brothers, was poisoned by his own Indian cook shortly after the man had been subjected to 124 lashes over a period of twenty-four hours.

The profoundly disturbing and destructive mission system persisted into the 1830s. Then a revolutionary Mexican government secularized the missions, sent the friars away, and gave essential control of Alta California over to Mexican hidalgos. These huge landholders would be much romanticized over the years, while the former mission Indians became day laborers and servants at best and nearly invisible pariahs at worst. But none of this would hold a candle to the devastation awaiting the Indians as the United States achieved what it took to be its manifest destiny, and California was flooded with gold-hungry, land-hungry Americans.

PART FOUR

Indeh

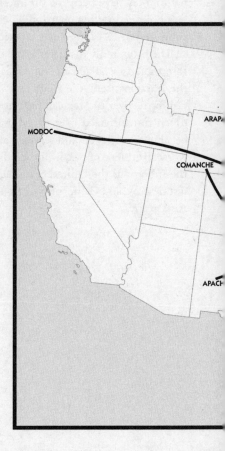

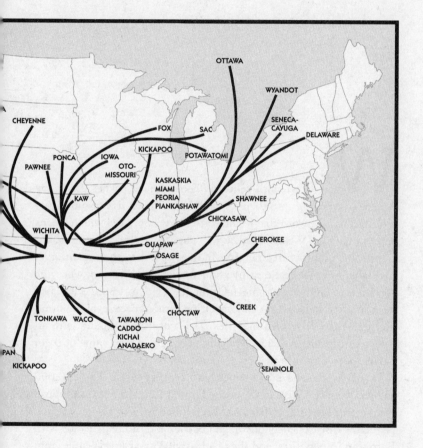

CHEYENNE

OTTAWA

WYANDOT

FOX   SAC

SENECA-
CAYUGA

DELAWARE

PONCA   IOWA   KICKAPOO   POTAWATOMI

PAWNEE   OTO-
MISSOURI

KAW

KASKASKIA
MIAMI
PEORIA
PIANKASHAW

SHAWNEE

WICHITA   CHICKASAW

OUAPAW   CHEROKEE

OSAGE

TONKAWA   WACO   TAWAKONI   CREEK
CADDO
KICHAI   CHOCTAW
ANADAEKO

PAN

KICKAPOO   SEMINOLE

REMOVAL

When nineteenth-century Chiricahua Apaches first saw Americans moving into their lands in the arid country of southeastern Arizona, the word that occurred to them was *indeh,* which means approximately, "We are dead now." The Chiricahuas were the last significant group of free-ranging Indians to fall to the expansionist juggernaut of manifest destiny and American civilization, when the charismatic Geronimo came in from the cold in 1886. They had been shipped to two dank concentration camps at sea level in humid Florida, where they died like flies. The century would end with all living Chiricahua Apaches officially prisoners of war, some of them having been *born* into that civic condition.

In all, by the end of the nineteenth century fewer than 250,000 Indians were still alive in the entire United States. Since Columbus's inadvertent landing, Indians had been killed by internecine warfare, pandemic diseases, alcoholism, and battles and prolonged wars with European imperialists, and they had survived—at least people from most of the original tribes had. The nineteenth century would bring forth the most severe obstacles yet. There would be more disease, more battles, more bloodshed, to be sure. But mainly there would be laws—some of them outright malevolent, but most of them thought to be helpful by the lawmakers—that would come very close to extinguishing American Indian cultures for good. There would be, as well, further nativist movements, fundamentalist summonses to an imagined purity by charismatic shamans who asked Indian people to look only backward. These would fail, however magnificently. Those Indian people who were able to look inward to the fundamental essence of their ancient ways and at the same time adapt to unforeseeable conditions would have a better hope in a world gone mad.

This particular stage of the madness began in 1813, when a man whose name meant Panther Springing Across the Sky perished from multiple gunshot wounds in a wooded swamp near the Thames River in Canada.

The Rise and Fall of Tecumseh

Tecumseh was one of the most cosmopolitan of the Indians of his time, in part because he was a Shawnee. Over the centuries, his people had split up, with some living in the South, even in Florida, some in Pennsylvania and Ohio, and some across the Mississippi in Arkansas and beyond. Nonetheless they stayed in touch, traveling back and forth. Evidently the various colonists, including Americans, never really figured out the connection. Tecumseh (whose mother was a Creek) was the sort of person to stay in touch with his relatives. By dint of thousands of miles' traveling, he knew most of the Shawnees and many of the tribal peoples west of the Appalachians and east of the Mississippi, the main Indian country contested before and after the American Revolution. He would become—by most measures—the best-known pan-Indian organizer in history, and his accomplishments would be adorned both during and after his life by legends, myths, and folktales created by the Americans he fought against, his allies the British Canadians, and Indians of many tribes. Probably more biographies have been written about Tecumseh than about any other American Indian (with the possible exception of Geronimo), and only recently have biographers made a serious attempt to separate the legends from the real story. That may finally be an impossible task since many of the legends began with what might be a kernel of truth, to be exaggerated by the man's admirers, not to mention his enemies who realized soon after his death that he was an extraordinary human being.

One story, which one can earnestly hope is true since it is so truly emblematic of the style of many Indian leaders, harks back to when Tecumseh was at the height of his renown and powers and sat down for a talk with the man who was essentially his nemesis, William Henry Harrison. Harrison was a thin-lipped Virginian general who would one day become the ninth president of the United States and promptly thereafter become the first president to die in office (from pneumonia caught while giving his inaugural oration in the late winter rains of Washington, D.C., without a hat or coat). William Henry Harrison was not the sort of man to kid around.

The event in question occurred in mid-August 1810, after a night (or it may have been several days) of public disagreement between the two leaders, in the town of Vincennes, on the Wabash River, capital of the newly established Indiana Territory, of which Harrison was the governor and also Indian commissioner. The commissioner's job was largely to create treaties with the local Indians. The old "civilization" policy had taken an interesting turn. Whereas Jefferson and others had expected that civilized Indians would tend to stay put on smaller tracts of lands, and then cede the excess to the United States, that had not worked as planned. Most of the male Indians of the Northwest did not turn to the female job of farming. By 1810, the government's thought was that if the Indians' hunting grounds were *taken* from them, they would have only two choices—get civilized or leave.

Tecumseh arrived at Vincennes with some eighty canoes bearing a multitribal force of several hundred warriors for this parley. Previously, Harrison had busily been signing treaties with individual tribal leaders. He convinced them that their only hope of continuing life as they knew it in their villages was to sign away large tracts of hunting grounds and other traditional tribal lands. When persuasion failed, he resorted to bribes and threats.

Tecumseh arrived like few before him. He was not weakened by war and alcohol, but the self-proclaimed leader of all Indians. He announced that all Indian lands were the common property of all Indian people and could not be signed away by any merely tribal chief, and that all the previously signed treaties were therefore invalid. He explained to Harrison that just as the United States had joined together in a union, Indians should not be denied the same right to unify. They insisted upon their own sovereign and inviolable territory—in short, a separate Indian nation. He made clear that the Indians did not wish to fight the Americans but would do so if they continued to be pressed by the uncontrolled onslaught of settlers and the injustices of the American government. Harrison replied that Tecumseh's notions about Indian land were demonstrably untrue. If all Indians owned land in common, why did they speak in different tongues? The treaty making would go forward as before, he said, and the Americans had always treated the Indians fairly.

(Such speeches, it should be pointed out, could go on for hours, particularly those of Tecumseh, whose oratory was described as a cascade of historical events passionately recounted, along with sharp reasoning and soaring poetry. Translators could never keep up with him, and so fairly untrustworthy reconstructions of his eloquence survive. In the midst of one speech that has come down to us he reportedly said: "Brothers—the Great Spirit is angry with our enemies; he speaks in thunder, and the earth swallows up villages, and drinks up the Mississippi. The great waters will cover their lowlands; their corn cannot grow; and the Great Spirit will sweep those who escape to the hills from the earth with his terrible breath." This was a reference to the great earthquake of 1811, which struck the lower Midwest. Centered at the frontier town of New Madrid on the Mississippi River, the quake rang church bells in Boston. Tecumseh legendarily predicted it.)

Evidently, while Harrison was explaining how fair the United States was to Indians, Tecumseh had enough and leapt to his feet, gesticulating and calling Harrison a liar. The two men confronted each other, sword and tomahawk raised, and the assembled forces glowered at each other. Finally, Harrison adjourned the meeting.

The next morning, some say, the two men had calmed down, and Tecumseh sent apologies to Harrison, who accepted them. Later, the two sat down together on a bench in the Indian camp to talk privately. Tecumseh kept sitting closer and closer to the general, pushing him toward the end of the bench. Finally Harrison—about to be shoved off the end of the bench—protested. Tecumseh laughed and said that was what the American settlers were doing to the Indians.

Indeed, by this time, Tecumseh did lead an enormous number of Indian warriors, younger people who had also listened to Tecumseh's younger brother, who was by then known as the Prophet. The brother, who had taken a Shawnee name, Tenskwatawa, meaning Open Door, was a nearly hopeless alcoholic until 1805, when he was visited by supernaturals and forswore alcohol and all other aspects of the white man's culture. He became one of the leading nativist preachers in Indian country.

Throughout the northern woodlands, a tradition of prophets and prophecies had long existed, and it flourished now at a time when religious revivalism was sweeping through both white and Indian country. One of the most successful prophets was a contemporary of Tenskwatawa who arose east of the Ohio Valley and the Great Lakes among the Senecas. He came to be known as Handsome Lake, and until 1799 he also was crippled by alcohol, a down-and-out drunk. Then, near death after four days lying in bed nearly comatose, he had the first of many visions in which supernaturals showed him the path out of his miseries. He began to preach a new morality and a new society, based on both traditional Iroquois rituals and elements of Christianity. He asked Senecas to forswear drinking, wife abuse, witchcraft, adultery, and other sins, and pointed to the blessings of marriage, children, and other common family values. Over time and with subsequent visions, he adumbrated what was called "the new religion" (and what is today in some Iroquois quarters called "the old faith"). He also preached the need to learn the white man's ways, to send some sons to white schools. It was all right, for example, for Senecas to farm and live in the white man's houses, but they should keep their own traditional clothing. Handsome Lake's vision would eventually, after his death, spread throughout the Six Nations and become the bulwark of their reinvigoration over the coming centuries. Indeed, some scholars are confident that without Handsome Lake, the trajectory of the nations of the Iroquois Confederation would have been downhill, and as devastating as life became for many of the other eastern tribes. Few nativist preachers had Handsome Lake's lasting influence.

In contrast to Handsome Lake, Tecumseh and his brother molded a straightforwardly nativist, antiwhite sentiment into a sense of racial unity, hoping to reinvent the western alliance that had collapsed a decade or so before at Fallen Timbers. By 1808, the two brothers had founded Prophet's Town on Tippecanoe Creek in Indiana, where the townspeople lived in the old ways, without domestic animals or any of the white man's products, even guns. The antiwhite message was spreading rapidly throughout the Northwest Territory, much to the dismay of American officials.

After the historic meeting with Harrison, Tecumseh took to the road again, traveling thousands of miles, trying to persuade tribes from

Florida to Missouri to take up the cause and to repel the expanding white presence. In the South, he had success among the Southern Shawnees, Creeks, and Seminoles, but little success among the Cherokees and the other southern tribes, who were trying to take the advice of Thomas Jefferson and become "civilized." On the other hand, the vast majority of Indians in what was then thought of as the Great Northwest took up Tecumseh's cause, and on one occasion at least, he led a force of three thousand warriors into battle, the largest known aggregation of American Indian fighting men ever assembled in one place.

In 1812 Tecumseh returned from his travels to Prophet's Town. He found that, acting on what amounted to a pretext—a charge about a couple of Indians who killed a white—Harrison had sacked the village. War ensued, but sadly it began before Tecumseh and the Prophet had finished cementing the pan-Indian alliances. Immediately following, the Americans declared war on the encroaching British, and the War of 1812 was on. Furthering his own goals, Tecumseh quickly joined with the British, who gained a useful ally in their capture of Detroit.

The tide of war, however, was against the British, who, in the East, had even managed to burn the White House. Their back was soon broken in September 1814 when Commodore Perry defeated a British fleet on Lake Erie. Tecumseh and his warriors reluctantly followed Colonel Henry Proctor, an especially weak British officer, as he retreated back into Canada north of the lake, pursued by Harrison. It was there that Tecumseh was killed in battle.

The mythologizing began almost immediately, with the Americans happily engaged in the process along with everyone else. Tecumseh was, after all, a truly worthy opponent—and indeed a man of rare humanity as well as courage and all the other attributes of heroes through time. In one instance, for example, when in Tecumseh's absence the contemptible Proctor had failed to keep some Indian warriors from massacring captured Americans, Tecumseh publicly excoriated him, telling him he was not fit to command. "Go put on petticoats," Tecumseh raged. On another occasion, hearing that some of his warriors were again killing captives, he rode straight into the melee and put an immediate stop to it.

Tecumseh's heroic efforts amounted to little. Once he was killed in battle in Canada, there was no one of sufficient stature—not even his brother, the Prophet—to replace him and hold together so fragile an alliance of Indian tribal groups against the overwhelming onslaught of

America and the centrifugal force of ethnicity. The tragedy of Tecumseh was twofold: in urging Indian people to put aside their age-old differences, he was, like his predecessors, ahead of his time; in trying to carve out a separate Indian country in the Ohio Valley in the face of a rapidly growing white presence, he was too late.

Red Sticks and Civilized Tribes

Visiting his mother's people, the Creeks, Tecumseh had stirred the embers of resentment and nativist religious fervor among many younger men of the confederation, as well as the closely related Seminoles in Florida. These angry warriors came to be known as the Red Sticks. Tecumseh is said to have given various of their leaders bundles of red sticks that would mark the time when they should rise up. Red was the color of war. Local prophets (or more aptly, shamans and war leaders) echoed the puritanical and antiwhite sentiments of Tecumseh and Open Door. They explained that the current plight of the Creeks had arisen from the failure of leaders to honor the spirit world. They had not paid the proper ceremonial respect to the sun, the Corn Mother, and the sacred fire. Few of the local nativist leaders went so far as to suggest (as the Shawnee Prophet did) that the Creeks drop all European trade goods and livestock. But the Creeks themselves were by no means united. The majority (including most of the Lower Creeks and about half of the Upper Creeks) saw the future in terms of adaptation to the white man's world. Civilization as specified by Jefferson and others beckoned strongly to these Indians. Some prominent members of this faction were able to avoid the problem of men engaging in agricultural labor by owning black slaves. In June 1813, a civil war broke out among the Creeks. The Red Stick minority attacked an army installation, Fort Mims, near Mobile, killing more than 350 soldiers, civilians, and slaves.

The world proceeded to fall in on the Red Sticks. Georgian militia joined by anti–Red Stick Creeks attacked from the East. A federal army pushed up from the South, joined by Choctaw warriors. From Tennessee came Andrew Jackson, a rawboned frontiersman, at the head of a large contingent of volunteers, along with some six hundred Cherokees. After repulsing the attackers twice, the Red Sticks were finally annihilated at the battle of Horseshoe Bend on the Tallapoosa River in Alabama. The remaining one thousand Red Stick people fled to Florida to join the Seminoles, and Jackson proceeded to force a treaty down the throats of the other Creeks (some of whom had, of course, fought with the United States). They had to sign a confession of war guilt and cede two-thirds of their ancestral territory, mostly westerly hunting lands that were by now overhunted, to the United States. Soon thereafter, Jackson went on to achieve celebrity status by his (and the Choctaws') heroic defense of New Orleans against the British. Once the War of 1812 was over, he returned to the business of stripping southern Indians of their lands, pressuring the Choctaws, Chickasaws, and Cherokees to sign away similarly vast tracts of traditional hunting grounds to the United States.

Jackson tried to persuade the Cherokees to move west of the Mississippi, and about a third of the tribe did move to Arkansas. The rest, along with the other major southern tribes, continued on their chosen paths to civilization, prospering on less land as farmers, and even requesting that missionary sects like the Moravians and Presbyterians open schools for them. The Cherokees took up the civilization program most wholeheartedly of all the southern tribes. By the turn of the nineteenth century, they had a formal National Council and soon instituted a national police force to see to it that Cherokees did not engage in horse stealing and other activities that would cause trouble with the surrounding white people. The council went on to take more powers to itself, such as outlawing clan vengeance and making itself (in the form of an executive committee) responsible for dealing with the United States government. In 1827, a con-

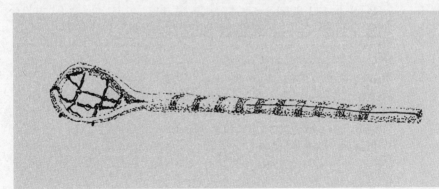

Cherokee stick for "Little Brother of War"

stitutional convention designed a Cherokee government consisting of an elected principal chief, a bicameral legislature representing eight districts, and a court system including a supreme court. The constitution proclaimed the sovereignty of the Cherokee Nation.

Meanwhile Sequoyah, an illiterate Cherokee, had developed signs for the eighty-six Cherokee syllables and introduced his system in 1821. In 1828, the Cherokee government launched its bilingual newspaper, the *Cherokee Phoenix,* in their newly founded capital town, New Echota. A man named John Ross, one-eighth Cherokee but with the complete trust of even the most traditional full-bloods, was elected principal chief and held that position until 1866, guiding the tribe through the most calamitous period in its history. By the 1830s, some sixteen thousand Cherokees owned thousands of hogs, cattle, and horses, maintained roads, owned stores, and worked in a variety of skilled trades. The average size of Cherokee farms was about fourteen acres, and the compact Cherokee towns of old not only had lost their autonomy to the national government but were far more spread out. Somewhere between 5 and 10 percent of Cherokee agriculturalists were slave owners with larger plantations, leading lives much like those of their white counterparts in the South. In short, the Cherokees took on most of the trappings of the European version of a nation. The tribe reinvented itself economically and politically in the hope of maintaining much of its deeper culture, its independence, and what remained of its original territories.

The other large southern tribes—Creeks, Chickasaws, and Choctaws—did not feel the need to go quite so far in the Cherokee direction. The Creeks created a National Council that attempted to undercut the influence of local towns and of clans, established a police force, and in many cases took up plow agriculture. At this time they did not seek to create a government based on the model of the United States, and had little interest in allowing missionary schools in their midst. To the west, the Chickasaws and Choctaws encouraged mission schools, took up plow agriculture, and drafted national codes of laws.

Most of these large and small economic and political changes were initiated by those tribal members who were the children of Indian mothers and white traders, people who developed a facility for dealing with both worlds. These too tended to be the elites in their tribes, the leaders, the plantation owners, the ambitious. But civilization was a tribal ambition as well as a personal one, and they were in one degree or another leading their people into what they hoped was a way of life that would discourage their ever-growing numbers of white neighbors from relocating them. Of course, that frail hope was not to be fulfilled, regardless of the tribes' efforts to play the game by the Americans' rules.

The Marshall Trilogy

In 1828, the same year as the Cherokees' constitutional convention, Andrew Jackson was elected to his first term as the seventh president of the United States. He was the first president from west of the Appalachians, a man in the mold of the frontier hero, who derided the treaty system for dealing with Indians as "absurd" and the notion of Indian tribes as sovereign nations as nonsense. He set out to clear up the confusions inherent in American Indian policy and laws, and to get as many American Indians out of the East, and particularly the Southeast, as he could—by persuasion, law, the overruling of treaties, or main force.

Thomas Jefferson is credited with thinking up the idea of removing Indians from east of the Mississippi—contingent, of course, on their decision to remain hunters. For those who chose to remain, the process of civilization would reduce their need for large areas of land. But it would also lead, as Jefferson explained to a delegation of Delawares and Mahicans, to a time when "you will unite yourselves with us . . . form one people with us, and we shall all be Americans." When the Ohio and Great Lakes tribes turned up their noses at civilization, policy makers thought the outright loss of their hunting grounds would nudge them toward civilization. Within all this, a complex series of considerations arose, many surrounding the notion of *fee simple.* Land awarded in fee simple could be sold or left to one's heirs. Sections of land were offered to various individual Indians in fee simple if they elected to become U.S. citizens—particularly influential Indians who could also sign treaties ceding Indian lands to the United States. A few Cherokees and a few Choctaws took this route, and larger numbers (but by no means a majority) of members of the southern tribes took the option also offered of moving to lands reserved for them west of the Mississippi. Those tribal people who remained in the South, the majority, were the most adamant about their tribal sovereignty and their rights to their land. A collision was in store.

Another aspect of the inevitable collision was that Georgia had agreed in 1802 to give up its claims to charter lands to its west that would soon comprise the states of Alabama and Mississippi, in return for a federal pledge to obtain for Georgia the Indian lands east of the Chattahoochee River as soon as that could be arranged peaceably and reasonably. Known as the Georgia Compact, this guarantee flew exactly in the face of the federal pledge—often reiterated—to protect from illegal and unreasonable seizure those Indian lands remaining after various tribal land cessions.

The administration of James Monroe was taken to task by Georgia for failing to enforce the 1802 guarantees to the state. For a while Monroe protested that if the Indians refused to sell, there was nothing the United States could do. Tempers flared and soon, in 1824, Monroe caved in, called for relocation of the southern tribes, and rationalized this policy as the only way to avoid their "degradation and extermination" by the whites. The federal government's powers—on paper and in fact—remained severely limited.

The following year, the Creek National Council ordered the execution of one of the Lower Creek leaders who had signed a treaty giving practically all the Creek land to the United States: Creek law specified that any sale of Creek land had to be authorized by the National Council. Georgia responded to the execution by threatening to invade the Creeks, which in turn put a new U.S president, John Quincy Adams, in a pickle since he was enjoined by treaty to protect Creek lands. The matter simmered without resolution until the election of Andrew Jackson in 1828.

From his inaugural address onward, Jackson offered the tribes—and in particular the Cherokees—two choices: migrate west of the Mississippi or stay and be subject to the laws of the states. The idea of the tribes establishing separate governments and laws was unacceptable. The southern states soon enough enacted laws subjecting the Indians to state laws that in effect made them second-class citizens, on a par with freed blacks. That is, they were not allowed to vote or to bear witness in state courts, among other indignities. Proponents of relocation (who included virtually all the white people in Georgia, Alabama, Mississippi, and Tennessee) claimed that civilization had not worked, that even if the likes of the Cherokees had produced the trappings of civilization, underneath they remained savages.

So virulently did the "Freemen of the State of Georgia" detest their

Creek neighbors that in 1789 they had basically legalized the hunting of Indians. The law read, in part, "It shall be lawful for the Government and the people of the same [Georgia], to put to death or capture the said Indians wheresoever they may be found within the limits of this state; except such tribes of the said Indians which have not or shall not hereafter commit hostilities against the people of this state, of which the commanding officer shall judge."

No issue was more tendentious in the early years of Jackson's first term. Those who opposed the removal policy, pointing out that the Constitution made treaties part of the supreme law of the land, were Jackson's eastern political opponents, and the tide of politics had moved west. The new egalitarian Jacksonian democracy, so loudly trumpeted in American textbooks, was a democracy of the many, but not all. On May 28, 1830, Jackson signed a removal bill that called for the expulsion of about a hundred thousand southeastern Indians— which is to say, essentially all of them—to lands in the West that would be set aside for them "forever." (At the time, the population of the United States was more than 12 million.) The costs of the migration would be paid by the federal government, along with a year's sustenance, and once they were in their new lands, the Indians would be protected from any troubles brought on by whites or western Indians. There was talk (but no action) in Congress of formally establishing a region, made up of what is now eastern Oklahoma and parts of Kansas, to be called the Indian Territory, which might one day become its own state of the Union. Desultory discussions began between representatives of the United States and the tribes—Comanches, Kiowas, Pawnees, and others of the southeastern Plains—who used the new homelands of the eastern Indians for hunting.

Soon some fundamental questions raised by the policy of removal found their way to the United States Supreme Court: Who owned the real estate of the new nation? Were Indian nations independent? Were treaty rights sanctified, or subject to change in new circumstances? These questions soon came before Chief Justice John Marshall, who had already ruled in 1823 that, despite centuries of treaties, the Indians did not retain "complete sovereignty, as independent nations." The Europeans had gained title to sovereignty by the ancient right of discovery. Indian sovereignty was thus limited. In 1831, after the Cherokees asked the Jackson administration for federal help against the coercion of Georgia and were rebuffed, they sued. Marshall ruled that the Cherokee Nation was a "state" but not a foreign one. It was instead a "domestic dependent nation," and for the time being, the Supreme Court left the matter of federal or state authority unaddressed. Marshall explained in his opinion that he was sympathetic to the question of federal authority and would appreciate a case being brought before him that went to the heart of that matter. Another suit, brought the following year, did provide some clarification. Georgia demanded that two missionaries among the Cherokees comply with state law and obtain a state license and take an oath of allegiance to the state. Marshall ruled that the state law was unconstitutional because sole authority over the tribe lay exclusively in the hands of the federal government. The three Marshall decisions are referred to by the legal community as the Marshall Trilogy and are part of the bedrock of Indian policy to this day, though throughout the years the principles set forth have often been blurred, contradicted, or ignored.

In response to this last judgment of the Marshall Trilogy, President Jackson legendarily said something to the effect that "Chief Justice Marshall has made his law; then let him enforce it." Whether Jackson's words or not, the statement reflects Jackson's view of the matter. He wanted the Indians out of Georgia and the other southern states, and he never intended to enforce the court's decision—probably the first impeachable offense by a United States president. Such a drastic and unprecedented response to Jackson's failure to enforce the law was not raised, however, and the question of sovereignty would continue to haunt the American Indian tribes and the federal and state governments until this very day.

Trails of Tears

The Choctaws were the first to go en masse. Over the years since the American Revolution, small groups of Indians from both the Northeast and Southeast had, as noted, trekked across the Mississippi, impelled by crowding, hostilities, overhunting of ancestral territories—lighting out for the territories, as Huck Finn would put it, to seek a freer, less trammeled, perhaps simpler life, in any case a life free of white intrusions. Many of the people who stayed behind were nonetheless familiar to one degree or another with the western lands, having ventured there on hunting and trading trips over the centuries and perhaps for millennia. By the time of Andrew Jackson, groups of

Cherokees and other southern tribes not only had specific western lands set aside for them by treaty but considerable numbers of people making a new world there for themselves. In a process vaguely analogous to biological speciation, in which groups of creatures that become isolated from one another evolve differently over time, the western branches were developing their own ways, their own traditions, and it was not uniformly taken as especially good news that their onetime tribe mates would be taking up residence in their midst.

Astonishingly, an estimated twenty-five hundred Choctaws died of exposure, starvation, and marauding by whites during the trek of more than five hundred miles that three groups made between 1831 and 1834. Those yet to leave their ancestral homes for the new Indian Territory heard of the hardships inflicted on their people by the confusion and federal mismanagement of the journeys and chose to stay home, as landless squatters. Many of these finally did leave, trickling west throughout the 1840s and 1850s, leaving some two thousand in Mississippi, where their descendants remain on tribally owned land.

The Creeks were not at all interested in going west and in due course worked out an arrangement with the federal Indian commissioners whereby they would be permitted to remain in Alabama on

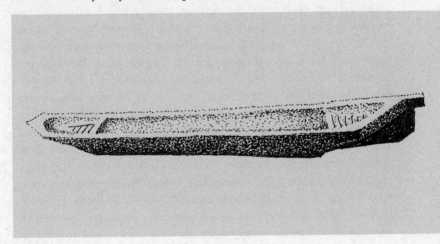

Seminole pirogue

clustered individual reserves (that is, towns). The federal government went along with this, knowing full well that the Alabamians would have none of it. In 1832, harassment by the citizens of Alabama included the forcible eviction of Creeks from their allotments by mobs, robbing graves of jewelry, outlawing hunting by Indians, and other measures that, after four years, led to a brief and disorganized uprising by some young Creek warriors. This was termed the Creek War and was ample justification for Jackson to send in troops. Creeks were rounded up and marched off to the west, forced to leave everything behind—from possessions and homes to the graves of their ancestors. Once again, some Creek holdouts fled, joining the Seminoles.

The Chickasaws agreed to go, but insisted upon a site report by tribal elders. On two occasions the elders investigated the lands in the West and found them wanting, but finally in 1837 they purchased the right to live among the Choctaws in the Indian Territory, sold off their properties in Mississippi, bought slaves and cattle, and moved. After almost two decades of discomfort at being part of the Choctaws, the Chickasaws became their own nation once more.

The Seminoles, mostly refugees to begin with who had already migrated into what was Spanish Florida, were looked upon with great suspicion (and land hunger) by the settlers of Georgia. Seminole towns had become a haven for runaway slaves, and indeed there was much intermarriage between the Seminole Indians and blacks. Georgia planters organized various raids on the Seminoles' northern towns, and in 1818, Andrew Jackson led a small army of American soldiers and Creek warriors in an outburst called the First Seminole War that persuaded the Spanish to sell Florida to the United States. By 1823 the Seminoles lived on a reservation to the south in the approximate middle of the Florida peninsula. The poor land of their reservation was not in demand but Florida settlers nevertheless sought their removal, largely for racist reasons. This was arranged as part of a treaty in 1832. Among other things, the treaty called for the Seminoles to begin leaving by 1836 and to settle among the Creeks. This alarmed the Creeks, who feared, for good reason, that the Seminoles might seek vengeance on them, and it alarmed the black Seminoles, who, for good reason, feared that the Creeks would enslave them.

Like other tribes, the Seminoles were split over the question of removal. On the anti side was a young warrior, Osceola, the son of a white trader named Powell and a Creek woman who had grown up among the Seminoles. Osceola was headstrong and self-confident, a flamboyant dresser and a persuasive speaker. He was opposed both to any emigration or talk of it, and also to the loss of any black compatriots to slave hunters. On one occasion he said, "I say, we must not leave our homes and lands. If any of our people want to go west, we won't let them; and I tell them they are our enemies, and we will treat them so, for the Great Spirit will protect us."

Good as his word, in November Osceola killed one of the tribe's leading proponents of emigration, and it became clear to the American settlers, Florida officials, and the United States government that the antis were by far in the majority. The United States sent in some troops to force the Indians to leave. On December 28, 1835, a group of 180 Seminoles hid in the tall grass along a road, where they waited for three companies of 108 soldiers under the command of Major Francis Dade. Beyond the road was a pond. At about eleven o'clock, the soldiers were stunned when the Seminoles rose up from the grass and poured fire on them. According to a Seminole named Alligator, writing about the attack, the first volley "laid upon the ground, dead, more than half the white men." Cannon fire was returned until the Indians shot the artillery men. Finally only three soldiers were left alive. They tried to build a small barricade or fort of logs but were killed. "The firing had ceased," Alligator wrote, "and all was quiet when we returned to the swamp about noon." The same day that Dade's column was slaughtered, Osceola killed the Indian agent and several others. The Second Seminole War was under way and it would last for six years of lethal skirmishing in hostile country.

Over the years, small bands of Seminoles would attack and then melt back into the swamps—Big Cypress, the Everglades. They knew the terrain and could disappear like shadows into a hummock of grass or into cypress groves. Whatever American military men had learned about fighting Indians in the South—such as establishing small forts in Indian country and patrolling from there—was of little use. The entire U.S. army at the time consisted of no more than eight thousand men and it had other important chores, so it was never able to commit the total of troops necessary. Many of the troops came down with diseases to which they had no immunity, such as malaria, yellow fever, and other plagues of the subtropics. But those soldiers on the scene did have the advantage of regular supplies, whereas the Seminoles had to scratch a living from the land as best they could and to trade with

Cuban smugglers and fishermen for guns and ammunition. At this time, the Seminoles apparently gave up the old Creek log cabin and returned to the local form of house, called a *chickee*. These are open-air houses with thatched roofs that archaeologists have found were in use in this region as far back as 2000 B.C. They are quick to build, less painful to leave behind, and are still in use today. So impoverished were the surviving groups that they evidently made clothes by sewing rags together, which later they would turn into a highly original and distinct style of clothing akin to the finest quilting.

During this extended if sporadic war, those Seminoles who were captured were soon shipped off to the Indian Territory—in all, some four thousand. In one dark moment, on October 25, 1837, Osceola was persuaded to approach with a white flag of truce to parley with the officer then in charge of the Florida campaign, Brevet Major General Thomas Jesup. The fighting had worn out the Seminoles, and Osceola was apparently ready to discuss (if not agree to) removal. But 250 soldiers formed a circle around Osceola and captured him and his party without a shot fired, hauling them all off to jail, but for two who escaped and spread the word. Osceola was already ill, probably with malaria, and died later in prison. In the meantime, people throughout the East protested the duplicitous manner of Osceola's capture and Jesup would never escape criticism for the rest of his life. These protests were among the first signs of an eastern faction of the American public that would over time become champions of the Indians even as they were being forcefully shoved aside thousands of miles from the east coast (from which, of course, they were long gone).

The Seminoles had other leaders, though, and continued to resist. Finally in 1842, President John Tyler concluded that rousting the remainder out—in all about five hundred—was hopeless. The American troops simply were withdrawn. This was, in fact, the only permanently successful resistance that any American Indians ever accomplished against the United States. It and the Pueblo Rebellion of 1680 stand as the only times armed resistance against Europeans paid off. The remaining five hundred Seminoles agreed to move to what today are three reservations in the South, near Big Cypress Swamp and the Everglades, and their descendants, Seminoles and Miccosukees, live there to this day.

All of these forced migrations were catastrophic for the émigrés. In most cases, when groups of them were rounded up they were put in what amounted to concentration camps, where maltreatment from exposure, hunger, and rape was common. Along the way they were preyed on by horse thieves and mobs of lawless settlers, lethal diseases, and in many instances foul winter weather for which they were not prepared. Such conditions are invariably worse for children, the elderly, and women, especially pregnant women. No one knows exactly how many died in these treks, and the despair and agony of these removals is beyond most people's imagination today. In no case was the despair and agony of removal any greater (or better documented) than that of the Cherokees, the last of the five major southern tribes to go.

During the half century or so before the 1830s, thousands of Cherokees had voluntarily moved west of the Mississippi, establishing there essentially a separate nation, the Western Cherokees, also called the Old Settlers. They numbered some five to six thousand. In 1835, about sixteen thousand Cherokees remained in the East, the majority of them led by John Ross, who had been elated by the decisions of the Marshall court and refused to negotiate further with the United States about removal but, instead, depended on the goodwill of the American people. A small number of Cherokees believed Ross was naive, that the American people were essentially racist and that a failure to negotiate satisfactory terms for removal endangered the Cherokee people as a whole. These dissenters, including Ross's brother, in the capital town of New Echota signed a treaty on their own with the United States in late 1835 that called for the removal of the Cherokees to the Indian Territory by 1838. And soon enough some two thousand dissenters left. The vast majority of eastern Cherokees remained faithful to Ross and his vision of eventual justice. The treaty was ultimately ratified by only one vote in a hotly contested Senate decision.

In May 1838, however, General Winfield Scott was sent to oversee the removal of the remaining Cherokees, asking them in writing to leave peacefully and "spare me, I beseech you, the horror of witnessing the destruction of the Cherokees." Scott's men built stockades throughout Cherokee country and proceeded to arrest the Cherokees. Men were hauled out of their fields, women and children from the houses, prodded by bayonet along the trail to the stockade, their homes burned. Rich or poor received the same treatment. Cattle and other possessions were taken by mobs who also dug up graves to rob them of valuables. A soldier who participated wrote:

> In one home death had come during the night, a little sad faced child had died and was lying on a bear skin couch and some women were preparing the little body for burial. All were arrested and driven out leaving the child in the cabin. I don't know who buried the body.
>
> In another home was a frail Mother, apparently a widow, and three small children, one just a baby. When told that she must go the Mother gathered the children at her feet, prayed an humble prayer in her native tongue, patted the old family dog on the head, told the faithful creature good-bye, with a baby strapped on her back and leading a child with each hand started on her exile. But the task was too great for that frail Mother. A stroke of heart failure relieved her sufferings. She sunk and died with her baby on her back, and her other two children clinging to her hands.

The suffering continued in the stockades, which by June housed some five thousand Cherokees, who developed what was called "serious mortality" from a variety of diseases. The first groups to be evacuated by steamer had to be forced onto the boats, with children often separated from parents. About 10 percent on such trips would die from dysentery and other diseases. The Cherokee National Council soon begged to be allowed to manage the removal themselves. Their wish was granted and some thirteen thousand Cherokees began to move out, mostly across Tennessee, Kentucky, southern Illinois, and Missouri, to the Indian Territory. Along the way they were beset by starvation, cold, accidents, deliberate murders, and a host of diseases ranging from measles to flu, cholera to colds. Few old or very young people survived. When the Cherokees arrived in their new country, they and the other tribes there were struck by an epidemic of smallpox. The $200 that Congress had appropriated years before for inoculating Cherokees had long since run out.

The Cherokee death toll directly attributable to the removal has been estimated at approximately four thousand, or one-fourth of the entire population. Nor were the troubles over. The national group led by John Ross contained by far the majority of Cherokees and expected to be in control of Cherokee destinies in the Indian Territory. But the Old Settlers had different ideas, and so did those dissidents who had illegally signed the treaty with the United States. Friction developed and erupted in violence when the leaders of the dissidents were murdered (or executed, depending upon the political viewpoint) in 1839. While Ross claimed to have had nothing personally to do with these executions, they led to violent strife between the factions. This Cherokee Civil War persisted until 1846, when the parties made peace and founded a new and united Cherokee Nation.

Meanwhile, pressures from settlers and land companies had impelled many people of the northern tribes to relocate themselves. Shawnees, Delawares, Potawatomis, and other Great Lakes tribes poured into Missouri and, when that became a territory, into eastern Kansas, north of the lands of the Cherokees. Even some of the Iroquois moved west to the Indian Territory, though many remained behind. About a thousand Cherokees had escaped removal by hiding in the mountains of North Carolina. A handful of Catawbas remained in their old lands in the Piedmont, a few Choctaws in Mississippi.

Those Indians who remained in the Northeast were engulfed. They inhabited small settlements on the periphery of things, forgotten little villages in New England where the remnants of Pequots and Mahicans interbred with other pariahs, the blacks. A few tiny reservations were also tucked away out of sight.

Today one can look at a map of the United States showing the whereabouts of American Indian lands and see that east of the Mississippi it remains almost blank. This was accomplished by the 1840s by relentless and often ruthless American pressure against people who no longer had the means of physical resistance. East of the Mississippi were only the tatters of what had once been. Indeed, east of the Mississippi, what the United States would continue to refer to as "the Indian problem" did not, as far as anyone could see, exist.

As historian Michael Green has pointed out, in the United States (a country by now only about fifty years old) it was the Indians who were the aliens, strangers in a strange land. European Americans were pushing westward into the Plains, snaking through those vast grasslands, trapping in the cold streams of the Rocky Mountains, exploring the coastline of the Pacific, trekking into the Southwest. By midcentury they owned it all.

CHAPTER ELEVEN

AN AMERICAN SOUTHWEST

The New Mexico Territory

In 1805, a Spanish lieutenant, Antonio Narbona, led a military
expedition into Canyon de Chelly, in northeastern Arizona. The
canyon is vaguely *Y*-shaped, one thousand feet at its deepest and
some fifty miles in overall length. Anasazi people had lived in open
sites and the rock shelters here and there along the canyon floor
above the small rivers that run through it. Navajos now farmed
there and ran sheep in the summer. Narbona's raid was a retaliatory
one, as had been the Navajo raid on the Spanish that preceded this
one, the latest in a cycle of attack and counterattack that went back
a long, long time. Spanish ranches were now encroaching on lands
the Navajos had long used, and the slave trade—capturing Indians
for domestic work or, if they were male, for killing labor in the Mexican silver mines—was alive and well. So what had been sporadic
violence was now far more common throughout the region to the
north and west of Santa Fe where Navajo bands were proliferating.
But this was the first Spanish attack on the area of Canyon de Chelly,
an especially revered place of refuge for the Navajos.

With Narbona's approach, the Navajos fled to a high and deep
shelf in the red sandstone wall of the canyon where they had successfully withstood raids by Utes storming down from Colorado.
But Narbona's troops went to the top of the canyon and rained bul-

Navajo rock art, Canyon del Muerte

lets down through the course of an entire day. The lieutenant's official report listed the killing of ninety warriors and twenty-five women, and the capture of twenty-two children along with eight adults. The rock shelter is still known as Massacre Cave, but the Navajo version of the carnage is that in all some 120 Navajos died, only ten of them warriors, the others having been off hunting. The rest of the dead, the Navajos say, were women, children, and elderly men.

Narbona went on to be governor of New Mexico, which, more than a century after the return of the Spanish from the exile imposed by the Pueblo Rebellion, was still a remote, poverty-stricken, and mostly forgotten outpost of New Spain. Indeed, the few missions the Spanish had established in Texas, as well as the aging colonies in Florida and New Mexico, were all looked upon by the Spanish crown as money-losing enterprises of a purely defensive nature. They were buffers between the new United States and other European claimants to the lands west of the Mississippi. This was particularly true of the three missions in Texas, inhabited in all by a mere twenty-five hundred Hispanics in the year 1790, a time when New Mexico boasted almost eight times that many.

After the Pueblo Rebellion, the Spanish had returned with sufficient vengeance to bring to heel the few pueblos like Jemez that remained rebellious (a task accomplished with the military assistance of other pueblos, for the area had returned to its normally fractious state of affairs). During the eighteenth century, the Spanish and the Pueblo people along the Rio Grande of New Mexico reached a more or less peaceful modus vivendi. To the west, when the Franciscans returned to the Hopi mesas after the rebellion, most of the people in the easternmost village, Awatovi, welcomed the church back. But not the other villages. Soon, in the year 1703, the village leader of Awatovi concluded that his people's reconversion to Christianity meant they had become witches, and he arranged for the other Hopi villages to launch a surprise attack, during which every male in Awatovi (including the village leader himself) was to be killed. Most of the Awatovi men were trapped in their kiva, which was burned. A few Awatovi families escaped and went to Canyon de Chelly, where they eventually became a Navajo clan; most Awatovi women and children were split up among the other villages. All in all, it was a deeply wrenching event of which the Hopis say little even today. Once the deed was done, however, the Hopis returned to their mesa-top villages looking out over the desert and remained relatively isolated well into the nineteenth century, free of Christianity and of most Spanish influence (except for some livestock and fruit trees), their ancient ways intact and unchallenged. They were considered *the* great apostates by the Spanish, who simply stopped bothering with them. Thus did the western reach of Nuevo México shrink by some two hundred miles.

The missionaries, settlers, and Spanish authorities continued to exploit the Pueblo people for labor and various forms of tribute, but the Franciscans had been sufficiently chastened to look the other way when the Indians performed their own ceremonies, and the two religions were allowed to coexist, as they do today. By the beginning of the nineteenth century the missionary effort in New Mexico had largely run out of steam, with diminishing numbers of friars in the province. The Hispanics and the Pueblos found themselves on the same side, trying to protect themselves from raids by Navajos to their northwest, Apaches to their south, Utes to the north, and Comanches to the east. Pueblo warriors supplied the bulk of the troops in most circumstances. The raids were sporadic, separated by periods of intertribal trade, especially between the Pueblo people and visiting Comanches and Utes at annual fairs at Pecos and Taos Pueblos.

New Mexicans continued trade with Chihuahua to the south, shipping wool, pottery, hides, and slaves southward for Spanish goods in a fixed-price system that left New Mexican traders permanently in debt. Over the years, a handful of French and then American adventurer-traders had shown up, trickling down from the North and East, but the Spanish authorities in Santa Fe made it clear that they were not welcome, basically maintaining the province in a state of isolation from other Europeans into the early decades of the nineteenth century.

Zia Pueblo bird motif

For reasons that probably would have meant little to the Indian inhabitants of New Mexico, the American and French Revolutions had lit rebellious fires all over the world. In 1810, independence movements began in Mexico and throughout much of South America that would soon doom the Spanish empire in the New World. Even as late as 1800, in the greater American Southwest, the Spanish hand had a grasp of only the thinnest strips of land. Spain could claim it held the pueblo country along the upper Rio Grande, and a small sliver of Arizona reaching no farther north than Tucson, where they had built a presidio (or fort) to guard the few missions among the Pimas and Papagos (people today known by their own name for themselves: O'odham). Over the centuries, Apaches and Yuman Indians had effectively kept the Spanish out of the rest of Arizona as well as large parts of southern New Mexico. Lastly, Spanish missions dotted a narrow strip of California coastline from San Diego to San Francisco. Spain had long since given up any practical claim to the coast of today's Oregon and Washington. All the rest of the area claimed by Spain, a vast stretch of land that included what is now the interior of California and its northern coast, all of Nevada and Utah, most of Arizona and New Mexico, and some of Colorado and Wyoming, was in the hands of untamed Indian tribes. Within a half century, this enormous piece of land would become part of the United States, but for a brief two and a half decades it was the northernmost range of the new revolutionary nation, Mexico.

In 1821, the Pueblo people of the Rio Grande learned that they had been given Mexican citizenship and a guarantee that "the person and property of every citizen will be respected and protected by law" and that Mexican administrators and soldiers were now to help protect them against the depredations of the "wild tribes." Before long, the last of the Franciscans left the region, replaced by a handful of secular (diocesan) priests, not members of an order of friars. The missions were thus "secularized." Indeed most of them went unstaffed by clergy except deacons, who could perform baptisms but could not celebrate mass or hear confessions. The Pueblo people also soon found that the Mexican authorities were far less capable than the Spanish had been in containing the wild tribes that ringed the world of the pueblos, and lackadaisical as well about non-Indians usurping pueblo lands. At the same time, the Mexican regime brought with it more liberal notions of trade. They opened New Mexico up to a strange breed of foreigners—mountain men and traders, who began arriving via the Santa Fe Trail from Saint Louis and pressing their commercial interests south into Chihuahua.

On August 18, 1846, a twenty-seven-hundred-man American army called the Army of the West, led by General Stephen W. Kearny, arrived unopposed in Santa Fe to occupy the territory of New Mexico and set up a civilian government, one of the early maneuvers of the Mexican War. Indians were not allowed citizenship in the United States, so the Pueblo citizens of Mexico soon became noncitizens again. Two years after the hostilities with Mexico had petered out, the United States dictated the terms of the peace. The Treaty of Guadalupe Hidalgo was proclaimed on July 4, 1848. In it, the Pueblos and others in the new U.S. territories were to have "free enjoyment of their liberty and property." The treaty also promised that the Pueblos would continue to possess whatever lands they had been given in grants by the king of Spain and the Republic of Mexico. The Pueblos were clearly village-dwelling agriculturalists and apparently devout Catholics as well, so they were not considered Indians (in the sense of wild savages) either. They would remain in an ambiguous position in the minds—and the laws—of the makers of Indian policy well into the twentieth century. For example, they were denied the protections of the various federal intercourse acts that protected Indian lands from usurpation by states (and territories).

On the other hand, General Kearny's announced task was to protect all settled New Mexicans from the depredations of the savages, and the peaceful Pueblo people were included as New Mexicans. To this end he and his successors endeavored to make treaties with the Navajos and Apaches, and they repeated the same mistake that British and Spanish treaty makers had been making since the outset. They would deal with an Indian leader, assuming that he was the chief of all the people in the tribe. But like so many other Indian peoples from time immemorial, the Navajos and Apaches were loosely affiliated, autonomous bands, and no one spoke for all of them. Typically a Navajo band that was relatively wealthy (in sheep) and settled would see the value of peace and make a treaty with the soldiers. Then another, less settled band would go forth seeking vengeance for some crime against them, and the Americans learned that the word of a Navajo "chief" was no good. And then soldiers would go forth to exact punishment, as often as not attacking a peaceful band and thereby confirming that white men were not to be trusted. To better control the raiding, the army established forts in Indian country, such as Fort Defiance in northeastern Arizona (still at the time part of the New Mexico Territory), but matters continued to deteriorate. In 1860, two thousand Navajo warriors—a wholly unprecedented gathering—attacked Fort Defiance. After nearly succeeding, the Navajos were driven off, suffering major losses from the United States artillery. It appeared to the Navajos that though they had lost the battle they had somehow won the war. Soon the blue-shirted troops abandoned Fort Defiance and other forts throughout the region. A more important task awaited the troops to the east—the Civil War.

Navajos and Apaches now began to raid undeterred. To the south, a group of Apaches called Chiricahuas, led by a man named Cochise, had been cooperating with the white Americans who had begun streaming through their country in southeastern Arizona. Precious metals had been discovered not just in California but in the northern hills and mountains of Arizona. The rush west was on. As for Cochise, so long as the Americans kept going and did not interfere with the Chiricahuas' raids south against the Mexicans, he gave no one any trouble. Yet in February 1861, Cochise's Chiricahuas were erroneously blamed for the abduction of a white child and the theft of some cattle. A hotheaded army lieutenant called for a parley, only to arrest Cochise and his small party and accuse him of lying. To an Apache, a liar is utterly hateful, and not fit to carry even a message. Furious, Cochise escaped, captured three soldiers, and offered them to the army in return for his companions (including his wife and son) who had not escaped. The lieutenant refused and hung three Apache men, letting the wife and child go free. Cochise responded by killing the three soldiers. A war of terror and vengeance was unleashed, and soon enough the Chiricahuas' lightning raids on ranchers, miners, Americans, and Mexicans went unopposed once the soldiers manning forts in the area disappeared. The only safe place in the region was Tucson, and even there the few inhabitants lived in a state of terror. This installment of the Chiricahuas' attempt to keep their ancestral lands free of interference would last eleven years in all, nine years after the American soldiers returned to the Southwest.

In 1863, General James H. Carleton was ordered to lead a regiment of California volunteers into New Mexico to decide matters there for the Union (a task that had already been taken care of by the locals) and to put an end to the raiding by "savages." His plan was to round up the Apaches and Navajos and stow them on a forty-square-mile reservation along the Pecos River in eastern new Mexico, a place called Bosque Redondo and known also as Fort Sumner. To this end, he employed the famous mountain man and Indian agent Colonel Kit Carson, of Taos, to start with the Mescalero Apaches in southeastern New Mexico. With local volunteers, Carson promptly ran some five hundred Mescaleros into Fort Sumner. He then set out for Navajo land, ordered by Carleton to explain that the Navajos had two options: surrender or be exterminated.

The campaign began in the autumn of 1863, with Carson's troops systematically destroying cornfields, fruit trees, and sheep by the thousands, and killing at least three hundred Navajos. Another seven hundred were captured. In January, Carson led his men through Canyon de Chelly, destroying fields, orchards, and livestock. The unstoppable invasion of the Navajos' most secure refuge essentially broke their spirit. (About two thousand Navajos, however, escaped and fled into the Grand Canyon and Utah.) By spring of 1864, a series of deportations began, called the Long Walk, one of the most traumatic events in all of Navajo history. In all, eighty-five hundred men, women, and children were marched hundreds of miles to Fort Sumner, what amounted to a concentration camp, there to learn (in Carleton's words) "the arts of peace" and "the truths of Christianity." There, the general said, they would learn the skills of the farmer, and once the old ones had died, they would become "the happiest and most delightfully located pueblo of Indians in New Mexico."

In fact, about 10 percent of the marchers died on the way—from dysentery, fatigue, exposure, and murder. Stragglers were picked off by Hispanic slavers while the soldiers looked on. Complainers were simply shot. In one incident the army evidently would not allow a pause in the march for a young woman to give birth. She paused anyway and was shot by one of the soldiers. Many more would die at Fort Sumner during an ordeal that would continue for four years until even the New Mexicans themselves rose up in protest.

Meanwhile Carleton turned his attentions south, trying to stem the marauding by the Chiricahuas. In this he had virtually no success. A contingent of his soldiers was ambushed at Apache Pass, and he was shorthanded to begin with, what with most soldiers still engaged in the Civil War. And they were up against a remarkable enemy in a hostile and sometimes bewildering landscape. As one officer explained about the Chiricahuas:

> They can live on the cactus; they can go more than forty-eight hours without water; they know every water-hole and every foot of ground in this vast extent of country; they have incredible powers of endurance; they run in small bands, scattering at the first indications of pursuit. What can the United States soldier, mounted on his heavy horse, with the necessary forage, rations, and camp equipment do against this supple, untiring foe? Nothing, absolutely nothing. It is no exaggeration to say that these fiends can travel, week in and week out, at a rate of seventy miles a day, and this over the most barren and desolate country imaginable. One week of such work will kill the average soldier and his horse; the Apache thrives on it.

In 1848, Mexico had ceded about one-fourth of today's lower forty-eight to the United States. Mexicans and many American historians have since looked upon this treaty as something akin to highway robbery. Yet most of the lands ceded had barely even been visited by Spaniards or Mexicans, much less settled. They were inhabited by Indian tribes, very few of which had ever been subdued by Europeans or Americans. In the New Mexico Territory, especially in its southern reaches where the Chiricahua Apaches roamed, the Americans might have been forgiven for thinking they had bitten off more than they could comfortably chew.

Pariahs and Paiutes

It was not just Indians whom the new nation of the United States was bent on running off. In 1847, just after the hostilities between the United States and Mexico had stopped, a charismatic leader named Brigham Young led members of the Church of Jesus Christ of Latter-day Saints into Utah. The Mormons, as they came to be called, had suffered religious persecution, violence, and ostracism as they sought to locate their communitarian societies in Missouri and Illinois. Finally they trekked westward to a place where they hoped they could lead their lives as they saw fit, beyond the influence of Americans who despised their esoteric teachings (for example, that God evolved from mankind) and who were morally opposed to their practice of polygamy.

In this new arid landscape, they established the state of Deseret, a vast area that included all of Utah, much of Nevada, parts of northern Arizona, and even a fragment of California—in short, most of the Great Basin that lies between the Rocky Mountains and the Sierras. Their hope for exclusive residence was short-lived. Other Americans were soon streaming through on the Oregon Trail and on their way to California, and some of these stopped off and stayed. And of course the Great Basin was already inhabited—by numerous small bands of Shoshones, Utes, and Paiutes. (Utah got its name from the Spanish name for these tribes, Utahs.) These were people who lived much as people had always lived in this difficult region. They were hunters and gatherers, some of whom also practiced a

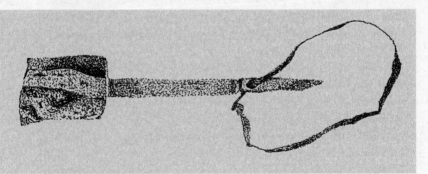

Southern Paiute war club

very limited horticulture near the springs that erupted here and there among the mesquite and creosote bushes. But these Numic speakers were basically a nonagricultural people.

The people who came to be called the Southern Paiutes were typical of these first inhabitants. Some twenty separate bands lived in the high desert country along the north rim of Grand Canyon, from Utah west into California, with one band south of Grand Canyon. At the time of the Mormon arrival they hunted anything from ant larvae to elk, and placed great reliance on gathered plants—for food and for fiber products, chiefly baskets, cordage, and knitting. The first Europeans to visit them were Spanish priests who arrived in 1776 to attempt a mission. By 1830, the Spanish had opened up the Old Spanish Trail through Paiute territory to link their failing enterprises in New Mexico and California. By the time the Mormons arrived in the area to the north, the Paiutes were accustomed to seeing Spaniards, American mountain men like the trail-blazing Jedediah Smith and Joseph Walker, and miners seeking gold in California. Added to the depredations of Utes seeking slaves for sale to the Spanish, livestock passing through with the wagon trains was trampling the wild plants they relied upon—such as marsh plants and, in drier areas, sickleweed and other seed bearers. The Paiutes took trespassing livestock as fair game, and the miners and others passing through took Paiute theft of their livestock as an excuse to shoot Paiutes on sight. Perhaps impressed by the elegant, colorful, and powerful Indian groups they had seen on the Plains, the people who streamed through the Great Basin had little but contempt for the Great Basin tribes. Diggers, they were called, a term of disparagement that was soon attached to most of the California tribes as well. Later, Mark Twain would call the Paiutes "inferior to all races of savages on our continent." On the other hand, when Paiutes rose up in anger and killed a settler or two, they were branded as exceedingly dangerous, marauding savages given to massacring innocent whites. For protection, some of the Paiutes turned to the Mormons, who within ten years of their first arrival had grown greatly in numbers and had established settlements throughout the Southern Paiute country.

According to Mormon reckoning, all Indians were derived from one of the lost tribes of Israel, and were thus to be honored. By 1850, Brigham Young was the governor of the Utah Territory and also took on the duties of superintendent of Indian Affairs. One of the first things he and the Mormons set out to accomplish was to bring the slave trade to a halt, which they did. They encouraged the Paiutes to live near them so they would be safe from the interlopers moving through, and in many instances made efforts to convert the Paiutes to the Church of Latter-day Saints. (This missionary work among Indians and others here and abroad continues: until the 1970s, Indian were told that if they did become Mormons, their skin would begin to lighten.) But regardless of Mormon protection, individual Mormons and non-Mormon settlers took over Paiute lands, particularly those located near springs and along rivers. The Paiutes were soon enough almost entirely dispossessed. In addition, cattle had begun severely overgrazing the grasses in the region on which the Paiutes depended for seeds to eat, and settlers chopped down much of the piñon pine forests upon which the Paiutes depended for nuts.

Few places were left where the Paiutes could live as they once had, and most of them had to eke out a living by doing menial labor in Mormon and non-Mormon towns and on ranches and farms.

Southern Paiute toy

Indian agents sent out to Utah from Washington, D.C., complained about Young's usurpation of total control over the Indians, but it was the Mormon institution of polygyny that eventually led to an outbreak of war between the Mormons and the federal government in 1857. In 1858, with the war over, Young was replaced as governor of Utah Territory and superintendent of Indian Affairs. But by then, despite some efforts to locate them on reservations where they would be safe, the Southern Paiutes lived a marginal, mostly landless, and penurious existence on the fringes of white society—and this would be their lot well into the latter part of the twentieth century.

The American West was turning out to be a big problem. Well before the Civil War erupted far to the east, the notion began to penetrate minds in Washington, D.C., that the old policy of moving Indians into territories west of the Mississippi was no longer functional. The West had its own Indians and the entire continent was now open to white settlers swarming westward. The settlers needed protection from Indian tribes that American settlers had hardly ever heard of before. Somewhat closer to home, many Plains tribes were by then raiding the farms of the relocated "civilized tribes" in the Indian Territory, making farming precarious and creating a situation where the tribes had to rely more on hunting, which in turn put them further in competition with the surrounding Plains people and, ironically and by definition, made them less civilized. The so-called Indian problem was by no means solved. Indeed, in far off California, Indian affairs were entirely out of control.

California Onslaught

During the decade between 1845 and 1855, the population of Indian people in California dropped from an estimated 150,000 to one-third of that—about fifty thousand. This constitutes probably the worst and most rapid mortality among a large area's native inhabitants since the first onslaughts of European diseases on the continent. One difference is that a great fraction of the deaths among the California Indians was deliberate.

The decade in question spanned California's transition from being part of the independent nation of Mexico to being the thirty-first of the United States. For the Indians, life during the brief hegemony of Mexico had hardly been an improvement over life in the missions. Once they got around to it, the Mexicans began secularizing the missions, sending the padres home and putting priests in their place who were not part of any order. In sixty years, the missions had put some fifty-six thousand Indians on their rolls; when the Mexican Republic took charge, there were about fifteen thousand still enrolled. The rest were dead. One of the announced goals of the revolution was land reform. The idea was to put such holdings as the huge mission properties in California equally into the hands of settlers and the Christian Indians. But the egalitarian winds of the revolution petered out before reaching so far north. The mission lands, livestock, and other assets were given instead to Mexican political favorites, and the mission Indians were dispossessed. They were left with few choices but to submit to a system of medieval-style peonage, working on the great *rancherías* that came about or in towns, or to head back into the hinterlands, where the other Indians regarded them with suspicion at best. As one old ex-neophyte explained: "I am very old . . . my people were once around me like the sands of the shore . . . I am a Christian Indian. I am all that is left of my people. I am alone."

Indian mortality in the civilian towns was high, as it was on the *rancherías,* and the Mexican military obligingly raided the hinterlands for fresh peons. It appears that some Mexican colonists and soldiers took to killing those who must have been regarded as surplus Indians largely for the sport of it. One Mexican colonist, José María Amador, bragged that he had invited a group of Indians for a feast and proceeded to execute a hundred Christians among them, and then executed a hundred non-Christians. In response to Mexican brutality, native resistance stiffened; raids and counterraids became more frequent; but even with such mayhem, disease accounted for more than five times the deaths as homicides. Smallpox, measles, and a host of respiratory and venereal diseases were all nearly omnipresent stalkers, as were hunger and starvation.

By the time of the outbreak of the Mexican War in 1846, enclaves of American settlers in California and some in Sonoma had already proclaimed California to be an independent republic. The Mexican settlers, called Californios, gave up in early 1847. Eight days before the Treaty of Guadalupe Hidalgo was signed in 1848, a man named James Wilson Marshall picked up some nuggets of gold from the American River, where he was building a sawmill, and the world of California was suddenly thrust into what today we might call fast-forward. Within a few months four thousand miners were combing the river. In 1849, some forty thousand gold seekers arrived in San Francisco by ship, another forty thousand came by wagon from the East over the California Trail, and thousands of others straggled in. So vast was the influx that California was made a state of the Union in 1850. By the time the gold petered out a few years later, about $2 billion worth of it had been extracted. An astonishing one hundred thousand California Indians had died. Most of those who remained were landless.

When California became part of the United States in 1848, the responsibility for Indians rested with the War Department. In California, it rested with General Kearny, who appointed three Indian agents and then marched eastward to protect the New Mexican populace from Navajos and Apaches. California was a long way geographically and administratively from Washington, and the federal government was no powerhouse. It was largely incapable of protecting the California tribes from the catastrophes that began immediately. Indeed, the federal government even financed some of the more calamitous events.

In 1851, the new state's governor, John McDougall, explained to the legislature: "That a war of extermination will continue to be waged between the races until the Indian race becomes extinct, must be expected. . . . the inevitable destiny of the race is beyond the power or wisdom of man to avert." In order to avoid slowing down destiny in any way, the state gratefully reimbursed any white man for his expenses

Arrow straightener, Tubatulabal

in raising a group of vigilantes to go forth and slaughter some Indians, thus suppressing alleged Indian uprisings. Large and small massacres were common, especially in the first decade of statehood, and while some of the Indian agents reported some of these events to Congress and to the commissioner of Indian affairs, Washington was helpless. Worse, in many instances, the federal government reimbursed the state for reimbursing the vigilantes. By 1860, more than four thousand Indians had been killed in such engagements.

In one of the most egregious incidents, called the Clear Lake Massacre, a group of soldiers sought retribution against the Pomo Indians, two of whom had murdered a white man who enslaved and abused a number of Pomos. They set out in canoes to an island where several hundred Pomos were camped and asleep, and slaughtered men, women, and children, much like shooting (or knifing) fish in a barrel. More than 135 Pomos were killed. In another typical incident near Humboldt, some vigilantes snuck into an Indian camp, shot as many men, women, and children as they could, and then cut the throats of those remaining. Next morning, a special government investigator later reported, "60 bodies lay weltering in their blood—the old and the young, male and female—with every gaping wound a tale of horror to the civilized world. Children climbed upon their mothers' breasts and sought nourishment from the fountains death had drained; girls and boys lay here and there with their throats cut from ear to ear."

In 1850, the state passed laws permitting Indians to be indentured for months, even years, on the say-so of any white man who claimed that an Indian was a vagrant, or that he had Indian parents' permission. A newspaper editorial in 1861 noted that "there are parties in the northern countries of this state, whose sole occupation has been to steal young children and squaws from the poor Diggers . . . and dispose of them at handsome prices to the settlers." A pubescent Indian girl could be legally obtained from these specialized kidnappers as a slave-concubine for $100. In all, some four thousand Indians were enslaved until 1867, when the Fourteenth Amendment to the U.S. Constitution forced California to disallow such practices.

Unknown numbers of Indians died from starvation and disease brought on by malnutrition. No matter where the Indians tried to go to live, the obstacles were enormous. With the end of the gold-mining frenzy, thousands of white men and women needed work, and took the more menial jobs that some Indians had learned to fill. If Indian labor was called for at all, it was seasonal, and for subsistence wages if that. With the season over, the laborers were cast adrift, and Indian agents' reports speak of untold numbers dying. Alcoholism was encouraged and ran rampant— some Indians received no wages but liquor instead. Diggers, after all, were replaceable.

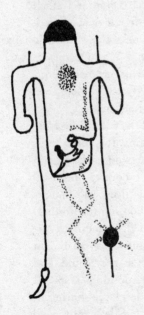

Chumash rock art

In the backcountry, mining operations destroyed the salmon fisheries, and out-of-work miners moved into farming. California was soon aswarm with white Americans, whereas under Spain and Mexico the inland areas had been more or less free. Now pigs ate up available acorns and other forest mast products, long a source of food for the tribal people. Fences prevented communal hunting. Food stores were often destroyed by vigilantes. Desperate tribesmen killed American livestock and were slaughtered in return.

In the face of all this, a small series of superintendents of Indian Affairs established a handful of awkwardly multitribal reservation lands, and by the end of the Civil War it was clear that this program was a monumental failure. The superintendents themselves were corrupt, slicing off pieces of planned reservations for purchase by their cronies, skimming from federal funds and from such necessities as deliveries of beef to the few Indians who tried to live on the reservations. These were typically located on marginal lands at best, making self-sufficiency a cruel dream. Worse, squatters simply invaded the reservations, taking over the best land. In 1866, a federal report concluded that the California Indians' sorry state "is the result of their intercourse and contact with the lowest class of the white population. . . . The Indians in this superintendency are placed, by circumstances over which they had no control, under peculiar hardships. . . . with no lands, no treaties, no annuities, no power or means of extricating themselves from the influences with which they are surrounded." Again, knowing all this, the federal government found itself unable to act.

These early decades in the new state of California were as close as citizens and officials of the United States would ever come to deliberate, region-wide, physical genocide. But that word also includes the death of culture, not just people. By the time (near the century's end) when anthropologists took an interest in the Indians of California and sought to create a picture of them as they had once been, their cultures had virtually all been scrambled like so many eggs, and all but the merest handful of Indians living in the remotest regions of the state had suffered through a century of unrelenting trauma and malevolence. That any tattered recollections of their original tribal lifeways remained constitutes a miracle that defies explanation.

CHAPTER TWELVE

THE LAST OF
THE GREAT HORSEMEN

The Big Treaty

A strange thing happened on the way to the final defeat of the charismatic horsemen of the Plains. In the late 1830s and early 1840s, and for a terrible reason, peace broke out between the tribes—or at least most of them. The tribes all had other reasons for making peace, but the greatest need was probably a smallpox epidemic, the worst outbreak of pandemic disease that had ever struck the Plains. It came on a fur-trading steamboat plying the Missouri River in 1837, and the death toll was appalling. The Indian agents had set out to inoculate the northern Indians but the medicine ran out after some of the Sioux were inoculated, which left the northern villagers to suffer staggering mortality. The epidemic took half the Arikaras and Hidatsas and reduced the Mandans from about sixteen hundred to less than 150. From there it moved north, taking half (four thousand) of the Assiniboines, some six thousand Blackfeet, and two thousand Pawnees. The Crows lost a thousand, and the Sioux lost many, but nothing like the other tribes. The disease continued to move, striking the Osages, Kansas, and others; and from there, in the winter of 1839–40, it ravaged the people of the southern Plains—Kiowas, Cheyennes, Arapahos, and Comanches. In all, about half the entire Indian population of the Plains was wiped out.

In addition to disease, the Plains tribes were being crowded from the East. Increasing numbers of whites were passing through and often staying. Homesteaders were pressing westward onto the Plains, pushing into the Indian Territory. Army posts sprang up along established routes. At first, most of the tribes saw little reason to complain of these intrusions, and many had agreed to keep the routes open, but the United States Army presence did nothing to forestall intertribal warfare. Then the Sioux made peace with the Cheyennes and Arapahos, freeing themselves to press their hunting territories outward to the west and north at the expense of the Assiniboines and others. The Cheyennes and Arapahos were now free to fight the Pawnees and the Crows, with whom they struggled for prime bison hunting grounds. The Cheyennes had a special reason to hate the Pawnees, for they had earlier stolen the Cheyennes' Four Arrows bundle, one of the tribe's most sacred and necessary objects. Continuing assaults on these village-dwelling part-time hunters left them weakened and in disarray.

To the south, the Southern Cheyennes made peace with the Kiowas, with whom they had been exchanging ferocious raids. This gave them access to better hunting grounds to the south of the Arkansas River. It also gave the Kiowas access to Bent's Fort, a major trading center in the Cheyenne country of southeastern Colorado. It had been founded in 1834 by trader William Bent, who married a Cheyenne woman. Indians, mountain men, merchants on the Santa Fe Trail, and a host of others used the huge adobe fortress as a major stopover and marketplace. Farther to the south, the Comanches, who had long been raiding the settlers in Texas (then part of Mexico), lost twelve of their most important leaders in a massacre that broke out during peace negotiations with Texans in San Antonio in 1840. Determined to retaliate, the Comanches realized they did not need to be fighting at the same time with the Cheyennes to their north.

A grand council was convened near Bent's Fort in 1840, with some five thousand Indians in attendance. Hundreds of horses and other gifts changed hands, and for a time peace reigned among most of the tribes of the Plains. Then, in only a few years, the waves of whites crossing their lands became a tidal bore. People streamed along the Oregon Trail now that the Pacific Northwest had become part of the United States, as had the huge region of the Southwest. Gold seekers flowed into California, crossing the plains in unprecedented numbers. The flood of forty-niners destroyed game, eliminated stands of trees, and trampled the grasses as they swept through. The Platte River Valley was turned into a barren strip, splitting the bison herds in two. To the south, the Santa Fe Trail became another such barren strip.

It was becoming clear to the U.S. government that yet more needed to be done to keep the Indians separate from the swarming hordes of whites. In 1849, with the Indians generally in a state of peace with the United States, the Indian Affairs office was transferred from the War Department to the newly established Department of the Interior, and the new commissioner, Luke Lea, recommended that the Plains tribes be persuaded to retire to permanent homes of "limited extent and well-defined boundaries"—in other words, reservations. Four months later, in February 1851, Congress happily passed the Indian Appropriation Act, which called for the tribes of the Plains to be "concentrated," and provided the then-large sum of $100,000 to negotiate the needed treaties.

A man well known as Broken Hand to the Indians of the northern Plains was assigned to carry out this new policy. He was Thomas Fitzpatrick, the Indian agent for the Upper Platte and Arkansas agency and a knowledgeable frontiersman, and he called for a grand council meeting at Fort Laramie, along the North Fork of the Platte in Wyoming. Some ten thousand Indians showed up, their tepees stretching for miles along the river, and people from nine separate tribes challenged one another to races, gambled, feasted and

Sioux horse fetish

caroused, and looked eagerly at the enormous supply of gifts that Broken Hand would dole out to them. By this time, the tribes knew that most of the gifts would be withheld until the Indians signed whatever treaties the agent had in mind; he would not initiate the council with gift giving, which was the Indian way. So it was, after days of speeches and rituals, that the tribes present (the Comanches and Kiowas had stayed home fearing their horses might be stolen) signed the Treaty of Fort Laramie on September 17, 1851. The Cheyennes referred to it simply as the Big Treaty.

The tribes were to receive gifts and annuities of $50,000 for ten years. In return the tribes agreed not to molest travelers or wagon trains crossing through their territories, and most important, to accept definitive boundaries to their territories. The treaty did nothing to keep the Cheyennes from attacking their chief enemy, the Pawnees, nor did it keep the Sioux from raiding the Omahas, Otos, and others to the east who resided in lands the Sioux had taken to claiming as their own. (By this time, while the populations of other Plains tribes had diminished, the Sioux bands had grown to some twenty-five thousand, from about five thousand a half century earlier. The various Sioux bands operated independently as before, but they were virtually all driven by the same forces: chiefly the need to expand into the hunting grounds of other people as the bison herds diminished and moved.)

Two years later, in 1853, Fitzpatrick arranged similar treaties with the Comanches, Kiowas, and Kiowa Apaches in the southern Plains, and two years after that, the Blackfeet signed the same kind of agreements. Also in 1853, a new commissioner of Indian Affairs, George Manypenny, signed treaties with the Otos, Kansas, Miamis, Shawnees, and other tribes of the eastern Plains region; these tribes ceded over 15 million acres to the federal government, which effectively eliminated the northern part of the Indian Territory, restricting it to present-day Oklahoma without the panhandle.

The Big Treaty (of Fort Laramie, in 1851) and those that followed hard on its heels have been interpreted as an American strategy to divide and conquer the tribes of the Plains. Certainly the Americans had no especially noble plans in mind for the Plains tribes, but they were already divided and were largely bent on conquering one another. In particular, the Sioux and their allies, the Cheyennes and Arapahos, were rapidly taking control of the central Plains at the expense of the other tribes.

One of the tribes that was consistently pushed around by the Sioux and the Cheyennes was the Pawnees, who seem to have taken some comfort, as the oppressed sometimes do, in stories that made their oppressors look foolish. In the 1880s, the Pawnees told folklorist George Bird Grinnell a relatively mild and amusing story of the Cheyenne blanket. It was known by the Pawnees and other tribes that if a Cheyenne man left his camp and, wrapped in a Cheyenne blanket, stood by himself on the top of a hill, he wanted to meditate or pray. No one spoke to him or went near him. One day, a Pawnee boy decided to go on the warpath (essentially a raid) against the Cheyennes, so he snuck up on their camp and hid. After a while he wrapped himself in a Cheyenne blanket he had somehow gotten earlier, and stood on the top of the hill overlooking the camp. He stood there for a couple of hours, when he saw some buffalo hunters returning to camp. One was on a beautiful spotted horse—what was known as a running horse, ridden only on the hunt or on the warpath. The Pawnee boy decided that the spotted horse was the one he wanted.

As was the custom, the Cheyenne rider led the horse into camp and up to his lodge, where he dismounted, handing the reins to the women and going inside. The Pawnee boy, still wrapped in his Cheyenne blanket with only his eyes showing, strode down the hill into the camp and right up to the rider's lodge. He walked right up to the women and took the reins of the spotted horse. As he had planned, the women thought he was a relative of the owner and was going to take the spotted horse to the river for a drink. As soon as he went over the bank of the river and was out of sight, he leapt up on the horse and rode away, having stolen this fine Cheyenne horse in broad daylight.

For the Pawnees, such grand moments were all too rare. Their territory (mostly in Nebraska) was continuously reduced, as were their numbers, in the increasingly violent cycle of attack and counterattack that became the norm on the Plains. Outbursts of intertribal war also posed dangers for white travelers and settlers. Also, many of these Americans were well aware that their very presence on the Plains, and particularly the hunting by whites of the bison, was at least in part responsible for the intertribal hostilities. But the Big Treaty was largely irrelevant, as historian Richard White has pointed out, chiefly because the Sioux had no intention of sticking to the boundaries set for them or of giving up warring on others who were in their way.

At some of the treaty signings, Indian elders pointed out that it might be increasingly difficult to constrain the younger warriors from seeking status through hunting in the territories of other tribes, and through raiding. Even sheer misunderstanding could lead to a violent outburst. In 1854, a young Lakota (Sioux) shot a cow along the Oregon Trail that was later claimed by a Mormon settler. A green and hotheaded young officer, John Grattan, rode out with thirty men to the camp of Conquering Bear, where the young Lakota was found, and demanded either payment or the surrender of the offender. Conquering Bear did not immediately respond. Grattan ordered his men to open fire,

Pawnee bear in stone pipe

and the Lakotas promptly killed Grattan and all the rest. The army then sent out a larger force that attacked several Lakota villages and arranged a peace treaty that kept the Lakotas quiet for a year or so.

All the while, the Plains grew more crowded, the bison herds continued to diminish, and the promised provisions and annuities to the concentrated tribes were delayed. The Plains would soon be in flames once again. By this time, many if not most of the best places to spend the harsh winters of the northern Plains had been taken over by fort-building American troops, and even those tribal people who stayed near the forts fared poorly, since the army was ill equipped to feed them. On the restricted areas where some tribespeople did attempt to live according to the treaties, the bison herds were generally poor if not altogether missing, and they were forced to go off-reservation to hunt. Most of the tribes, as well, were split between what would come to be called *hostiles* and *friendlies*.

It was not uncommon for the younger warriors to want to stem the onslaught of whites, while older heads, recalling such things as the astounding size of the Army of the West (twenty-seven hundred men) that had crossed through the Plains on its way to New Mexico in 1846, sensed that the white man was just too powerful and numerous and the tribes would have to accommodate themselves to the growing white presence in their midst. For example, one of the great leaders of southern Cheyennes, Black Kettle, was a lifelong proponent of peace, while one of the Cheyennes' long-standing military societies, called the Dog Soldiers, staunchly avoided settling on the reservation lands and instead insisted on the nomadic hunting-and-raiding style of life that had now for more than a century been the Cheyenne way. Conflict was inevitable, and by the time it broke out seriously in a series of wars, the Plains Indians were hopelessly outnumbered. By 1860, almost a million and a half whites lived in the West and in all some 350,000 Indians—of whom seventy-five thousand rode the Plains.

The major conflict was between the Sioux and their allies and the Americans, and the Americans would often be aided by those tribes that had so long been punished by the various Sioux and Cheyenne bands—the Crows, Pawnees, and Arikaras, who, in joining with the Americans as scouts or even as warriors, were fighting for what they perceived were their tribal interests. But even with such assistance, the American army fared badly in its early forays against the Sioux and the Cheyennes. Many factors contributed to the early military failures of the United States on the Plains. Primarily, the U.S. Cavalry was ill-equipped in terms of both their horses and their tactics and strategy to overcome those who have since been judged to be among the world's most accomplished guerrilla warriors.

Honor was given to a Plains warrior who died in battle (as opposed to some other way, such as disease or accident), but Plains warriors hardly ever went forth into a battle planning to die. It practically never occurred to Plains warriors to lay siege to a United States fort or other installation, for example, and in only a few instances—such as the battle at Beecher's Island on Colorado's Republican River in 1868—did a large group of Indian horsemen besiege a large group of dug-in soldiers, as one used to see in western movies. The Plains warriors were not interested in prolonged battles. In most conflicts Indians would sweep down in a lightning strike, and if they perceived that the battle was going against them, they scattered to the four winds. Even when they won, they soon retreated to more familiar ground to replenish their supplies of food.

It was inevitable, however, that the military tide would change in favor of the United States. The warriors simply could not have prevailed in any protracted war. Any victory was short-lived since they had no concept of holding on to strategic areas, like river crossings, that they might have won. They had no industrial or agricultural base by which a long campaign could be maintained. Eventually their weapons and ammunition even had to be obtained from their enemy. Finally, the bluecoats realized the strategic value of attacking the Indians in their winter camps.

The Civil War and Western Massacres

The primary effect of the Civil War on the Indian tribes of the far West was to withdraw troops from the forts from which the army policed Indian affairs. Navajos, for example, saw the troops mysteriously disappear from Fort Defiance, and the army left southeastern Arizona to the Chiricahuas. On the other hand, many members of the Iroquois Confederation joined the Union Army, seeing the war as an appropriate outlet for their long-suppressed military abilities. The most famous of these was Ely Parker, a Seneca known to his people as Reader and who rose through the ranks to become General Ulysses S. Grant's military secretary. Parker was the person who actually wrote down the final copy of the surrender agreement that Robert E. Lee signed at Appomattox, and it is said that when Lee spotted the Seneca, he said to Grant, "At least there is one real American here." To this, Parker said, "We are all real Americans here." Parker rose to the rank of brigadier general after the war, and in 1869 became the first Indian to serve as commissioner of Indian Affairs.

On the Confederate side, many groups and especially men from the Five Civilized Tribes fought for the South, though the Cherokees, for example, were split in allegiance between North and South. The archrival of the Cherokee leader John Ross, Stand Watie, became a calvary general brigadier for the Confederacy, raising two cavalry companies called the Cherokee Mountain Rifles, which fought more battles in the West than any other Civil War unit. On June 23, 1865, Watie became the last Confederate staff officer to lay down his arms, thus marking the literal end of the Civil War.

Before the Civil War, hostilities between whites and Plains tribes were relatively minor and short-lived. But as U.S. troops left their forts to go fight in the East, some of the warriors in some of the tribes took to more daring raids on settlers and other installations. They (and some white settlers) burned down some of the empty forts. In Texas, Comanches and Kiowas (and other Indians that had been forced into

Mexico—Lipan Apaches and Kickapoos, who were originally from Illinois) drove the white settlers back eastward a hundred miles. In 1862, more than four hundred whites died in an uprising of the Santee Sioux. Since 1837 the Santee Sioux had been forced ever westward from their original homes east of the Mississippi River. Stuck on a diminishing reservation, they exploded when promised federal monies and provisions did not arrive. It was too late to hunt buffalo, their credit had been stopped, and they were starving. Besides the loss of life among whites, some ten thousand settlers fled their homes, leaving twenty-three counties practically unpopulated for years.

The federal government sent some sixty-three hundred troops to put down the uprising, and while only a handful of Santee Sioux were casualties, once order was restored the authorities tried and convicted some four hundred Sioux for murder and other crimes. In all, 306 of them were sentenced to be hanged. President Abraham Lincoln intervened. Since in his view the crimes were in fact acts of war, most sentences were commuted, but even so, around Christmas of that year, thirty-eight were hanged at Mankato, Minnesota, in the largest single execution in the history of North America. (Each year to this day, tribes of many Indian nations, but chiefly Sioux, gather at Mankato for a pow-wow to commemorate these and other Indians who have died in wars through history.)

Meanwhile, in the central Plains, where tidal waves of settlers had begun to arrive with the Colorado gold rush of 1859, the Sioux-Cheyenne-Arapaho alliance, as well as the Comanche-Kiowa alliance in the South, had taken to making serious raids of wagon trains, ranches, and towns. Chaos reigned, and some (as it turns out, alarmist) authorities from Minnesota to Texas expected the Indians to rise up in unison at any moment and try to murder every white east of the Rockies and west of the Mississippi.

In one response to the raiding in Colorado (chiefly by Southern Cheyennes), a division of volunteers was sworn into federal service—the Third Regiment of Volunteer Cavalry, with headquarters in the town of Denver. Since it was to be in business only to put down the Indian raiding, it was commissioned for a period of one hundred days. For about three months it saw only one action—the slaughter of a small camp of men, women, and children. The so-called hundred-dazers began to be seen as something of a laughingstock around Denver, and they seethed under the rubric "the Bloodless Third." In fact, they were a fairly ragtag collection of lowlifes, but they were under the command of Colonel John Chivington, who had seen action in New Mexico, helping to drive a Confederate force out of the territory in 1862. Chivington was a large, burly man, by profession, a Methodist minister, who looked upon the rightness of his task with all the certainty of the religious fanatic. He devoutly hoped that the Plains Indians would be exterminated, and was determined to do his part.

Near the end of autumn, several Cheyenne groups, including those who followed the peaceful leader Black Kettle, came into Fort Lyon in southeastern Colorado seeking a place to stay for the winter. The commander of the fort, evidently realizing that he hadn't enough supplies to take care of Black Kettle's people, told them to settle down for the winter some fifty miles off, near the sandy bluffs of Sand Creek. It was perfectly likely that there were a few among Black Kettle's followers now who had spent the summer out raiding on the Plains. This was, in fact, fairly standard practice among the raiders—to split up and move in for the summer with peaceful groups of relatives and friends. But everyone in the region knew that Black Kettle's people were the most peacefully inclined of all the Cheyennes and that the militants were mostly concentrated in the north, in a place called Smoky Hill. The commander of Fort Lyon, Major Scott Anthony, had told Black Kettle that, in moving to Sand Creek for the winter, he would be taken care of, that "no war would be waged against them." By now, as well, Black Kettle's people included many people similar to Owl Woman, who had married William Bent and begun a Cheyenne lineage of mixed-bloods. Even though miscegenation was a horrid affront to Chivington and others of his pious ilk, he hired one of William Bent's sons as a guide. Two other sons lived with Black Kettle's people.

On November 14, the hundred days almost up, Chivington ordered the Bloodless Third into the field. They headed south from Denver to Fort Lyon, not to Smoky Hill, where militants were known to be camped. At Fort Lyon he persuaded the commander, Major Anthony, that he would go first to Sand Creek and Black Kettle's camp for the sole reason of rounding up whatever militants had joined them. They set out, more than 450 strong and with a few men from the state's First Regiment, on the cold night of November 28—no doubt with the words of Chivington ringing in their ears: "Damn any man who is in sympathy with an Indian."

As historian Elliot West has said, Chivington's regiments were, among other things, "cultural shock troops." There would be but one way of life in Colorado, and that would be Chivington's brand of the Christian life. The attack began in the early morning. The approaching regiment's clamor caused the women in the 120-lodge village to believe their winter travails were over because a buffalo herd was approaching. The siege of the town lasted through the afternoon. Black Kettle survived but most of the other Cheyenne peace leaders did not. The details remain murky. Chivington claimed that he had seen to the death of five hundred Indians in this attack, only two of them women, one of whom had hanged herself. Other witnesses and the Cheyennes put the number at 150 or two hundred, with many women and children slaughtered. Chivington said there was no mutilation of the dead; others said that it was rampant. In any event, it is now well known that Black Kettle's people, and the Arapahos who were among them that night and day, believed they were sleeping under the protection of the United States flag. The Americans lost nine in the battle.

(Another murky aspect of what is now generally called the Sand Creek Massacre is where, exactly, it took place. In 1998, Congress passed a bill that would include the site of the Sand Creek Massacre in the national park system if it could be found and authenticated. Faulty maps from the time and conflicting accounts left the actual spot in some doubt. Working with locals and members of the tribes, Park Service archaeologists probed an area some of the Southern Cheyennes believed to be the site as described in the stories passed down from those days. Near a place called Dawson's Creek, they found not only the sure remnants of a Cheyenne camp of the period but also twelve-pounder cannonballs of the sort fired by Chivington's forces into the village.)

Once the surprise attack and massacre were over, Chivington's men took whatever they wanted from the village, burned what was left, including the dwellings, and left. They did not proceed to Smoky Hill or any other site of militant activity. Instead they made their way circuitously back to Denver, where the *Rocky Mountain News* hailed Chivington's triumph as one of the finest among "the brilliant feats of arms in Indian warfare." On the other hand, the net result of this brilliant feat was that the Cheyennes rose up in unbridled fury and scourged the landscape for a year.

Meanwhile, Major Anthony, feeling utterly betrayed, later asserted that Chivington had "whipped the only peaceful Indians in the country," even pointing out that Chivington's claim that his men had toiled though deep snow to effect this triumph was a lie. "The weather was . . . delightful for this time of year," the commander said. Later the U.S. government condemned Chivington's "gross and wanton outrages" at Sand Creek (he had by then resigned from the army and was beyond punitive reach) and tried, however feebly, to make amends, but it was far too late.

The succeeding Cheyenne-Arapaho war ended in the fall of 1865 when the tribes signed treaties with the United States not unlike those they had signed before—with promises of annuities and assistance, promises to stay on a reservation. Black Kettle was one of the signatories, ever optimistic that things could be worked out somehow. (He was killed a couple of years later in a battle with a flamboyant young cavalry officer, George Custer, in a wholly unwarranted attack on his village.) The Cheyenne-Arapaho war cost the federal, territorial, and state governments some $30 million. In its second and last year, 1865, with some eight thousand American soldiers in the field, it led to the death of about fifteen Indians at an expense, estimated the commissioner of Indian Affairs, "of more than a million dollars apiece"—probably the most expensive campaign ever waged by the United States in terms of kills-to-dollars ratio. Also, it was less a war that anyone had won than, militarily, a draw. But even so, most elements of the Cheyenne way of life, invented little more than a century before for an existence on the Plains, were now doomed. The day was not far off when Cheyenne warriors and hunters would ride free, fierce, and flamboyant over the windswept Plains under the limitless vault of the sky no more.

Peace Policy and Warfare on the Plains

That same year, 1865, the Comanches, Kiowas, and Kiowa Apaches signed treaties in which they accepted a reservation south of the Cheyennes, and nine separate Sioux groups also agreed to remain well to the north of the Platte River and its trails west. But almost immediately the Oglala Sioux, led by Red Cloud, began open resistance to the construction of forts and of a road running through their hunting grounds near the Powder River to the recently discovered gold fields in Montana. Red Cloud's warriors harassed troops and wagon trains, isolated the forts, and then destroyed an entire army relief party. This, of course, came to be called a massacre by white Americans. The embarrassment of such a loss to the Indians did not, as one might expect, lead to immediate revenge by the army but to a congressional investigation of the reasons for the Indian problems in the West. The investigation turned up a long list of treaty abuses by the federal government and the white settlers, and this led in turn to another round of peace treaties replete with fresh promises. As well, in late 1867 the army agreed to abandon the forts and the road to Montana—a rare victory for the Indians, however short-lived—and eventually even Red Cloud agreed to a treaty. Meanwhile, the government had created the Great Sioux Reservation (essentially the eastern half of South Dakota) and large numbers of Sioux took up residence there. But not all.

Followers of some Sioux leaders such as Sitting Bull and Crazy Horse remained on the loose, west of the Black Hills, hunting and raiding. Similarly several Cheyenne groups held out and continued their traditional attacks on the Pawnees and others. To the south, about a third of the Comanches, including the band led by Quanah Parker (son of a white woman who was captured as a girl and grew up as a Comanche), continued raiding in Texas, as did Satanta's Kiowas. The army's response was to call for total war on the Indians. General William T. Sherman, of Civil War fame (the *T* standing for Tecumseh, ironically enough), now commander of the Division of the Missouri—the armies on the Plains—determined that all Indians should be herded by force into the already crowded Indian Territory. The creation of some of the most important divisions enlisted to achieve this goal arose from the quiet and largely uncelebrated heroism of black troops in the Civil War.

Most of the work of fighting Indians involved chasing them endlessly and frustratingly over the dusty Plains. It was extremely tedious and unrewarding duty, since one might spend weeks or months in the saddle without ever making contact with the enemy. The desertion rate in the western armies in this period often reached as high as 30 percent. So arduous and tiring was the job that soon after the Civil War concluded, some of the task of chasing down "wild" Indians was assigned to the Buffalo Soldiers, so-called because the Cheyennes saw the similarity between the black troopers' curly hair and that of the bison. In all, two black infantry and two black cavalry divisions were formed, and they came to be known as the most effective Indian fighters in the West, despite the less than excellent mounts and cast-off equipment they received, along with poor food, severe discipline, and the most lonely postings. Even so, their desertion rate was by far the lowest in the frontier army. They were relentless in pursuit of their foes, and eleven of them received the Congressional Medal of Honor. The Buffalo Soldiers were always led by white officers, however. An up-and-coming officer, George Custer, whose famous comeuppance at the hands of the Plains Indians lay in the future, was offered the command of one of the black cavalry divisions and turned it down, believing it was not the best way to become a general officer. On the other hand, well after the Indians were subdued and living mostly on reservations, another white officer literally made a name for himself by leading the Buffalo Soldiers into Mexico to punish Pancho Villa for a 1914 raid on the United States. This was General "Black Jack" Pershing, so nicknamed because of his preference for the black troops. In any event, as the Indian wars raged throughout the West, it was the Buffalo Soldiers who delivered the final crushing blows to several Plains tribes and later to those in Texas and the Southwest, in particular the Mescalero Apaches.

The Buffalo Soldiers were capable of traveling light and long in pursuit of their quarry, but for the most part, the U.S. Cavalry began at a disadvantage in chasing down Indians. The bluecoats rode large, strong horses, which needed a great deal of feed, and not just the grass available for the taking almost everywhere in the warmer months at least. The soldiers also traveled heavy, and a cavalry unit would of necessity be accompanied by wagon trains of supplies and materiel to maintain them in the field. Thus the cavalry was simply too slow to catch up with the warriors whose smaller, fleeter horses did fine on nothing but the available grass and who also had the advantage of intimate knowledge of huge areas of land. Such chases rarely bagged more than one or two of the enemy.

During these years, too, the Indians were often just as interested in stealing horses as they were in fighting white soldiers, as interested in guile as in heroics. In July 1864, for example, some Kiowas, led by their storied leader Satanta, pulled a sensational con job on the U.S. forces at Fort Larned in southern Kansas. They told the soldiers that their women would entertain the men by putting on a dance for them in the fort. The women danced, the soldiers ogled, and the Kiowas ran off with the fort's horse herd. When the soldiers went in futile pursuit, the Kiowa women ran off in the other direction. One can imagine the hilarity at whatever celebratory dance took place when the Kiowas reassembled somewhere far off with their new remuda.

Once General Sherman was assigned to the West and the task of pacifying the Indians, he began lobbying forcefully to have the federal government's Indian Bureau returned to the War Department, believing the Interior Department too prone to accommodation and peacemaking. In late 1869, the president-elect, Ulysses S. Grant, seemed to agree with him. But once in office, Grant changed his mind and the Bureau of Indian Affairs remained in Interior and in exclusive charge of all Indians on the reservations. The army continued to be responsible for those off the reservation. Soon Grant announced his peace policy, or what some called the Quaker policy, since it was a group of Quakers who had caught Grant's ear. At this time there was a good deal of sympathy in the East for the Indians and a fair amount of resentment over the heavy-handed way the army treated them. A popular paean to Indians began, "Lo, the poor Indian." Many people on the ground in the West, with dripping irony, took to calling all Indians by the name Lo.

Grant's peace policy parceled out on-the-ground responsibility for the reservations to various Protestant sects, such as the Quakers and the Dutch Reformed Church. This, it was assumed, would solve the problem of greedy white traders and others who preyed on the tribes. Of course the responsibility for civilizing (that is, Christianizing) the tribes fell to the church groups, which avidly sought to convert their charges. This policy (putting churches in charge of administering government business) was not at the time construed as a violation of the establishment clause of the First Amendment. (The Dutch Reformed Church, for example, got a great leg up on other sects in converting the Mescalero Apaches and remains the most important Christian sect there. They did have to compromise in several ways, such as putting a curtain down the aisle of the church so that men and women would not be in sight of each other as they worshiped, a holdover from Apache tradition.)

The army resented all of this, of course, especially since the peace policy was not any more effective than any other in keeping all the Indians on the reservations. Worse in their eyes, since the military could not pursue raiders onto Indian land without the permission of the churchmen in charge, some Indians habitually used the reservations as sanctuaries from which to raid nearby settlements. The army was thus hamstrung for about three years, but then large-scale hostilities broke out again on the Plains—chiefly the result of continuing encroachment by whites on Indian lands, and also the frequent failure of the federal government to deliver on its other promises. In many cases as well, these failures to deliver food and other materiel lay at the hands of crooked Indian agents on the reservations.

Up until this point, in various skirmishes and battles, the Plains warriors had acquitted themselves quite well. They had several advantages. Of course, they knew the terrain better than the bluecoats. They could live off the land, which increased their mobility, especially in the warmer months. Most warriors had several horses and could shift to fresh mounts as needed; a cavalryman had one horse. Personal initiative was a key element among Indian warriors. At the same time, the U.S. military men had a difficult time understanding the chain of command among Indians. In fact, in a battle, there was really no such thing; the Indians' freelancing and unpredictable feints and attacks were often bewildering to the bluecoats. When several bands or tribes were able to get together for a battle, they were truly formidable—as when Sioux, Cheyennes, and Arapahos all took to the field at once.

On the other hand, the bands and tribes rarely did get together because old rivalries, old hostilities were hard to erase. Without stores of food and forage, they were unable to mount anything like a protracted campaign, and as such military historians as Robert Wooster have pointed out, "They deluded themselves into believing that minor tactical successes would deter" the white expansion into their lands. And finally, they were nearly helpless when attacked in their winter camps, where their horses were starving or dying and their mobility and strength were at a seasonal low. They were prisoners as well as masters of their particular environment.

At the same time, the army was hardly a perfect juggernaut. To begin with, it was typically undermanned on the Plains since it also had to help force Reconstruction down the throats of the former Confederacy, guard the nation's borders, and attend to other matters of public order. Communication and lines of command were often weak, officers in competition with one another for promotions often did stupid things, and most of them were simply untrained for fighting Indians, having come of age in the mindless sieges of the Civil War. Strategic and tactical planning was often on an ad hoc basis, arising in response to a specific problem. But the army did have utterly superior resources, not just weaponry but also rapid communication by telegraph, and huge pools of manpower to draw on. It had learned that offense rather than defense, attacking in winter, and attacking with multiple converging columns were highly effective strategies. And finally, the army shared in the general notion of the American public at large, and particularly those members of the public who were flooding the far West, that come whatever may, the Indians simply had to get out of the way.

In 1874, in Grant's second presidential term, three thousand troops under the command of Colonel Nelson Miles swarmed over the Texas panhandle and waged what came to be called the Red River War, chasing down and harassing Comanches, Kiowas, and Southern Cheyennes who had refused the reservation life. Instead they sought to live the old way, hunting bison, raiding, and stealing horses; but white hunters were now in direct competition for the bison, which led to what might be thought of as mini massacres on both sides. To the complaints of the white hunters and the settlers in the region, the army finally responded. Wherever the Indians tried to pause, they were chased away, their temporary villages burned. It was the last major engagement to occur on the southern Plains and it was over by June 1875 when the last holdout, Quanah Parker, led his Comanche band into Fort Sill in the Indian Territory.

Also in 1874, the flamboyant George Custer (having destroyed Black Kettle's village) went on to confirm that there was gold in the Black Hills. The following year, while Miles was concluding the campaign in the South, some fifteen thousand gold seekers began pouring into the Black Hills. The federal government offered the Sioux leaders $6 million plus a $400,000 annual stipend to relinquish the Black Hills, their sacred lands, known to them as Paha Sapa, but they refused. Meanwhile leaders like Sitting Bull and Crazy Horse were attracting young Sioux warriors into a large force of nontreaty Sioux in the northern region of the Black Hills. Preemptively the army ordered twenty-five hundred men in three columns to converge, and war broke out. Just before the nation celebrated its centennial, the most celebrated of all battles between whites and Indians took place when General George A. Custer with characteristic hubris took up an ill-advised position on the Little Big Horn River and was promptly slaughtered with all his men by Sioux and Cheyenne warriors.

Within months, the Sioux and the others were all located on reservations, except for Sitting Bull and his followers, who fled to Canada.

The war cost the Sioux their beloved Black Hills, though they would have lost them anyway. Furious at the massacre of Custer's force, Congress decided it would provide no further funds for the Sioux until they relinquished these sacred hills, and in 1877—faced with starvation— the Sioux complied. The Black Hills were gone, and with them the life of the free-ranging Plains Indian.

Holdouts—the Nez Perces

That same year, 1877, saw one of the longest, saddest, and most heroic attempts by an Indian group to escape from the whites—the embattled trek of the Nez Perces from Oregon to a point agonizingly close to the Canadian border and freedom. The Nez Perces (French for "pierced nose"—it seems that someone early on saw one of them with a bone through his nose, a habit that must have immediately been dropped) had always been great travelers. While the homeland of the several relatively independent bands was in the plateau region where Oregon and Idaho meet, they traditionally went south to fight the Shoshones, north to trade or fight with the Coeur d'Alenes, west to trade with the coastal Chinooks, and east across the Bitterroot Mountains to hunt bison with the Flatheads and the Crows. When they got their first look at horses, they quickly adopted many of the Plains cultural traits and proceeded to become the only Indians to develop a new breed of horse, the beautifully spotted and durable Appaloosas.

Ever since the Lewis and Clark expedition came their way in 1805, the Nez Perces prided themselves on having never killed a white man, even though white settlers were beginning to turn up all over their homelands by the 1850s. Some of them had even actively sought missionaries to help them become Christians, hoping among other things that the new religion would assist in the hunt. In 1855, when the governor of the new Washington Territory called on them to restrict themselves to a ten-thousand-square-mile reservation, they acceded without much ado. Eight years and a gold rush later, they were told they needed to reduce their reservation to a mere thousand square miles, all in Idaho. The revision was agreed to by many Nez Perce leaders but not by one named Joseph, who lived in the northeastern corner of Oregon in a land of lush grass and pristine streams.

Joseph led the Wallowa band, and today the northeastern corner of Oregon is named Wallowa County. Joseph had no intention of leaving, reminding his son, also called Joseph, never to sell the Wallowa Valley lands since (among other things) his father's bones would be buried there. After the old chief's death, a good deal of argumentation ensued between incoming white settlers and the Wallowa band—but no violence by the Indians. Soon President Grant said that the Wallowa Valley should be exclusively that of the Nez Perces who lived there. Yet this order from distant Washington, D.C., was ignored and whites continued to pour in, with the Grant administration finally reversing course and announcing in May 1877 that the Nez Perces had to decamp to Idaho in thirty days.

Young Joseph, backed by his fearless warrior brother, thought it better to comply rather than risk the loss of life from the conflict that would occur if the Nez Perces refused to go, and won the day against more militant members and bands. But then a young Nez Perce man was shamed by his band into avenging the murder by whites of his father. As so often happened on the tinderbox frontier, this small event ignited a blaze of killing. In days, some fifteen white settlers were dead, and most of the Nez Perce bands had decided to fight rather than capitulate. Joseph and his brother had little choice but to go along, and so one of the most protracted running battles in Indian history was under way.

Attempting to execute the orders from Washington was General Oliver Otis Howard, a devout, one-armed veteran of the Civil War who was known as "the praying general" and who proved in the long run to be a lackluster opponent for the Nez Perces. He sent some troops to intervene, and when the Nez Perces offered to parley under protection of a white flag, one hotheaded soldier took a shot at the Indians, who—even with their smaller numbers and older weapons—promptly overwhelmed the white troops. Thirty-four bluecoats wound up dead and two Indians were wounded.

Soon some seven hundred Nez Perces (including about 550 women, children, and elderly) under the leadership of several war leaders spent a month evading Howard's troops along the Salmon River. Trailed by some six hundred troops, the Indians then fought several engagements, which they won handily, and headed for the Bitterroot Mountains, which, once crossed, would put them close to the lands of the Crows, with whom they hoped to join. The Nez Perce strategy, when attacked, was for the women and children to go ahead, pushing the pack train, while the warriors fought and stalled the army. It fell to young Chief

Joseph, who had not been raised as a war leader, to take command of the women and others and see to their safety.

In late July, the Nez Perces led their horses along a narrow ledge to get past a fort that some volunteers from Fort Missoula had built across the trail on Lolo Pass in the Bitterroots. The fort came to be known as Fort Fizzle. News of the dramatic chase across the wild West had reached the public via telegraph and newspaper, and many in the East, who complained about the army's Indian policy as both brutal and feckless, were rooting for the Nez Perces.

Once in Montana, the Nez Perces paused in Big Hole Valley, thinking themselves safe from Howard's pursuit for the time being. But the telegraph that let the American public in on the melodrama also brought troops in Montana into the pursuit. Two hundred attacked the Nez Perces, only to be driven off by Indian sharpshooters, but not before several Nez Perce war leaders were killed. By now eighty-nine Nez Perces had died, most of them women, children, and elderly who were overcome by the difficulties of the trek. The Nez Perces ducked south and swept through the now five-year-old Yellowstone National Park (to the apparent amazement of some tourists there) and then headed north, where they were attacked on September 13 by Colonel Samuel Sturgis and 350 troops of the Seventh Cavalry out of Montana's Fort Keough.

Once again, the Nez Perce warriors outfoxed and outfought the cavalry while their families went on ahead, and Sturgis gave up. But the Indians had noticed Crow scouts among the American troops and realized that a safe haven in Crow country was not likely. Instead, the best idea seemed to be to head north and join Sitting Bull's Sioux in Canada. Winter comes early to this northern country, and the Nez Perces had been battling the cold and the snow of the region's early winter. They made it to a place called Bear Paw, thirty miles from the Canadian border, where, believing themselves temporarily safe, they paused to gain their strength.

But General Howard had telegraphed again to Fort Keogh in Montana and this time one of the most effective Indian fighters in the United States Army, Colonel Nelson Miles, was sent in pursuit—he of the campaign in the Texas panhandle and lately of Sioux country. He raced westward and north like a free safety crossing the field on an angle to intercept a wide receiver. Miles was also inordinately ambitious and seen by his peers as happily unethical when it came to gaining promotions. In any event he led cavalry, infantry, and Cheyenne scouts to block the Nez Perces' way into Canada, making great haste lest General Howard catch up with the Indians and claim credit for stopping them.

On September 30, Miles's forces came upon the Nez Perces and attacked. More war leaders and warriors were killed, but the attack failed and Miles withdrew to undertake a siege of the encampment. Some warriors and their families escaped and may have made it into Canada, or may have perished in the snow and cold. Others were killed by Assiniboines. Howard's troops arrived on October 4 and the next day, with only Joseph left among the leaders, the Nez Perces capitulated. The bloody trek of seventeen hundred miles was over—only thirty miles away from the safety of Canada. On horseback, Joseph approached Miles (whom Howard generously gave the honor of accepting the Nez Perces' surrender) and ended a heartbreaking speech by saying: "My people, some of them, have run away to the hills, and have no blankets, no food. No one knows where they are—perhaps freezing to death. I want to have time to look for my children and see how many I can find. Maybe I shall find them among the dead. Hear me, my chiefs. I am tired. My heart is sick and sad. From where the sun now stands, I will fight no more forever."

Most of the 430 remaining Nez Perces were allowed to return to the reservation in Idaho, but Joseph and his immediate followers were sent to the Indian Territory and later to the multitribal Colville Reservation in Washington. Joseph's speech was widely reported and brought him considerable national fame and sympathy—as well as credit for masterminding the marathon trek, credit he never claimed. But he was never allowed back into Wallowa country. Instead he died in Colville in 1904 of what the reservation doctor called "a broken heart."

Holdouts—the Chiricahuas

At the time of the American Civil War, some three thousand Chiricahuas roamed an area stretching from southwestern New Mexico and northeastern Arizona down into Mexico. They lived in relatively small bands that availed themselves of game in the highlands in summer and the lowlands in winter, and every so often they came together in larger units under the leadership of charismatic men like Cochise. In their worldview, farming or fishing was simply not done. Their country was

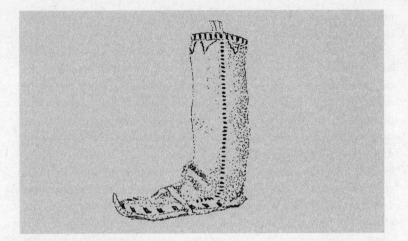

Chiricahua Apache moccasin

what is called basin and range, isolated mountain ranges like saw's teeth rising out of flat desert and grassland valleys, and they had defended it against encroachments from the Spanish-speaking south for centuries, raiding and being raided.

By the early 1870s, the Chiricahuas loyal to Cochise had also taken to raiding the Anglo population showing up in their midst, terrorizing wagon trains, towns, and ranches. They were, of course, raided in return. They were hated by virtually every non-Indian in Arizona and by the O'odham people too (then called Papagos and Pimas). But given the peace policy of President Grant, Cochise was offered and accepted in 1872 a reservation that consisted largely of the lands in Arizona where the Chiricahuas had always lived, in return for a cessation of raiding. The so-called Western Apaches had all been rounded up by General George Crook earlier and were located to the north of the Chiricahuas on a dry and unpromising reservation called San Carlos, while the eastern bands of the Chiricahuas were at peace at Warm Springs in New Mexico. But in 1874 Cochise died, which split the local Chiricahuas' leadership, and a fracas occurred two years later when a dissident group of Chiricahuas killed three white men. Fearing a general outbreak, the territorial governor howled to the federal government, demanding their removal. In October 1876, President Grant formally abolished the reservation Cochise had agreed to. A few months later, in 1877, silver was discovered in nearby Tombstone. The army set out in force.

Some of the Chiricahuas fled to Mexico, some were herded into the San Carlos Reservation, a grassless, gameless place with a brackish river and mosquito-breeding pools, where they were told they would be taught to farm—in a land that even they knew could support a few livestock at best, but little by way of farming. Many in the months to come would simply flee, including a man named Goyathlay, who came to be known also as Geronimo.

With a handful of fellow Chiricahuas, Geronimo (who was not a leader per se but a much respected tactician who had special shamanic powers as well) and one of Cochise's sons terrorized the Mexicans and retreated to Warm Springs. This brought federal troops down on the Warms Springs people and many of them, and Geronimo's group, were herded back in chains to San Carlos. But some of the Warm Springs Chiricahuas under the command of a war leader named Victorio went on a rampage and terrorized the country from west Texas to Arizona, as well as in northern Mexico.

Riding out of Fort Davis in west Texas, the Buffalo Soldiers went in pursuit of Victorio, who would later be cited as one of the greatest guerrilla fighters in history. Eventually, in July 1880, after thousands of miles of pursuit, they ran Victorio back into Mexico, where, almost by accident, he and his people were found, attacked, and annihilated by a Mexican force.

Meanwhile Geronimo was on the loose, raiding from Mexico's Sierra Madre and pursued vainly by four thousand Mexican troops as well as some American soldiers. In a highly controversial move, he and his group snuck back into the San Carlos Reservation (by then called the White Mountain Reservation) and forced other, highly reluctant Chiricahuas to leave with him at gunpoint. In the ensuing melee, many of the reluctant ones were killed by United States soldiers, and Geronimo became roundly hated by many of his own people.

General George Crook was soon called back to duty, and he managed in 1883 to bring Geronimo and his people back to the White Mountain Reservation. One of the restrictions imposed on the reservation was against alcohol, but the Apaches had traditionally spent a good deal of time under the influence of a corn-based alcohol called *tiswin*. Finally finding such confining rules too much, Geronimo again broke out with 130 Chiricahuas and about forty other Apache warriors. Most of the Chiricahuas, however, stayed on the reservation.

Whereas ten years earlier, when Cochise's reservation in southeastern Arizona had been abolished, virtually no whites lived in that region, now the Southern Pacific Railway ran through it, some four hundred thousand head of cattle grazed its grasses, and some twenty-six thousand Anglos lived there. Everyone in the region was in an uproar over this latest breakout. Crook, who had a great admiration for the military talents of the Apaches and who was admired in return as a formidable man of his word, called for scouts from the Chiricahuas remaining on the reservation, and they led what soon became five thousand United States troops on a ten-month trek in pursuit of Geronimo. Fully one-fourth of the entire standing army of the United States spent almost a year trying to catch a small group of Chiricahuas who numbered mostly women and children.

In March 1886, the renegades approached Crook for a parley. They were exhausted, ready to capitulate. Crook was under pressure to extract an unconditional surrender but believed he had room to negotiate. He told Geronimo that he and his group would be imprisoned in the East but if they did not surrender, they would be hunted down until the last one was killed, "if it took fifty years." The renegades insisted that the imprisonment in the East last only two years, and then they should be returned to their reservation. Crook agreed.

But the president, Grover Cleveland, wanted these renegades turned over to Arizona to be tried as criminals, which meant certain execution. Crook received a telegram saying that only unconditional surrender would be acceptable. While these communications were going on, Geronimo and some thirty others of the renegades bolted, and Crook told his superiors that a demand of unconditional surrender by the others would simply lead them to vanish into the landscape. While Geronimo and his group remained on the loose, the rest of the renegades, still believing that they would be stashed in the East for only two years, were loaded on a train and shipped to Florida.

Crook, whose reliance on Apache scouts had long irritated his superiors in Washington, was summarily replaced by none other than the vainglorious Nelson Miles, and with five thousand troops he pursued Geronimo over the next few months. To his credit, he explained to Washington that the desert-dwelling Apaches should not be located in so humid a place as Florida, but instead be sent to the Indian Territory. The governor of Arizona was unalterably opposed to such a plan, wanting the Apaches if not dead then at least as far from Arizona as possible.

The president and the commander of the U.S. Army, Philip Sheridan, insisted that *all* the Chiricahuas (now about five hundred), including those who had served the United States as scouts in the chase after Geronimo, be rounded up and sent to Fort Marion in Saint Augustine, Florida—except for Geronimo and the warriors with him. They were to be tried and executed. These plans were kept secret.

Eventually, in late August, two Chiricahua scouts approached Geronimo in his mountain redoubt in the Sierra Madre and got him to agree to meet with General Miles. The meeting took place on September 3, in a place just north of the Mexican border in Skeleton Canyon. Miles told the renegades that they would be reunited with their families in Florida, where they would have to stay for an indefinite period before returning to Arizona. The renegades agreed. A few weeks later, a tiny band from Warm Springs that had been on the loose turned themselves in to some men from the Tenth Cavalry, and the Indian wars in the United States were over. The last free-ranging American Indian bands to constitute a serious threat to life and limb were in prison or living on reservations.

(A few holdouts continued on, largely out of the public eye. Some Apaches, probably both Chiricahuas and Mescaleros, continued to live in the Sierra Madre in Mexico until the 1940s, when they apparently left to live among other Mexicans. One Apache man who came to be called the Apache Kid haunted the San Mateo Mountains of New Mexico into the twentieth century and may have killed a few prospectors there. The actual last free-ranging Indians in the United States were a handful of Yahis who lived near Oroville, California. They were able to hide from the depredations of American miners and others, and they included the famous Ishi, a Yahi man who "came in from the cold" in 1911 and was finally taken in hand by the anthropologist and believer in the ethnographic present A. L. Kroeber. Kroeber and Ishi—not his real name, which he never revealed, but a Yahi word for "man"— learned to communicate, and Kroeber was able to learn a great deal about Yahi life, while Ishi himself became a popular museum exhibit, dying in 1916 of tuberculosis.)

Once Geronimo's band had surrendered, it was put on a train, which was briefly held up in San Antonio while President Cleveland, hearing that Miles had promised Geronimo's band it would go to Florida, deliberated and finally gave in. The train proceeded east, but Geronimo and his men were taken off the train and confined at the Florida panhandle's Fort Pickens, on the opposite side of the state from the rest of their families, who went on to Fort Marion, on the east coast. Meanwhile the army had a bit more mopping up to do. Back on the reservation, the Apache scouts were disarmed and with all the others—the Chiricahuas who had not participated in Geronimo's escapades but on the contrary deplored them—were marched a hundred miles north to Holbrook, Arizona, and put on a train east. They, along with all the other Chiricahuas, combatants and noncombatants, and even children not yet born, would be confined as prisoners of war for twenty-three years—all in all, the most dishonorable treatment any Indian tribe ever received from the high levels of the United States government.

CHAPTER THIRTEEN

THE RESERVATION

By 1880, practically all the Indians of the West and some in the East were located on about one hundred reservations. In California and most of the Pacific Northwest, in the East and in much of the plateau country, the Great Basin, and the Plains, many tribes that had had little to do with one another or even were distinctly unfriendly in the past were sequestered together, as often as not on plots of ground where none of them had traditionally resided. And of course, this was also the case in the Indian Territory, which by this time consisted of Oklahoma minus the panhandle.

For the most part, the Southwest was something of an exception. Many of the tribes there were located on reservations that more or less coincided with at least some of their traditional lands—especially in the cases where those traditional lands seemed too poor in resources and other attractions to interest the white populations in them. The Pueblo people of the Rio Grande, as well as the Hopis, Zunis, and Acomas to the west, all remained on lands they had inhabited since before memory. Once the Navajos—or the Dineh, as they called themselves (the People)—were freed in 1868 from their concentration camp at Fort Sumner, they were awarded a large rectangular piece of land athwart the present state line between northern Arizona and northern New Mexico, a reservation that included at least some of what they referred to as Dinetah, the ancestral place of the People. Before long they began simply to spread out, mostly to the west, finally reaching almost to Flagstaff, north into Utah, and south almost to Holbrook. These remote and mostly arid areas were not especially attractive to white settlers at the time, and the spread of Navajo camps into them went largely unnoticed, or at least ignored. Today, the Navajos have the largest reservation in the country—the size of West Virginia—and they are the largest reservation tribe, with more than a quarter of a million members.

By the 1880s, the Navajo expansion had brought them into residential competition with the Hopis, however, and this led to even more strife than had existed previously between the two peoples. The Hopis, who had managed to keep an extremely low profile for the forty-odd years that the United States had taken control of the Southwest, complained bitterly about the Navajo presence. In response President Chester A. Arthur created the Hopi Reservation by executive order in 1884. This was a rectangular area of some 2.4 million acres, set aside for the use and occupancy of the Hopis and "and such other Indians as the Secretary of Interior may see fit to settle thereon." These words would become the keystone of a land dispute between Hopis and Navajos that has not been totally resolved at the time of this writing.

The executive order—essentially a stroke of the presidential pen—was now the means by which lands were set aside for Indians. It had been thirteen years since the United States entered into treaties with Indian tribes. As an adjunct to Grant's Quaker policy, Congress in 1871 had attached a rider to an obscure Indian appropriations bill that almost completely altered the relationship between the United States government and the Indian tribes. Passed on March 3, it authorized the Indian department to expend $1,500 to transport some goods to the Yankton Sioux, "*Provided,* That hereafter no Indian nation or tribe within the territory of the United States shall be acknowledged or recognized as an independent nation, tribe or power with whom the United States may contract by treaty." The rider added, with either blind idealism or transparent hypocrisy or both, that the terms of those treaties already in existence were to be honored. In fact, the rider was interjected to satisfy at least two complaints. First, the House of Representatives had begun grumbling about the fact that arrangements with Indian tribes, if made by treaty, excluded the House from the process, it being up to the Senate alone to ratify treaties. (An executive order needed only to be approved by a majority in both houses, rather than two-thirds of the Senate.) Second, humanitarian groups in the Northeast had begun to rail against the way treaty obligations seemed always to be mishandled.

This stealth rider (one of thousands that Congress has launched into the miasma of federal policies over the years) seemed to constitute an attack on the philosophical and jurisprudential bases of the Marshall Trilogy and the special status of the tribes, referred to as sovereignty. Rather than clarify the status of the tribes, however, the rider simply made matters murkier. For what could be given by a stroke of the presidential pen could as easily be taken away by another stroke. (Cochise's reservation was taken away by this method.) In this sense, the Indians lived on executive-order reservation lands by sufferance or whim of the government, rather than by something as solemn as a treaty, which is at least morally a bit harder to break. Even worse was in store for the Indians and their remaining fragments of land, but in the meantime, the tribes now needed to go through the long, uncomfortable, but necessary business of reinventing themselves yet again. New lands had to be sanctified and populated with tribal spirits and meaning, while the remains of ancestors were left behind. New ways of living had to be imagined and implemented. Plains Indians who had long since given up agriculture for the raiding and hunting life now were told to plant and hoe. On most reservations, most of the daily round was now dependent upon and defined in Washington, D.C., and overseen by white Indian agents whose paramount interests were often their own gain, not their Indian charges. In Washington, a great deal of pressure was exerted by so-called humanitarian organizations, which had their own notion of what would be best for the Indians.

The Humanitarians

In 1884, two years before Geronimo and the last free-ranging Apaches gave themselves up (they were not, in that sense, defeated—as Geronimo liked to point out), the U.S. Supreme Court decided a case brought by a Ponca Indian named John Elk, who had voluntarily left his tribe where it had been relocated in the Indian Territory and moved to Nebraska. There he registered to vote and was refused by the Omaha city registrar because he was an Indian. His case was based on the equal protection clause of the Fourteenth Amendment (by which southern blacks were being given some of the rights of other Americans), but the court said that Elk and the others of his race belonged to "alien nations" to which the Fourteenth did not apply. Indians could not get the franchise, the court said, unless Congress explicitly allowed it.

It was the achievement of this very goal—citizenship and the vote—that almost everyone sympathetic to Indians in the United States in the nineteenth century bent their humanitarian, indeed Samaritan, efforts. There was near unanimity that the road to citizenship (for which *the* necessary precursor was that state called civilization) had to be paved by the adoption of Christianity and the sense of civic responsibility that, the well-wishers all thought, arise only in the breasts of those who understand the solemn but liberating responsibilities of owning private property. Most of the Indian rights groups that arose after the Civil War were in fact made up of former abolitionists, whose original goal was at least partly fulfilled by the advance of Reconstruction policies that put blacks in legislatures and on the land as owners of small farming plots. So now the reformers could look forward to that day when Indians were citizens and private land owners, burghers who sent their own representatives to legislatures and to Congress.

For these people of goodwill and high principle, the point of all Indian policy, all humanitarian efforts, all the sequestering of "wild" tribes on reservations, was assimilation. (It is not that hard today to look back on the certitude of such beliefs and to scoff at them, if not deplore them. On the other hand, it was by no means an evil impulse on the part of its adherents. They simply wanted what seemed at the time to be right, which was that Indians would melt into the general population. By way of comparison, once the policies of Reconstruction in the South had failed and been abandoned—and even during those attempts—there was no attempt whatsoever to assimilate blacks into the dominant white society. They were set aside as pariahs: out of sight and out of mind unless someone took it into his head to lynch one. This pariah status—the condition of being without any status, just ignored, not part of society at all—was the lot of most blacks until well into the second half of the twentieth century. Indians would wind up, by white thinking, at least, doing better than that in many ways, and earlier.)

The most important key to civilizing the Indians was, of course, education, and early on the well-meaning makers of policy and those on the reservations who carried it out saw schools as the place where new generations of Indians would happily (or not) learn to shed their tribal (that is, barbarous) ways. In boarding schools and day schools, those run by missionaries or other agencies, Indian children would speak and write only English and wear only Western dress. Boys would have their long hair cut, losing an important sign of Indian identity. In most reservation and other Indian schools, these educational initiatives were more often than not ruthlessly applied. The children would learn the practical arts and the mechanical arts, and being away from home, often for years at a time, they would *not* learn from uncles and aunts and other elders the old stories of tribal origins, the old morality tales, and other pieces of mythological wisdom. In far-off schools they would be kept from the traditional rites of adulthood and tribal initiation. They would be bluntly and consistently told that being an Indian was not something they could be proud of. In off-reservation boarding schools they would meet children of other tribes and later intermarry, breaking down tribal identities and creating the beginnings of a pan-Indianism that, it was hoped, would be a prelude to breaking down allegiances to any particular group. The word "culture" as used in the anthropological sense—a kind of valuable group ethos—had been defined by Franz Boas in the 1890s but was not in wide use outside of academic anthropological circles until well into the twentieth century. The education policies set out for Indians by their humanitarian supporters, however, were designed precisely to bring Indian cultures to a complete end within a generation or two.

The first, and most famous, off-reservation boarding school for Indian children was the Carlisle Indian Industrial School, founded in 1879 on the site of a former military base near Harrisburg, Pennsylvania. It was run by an army officer, Richard Henry Pratt, who had previously run an Indian prisoner-of-war camp in Florida and who firmly believed, as did many others of this era, that the solution to the "Indian problem" was to "kill the Indian and save the man." This applied as well to women, of course. In addition to cutting off the boys' long hair and putting them in uniforms, Pratt forbade the use of native languages. Girls learned to sew, cook, and do housework, while boys learned to farm or be mechanics. Student labor was important for maintaining the schools and feeding the students. In the summer, students would be placed with white families, and upon graduation they were encouraged to find work away from the reservations. The standard use of corporal punishment for laggards or malefactors was what upset visiting Indian parents the most. Corporal punishment as a means of child rearing was unheard of in most traditional Indian societies. Many of the government-sponsored schools maintained cemeteries to bury the students who died there, the result of outbreaks of diseases such as tuberculosis that occurred in the overcrowded conditions. By 1899, twenty-five such boarding schools in fifteen states had an overall enrollment of some twenty thousand Indian students, some worse than others in terms of living conditions and educational programs. Mission schools and government-run schools virtually all had the same goals and much the same programs to achieve those goals.

The chief effect of the physical and cultural hardships imposed on untold numbers of Indian children by these schools was a sense of low esteem for their very Indianness, a divided sense of self. Elders were saddened when students would return to the reservation, unable to speak their native language or pretending to be unable. One Sioux woman recalled that the beatings administered by her Christian teachers taught a grim lesson. "They hurt our young and as we grew up we in turn learnt to beat our kids, which is not a good way to be." It seems that those children who could return to a society still culturally intact, where the old teachings and the old ceremonies still held sway over life on the reservation, had a better chance of overcoming the experience. The Hopi Don Talayesva, whose autobiography, *Sun Chief,* is a classic of the genre, was educated at the Indian boarding school in Riverside, California, far from home and far from the ceremonial round into which he would have been initiated as a youth. He was well on the way to forswearing his Hopi heritage in favor of Christianity and a fluency in the ways of the white world when Hopi supernaturals visited him and called him back to the Hopi way.

In the nineteenth century only one of the Indian organizations that sprang up, the National Indian Defense Association, held the idea that Indian tribal life was of value in itself, and it was soon out of business. All the others were staunchly in favor of assimilation as soon as possible. The Women's National Indian Association pushed education, social welfare, and the fulfilling of treaty obligations—all unexceptionable, even forward-looking goals in 1879, when it was founded. The Lake Mohonk Conference of the Friends of the Indian first met in 1883, convened by a Quaker who served on the federal board of Indian commissioners. These conferences, held annually until 1917, were a forum for members of old and new rights groups to air their views and influence government policy with agreed-upon platforms. Most influential was the Indian Rights Association, founded in 1882. It sent investigators into the field to assess conditions on the reservations, created a cadre of lawyers to draw up legislation and handle legal cases, and undertook a sophisticated program of public information about the state of Indian country. It was another strong advocate of education as well as legal protection. Like almost everyone concerned, from church ladies to politicians and even some Indian people who had gone through the white educational system and emerged as professionals of one kind or another, the Indian Rights Association looked forward to the day when the reservations would be divided among individual Indians as private property, putting an end to the communal ways of tribes. Once this was accomplished, and Indians were on their way as solid yeomen into the mainstream of American life, citizenship could be granted to these first Americans. Without seeing the irony of it, the Indian Rights Association and other such groups were seeking the protection of the tribes even as they advocated their ultimate disappearance. If the finest and most generous souls held so unreconcilable a set of attitudes, it could not be surprising that less generous people—such as western ranchers and cynical Indian agents—held less benign views.

The Ethnographers

From nearly the beginning of European contact with the native populations of the New World, the occasional priest, soldier, naturalist, or traveler made a serious attempt to look at the Indians without the usual blinders, to see them as they were. The first of these, or at least the most notable of his era, was the Spanish Fray Bartolomé de Las Casas, in the sixteenth century, who championed the native populations as having souls as well as merit, taking their cause to the crown and the Vatican and influencing both institutions favorably. Later on, soldiers had entirely different reasons for trying to understand Indians, their customs, and their thought processes. One of these, John C. Cremony, was a major in the California Volunteer Cavalry operating in Arizona, New Mexico, Texas, and Arkansas into the 1860s, and earlier had served as an interpreter to the U.S. Boundary Commission from 1849 to 1851. In 1868 he wrote a remarkably detailed and perceptive book, *Life Among the Apaches,* which, while hardly a systematic report, was filled with insight into their ways and written with something akin to awe. He wrote during the time that Mescalero Apaches and Navajos were sequestered in the festering camp called Fort Sumner, which he found an appalling "solution," explaining with some exasperation that "we have never striven to make ourselves intelligently acquainted with those tribes. . . . If this volume shall have the effect of bettering our present deplorable Indian policy, by letting in some light, it will accomplish the author's object."

In the meantime, curious naturalists combined their interests in flora and fauna with observations of Indian life as they encountered it. Earlier in time, John Bartram and his son William were among these, the latter pointing out correctly that the huge Indian mounds he encountered in the South were clearly recent, which led him to the opinion that all such edifices were the work of the Indians and not some lost race of Israel or Vikings or any of the other builders imagined well into the twentieth century by people who simply could not believe that American Indians could ever have been capable of such engineering feats.

It was the Bureau of American Ethnology that put at least a scholarly end to such speculation. The bureau was the brainchild of John Wesley Powell, a midwesterner who had been trained as a naturalist, lost an arm in the Civil War, and nonetheless led the first successful expedition through Grand Canyon by boat in 1869. During his adventures in the West he became fascinated by and later expert in both the geology of the Colorado Plateau and the languages and lifeways of the Indians, particularly Paiutes, who lived there. Before Powell, of course, many people had made systematic attempts to describe what we now call Indian cultures. Henry Schoolcraft made detailed studies of the Great Lakes tribes and Lewis Henry Morgan did the same for the Iroquois, studies important not the least because they dealt with individual tribes for their own sake, rather than thinking of them simply as one group of a more or less uniform race called Indians. Few white Americans were interested in seeing the Indian populations as so vastly diverse; instead, they preferred to see *the* Indian problem and seek *the* Indian solution.

It was Powell, with the Bureau of American Ethnology, which was housed in the Smithsonian Institution, who began long-term, wide-ranging, systematic studies of the American tribes, their languages, their material culture, their oral history. (He did this while also becoming the second director of the United States Geological Survey and putting the federal government squarely and ever thereafter in the business of scientific research.)

The annual reports of the BAE, which continued in existence well into the twentieth century, contain wonderfully detailed and useful information about a host of tribes that would otherwise almost certainly have been lost as the world changed for the Indians as well as everyone else. The general attitude of the investigators was like that of most other non-Indians involved with Indians: that their ways would soon disappear. And indeed, some of those old ways did over time disappear, and it was not unusual in the twentieth century for Indian delegations to arrive at the Smithsonian seeking information by which they might revive a ceremony not performed in several generations. By the end of the nineteenth century, some tribal elders—seeing the younger generations coping with new circumstances and going new ways—also believed their traditions were probably over. Some even saw the researches of the BAE and other anthropologists, such as Franz Boas of Columbia University, who studied tribes in the Pacific Northwest, as useful to keep their traditions from disappearing altogether from memory.

The BAE sponsored what can well be thought of as the first truly hands-on piece of modern ethnography. In 1879, shortly after the Bureau of Ethnology was founded (the word "American" was added later), Powell sent a group of people to the Southwest, and first off to the Zuni Reservation in western New Mexico. This was the Stevenson collecting expedition, led by Colonel James Stevenson of the United States Geological Survey, and it included his wife, Matilda Coxe Stevenson. The expedition was accompanied by a frail and rather strange young man named Frank Hamilton Cushing, who at the time was a mere twenty-two years old. Cushing had weighed a mere one and a half pounds at birth and miraculously survived to become fascinated as a boy with things Indian. By the age of nineteen he had already published a serious article in the antiquarian press, and he soon caught the eye of the Smithsonian.

The purpose of the Stevenson expedition was to collect daily objects of southwestern Indian life, and to delve into the Indians' more closely guarded customs and beliefs. Both the Stevensons and Cushing were pushy in their own way—as many (though not all) such field investigators were then and have been ever since. Matilda, in particular, was direct and relentless in pursuing her task of collecting material objects from the Indians. She would offer money and, if that failed, threaten reprisals by the military. She would even, it is said, confidently march into the midst of ceremonies being performed in the sacred space of kivas and make her demands. In one year, she and her husband collected an astonishing eighty-five hundred objects from the Pueblos. Meanwhile Cushing, who had expected to spend about three months learning everything there was to know about the Zunis from the tents in the expedition camp outside the pueblo, found that he could learn little as an outsider. So he simply moved into a room owned by the tribe's governor, evidently unannounced. This secular tribal chief, on discovering Cushing there, asked, "How long will it be before you go back to Washington?"

Except for an occasional visit home, it would be some four years before Cushing left for good. He became essentially the first participant observer, the first anthropologist to have lived among his subjects for a long period. From the outset, and in the largely antagonistic manner of competing naturalists in nineteenth-century America, he and Matilda Stevenson were at odds. Later, she would write on the back of a famous photograph of Cushing adorned in Zuni costume, "This man was the biggest fool and charlatan I ever knew." Meanwhile, in letters to his superiors in Washington, Cushing complained bitterly about the "presence in our party" (meaning Matilda), accusing her of "gossip and intentional malice" that he could "never cease either to remember or resent."

The falling-out was soon of such intensity that John Wesley Powell himself had to go to Zuni, where he soon persuaded the Stevensons to go elsewhere to collect. They did so, leaving Cushing alone to pursue his researches but also without any of the expedition's resources. Completely on his own, he learned the Zuni language, their own version of their history, and their worldview (that is, their culture). He barged in on otherwise secret affairs and made himself part of them. In one instance he was observing a supposedly secret ritual that involved flagellation and bloodletting. Upon being discovered, he began whipping himself, evidently to the surpise and even pleasure of the Zunis. He became a prominent member of the tribe's deliberative councils as well as a member of the Bow priesthood, a secret warrior society, and the only white man ever to be so included. He became so staunch a defender of the Zuni land and life that at least once he took a shot at someone he thought was intruding. He lobbied so successfully to keep ranchers and others (including Apaches, who were still at this time on the warpath) from encroaching on Zuni lands that he ran afoul of powerful politicians in the territory and finally was recalled to the Smithsonian.

Cushing was unusual among the nineteenth-century ethnographers of Indian life in many ways. For one, he did not think that Zuni culture should or would disappear, but on the other hand believed it should be supported as is, not missionized or otherwise pressured out of existence. He became a forceful Zuni advocate in the greater world beyond. So Cushing, along with Lewis Henry Morgan and Henry Rowe Schoolcraft and a few others, started the field of American anthropology on the road to an emphasis on the great plurality of cultures. Other contemporaries of Cushing also were beginning to see the various tribal cultures as worthy, complex, and valuable in themselves, but for the most part they believed they were seeing the last vestiges of dying ways of life.

Matilda Stevenson was of this opinion. She later published voluminous descriptive accounts of Zuni life as she had seen it, particularly the domestic sphere. For this she had a collaborator named We'wha, whom she once took back to Washington as "the Zuni princess" to discuss the female domain at Zuni. Ironically, Matilda never knew that We'wha, while perfectly comfortable in the Zuni woman's world, was in fact a man-woman. That is to say, *he* was a man who lived as a woman, sometimes called a *berdache,* which is a derogatory term from the French. This was a role common in native America, such individuals usually referred to as *twin spirits.* Their inclusive treatment in their societies highlights the fact that in small societies every individual is valuable; there simply are not enough people to exclude someone for something as unimportant as sexual orientation. In any event, Matilda Stevenson was appointed a staff member of the BAE (though unpaid), which made her essentially the first female professional social scientist. Later she would found the Women's Anthropological Society of America in 1885.

This was all taking place at a time when white policy makers virtually unanimously believed that it was already high time the reservations were eliminated and the Indians turned into small-time yeomen. The faux Darwinian notion—savage, barbarian, civilized—still lurked in the minds of scholars, and most saw little reason not to hasten the course of social evolution along. Eventually, however, American anthropologists, who in fact owed most of the nature of their discipline to the Indian tribes they studied, would be among the staunchest supporters of the tribes in a variety of ways. Indeed, the relationship would veer back and forth over the decades to the very present, from love to hate and back, just as historians veer back and forth about many matters. Today, for example, Cushing, though one of the most successful ethnographers ever, is perceived by some Zuni and friends more as the bully and less as the preternaturally gifted student

Hopi tile showing anthropologist J. Fewkes

and pioneer. Indeed, anthropologists have not been especially popular on the reservations for a few decades, particularly with younger and more militant Indians who see anthropology as a vestige of an imperialist past. Meanwhile Matilda Stevenson's autocratic ways are often overlooked by present-day white colleagues in the glow of her pioneering role as a female social scientist.

In these early years of anthropology as a professional discipline, and well into the twentieth century, ethnographers visited the tribes in increasing numbers. (A joke arose after several decades, shared by both sides, that a typical Navajo household consisted of a man, his wife, their children, and an anthropologist.) Typically, these early anthropologists sought out informants who were old enough to recall how life had been before it was altered by European influence. It came to be thought that the tribes had long experienced a kind of pre-Columbian cultural stasis, what came to be called the *ethnographic present,* and this was the elusive picture anthropologists sought to reclaim, though it had never really existed. Preoccupied by this ideal, however, the anthropological community tended to pay little attention to the younger members of the tribes, precisely those who were of necessity the ones coping with the rapid and wrenching changes brought about by the need to adapt to life on the reservation. The notion of acculturation was yet to be imagined.

By the 1880s, some tribes had been on reservations for decades and others were just entering this new state of affairs. The effects of this new arrangement differed widely from region to region, from tribe to tribe, but further cultural adaptation, further social change, was the fate of virtually all of them. In this, as in all social change, there were winners and losers.

On the Reservations

One of the great geographical winners in the late nineteenth century was the Navajo tribe. They returned from the horrid ordeal at Fort Sumner to a reservation of about 3.5 million acres, which is to say an area somewhat larger than the state of Connecticut. It consisted of some but hardly all the land where the Navajos had lived previously and lay athwart the current border between New Mexico and Arizona. Within months they had begun to move beyond its still pretty vague boundaries—mostly to the west instead of back toward the heart of the Dinetah, to the east, in the New Mexican badlands. They simply turned up here and there with their herds of sheep, building their lonely camps among the mesas, grasslands, and canyons. By 1880, more than one and a half million acres had been added to the Navajo Reservation by executive order. By 1900, the reservation had been increased to more than twice the size of Connecticut. In all, there have been some eighteen separate additions to Navajo land, and today it is approximately the size of West Virginia, a medium-sized state of more than twenty thousand square miles. This is perhaps the most successful example of passive aggression in American history, for the Navajos never again took up arms against the whites. They just moved onto lands that were empty and, essentially, waited for squatters' rights to be confirmed.

The Navajo population grew rapidly, doubling from fifteen thousand in 1870 to some thirty thousand at the end of the century. Theirs was not land that was suitable for farming, and white Americans had yet to take note of its physical beauty or develop a tourist interest in the Southwest. It was mostly a region of arid lands, extreme heat, extreme cold, and savagely high spring winds, and no one at the time was aware of the wealth of mineral resources underneath its near-desert surface. The herds of sheep and goats grew enormously and soon began to change the nature of the ecosystem there. Sheep in particular were central not only to the Navajo subsistence economy but also to much of Navajo social philosophy. For example, a sheep herd included those owned by various members of the extended family who lived together in the camp, including animals owned by young children. In tending his or her own sheep and those owned by the rest of the family, a Navajo child had a lesson in the delicate balance between individual autonomy and communalism that is the earmark of Navajo and most other Indian cultures. When a child's personal sheep was killed and butchered, the child was honored for making possible the feast for the entire family.

For the most part, the latter half of the nineteenth century was, for Navajos, a good time. But for the occasional scuffles with whites at the borders of their land, they lived as they wished, little trammeled by the white world beyond. Of course, they had agreed in the treaty of 1868 to send their children to white-run schools, and a few of these were built. But given the need for their children to be tending sheep and thus learning the Navajo way, and disliking the kind of discipline white teachers tended to dole out, most Navajos kept their own children home and some sent orphans to the schools. By 1900, only 3 percent of Navajo children attended school, and only a handful of Navajos spoke English. The Navajo ways were, for the most part, intact. Exquisite sand paintings were rendered on the floors of hogans, and healing ceremonies, some lasting as long as nine days, still were held, during which medicine men recited the entire history of the Dineh from time immemorial to the present.

Smaller parts of the long history that some commentators take as the quintessential American epic served (and still do) as the background for less august activities. For example, the Navajos' version of a gambling game called the moccasin game or shoe game goes back to the time of creation, long ago, when the there was no light or dark. The game involves two teams, one of which hides a big round yucca seed in one of three moccasins that have been lined up and covered with sand. The other team has to guess which moccasin the seed has been put in. Back then, the animals had to decide whether the world should be permanently dark or permanently light. This was before the animals had taken on their present form, but there were some that we think of today as night animals (like owls) and some day animals (like badgers). Even though the day and night animals played the moccasin game throughout the day and night, neither side could win. As a result there is both day and night now. For the Navajos, the gambling game is a reminder, even a kind of iteration, of an important moment in their creation story and therefore part of what white people call religion.

While Indian ceremonies were generally discouraged in the 1880s and even actively banned, the Navajos, living miles from one another and even farther from any white authorities, were largely left to their own devices. The main intrusion of the Anglo world into that of the Navajos—besides the arrival of the railroad pushing through the southern part of the reservation and providing some Navajo men with a new kind of work—was that of traders. These men established trading posts on the reservation and participated in a unique credit-bartering scheme wherein Navajos could obtain supplies they desired against the day when they sheared the sheep and brought in wool or mutton. In the early days most traders were honest and were held in high regard, though later the federal government had to step in and regulate these affairs. Good traders would, for example, keep pawned Navajo jewelry until the owner repossessed it, died, or moved away—not just sell it to the first taker. Also, in league with the local women, the traders developed unique local designs for rugs that they marketed, creating an awareness in the outside world of the beauty of Navajo crafts and, to a degree, of Navajo culture.

The adrenaline-filled moments of raiding were gone, but no one was raiding the Navajos either, and some men had other ways of achieving status, some traditional, like becoming a medicine man (or "singer") or increasing one's sheep herd (a sign of wealth), and some new, like working as a silversmith. But for many Navajo men, their role in society did not change so much as it diminished. On the Plains, in the Northwest, in the Great Basin, and elsewhere in the Southwest, the story was much the same. Men who had provided venison from the hunt and other riches from raiding now often found themselves unable to provide for their families. A Mescalero Apache named Big Mouth recalled the early days on the reservation among the Sacramento Mountains in southern New Mexico, where at Fort Stanton the White Eyes were in charge of the Apaches:

The officer said that every Mescalero must come to the fort, babies and all, to be counted and tagged and that once in seven days one member of the family was to come and get food for those of his group. We did as they said, but we got no food. "Come again on the seventh day and there will be cattle for you."

Seven days is a long time to be hungry, but we gathered what we could in the woods. There were no piñons [piñon pine nuts] that year, but mesquite beans and acorns could be found. Apaches had always lived largely on venison, and without meat we were weak. But most of our people had enough to enable them to live.

On issue day, Saturday, we went and we got some cattle; but they were poor and thin, and there was little meat on them. In two days we were without food again.

One erstwhile Crow warrior lived for four decades on the reservation in Montana but ended his autobiography with the end of the old lifeways: "Nothing happened after that," he wrote. "We just lived. There were no more war parties, no capturing of horses . . . no buffalo to hunt. There is nothing more to tell."

Without the hunt, much of the seasonal work of the tribes was gone—both male and female work. New ways of achieving status—or forgoing it—had to be devised. War leaders, and the warrior societies and indeed most of the men's societies, all lost their reasons for being and began to disappear. When tribes took to electing councils, making laws, and holding meetings, their actions needed the approval of the local Indian agents and thus were largely hollow exercises. Government agents pushed the Plains people to live in single-family dwellings rather than in camps of extended family groups. In 1883, the government issued a bulletin, *The Code of Religious Offenses*, that outlawed most Indian ceremonies. For example, Sioux burial practices, marriage practices (polygamy), and the use of intoxicating substances were suddenly criminal acts. The sun dance, if held at all, had to be held in hiding, and became little more, as historian Paul Carlson has pointed out, than "a summer pageant." The healing ceremonies of shamans were, of course, against the law. The vision quest, in which a young man went into the wilderness to get in touch with his guardian spirit, was no longer in behalf of the hunter or warrior, and became something new and perhaps a bit watered down.

The white presence around—and on—the reservations of the Plains and elsewhere was greater than that in most parts of the Southwest (the Apache reservations being the exception). Ranchers and others coveted any stretches of good grass on the reservations. Many reservations were shrunk in size. The Great Sioux Reservation in South Dakota was shredded into five separate reservations that, in total area, were much smaller than the original. While the tribes came to regard these lands as homeland, and reinvented ceremonies to take the place of those that had disappeared through their loss of meaning or their being banned, the reservations continued to be shortchanged by the federal government. Farming equipment—and training—was slow to arrive, as were provisions. Hunger was a familiar companion. Rumors that land was to be taken away or people moved elsewhere discouraged men from becoming active tillers and stewards of land, and those who made an effort at farming more often than not failed under the poor conditions and climate. Stock raising was more promising, but in the 1880s most Indians had to use their livestock to feed their families: by 1885, most of the Indian cattle-grazing lands from the Cheyenne Reservation to the Comanches and Kiowas was leased to Texas cattlemen, the fees used to feed band members. In eking out a life for themselves, in trying to hold on to old ways, in guarding as best they could the old and new ceremonies and the secrets upon which much of traditional life depended, many Indians did manage to withstand what amounted to a largely legal onslaught on their world. They were not altogether powerless, but their strength lay in the steadfastness of their basic beliefs and their ability to cope day to day, not in anything resembling political power. Surely, too, a sense of humor was a vital component of their survival, particularly when it came to the white man. As the Chiricahua Daklugie said: "In addition to the characteristic hypocrisy of the White Eyes they had the queer custom of changing chiefs every four years. It takes that long or longer for a man to learn how to be a chief. Perhaps they were still trying to find one they could respect and trust. Perhaps they never will. That's the way it looked to me."

In California, matters were worse. In 1883, the government formed a commission to look in on the California Indian tribes—by now most of them were thought of not as particular tribes but as Mission Indians. On the commission was Helen Hunt Jackson, a woman who lost her husband and children in 1863 and turned to writing, producing in 1881 a book entitled *A Century of Dishonor,* in which she arraigned American Indian policy. Her own report on the California Indians was extracted by the commissioner of Indian Affairs in his annual report in 1883. Many of the Mission Indians, the report said, "have been driven from lands occupied and cultivated by them for years, to which they had at least a color of title from the Spanish government, and the ejectments have often been made with force and violence. . . . The few little villages left to them in the cañons of the mountains, from long years of cultivation have become extremely fertile, and are looked upon with longing eyes by the surrounding white settlers." In short, the Mission Indians lived on plots too small to be called reservations and known instead as *rancherías,* some being no more than a few acres. They lived in almost total penury, and terror that what little they had would be taken away. Jackson called for the removal of all white settlers from such lands, the resurveying of the lands awarded to the Indians, the patenting of the lands to the Indians, the establishment of schools, and even made the remarkable suggestion that the Indian agent be required to inspect such places "at least twice a year."

Not until seven years had gone by did Congress, in 1891, pass an Act for the Relief of the Mission Indians in the State of California, which appointed yet another commission, this one empowered to select reservations for all the Mission bands of a size sufficient to meet their requirements and to be patented to the Indians. The results were, in many cases, long in coming, and the life of the California Indians continued to deteriorate.

In much of Indian country, in the Great Basin, on the Plains, and elsewhere in the West, many Indians yearned for the old days, even fantasized that they would return, that something would send the white man packing and bring back the buffalos and the old lifeways. The old ceremonies would be recalled in detail, learned anew, and would embody their original purposes. People whose autonomy and religious lives had been so severely curtailed, people who were hungry, discouraged, and bored, people whose sons and daughters were veering into boredom, pointlessness, and alcoholism—such people were ready for new prophets, for answers, for new prayers and ceremonies that might bring such a desirable world about.

Peyote and Ghost Dances

No one knows how long people in Mexico and Texas ingested the dried top, or button, of the peyote cactus *(Lophophora williamsi),* which provides a non-habit-forming mild vision, or hallucination, and can also act as a purgative, causing vomiting. It was in use, archaeologists know, by 1 A.D. and probably earlier. The use of hallucinogens goes back much farther in time than that. Paleo-Indians in the Trans-Pecos and lower Pecos areas of Texas used Mexican buckeye (*Ungnadia speciosa*) not only to kill fish (spread on the water, it made fish gills fail) but also to gain hallucinations. Taken in excess it would have the same effect on lungs as on gills. Later, Mexican buckeye was replaced by red bean (*Sophora secundiflora,* and not a bean), which was also potent as a hallucinogen and lethal in excess. Then came peyote, which produces hallucinations but is in no way lethal. It was used by many throughout the Southwest, and in 1875 the Comanches, and in particular Quanah Parker's band, began using it, having picked it up from other Indians of the region. It provided a new kind of spirituality, a way of establishing an identity separate from the surrounding white culture, a means of insisting on one's Indianness. Peyote soon came to be used in healing ceremonies and rites of thanksgiving, spreading to the Kiowas, and from there throughout the West. It would later, in the twentieth century, become a key feature of the Native American Church, what is today *the* pan-Indian (as opposed to any purely tribal) religion.

Other spiritual responses to the new, restricted world of the American Indians sprang up. In the late 1860s, a Paiute named Wodziwob—also known as Fishlake Joe—experienced a trance state

Silas John cult (Apache) symbol

in which he found that Indians could create a new paradise by performing certain rituals, the main one of which was a dance in which the performers joined hands, forming a circle, and stepped sideways to the left. If performed for five nights in a row and overall twenty times a year, the dance would result in the return of deceased Indian ancestors but not whites. This, the first version of the Ghost Dance, and Wodziwob's other teachings, especially the promise of a world without whites, found fertile ground and was soon taken up by many tribes in California and Oregon. After a few years, the popularity of his teachings faded, but the yearning remained and became more widespread as more and more tribes were sequestered on reservations.

On January 1, 1889, during a solar eclipse, a young Paiute named Wovoka (the Woodcutter) was cutting wood for use in a Nevada mine near the Walker Reservation. The mine was owned by a family named Wilson. Wovoka had grown up with the white family, also receiving the name Jack Wilson. He was a tall, dignified man with piercing eyes and a deep voice. During the eclipse, he went into a trance and received a revelation in which he entered heaven. There he saw his ancestors alive and well, and was instructed by God to not fight, but to work with the white man, and to dance in the manner that Wodziwob had called for. He and those who did this would then be rewarded in the next life.

This was the time of a severe drought, and Wovoka predicted rain, a matter to be taken seriously because it was believed that he had already shown that he could make ice fall from the trees in summer, not to mention that he was invulnerable to gunshots. People came from far and near to listen to Wovoka preach. Wovoka apparently did not think it inappropriate that some of his visitors took him for the Christ come again. In November 1889 a Cheyenne named Porcupine journeyed by train to Pyramid Lake in Nevada to see this messiah.

I had always thought the Great Father was a white man, but this man looked like an Indian. . . . He was dressed in a white coat with stripes. The rest of his dress was a white man's except that he had on a pair of moccasins. Then he commenced our dance, everybody joining in, the Christ singing while we danced. . . . In the night when I first saw him I thought he was an Indian, but the next day when I could see better he looked different. He was not so dark as an Indian, nor so light as a white man. He had no beard or whiskers, but very heavy eyebrows. . . . He told us . . . that all our dead were to be resurrected; that they were all to come back to earth . . . that there was to be all good hereafter, and we must all be friends with one another . . . the whites and Indians were to be all one people.

Soon thereafter, Wovoka was visited by some Sioux leaders, who took the Ghost Dance, as they called it, home with them. (The Paiutes continued to call it the Round Dance.) The Sioux and other Plains tribes who took it up, however, gave it a noticeably different meaning. For them, performing the dance would (as in Wodziwob's vision) lead to the destruction of the whites, the resurrection of the ancestors, and a nativist return to the pure old ways of the tribes. The Ghost Dance soon spread far and wide on the Plains, only the Southern Cheyennes and the Comanches shunning it. For the disaffected young in particular, who tended to be fed up with reservation life, the Ghost Dance represented, even embodied, hope, promise. In the Sioux version, people danced in a circle, holding hands. Many wore American flags wrapped around them upside down—an ironic statement based on the nautical distress signal. The ceremony lasted for as long as two and a half days, during which the dancers fasted completely and many fell into trances or dropped from exhaustion, in a sense dying and visiting old ancestors among the stars. Porcupine's account points out that in Paiute country, whites and Indians together performed the dance, but on the Plains and especially among the Sioux, it was an exclusively Indian affair. While it was not a war dance as such, the Plains version did have ominous overtones for any whites who found out its meaning, and the Sioux Ghost Dancers also took to wearing buckskin shirts with special painted designs that bestowed on them an imperviousness to gunshots.

As always, such considerations led to a general nervousness on the part of the whites on the reservation and nearby, to add to their normal hostility. A new agent had recently been installed at the Pine Ridge Reservation, and the Oglala Sioux there were wearing their holy shirts. The agent panicked, announced that the reservation was out of control, and called for a thousand troops to restore order. In mid-November, troops under the command of Nelson (Bear Coat) Miles had surrounded both the Pine Ridge and the Rosebud Reservations. Hundreds of Sioux fled to the Badlands, north of Pine Ridge. Elsewhere, on the Standing Rock Reservation, to which Sitting Bull had returned earlier from Canada, police attempted to arrest the old chief and wound up killing him. With news of this spreading quickly, hundreds more angry and scared Sioux headed for the Badlands. The winter weather was particularly fierce and some 340 turned back, to be met by soldiers and ordered to camp at Wounded Knee, not far from the Pine Ridge Reservation. The following day, as so often had happened in these encounters through the years, shots rang out, hell broke loose, and Indian men, women, and children wound up dead in the snow. The frozen bodies of some three hundred people—mostly women and chil-

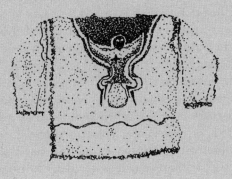

Ghost Dance shirt

dren—were unceremoniously dumped by the whites into a long
ditch and buried.

Most of the Sioux in the Badlands were on their way back to the
reservations when they heard of the massacre at Wounded Knee, and
soon enough four thousand people, including about five hundred
Cheyennes, were stalled near Pine Ridge, surrounded by five thousand troops. After an uneasy week the impasse was over. On January
15, two columns of Indians four-thousand-strong marched in a four-
mile-long procession soundlessly into Pine Ridge. The Ghost Dance
soon faded out except as a remnant among a few tribes. The Sioux
breakout of 1890–91, or what came to be called Wounded Knee,
was also the end of a dream—but it was a dream that a new breed of
Indian warriors would rekindle at the very same spot some eighty
years later.

Final Solution Number One

By the end of the 1870s most Indians were ensconced on reservations, the purpose of which was at least twofold: to keep Indians
from bothering white settlers and to keep white settlers from
bothering Indians. But the system begged many questions. For
one, could Indians leave their reservations? This matter came up
when a Ponca group led by Mochunozhin, or Standing Bear,

headed north from Indian Territory to their earlier reservation in the Dakotas. Standing Bear was arrested and jailed. Reform groups were aroused and rallied to his cause. Standing Bear won a legal battle for the right not to be held on a reservation against his will. Even so, officials from the Indian agency continued to make it difficult for Indians to come and go.

Similarly, the Indian Bureau insisted on enforcing federal laws on Indian reservations, even though this constituted a breach of most treaties, which guaranteed Indian self-government—at least up to a point. In practice, of course, that point shifted at the whim of the United States government. The Indian Bureau believed that the use of Indian police forces on the reservations would not only relieve the army of some onerous duties but also put the Indians on the path of civilization. (The notion of an Indian police force was that of a Dutch Reformed man, John Clum, who was appointed Indian agent on the San Carlos Apache Reservation though he was only in his early twenties. In the early 1870s he created an Apache police force by way of putting men to useful work as well as having civilians, and not the U.S. Army, keeping order. There were intertribal Apache tensions, which added to hunger and crowded, unhealthy conditions, but Clum had each separate group of Apaches appoint its own police officers. This was a considerable success, despite which Clum found himself in constant argument with the army over who should control the reservation.)

In addition to establishing Indian police forces, in 1883 the Indian Bureau instituted tribal courts, typically made up of three judges drawn from the ranks of the tribal police. The tribal courts were to impose penalties on those who persisted in tribal ways (such as ceremonies) that were banned, as well as those who committed petty crimes. But major crimes, such as murder, were a different matter. In the same year the tribal courts were decreed, a Sioux named Crow Dog killed another Sioux, and the matter was settled by the two sets of relatives in the traditional manner of providing acceptable compensation for the lost life. But territorial authorities took Crow Dog to court and a federal jury convicted him of murder. The case quickly reached the Supreme Court, which ruled that the federal government did not have sufficient jurisdiction to prosecute a crime committed by one Indian against another on Indian lands. This kind of political independence was not what the Indian agents and many whites had in mind at all, and two years later, in 1885, the U.S. Congress passed the Major Crimes Act, which made seven crimes, including murder, manslaughter, and larceny, subject to the laws of the state or territory in which an Indian reservation was located.

In practice, then, Congress was steadily whittling away what shreds of sovereignty were left to the tribes, but the year 1887—one year after Geronimo surrendered and three years before Wounded Knee—was the beginning of what was the greatest calamity American Indians had faced since the importation of the smallpox virus. The state of American Indians was by no means the major preoccupation of the United States government in 1887. The American frontier was about to close for good. From the American government's point of view, Indian affairs were a relatively paltry concern compared to the problems caused by the rapid and massive industrialization and urbanization of the nation. Labor problems were erupting into violence, the rights of southern blacks still needed adjudication, immigration politics (especially in regard to Chinese laborers) were explosive, and the legal status of corporations needed to be fixed. In 1887, ordinary Americans paid more attention to Queen Victoria's celebration of her fiftieth year as England's monarch and to Sherlock Holmes, who made his first appearance in print. Few Americans noticed the congressional passage of the General Allotment Act that year, a bill crafted with the intent of eliminating the remaining vestiges of Indian cultures in America, a goal devoutly desired both by those who wished the Indians well and by those who wished them ill.

Known also as the Dawes Act, it called for the *allotment in severalty* of the Indian reservations, meaning essentially that heads of nuclear American Indian families were to select plots, most often of a quarter section (160 acres), on the reservation, which would be patented to them and on which they were to make a living, in return for which they would become American citizens. If an Indian did not choose a lot, the Indian agent on the reservation was charged to do it for him. Additionally, smaller plots were to be hewn out of the common tribal lands for children and single Indians. Once this was done, all remaining land on the reservation was to be made available for sale to whites, the proceeds to be held in trust for the tribes. To keep greedy whites from preying on the Indian allotments, they were to be held in trust by the Indian Bureau for each Indian owner for a period of twenty-five years. In due course, competency commissions would patrol Indian country and determine when an individual Indian was in fact mature enough in the ways of the world to have the right to sell his property. (The greater the white pressure applied to such lands, it usually turned out, the quicker the Indian owners became competent.)

This process, it was assumed, would accomplish many goals. It would bring the Indians into the mainstream virtually overnight, giving them the civil rights all other Americans enjoyed, loosening the heathen bonds of communal tribal life, and freeing up millions of surplus acres to whites. The Bureau of Indian Affairs would manage the funds accruing to both tribes and Indian individuals from the sale of lands. Of course, this process also promised an early arrival of the blessed day when the federal government would no longer be liable for providing those services—such as rations, medical care, education—that had been guaranteed in almost all treaties between the government and the tribes. Not everyone was in favor. President Cleveland saw the Dawes Act as essentially a scam for land-hungry whites to get more land—but he signed it anyway. The ethnographers in Powell's Bureau of Ethnology and a small minority of senators and representatives opposed it; and virtually all reservation Indians perceived it as a catastrophe in the making.

The extent of the catastrophe can barely be imagined. Sheer numbers only give the grossest idea. In 1887, Indian lands totaled 154 million acres, a combined area of a quarter of a million square miles, approximately the equivalent of the state of Texas. A half century later, less than a third of that land remained in Indian hands, in all 48 million acres, or the approximate equivalent of the state of Mississippi. Worse, by 1934, when the Dawes Act was repealed, 27 million acres of the 106 million lost had been plots originally allotted to Indians. Further, the Dawes Act had embodied precisely no thought about subsequent generations of Indian people, who would, in theory, inherit the quarter-section plots. Within a couple of generations, original allotments would be owned by numerous descendants in tiny fractions, a situation for which most Indian traditions held few solutions. Growing numbers of Indians were simply not part of the picture in the minds of those who applauded the notion of allotment in severalty, though by 1891 the Dawes Act had to be amended to permit allotment of one-eighth sections to heads of families.

Allotment in severalty did not take place immediately throughout Indian country. It never took place at all in the Southwest, since not even the Indian Bureau could imagine anyone making a living on 160 acres or so of desert (where evaporation generally equals or exceeds rainfall) or of other arid lands, where annual precipitation practically never exceeds twelve inches. Elsewhere, west of the hundredth meridian, a 160-acre farm was usually a losing proposition. Indeed, the slicing up of the western lands into 640-acre sections to be parceled out to homesteaders had been for the most part a huge and disastrous bust for the old Jeffersonian notion of a nation of yeoman farmers. Rain did not, as contemporary wisdom had it, follow the plow. Those alert and entrepreneurial folk who had managed to take control of water, the West's most precious resource, had every homesteader and rancher over a barrel. For the most part the individual sections soon fell into the hands of banks and became parts of ever-greater landholdings possessed by great barons in the East. The fact that many Indians were equally unable to make even smaller plots work is, in hindsight, no surprise.

The loss of land, the crowding in of white settlers, railroads, miners, ranchers, the breakdown of tribal authority and independence, the failure of the federal government to provide satisfactorily for the needs of the Indians as promised, the venality of many local Indian agents, and the mismanagement of most of the reservation resources—all brought about a sense of unease ranging from discouragement to despair among the reservation Indians. No one knows how many simply left for towns and cities, where they hoped to find some kind of employment, and essentially vanished from history.

That President Cleveland was right about the Dawes Act is nowhere better illustrated than in the subsequent treatment of the Indian Territory, the place where, among others, the Five Civilized Tribes had dwelled since their removal from the Southeast along with a host of other tribes. Once there, the Cherokees, for example, reconstituted themselves as a progressive tribe, still following Jefferson's advice to take on the trappings of civilization. Over time they grew, in part from welcoming into their tribal lands many Delawares and Shawneees. Like the border states to their east, they were divided between Union and Confederate loyalties, and in the Civil War their lands were devastated, with many people moving away to avoid the dogs of war, but once again they reconstituted themselves with all of the normal functions of a democratic state. By the time of the Dawes Act, the town of Tahlequah was the Cherokee political and business center, and there were more than 140 elementary schools and two academies of higher educa-

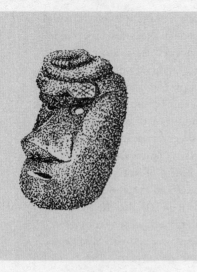

Cherokee booger mask

tion serving Cherokee youth. Cherokee presses produced two bilingual newspapers and hundred of books on religious and secular affairs. The tribe's judicial affairs were handled in its own court system, with no more or less smoothness than any state in the Union.

The original Dawes Act, of 1887, had exempted the so-called Five Civilized tribes (Cherokees, Creeks, Chickasaws, Choctaws, and Seminoles), leaving the task of allotting the lands in the Indian Territory to a commission designed to negotiate a settlement with the tribes. Negotiations were not successful, and in 1898 Congress passed the Curtis Act, which empowered the commission (now headed by none other than former senator Henry Dawes) to establish and manage town sites, abolish the tribal courts, draw up the rolls of the tribes, and allot the tribal lands to Indians on the rolls. Among the immediate questions was whose rolls to use. The Cherokees had performed their own census in 1880, and ten years later the U.S. census for the first time was to include all American Indians. Yet trouble arose over who was a Cherokee and who was not. The Cherokees included a number of blacks and intermarried whites, as well as Indians who had once been of other tribal designation. The result was that many of these nominal Cherokees were dispossessed. Another, more noticeable result was that surplus Indian lands were opened up for sale—which led to an unprecedented swarm of whites racing across the landscape to stake out their claims. The members of the Five Civilized Tribes, decreed now to be citizens of the United States, had little recourse but to sit back while the Indian Territory was joined with lands to the west and became the state of Oklahoma, a state that on its day of birth in 1907 was inhabited by almost a million and half people, of whom little more than 5 percent were Indians. In the ensuing years, by shady dealings too numerous to enumerate, many of these civilized Indians were cheated even out of their allotments. One old Cherokee, testifying before the Senate of the United States, explained that he had grown up on Cherokee land on a farm of three hundred acres. This had been taken away, allotted, sold, and he had only a few acres of land left to his name. He was exhausted, and for all his effort he simply could not make a living on his little plot. He told the Senate he was starving, and then pointed out that he spoke not as a single man sitting before them but for all the Cherokees.

Another dream that many of the Oklahoma Indians and some of their supporters in the dominant society had held—an Indian state of the Union, a state to be called Sequoyah—was gone. The effect psychologically on the Cherokees and others who had taken such pride in their governmental systems was devastating. Had the Cherokees and the others been allowed to follow their chosen destiny and create a self-contained and fully competent Indian state of the Union, it is not wholly improbable that Indian America might have become, by the beginning of the twentieth century, a place of promise and hope. As it was, however, at the turn of century the population of Indian America was at its lowest numerical ebb—some 250,000 souls—since sometime in the late Pleistocene or early Holocene. With few exceptions, such as for the Navajos and the Iroquois, the loss of Indian land, and with it important lifeways, was accelerating. At century's end, the common state of mind in Indian country was despair.

Nearly a hundred years after the passage of the Dawes Act, and sixty years after it was abolished, the scheme of allotment would come back to haunt the federal government like an angry ghost from the past. In the 1990s, a class action suit (representing some five hundred thousand Indians) was filed against the Department of Interior, saying that the Bureau of Indian Affairs had somehow managed to lose an estimated $3.4 billion it had supposedly been holding in trust for the Indian tribes and individuals who had sold their land off after allotment. A federal judge in Washington, D.C., would cite one secretary of interior, Bruce Babbitt, and the assistant secretary for Indian Affairs, Pawnee Kevin Gover, for contempt of court for not solving the problem. He would go on to cite the succeeding secretary of the interior, Gale Norton, with contempt also for failing to propose a plan to rectify the situation. By the early autumn of 2002, the matter remained unresolved, the Indians' money still lost somewhere in the warp.

PART FIVE

New Deals

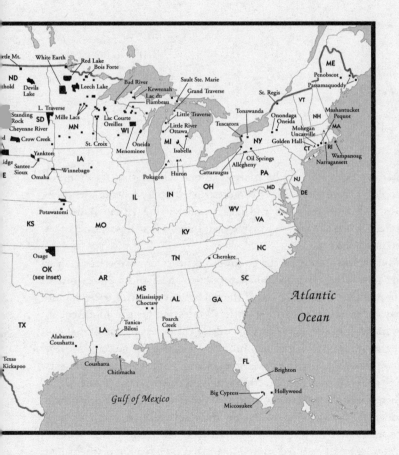

CHAPTER FOURTEEN

THE PROGRESSIVE ERA

It has been asserted by more than one scholar that no group of people in the United States is more trussed up by federal laws (perhaps like Gulliver with the Lilliputians' strings) than American Indians. Even the *identity* of American Indians is still governed to an extent by the feds.

By the beginning of the twentieth century it was perfectly clear that any future for the Indian people in the United States rested almost entirely in the hands of the federal government, even though that government was still relentlessly pressing for the allotment in severalty of Indian lands and the sale of the excess to non-Indians— all this under the flag of assimilation, meaning in effect *no separate future.* Traditionally the governments and major economic interests of the several states of the Union, and especially those in the West, where most of the Indians were, saw the reservations as unfortunate federally sponsored intrusions on their sovereign rights. In short, the states were no friends of the Indians in their midst. Many white westerners still recalled more-violent days, and some of them had even gone to court (with little success) seeking reparations for losses suffered not that long ago at the hands of the Indians when they had been free-ranging and dangerous. Only the federal government was powerful enough to protect Indian tribes from the states, and this remains largely true to this day.

Yet by 1900 violent outbreaks of Indians were unlikely, and the trials and tribulations of Indian country had continued to diminish as a topic of concern in the policy centers of Washington, D.C. The U.S. Army was essentially out of the Indian business. Of the three branches of the federal government, Congress was perhaps most in the thrall of those same interests that made the western states so inimical to Indians. Most congressional committees involved in Indian affairs were run by westerners. This was a time when the executive branch of the United States government was busiest with the tasks of bringing the United States onto the stage as a world player. Indian policy was something of an afterthought, a pesky perennial problem, but nothing had changed the government's idea that Indians should learn to be white. And the courts, in particular the Supreme Court, were no less likely to feel the political winds on their judicial cheeks then than now.

President Theodore Roosevelt, who as a young man had adopted the West and some of its frontier ethic, introduced the notion of conservation of resources and of reclaiming the lands of the West for development. (In the West, conservation has usually meant not letting a resource like water go to waste—almost the opposite of preservation.) The United States Forest Service was thus born; it would put millions of acres, including a good deal of Indian land, under the protection of the Department of Agriculture. In one instance of several, Blue Lake, in the mountains east of Taos Pueblo, in northern New Mexico, had been from time immemorial a place where the Taos Indians made regular pilgrimages for ceremonial purposes. By the end of the nineteenth century it was being visited and overrun by prospectors, lumbermen, and ranchers. When the Taos people complained, the Roosevelt administration incorporated the lake into the Carson National Forest; the Forest Service now controlled it, which meant merely that mining, lumbering, and ranching around the lake had to be done according to Forest Service rules. The lake continued to be overrun, and this interrupted any Taos ceremonies there. Out of Roosevelt's conservation policy what would later be called the Bureau of Reclamation arose as well, an organization that would, over the years, dam every major western river to provide irrigation and electricity.

By 1903, the English-only educational program of the government was in full swing, and not just children in boarding schools but adult Indians on their reservations were being assigned Anglo names as a matter of federal policy. That simple survival was the primary concern of most tribes at the beginning of the twentieth century, whereas the complex legal and political notion of tribal sovereignty was a major concern at the end of the century, suggests that the overall trajectory of Indian affairs rose in the intervening hundred years. Indeed, it did in many respects, but not in others, and the path has veered in both directions abruptly and almost inexplicably—a wayward, even dizzying trail that might well suggest to Indian people that the white man has a terrible problem making up his mind, much less keeping promises solemnly given. In the twentieth century, the world of the Indian would echo with such heavily laden terms as "allotment," "reorganization," "termination," "relocation," "reparations," "self-determination"—each signaling a switch in federal policy. Indians would see that the Supreme Court of the United States could easily, as it always had, both give and take away. Indians would have to learn to live with paradox after paradox, mostly the result of the unspoken assumptions of modern Anglo-American law as opposed to the ancient precepts of tribal existence. While the noted (and even sometimes exaggerated) Indian regard for nature would become one inspiration for a vigorous environmental movement, Indians would often find themselves attacked by the new environmentalists. They would see one president seek the utter end of government trust responsibilities for the tribes and another president—of the same political party—promise them a future of self-determination and partnership. They would see some historic rights restored by a nation not much given to historical consideration, and they would have to prove even to white friends that they too, just like whites, were entitled to change as history marches along. Larger percentages of Indian men would fight America's wars from midcentury on than of any other ethnic minority, even as new stereotypes would come into vogue to add to the widely held stereotypes of old. In awe of native spirituality, large numbers of disaffected whites—from hippies to New Agers—would seem to hijack Indian ceremonies and other parts of their cultures, and for many tribes old addictions would continue to be destructive and demeaning, while a different addiction would become a weapon for achieving a new strength.

Legalities

A notable twentieth-century legal triumph for the Indians had its beginnings in 1889, when a newly arrived farmer named Winters and several others began to dig irrigation canals that carried water from the Milk River in Montana to their fields. This was only a year after the Fort Belknap Indian Reservation had been established downstream, a few miles from the farmers, for the formerly nomadic Gros Ventres and Assiniboines. These Indians set out vigorously to make the transition from hunting and gathering to farming and raising livestock. Within a few years, the reservation was flourishing and drawing more and more water from the Milk River. In 1904, however, a drought cycle began, and soon the reservation was suffering from a lack of water. The tribes' agricultural efforts were foundering while the farmers upstream siphoned off the Milk River's flow for their own purposes. The local Bureau of Indian Affairs superintendent insisted that the Justice Department uphold the Indian rights to water. The Indians' side won, and the case was thereafter appealed all the way up to the U.S. Supreme Court.

The basis of the original court's decision, and the appellate courts' as well, rested chiefly on the general principles embodied in water doctrine and riparian rights in the West, the doctrine of *prior appropriation.* This in essence said, "First come, first served." Latecomers could use water only if it did not interfere with the use of previous users. (The users typically needed to show that their use was both continuous and beneficial.) On its face, such a doctrine would seem to benefit the first Americans, and particularly those who were on reservations that included land that a given group had inhabited aboriginally, but Indian claims were more often than not overlooked. The Supreme Court's 1908 decision in the case, *Winters v. United States,* therefore came as something of a surprise.

The court said, in effect, that the Fort Belknap Reservation had been set aside for the benefit of the two Indian groups—indeed, for their very sustenance—and this implied the use of sufficient water, regardless of whether water use was mentioned in the original language setting aside the reservation. The water was exempt from appropriation by state laws, the court went on, and the Indians' rights to it took precedence over other uses even if they had not yet begun to use the water or had stopped using it for some period. The Winters Doctrine, as it came to be called, did not explain how to quantify the amount of water to which a given reservation had a prior claim, nor did it specify the uses to which such water could or could not be put. The Bureau of Indian Affairs assumed the court meant only agricultural use, in farming and for livestock, and set out to survey reservations with this in mind. Yet, over the years in the West, the Winters Doctrine was largely ignored, especially as the Bureau of Reclamation got under way and began rearranging the flows of all the major Western rivers and parceling out to the states more water than the rivers contained. The doctrine was something of a time bomb, quietly ticking away through the century while Indian tribes bided their time.

The Supreme Court's upholding of Indian water rights was all the more surprising since only five years earlier, in 1903, it had substantially modified any Indian claim to sovereignty or any rights that were not subject to the whim of the United States Congress. This new state of affairs was the result of a case, *Lone Wolf v. Hitchcock,* involving the abrogation of treaty rights of the Kiowas, Comanches, and Kiowa Apaches. The case was brought by a Kiowa leader, Lone Wolf, with the assistance of the Indian Rights Association.

The problem went back as far as 1867, when Kiowas and Comanches agreed by treaty to reservation boundaries within which they would enjoy "absolute and undisturbed use and occupation." The reservation lands could not be alienated or ceded in any way without the signatures of "at least three-fourths of all the adult male Indians occupying the scene." But then along came the Dawes Act and the commission empowered to deal with the Oklahoma tribes, of which the Kiowas, Comanches, and by then the Apache Reservation were part. The commission obtained an agreement that the reservation could be allotted, but it failed to obtain the signatures of three-fourths of the adult males. To their credit, government officials, including Interior Secretary Hitchcock, advised Congress that the allotment agreement was improper and inadequate—but Congress ratified it anyway. In 1901, Lone Wolf sought an injunction against the implementing of the allotment agreement by the secretary, and he lost. The matter went swiftly to the Supreme Court, which announced its ruling in 1903. It said, essentially, that the Indians had not gotten very far along the path to civilization while enjoying all of their reservations lands, and that Indian tribes were mere remnants now of their former selves and unable to manage their own affairs, and were in all respects wards of the federal government, and furthermore that Congress had always had plenary power over all the affairs of Indians. Therefore, Congress could abrogate any treaty or other rights of Indians at will, and had full administrative power over all Indian property.

In other words, if a tribe wanted at some point to exercise its Winters Doctrine water rights, and the whites in the surround exercised sufficient political pull over their congressional representatives, Congress could solve the problem simply by declaring that the Indians would have to move to a new reservation. Later decisions would make it more or less clear that Congress could not act with utter impunity in such matters, however, but had to observe the federal government's necessary role as guardian and trustee of the tribes. Still, with their existence held together by such fragile threads, the Indian tribes had fewer rights and powers as they faced the task of living through what American historians refer to as the Progressive Era.

The legal and political obstacles Indians faced were daunting. In the first place, this was still a time when most western states and their representatives in Congress had a handful of issues dear to their hearts— mining, ranching, and a few others. Given the narrow concentration of their interests, this left them with the ability to trade their votes on matters of greater import in the East and Midwest in return for eastern and midwestern votes for their interests. Congressmen began to assume a notion of proprietorship over Indian affairs in their particular states. So the Indian tribes, most of which were in the West, were thoroughly in the thrall of western congressmen, for (or against) whom, of course, most of them could not vote. And if the federal government acted against the interests of the Indians, or if the government had previously acted against their interests, there were very few avenues open to the Indians to obtain redress. One of the rights accruing to a *real* sovereign is that it cannot be sued in court without agreeing to be sued. Indian tribes simply could not haul the Bureau of Indian Affairs or any other branch of government into federal court. Any such suit had to be taken to the United States Court of Claims, especially established to hear complaints against the federal government, but suits could not be brought in that court without a special act of Congress permitting them. This cumbersome arrangement would eventually lead to an attempt to redress more efficiently all such Indian claims against the government, but that would not take place until two world wars had been fought.

Chiricahua Destiny

One area where the U.S. Army remained in the Indian business in the early years of the twentieth century was as jailers of the Chiricahua Apaches, all of whom would remain prisoners of war until 1913. Their first years, as noted earlier, were spent in Florida. Geronimo and seventeen other warriors were interned in Fort Pickens, located on an island off Pensacola, a city that lobbied to get Geronimo, sensing correctly that his presence would bring tourists to the city. The rest of the Chiricahuas, less than five hundred, were located in Fort Marion, a 180-foot-square installation located in Saint Augustine (Europe's first successful colony in the continental United States). Conditions for the prisoners were appalling, the unaccustomed humidity and boredom being only part of the problem. Overcrowding and despair led to disease and death. Eighteen Apaches died at Fort Marion in the first seven months. Public complaint over the government's failure to civilize these prisoners of war led to a visit by Captain Pratt of the Carlisle School. He was dispatched to Florida, and there he selected about a hundred youths, girls and boys, to go to Carlisle. Later the public outcry, impelled in large part by the Indian Rights Association, led the administration in 1888 to remove the Chiricahuas from both Florida sites to a swampy and forested former barracks called Mount Vernon, in Alabama, where the prisoners of war would have the run of slightly more than two thousand acres. Here, babies died from all the insect bites they received; it rained much of the time and was more humid than Florida. In all, of 498 Apaches imprisoned in the first place, 129 were dead three years later. Thirty also died at Carlisle, which Pratt blamed more on hopelessness than on climate: "They have no home, no country, no future, and life has become hardly worth living," he wrote. Forty-nine Chiricahuas had already died in Florida, and within another year (spent at Mount Vernon), yet another fifty perished, mostly from malaria and tuberculosis. In 1894, after eight years of imprisonment, they had a population of three hundred, an overall loss of 40 percent.

Pressure rose to move the Chiricahuas to the Indian Territory, but Arizona and New Mexico were unalterably opposed to such a move, evidently fearing that these few sickly people, many of them children, would escape and make their way back to their old hunting grounds and massacre the now much larger population of the Southwest. Some suggested moving them to North Carolina. Meanwhile, the Indian

Service happily continued to leave the Chiricahuas to the military, which had no other authority for housing them except on an army base, and so they had to remain prisoners of war. Finally, Congress overrode the howls of the western delegations and decided that the Chiricahuas should be sent to Fort Sill, Oklahoma, to be located on some unallotted land the Kiowas, Comanches, and Kiowa Apaches were persuaded to give up for that purpose.

Apache doll

At Fort Sill, formerly a cavalry post and still in occasional use, the Chiricahuas would remain as prisoners of war for another nineteen years. Here Geronimo, still much lionized by the press, would become the first (and last) prisoner of war to be featured in a presidential inaugural parade. In 1905 he nearly upstaged Teddy Roosevelt in the parade from Capitol Hill to the White House. To complaints that the prisoner of war status was absurd, the army claimed it was merely nominal, but even at Fort Sill, where life was far more pleasant and freer, there were major problems. Some of the Chiricahua men enlisted in the army, and once their tour of duty was over, they had to return to their earlier status as prisoners of war. Though Chiricahuas could leave Fort Sill if they obtained permission from the military commandant, their status made such things as marriage tremendously complex. Not only was it difficult to meet other Indian people from the surrounding area, but who would want to marry *into* captivity? They were forced to marry mostly within their own (small) group.

Soon, the Kiowa, Comanche, and Kiowa Apache lands were allotted, and the rest sold off to whites. White towns sprang up, Lawton being nearest to Fort Sill, and the Chiricahuas and other tribes were being sold liquor. Evidently, Geronimo obtained some whiskey one February night in 1909, drank it, and fell asleep in the open. It rained, he caught pneumonia, and he died soon afterward.

Overall, the Chricahuas were relatively comfortable at Fort Sill, where they had been promised they could stay on permanently. The army had plans to abandon the place, leave it to the Chiricahuas, and return them to the guardianship of the Interior Department. But then the army changed its mind and decided to make Fort Sill an artillery training school, and the presence of the Apaches would no longer be tenable there. Eventually, after a great deal of argumentation in Congress and the White House, and more howls of pain from the New Mexicans, the Chiricahuas were given a choice. They could individually choose to remain in Oklahoma (on allotted lands of the Kiowas that had come free) or move to the Mescalero Apache Reservation in central New Mexico.

Those who had been six years old or older in 1886 mostly chose to go to New Mexico, where they would be as free as any other reservation Indians and dwell on unallotted land among people who were not utterly foreign to them. In all, 187 Chiricahuas took up life on the reservation starting in 1913. The younger adults disproportionately elected to remain in Oklahoma. By 1914, sixty-nine Chiricahuas were settled on scattered allotments in the Fort Sill area with little organization to keep them bound into a community. The Chiricahuas were split into two groups living hundreds of miles apart. From a proud, warlike, and distinct collection of closely related bands—what we would call, among other things, a culture—defending their lands and their lifeway for centuries from waves of intruders, the remaining handful of Chiricahuas would soon enough be largely absorbed into the worlds of the Mescalero Apaches and, in Oklahoma, other Indians, though retaining there a separate tribal status.

The Mescaleros had already welcomed into their midst other Apache groups, the Lipans as well as the Jicarillas (who would later all move to northern New Mexico), and the Chiricahuas felt they could be trusted to provide a warm welcome. Among the Chiricahuas who took the train to New Mexico was a man known as Daklugie, who Geronimo had insisted go to school to learn the ways of the White Eyes, the better to avoid being tricked by them. Daklugie later recalled that the Chiricahuas "looked forward to this move as did the Hebrews to the Promised Land." While leaving behind their "beloved dead," the Chiricahuas saw ahead of them "a permanent home, a home among our brothers, a home where we could be free, a home where we could go to the mountains and pray to Ussen as our ancestors had done and as our mothers had taught us to do." Yet joining the Mescaleros had its draw-backs, which Daklugie later discussed:

> . . . though we hated the White Eyes and their life-way in general, we had been in contact with them for twenty-seven years and had learned to like and adopt some of their customs. We found houses comfortable and convenient. And we gladly conformed to their standards of cleanli-ness.
>
> On my visit to Mescalero four years previous, I had found the people still living as primitively as we had before being forced into cap-tivity. They still used tepees. There were few who attempted to conform to our standards of cleanliness. They still ran sheep, and we exceedingly disliked sheep.

At first the Chiricahuas moved to a more remote part of the reserva-tion and maintained a largely separate existence. But inevitably their world changed; intermarriage became frequent. They soon had more important matters to deal with as a unified group—in particular the attempts by the White Eyes they so disliked to cheat them out of their land and other resources.

World War and Two Dreadful Senators

One of the most important names in twentieth-century Indian affairs is that of Senator Albert Fall, who became secretary of the interior under President Warren Harding and perpetrated the Teapot Dome Scandal. This involved the leasing of federal properties in Wyoming and Cali-fornia to private oil interests without competitive bidding and also, it turned out, with at least $100,000 in bribes to Fall, who became the first American to be convicted of a felony committed as a cabinet offi-cer. But Fall was, if nothing else, consistent in his desire for financial gain at almost any cost, in his realization that there was plenty of money to be had from the extraction of fossil fuels, and in his distaste for American Indians. Active in the local politics of his adopted terri-tory, New Mexico, he was elected a U.S. senator in 1912, the year the territory became a state—incidentally the same year that a Sac and Fox Indian, Bright Path, from the Carlisle Indian School (with the Angli-cized name of Jim Thorpe), won Olympic gold medals for the pen-tathlon and decathlon.

Fall owned a ranch near the Mescalero Apache Reservation in southern New Mexico. As a senator he made repeated efforts to have part of the reservation made into a national park, with some of the rest of the reservation sold off to pay for a road between that national park and another, to its west, that would include part of White Sands and a man-made reservoir called Elephant Butte. Not incidentally, the road would add value to Fall's ranch. What is more, his proposal would have withdrawn from the Mescaleros $3 million worth of timber and opened the reservation to mining with no royalty payments to the Indians. Aside from his own personal gain, this effort was also tied to his belief that executive-order reservations (as opposed to those arranged by treaty) were public domain land just like any other federal property, so that the federal government could lease mineral rights to private companies without any obligation of any sort to the Indians, who lived there (in his view) simply at the sufferance of the government. This was essentially a new kind of land grab. Homesteading in the West had proved a tremendous failure. More than a hundred thousand homesteaders had failed in the Dakotas between 1900 and 1915. Settlers' pressure on Indian lands was largely a matter of the past. Now it was big business, big money, that looked covetously at Indian land. Fall's senatorial initiatives never made it through both houses, but when he became secretary of the interior in 1922 he set out to make good on all his thwarted dreams. In the meantime, however, the United States entered the world stage by joining Britain and France and others in the "war to end all wars."

In all, between eight and ten thousand American Indians fought in the Great War—the tradition of patriotism on the part of the first Americans continues, even grows in intensity, to this day and often amazes white people who are aware of how badly the nation has treated the Indians. The reservation Indian agencies became registration centers, and all able-bodied Indians of a certain age were required by law to register. Many resisted, believing that if they registered they would automatically be sent to war, which was not the case. Only Indians who were already citizens could be drafted, and by no means all of them would be, and as often as not the registrars were not sure which Indians were citizens and which were not. Many who were legally citizens did not consider themselves such since they were not allowed to vote. (Citizenship was something granted by the federal government, but the states were empowered at this time to specify the qualifications needed to vote, and most states at this time disqualified Indians for one reason or another.) It was a grand mess, and there were several instances of outright resistance to registering or being drafted, especially in the more remote reservations—usually a matter of misunderstanding. In effect, only those citizen Indians who then volunteered were taken into the armed forces, and of those that served, some four thousand came from the Five Civilized Tribes. Cheyennes and Arapahos also volunteered enthusiastically, the Cheyennes even inaugurating a new war society. Indians from the East also served in large numbers, particularly Iroquois.

In the society at large as well as among Indians, a dispute erupted over whether Indians should serve alongside whites as regular soldiers or should be segregated into special Indian units. One of the strongest opponents of Indian units was the Society of American Indians, which had come into being in 1911, a large multitribal group of mainly Indian professionals, ranging from doctors and lawyers to anthropologists and writers. It claimed that the idea of such "a spectacular Indian regiment or battalion arises from the showman's brand of Indian as seen in the circus." (The Oklahoma Indian soldiers, most of whom were already in the National Guard, would have preferred to serve in separate Indian units.) In fact, the Society of American Indians had already begun to fall apart over several issues, including the propriety of using peyote (the society thought it was backward) and the question of working with the BIA or trying to eliminate it. The society was largely assimilationist; after the war it would fade away, a brave, early, and unsuccessful effort at pan-Indianism. Meanwhile many Indians found that their proficiency with firearms and their reputation as hunters—attributes the assimilationists earnestly sought to root out— led to their service as snipers. Service in the war, proclaimed Cato Sells, the commisioner of Indian Affairs, would civilize the Indians, though exactly how shooting people would accomplish this was something he never explained.

Many more Indians served the war effort by taking jobs—chiefly in agriculture, typically performing stoop labor that today is more often than not performed by migrant workers. In addition, the Bureau of Indian Affairs leased Indian lands not being cultivated to outside interests to farm. The largest farming concern ever organized up to that time was created on two hundred thousand acres of the Crow, Fort Peck, Blackfeet, and Shoshone Reservations by the Montana Farming

Corporation, a New York company formed by virtue of a $2 million loan from Wall Street to the Great Northern Railroad. The world around the American Indians was becoming bewilderingly complex. Some things, however, changed little. Instead of receiving payment for the leasing arrangement by this early agribusiness behemoth, the Indians were entitled only to 10 percent of the actual crop.

Indians bought $25 million in war bonds, mostly by simply agreeing to the transfer to bonds of money the government held in trust for them through the Bureau of Indian Affairs. A handful of Indians worked in munitions factories, and many at home on the reservation produced clothing and other materials for the soldiers. Prices for most commodities rose significantly, and Navajo families, for example, benefited considerably from the rising price of wool. But inflation was a two-edged sword. The price of livestock skyrocketed as well, which led many Indian ranchers to sell off their herds, ultimately to their loss. At Pine Ridge, the Sioux had become thoroughly successful raisers of cattle, but during the war the Indian agent, representing the federal government, persuaded them to sell their herds and plant wheat. They lived well enough off the sale of livestock and accomplished the transition to wheat, but then the price of wheat fell precipitously and the now herdless Sioux had no option but to lease their rangeland at poor rates to whites. So for the second time in less than a half century, they lost their economic base—first the bison, then their cattle. The net effect of seeking to increase Indian agricultural products for the war effort was that Indian tribes found yet more of their land essentially invaded by whites.

Worse for Indians overall, with the budget for the Interior Department frozen for wartime, the cost of services such as medical care on the reservations skyrocketed and health workers were siphoned off to join the war effort. Not unpredictably, Indian health suffered greatly as epidemics of measles, typhus, and pneumonia struck, followed by the devastating global influenza pandemic of 1918 and 1919, so virulent that it struck down people in remote Eskimo villages of the Arctic.

The exigencies of war and the national war effort postponed the settlement of a matter of land ownership along the upper Rio Grande in New Mexico, where Pueblo Indians had been living for more than a millennium. In 1922, when Albert Fall assumed the position of secretary of the interior, he set out to solve the problem once and for all. In this, he had a willing stooge, New Mexico senator Holm O. Bursum. The problem went back to the original Spanish land grants, which were made over the centuries of Spanish rule both to Hispanics and to the Pueblo tribes. These were not the days of global positioning satellites and precision surveying, and the borders of these grants were often somewhat vague. But they were confirmed by the Mexican government after 1821, and confirmed by the United States in the Treaty of Guadalupe Hidalgo in 1848. They were confirmed yet again, after new surveys, by Abraham Lincoln, who sent the Pueblos silver-headed canes as a symbolic iteration of the authority of the Pueblos over their affairs, a traditional gift harking back to Spanish times. Even so, as noted before, the Pueblo people were evidently too civilized, or at least not savage enough, to be considered in the same category as Indians, and so they soldiered on in the manner of regular municipalities in the territory of New Mexico, subject to territorial laws and without the protection of the federal government.

The people of the New Mexico Territory, having no more interest in the Indian people within its borders than any other western state or territory, basically sat back while Hispanics and Anglos proceeded to move onto Pueblo lands and by one ruse or another claim ownership. One of the many fraudulent ploys employed was to borrow some land for grazing and then to pay taxes on it, thus getting one's own name on the rolls as owner. Over the years, squatters proliferated up and down the upper Rio Grande and complaints by the Pueblo people were of little avail, for the territorial courts were hardly friendly. In 1913, the United States Supreme Court determined that the Pueblos were indeed wards of the federal government, and the state courts and other authorities therefore had no jurisdiction on the Pueblo lands. This spelled calamity to Albert Fall and others who hoped that the non-Indian claims to Pueblo lands—and water—would be settled cozily by their cronies in Santa Fe. (Santa Fe had been long been the center of the "Santa Fe gang," basically a large group of Anglo and Hispanic land speculators led by a white, Thomas Catron, which wound up controlling vast tracts of the territory, chiefly by means that would make the Teapot Dome Scandal resemble an afternoon thunderstorm.)

After World War I, Fall urged Senator Bursum to introduce a bill into the Senate that would resolve these long-standing disputes and clouded titles. The bill, which came to be known as the Bursum Bill, gave non-Indian claimants title to the land if they could prove possession by June 10, 1910, by one means or another (none of which would stand up to much scrutiny, but scrutiny was not really called for in the bill), in which case the federal government would pay the Pueblos for the land in either land or money, but would not award the Pueblos additional water to irrigate any such newly acquired land. To get additional water, they would have to go back to the state courts. All of the bill's several other similar provisions were equally injurious to the Indians, and the bill slipped through the Senate almost as unnoticed as a ghost.

The Bursum Bill backfired. It never made it through the House, and its defeat can be taken as a major turning point in reversing the widely held belief that the American Indians west of the one hundredth meridian should all become good, detribalized yeomen working their plots of land. That this notion had persisted into the twentieth century is astonishing in retrospect. It was already clear that homesteading the West by whites was almost a total failure. None other than John Wesley Powell had made it clear in the 1880s, in a largely ignored government report, that small farming in the West could be accomplished only by cooperatives like those of the Mormons, who, like the Indian tribes, practiced a more communitarian style of life. Nonetheless, even the—albeit conservative—Indian Rights Association and other well-wishers continued to believe that somehow Indians could accomplish what white men could not. That others less friendly to Indians continued to hold to this doctrine is more easily explained: they saw that the inevitable failures would free up Indian lands.

The Senate passed the Bursum Bill on September 11, 1922. The Pueblos responded by drawing together in monolithic opposition, a unity of purpose not seen among them since 1680. They drew up an appeal and sent it out to the public press and to other Indian tribes in November. It accused Bursum of a major deception since he had reported to his Senate colleagues that the Pueblos themselves had requested such a bill. Instead, the Pueblo Council said, "We were never given a chance of having anything to say or do about this bill. . . . This bill will destroy our common life and will rob us of everything which we hold dear, our lands, our customs, our traditions." The appeal ended with a question: "Are the American people willing to see this happen?"

Many were not.

Seeing the Light, Dimly

Something quite new was taking place, not just in parts of the West but in places as far in distance and in other respects from Indian country as Greenwich Village in New York City. New, radical, even revolutionary thinking was percolating here and there in America, new causes were bursting onto the scene, and small vanguards of people who did not look kindly on the status quo or the mainstream were popping up, especially in the East in the first decades of the twentieth century. Among the troublemakers were people like muckraker Lincoln Steffens, the anarchist poet Emma Lazarus who wrote the poem ("Give me your tired . . .") that adorns the Statue of Liberty, "Big Bill" Haywood of the Wobblies, and Margaret Sanger, a feminist champion of birth control. Marcel Duchamp's nude had descended a staircase in New York City and the art world would never again be the same, and by the early 1920s the satisfied world of middle-class America would be skewered by Sinclair Lewis in best-selling novels, *Main Street* and *Babbitt.* The frontier that had always been somewhere out West was officially no more, and Frederick Jackson Turner had theorized about its (salutory) effect—now, of course, gone—on the (white) American character, while others would claim the American character had long been formed more by urban exigencies. Immigrants flooding the country—Italians, Irish, Chinese—were looked upon as uncouth and contemptible, while blacks were not looked upon really at all: invisible, as Ralph Ellison would later say. It was one of America's periodic heydays of dissatisfaction with itself.

Many—sometimes up to a hundred—of these left-leaning luminaries, including a young Walter Lippmann, fresh out of Harvard, turned up for evenings at the strange home in Greenwich Village of a strange woman then known as Mabel Dodge. From about 1912 to 1915, she operated the most successful salon in American history, hosting an changing assortment of socialists, anarchists, suffragists, poets, lawyers, anthropologists, psychoanalysts, artists, academics, and even government officials. Here, as bohemian as it sounds (and was), people carried on a fiercely conducted cross-fertilization of new ideas, where politics and political theory met psychoanalysis and the artists' new way of seeing the world, where art and science and the rights of the people were paramount questions.

One of the visitors to Mabel Dodge's salon was a young social worker, slight of build and a bit myopic, whose job with the People's Institute in New York City was helping immigrants adjust to American urban life. Like many of Mabel's guests, he was not pleased with the greedy individualism that characterized so much of American commercial, social, and political life, and in 1919 he left to work with immigrants in California. By this time, Mabel Dodge had also left New York, fetching up in Taos, New Mexico, where she built an elaborate house only a few miles from the Taos Pueblo and married a Taos Indian, Tony Luhan. She saw the Taos Indians as embodying an organic blending of art and nature, of community and ego, an antidote to the overall decay she saw in her own society. Ever the cultural channel, she invited everyone from D. H. Lawrence to Harold Ickes to come see this wonderful, ancient example of a coherent society. Among those she invited was the social worker formerly from New York, John Collier, who needed very little persuasion about the vibrancy and importance of Taos Indian life. Collier had accepted the prevalent view that Indian cultures were inexorably on the way out, but the Taos ceremonies struck him as "a new, even wildly new, hope for the Race of Man." He returned to California convinced that all the Indian cultures should be preserved, whole and living, at virtually all costs.

Collier was neither the first nor the last white visitor to Indian country whose life would be changed by the experience and who would become an avid supporter of Indian causes. But he was the first to be appointed, in due course, the commissioner of Indian Affairs. Meanwhile, as a private citizen, he became a forceful lecturer on the American Indians, so when Stella Atwood of Riverside, California, a leader of the General Federation of Women's Clubs, heard about the Bursum Bill, she eventually got the women's clubs to sponsor John Collier to study the state of the Indian reservations and to be a lead spokesman against the Bursum Bill. Collier soon was back in New Mexico and helped organize sympathetic groups in Taos and Santa Fe, and helped the newly formed Pueblo Council with its appeal to Congress, which soon appeared in the *New York Times* and led to a blizzard of news stories and petitions. The following year, Collier founded the American Indian Defense Association, which put him in a position to become a major strategist and publicist in defense of Indian rights.

Another source of support besides what many local whites thought of as meddling easterners and radicals came from a source that Fall and

Bursum either overlooked or discounted: the tourism business. Beginning in the early 1900s, people had begun to make their way west not to stay but to see some of the natural and other wonders of the region. Such expeditions were soon being heavily promoted by the railroads. The Santa Fe Railroad advertized an overnight stay at Grand Canyon in a new hotel on the south rim, El Tovar. This was one of the string of hotels from Kansas City to California that entrepreneur Fred Harvey built, staffed with what would become the famous Harvey Girls as hostesses and waitresses. In the Southwest, Harvey undertook a major effort to encourage southwest Indian crafts, and one of the pleasant experiences for a tourist arriving in, say, Albuquerque, was to detrain and buy a silver-and-turquoise bracelet or a traditional pot from the Pueblo women on the platform. Indian traders on the Navajo Reservation had by now developed the beginning of a national market for Navajo rugs and other Indian crafts, particularly Pueblo pottery, with Navajo and Zuni jewelry soon to come. Before long, cross-country automobile trips became not just possible but also relatively comfortable, and soon the West, and with it a notion of the value of Indian lifestyles, was becoming part of the American sensibility. Surely, those who were benefiting from tourism in the Southwest with its patina at least of exotic Indian culture did not want to see the Indians dispossessed. One of the most rewarding, exotic, and arduous Indian experiences a tourist or resident of the Southwest could have was to drive nearly a hundred miles over dirt tracks through the Painted Desert to the Hopi villages and there to witness a Hopi snake dance. Local support for Indians was, at least in the Southwest, on the rise.

Just before Christmas of 1922, and a little more than a month after the Pueblos' appeal, the Bursum Bill was withdrawn from the house. Secretary Albert Fall, furious but undaunted, threatened to take administrative and legal action that would evict the Pueblo people altogether, and warned of bloodshed if the white people of New Mexico were not rewarded with the land of the nontaxpaying Pueblo Indians. This evidently was too unseemly even for the Harding administration. There were surely other reasons (of no consequence here), but Fall's forced resignation in March 1923 was announced. Even in his absence, however, congressional machinations continued in the realm of Indian mineral rights, especially multiple attempts to lease Indian lands for oil drilling without paying the tribes any royalty or, in other instances, insisting that the Indians pay taxes on any such oil earnings to states. In the early 1920s another congressional plot was hatched whereby all Indians would be awarded United States citizenship but at the same time, by other mechanisms in addition to allotment, lose yet more of their tribal status and land. As it turned out, only the first part of this scheme passed both houses, and in 1924 all Indians were citizens of the United States, whether they liked it or not. Many Indian people were deeply concerned, seeing citizenship, with more shrewdness than they were given credit for, as a ploy to deprive them of their rights. But the bill as passed was explicit in this regard:

> *Be it enacted* . . . , That all non-citizen Indians born within the territorial limits of the United States be, and they are hereby, declared to be citizens of the United States: *Provided,* That the granting of such citizenship shall not in any manner impair or otherwise affect the right of any Indian to tribal or other property.

Even so, in many states, including Arizona, with its disproportionate number of Indian people, Indians were still denied the vote. States determined who was eligible to vote and one common excuse for prohibiting Indians from the polls was that, while they might be citizens, they were also legally wards of the United States government.

In the same year, 1924, Congress created a commission to resolve the clouded titles on Pueblo lands, and this process soon began, with far better results than would have obtained under Bursum's bill, but with a good deal of dissatisfaction arising on the part of the Pueblos as the commissioners still tended to tilt toward non-Indian concerns. These matters would continue to haunt all involved throughout the century, and in the 1920s there were other arrows of criticism in John Collier's quiver. Collier remained in the thick of all these bewildering and byzantine initiatives, usually with the ear and aid of progressive senators like Bob La Follette of Wisconsin. Collier noisily took up the cause of the Navajos, who would have had a $100,000 reimbursable loan forced on them by Congress to help fund a bridge over Lees Ferry, opening the north rim of Grand Canyon but not helping the Navajos in any way. Brimming with outrage, he fought for the Flatheads in Montana, who were threatened with the loss of water and land to a Montana power company. In each case, he helped persuade Congress to make better deals with the tribes than Congress had planned, and in the process kept the cause of the Indians in general and his overall criticisms of Indian policy in the public eye.

Meanwhile the process of allotment was proceeding, though more slowly than before, and Indians, especially those who lived on executive-order reservations, had no idea if they were going to retain any rights at all to what was left of their land as Congress wrestled with this issue in the context of oil extraction. For example, oil had been found in the northern (and executive-order) part of the Navajo Reservation, and the BIA fairly quickly appointed an agent whose orders were to organize the first Indian tribal council, whose powers were limited entirely to rubber-stamping the agent's leases to oil companies, once such leasing became legal. In the uncertainty over land, not to mention the near impossibility of making any kind of decent living on the reservation, many Indians (though how many is really not known) were heading for the cities, where they dropped below the radar of government awareness. From 1890 to 1920, the population of Indians had stagnated, hovering around a quarter of a million, a mere 0.3 percent of the entire United States population. Most people who spent much time thinking about it still assumed that Indians would not survive as an independent group of people, a notion elegiacally embodied in 1925 in best-selling author Zane Grey's novel *The Vanishing American*. Yet for various reasons and through the efforts of many Indian tribes and white organizations, Americans were beginning to take note that the first Americans—vanishing or not—were as always getting a raw deal. One result of this growing awareness would be what some have called the most important investigation and report of Indian circumstances in the twentieth century.

The Meriam Report

In a response to the increasingly noisy criticism of Indian policy and the government's responsibility for poor Indian conditions, Fall's successor as secretary of interior, Hubert Work, in 1926 asked the Brookings Institution to make a thorough study of economic and social conditions on the reservations and make recommendations for their improvement. The Rockefeller Foundation funded the study, and chosen to lead the study as technical director was Lewis Meriam, a statistician and student of public administration with the Institute for

Government Research, which had recently become part of Brookings. Given that the study was requested by Work, who was an avowed assimilationist, and was to be carried out by what could at the time be thought of as the establishment, John Collier grumbled that a white-wash was in the cards and persuaded the Senate to begin its own investigation (which would not be complete until 1943). But Collier and others were surprised when, in 1928, Meriam issued his report, *The Problem of Indian Administration.* It was highly critical of the government on several fronts.

The report retained not only a number of phrases but ideas and policies that today one hears as condescending to the tribes, such as the notion that the major purpose of the Indian Service should be education, broadly conceived, to assist Indians in the transition to living in white society. But it also, forcefully, pointed out that some Indians "wish to remain Indians, to preserve what they have inherited from their fathers, and insofar as possible to escape from the ever increasing contact with and pressure from the white civilization." The report cited the belief of many white people that this was a legitimate desire, and that Indian cultures—art, governance, and so forth—had a great deal to teach the white world. While saying that there was no point in trying to enclose Indian tribes in "a glass case," the report criticized the dictatorial policies of allotment and other schemes that forced, rather than led, Indians along the path to whatever accommodation they as individuals wanted to make with white society.

The report was especially hard on BIA education programs, calling them far inferior to public schools and useless in preparing Indian children for life either on the reservation or in white society. Boarding school conditions—overcrowding, poor hygiene, inadequate nutrition, forced labor to maintain the school plants—came in for extremely critical commentary, as did the generally poor delivery of health care to the reservations. High rates of trachoma, tuberculosis, and other afflictions were rife, and outside of smallpox vaccinations, other preventive medical practices were notable by their absence.

Poverty, the report noted, was far worse than "any reasonable standard of health or decency," with half of the Indian population having assets of less than $500. More than two-thirds of Indians earned less than $200 a year, and when questioned, BIA officials had no idea how they survived.

The commission also explored an area of Indian affairs that was almost totally overlooked by the government—those who had left the reservation for the cities. Off-reservation migrants they were called, what today we call urban Indians. The report was the first significant attempt to address this segment of the Indian population, finding a handful of squatters' camps in California and Arizona, plus a number of mostly Pueblo people working in railroad repair shops in the Southwest, but mainly a large group of city Indians. These people, of many differing tribes, had widely divergent opinions about most things except that the BIA was of no use but mostly harmful, and that they could not make a living on the reservation. The report noted that off-reservation Indians often competed for relatively low-level jobs with Mexican-Americans, and most employers found most Indian employees steadier and more fluent in English.

The Meriam Report would lead the incoming Hoover administration to take several actions that benefited the tribes, such as reorganizing the BIA field offices to be more efficient and increasing the BIA budget from $16 million to $20 million. Hoover's people also set out to improve conditions in the BIA schools, and particularly in the boarding schools. But they—from the secretary of the interior on down—believed in the assimilation model and hoped to see the BIA vanish in a quarter of a century. And for all the increased efficiency of BIA reorganization (and not surprisingly the BIA bureaucracy was slow to respond), little advantage accrued, or could have accrued, to the Indians on the ground, largely because the increased budget was used chiefly to raise the salaries of BIA employees. A rearrangement of the very basis of Indian policy had to wait for the Depression and the arrival of the Roosevelt administration.

CHAPTER FIFTEEN

WATERSHED

Arguably, the first two administrations of Franklin D. Roosevelt saved the cultures of American Indians from sliding into oblivion. American Indians tend not to like hearing that argument, and indeed many or some of their cultures might have survived anyway, but it is difficult to imagine how, given the preponderance of federal efforts and policies to destroy them, and even just the relative indifference over so many generations of Indian Bureau people to the worsening poverty and ill-health of their wards. Certainly, if the land bases of the tribes had continued to be eaten away by allotment and other means through the remainder of the twentieth century, few Indian cultures could have survived as recognizable entities. For each Indian tribe (or to some degree those tribes forced together on one reservation) was essentially a separate ethnic group—a land-based ethnic group. Most of those individuals who left for the cities—however much they may over generations have lost much of their traditional ways—thought of the reservation as a geographic and spiritual home base. In the terms of Robert Frost, it was where, when you had to go there, they had to take you in. It was, indeed, the wellspring of one's identity. The Meriam Report had pointed out the evils of allotment, focusing chiefly on the economic deprivation that typically followed in its wake, but the Hoover administration only continued the process.

The Trials and Triumphs of John Collier

With the backing of the lawyer and social reformer Harold Ickes, whom Franklin Roosevelt appointed secretary of the interior, FDR appointed John Collier commissioner of Indian Affairs. It was 1933, well into the Depression, and among Collier's first acts was to hasten emergency food and clothing, like surplus army clothing, to the reservations. He ordered the construction of a hundred new day schools, as well as new hospitals, and increased health staffs. He arranged to have an Indian version of the Civilian Conservation Corps established, and in due course this agency, the Indian Emergency Conservation Work program, put several thousand Indians to work on thirty-three different reservations. On the Navajo Reservation, where the first of these programs went into effect, Indians built roads, and earthen dams to trap the little moisture that fell on their land, for watering sheep and small farming efforts.

Collier's primary initiative was the Indian Reorganization Act of 1934; it essentially put Indian policy on an entirely new footing. Certainly its most immediate benefit was that it called a halt to allotment and the return of any unallotted lands to the control of the tribes. All this was, of course, to better the chances that Indian cultures could continue in all their diversity, rather than be absorbed into the greater society. In this, Collier met with the strong opposition of western congressmen and their constituents, of missionaries, and of churches, not to mention most of the current employees of the BIA, who were, for the most part, staunch assimilationists. The act also called for improved educational facilities that would help preserve Indian traditions, as well as educate Indian children for life on the reservation and, significantly, for jobs with the BIA. (Later, in what amounts to the first example of affirmative action in the federal government, Collier saw to the enactment of a law permitting the Bureau of Indian Affairs to give preference to Indian applicants for jobs, a law that was later reviewed by the Supreme Court, where it was upheld.)

The Indian Reorganization Act (IRA) also authorized $2 million a year to purchase additional land for the tribes, and a $10 million revolving credit fund to help the tribes develop economically. Perhaps as important as ending allotment, the act permitted the tribes to draft constitutions and bylaws that would make them the equivalent of self-governing municipalities, but federal ones. As such they would be able to negotiate with federal, state, and local governments, at the same time retaining all the powers vested in any Indian tribe. Once again, after years of tribal sovereignty being gnawed away by Congress ever since 1871, the Marshall doctrine of "domestic dependent nations" had been revived.

Not every tribe thought this was a good idea. It was popular in the northern Plains and the Great Lakes area, but notably the Klamaths, Crows, and Fort Peck group rejected it, along with several others. Perhaps the most devastating rejection was that by the Navajos in 1935, the margin of loss being a mere 518 votes out of almost sixteen thousand cast. In all, of 252 tribes that decided to vote on this new program, 78 voted against, 174 for, and thirteen did not vote at all for one or another reason. Some of the tribes voting against the program simply saw it as yet another white man program, calling for a white man type of government that was alien to Indian ways (though this particular criticism was more often heard after the fact). Overall, since the larger tribes voted against the IRA reorganization, the majority of Indian individuals were against Collier's program. On the other hand, the original IRA of 1934 had excluded the Oklahoma tribes—at their request—but once they saw the political benefits of having a tribal government empowered to negotiate with the feds and other governments, they sought to be included and were so in the Oklahoma Indian Welfare Act of 1936. By the middle of 1937, almost a hundred tribes had adopted constitutions or ratified corporate charters (the other option in the original act). Some of the votes to adopt constitutions and ratify corporations were by narrow margins—usually with opposition arising from those who were called *full-bloods,* or traditionals (who were typically older members of the tribe). The younger *half-bloods* were typically more fluent in English, better educated (in white ways anyway), and more progressive. Such was the case at the Pine Ridge Reservation, where reorganization was approved by about seventy votes out of some four thousand cast.

Disagreements of this sort do not always quickly fade away in Indian country. Forty-five years later, in the 1970s, a small faction of the Hopi tribe would still be bitterly asserting that the vote at Hopi (which went narrowly for adopting a constitution and a democratically elected tribal council and a tribal chairman) was in fact miscounted since it did not include all the people opposed who simply did not vote. This, they say, means that the tribal council has no legitimate authority—an assertion that has been proven inaccurate by resort to the actual voting records, which do not support this claim.

One of the worries that many antis had at the time was that those who had and were satisfied with allotments would be forced to lose them as their land was absorbed into the tribal common lands. Another criticism, probably more widespread, was simply that an elected council was not an Indian way of doing things. In any event, friction was common on the reservations over this issue.

Nowhere was friction greater than among the Navajos, who had a further reason to distrust the BIA and John Collier. As early as the 1880s, agents on Navajo land had mentioned overgrazing by sheep as a noticeable problem. By the 1920s, it was common knowledge among those non-Indians working on the reservation that its lands were seriously overgrazed—sheep were, of course, central to Navajo life since their introduction by the Spanish, and many Navajos had huge herds. Then came the Dust Bowl days and the land deteriorated yet further, until Collier agreed in 1934 that a major stock reduction was a necessity. The BIA met with the Navajo tribal council (in business since 1923 as a rubber stamp for oil leases) and offered the Navajos more land—to be taken from Arizona and New Mexico—if they would approve a significant program of stock reduction. They agreed and the program was soon under way, but the government's agents implemented it by force and without letting Navajo people know about it in advance or have any say in the matter. Since the market for livestock had collapsed with the Depression, the government (while it paid for them) simply shot the animals where they found them, leaving them to rot. Most Navajos believed the land wasn't overgrazed but simply had deteriorated because of the drought, and most of them perceived Collier as an enemy similar to Kit Carson and General Carleton of the Long Walk. In all, Navajo livestock (horses, cattle, sheep, and goats) were reduced by about 40 percent—a frontal attack on what on Navajo land passed for wealth and status, not to mention basic survival. To make matters worse, the Navajos did not get the added land they had been promised by the federal government, because the state governments balked. It was against this background that the Navajos voted on the question of reorganization, and that the vote was so close is a miracle. Later, Collier simply issued a set of orders to the Navajos under which their existing tribal council was to operate. Collier remains, along with Kit Carson and some others, in the Navajo pantheon of malevolent white oppressors.

These were tumultuous times throughout the nation, and Collier's administration was often attacked by right-wing whites as part of a Communist plot for being so favorable to communitarian principles. The Red-baiters—more noisy than numerous—also objected to Collier's policy of encouraging Indian languages, tribal arts and crafts, and Indian religious ceremonies, and on this latter issue they were sometimes joined by Christian groups that continued to see Indian ceremonies as nearly satanic rites. Even so, in 1935 Congress created the Indian Arts and Crafts Board to help promote and market Indian products and later to certify their authenticity against imitations. The board, along with other initiatives, was part of Collier's attempt to create economic successes on the reservations through traditional tribal skills.

Another idea broached in the halls of Congress resonated with the Indians' well-wishers for ethical reasons (sometimes called guilt feelings); it also pleased those who simply thought the American judicial system and in particular the U.S. Court of Claims was being overburdened; and it seemed like another spiffy ploy to those who wanted the Indians to "get off the federal tit" once and for all. More and more tribes were seeking the special jurisdictional acts of Congress that were necessary to bring a suit into the U.S. Court of Claims, and even with that cumbersome requirement, the court felt that it was besieged. Forty-nine such bills were backlogged in Congress in 1930, which considered them pestiferous, and as often as not, if Congress passed one, the president would not sign it. In all ninety-five such complaints had been heard by the court between 1880 and 1930. Collier wanted a special tribunal—an Indian claims court—to hear such claims, one that was easier to get to. No one listened. Several bills were introduced (but not passed) between 1935 and 1940, calling for an Indian claims *commission* to investigate all Indian claims, both legal and moral, and recommend to Congress the means to settle them. Then people began to realize that such a mechanism still left the decisions up to Congress and might just present another obstacle to resolution. Roosevelt himself believed that such a commission itself should be able to dispose of the claims with finality. There the matter rested on December 7, 1941, when virtually everything by way of reform gave way to the need to mobilize for World War II.

But well before that, as the Depression dragged on, the Roosevelt administration had had to cut back on many of its favorite reform programs. Less money was available for acquiring new lands for the tribes and for helping develop their constitutional or corporate governments. Overall BIA appropriations fell from $27 million in 1932 to $16 million in 1935. Retrenchment followed retrenchment, and an increasingly shrill Collier alienated more and more members of Congress, especially those Republicans who (up until FDR's attempt to pack the Supreme Court) had supported most of the administration's initiatives. After 1937, Collier was largely ineffective in implementing his programs and introducing new ones. One still hears noisome criticism in some quarters: Collier went too far; Collier did not go far enough; Collier did not listen to what Indians themselves wanted; he listened too closely to the Indians.

On the other hand, as anthropologist Nancy Lurie has pointed out, Collier was instrumental in bringing into public consciousness a new view of Indians and a respect for their traditions, and in reasserting the rights of Indians to operate as tribal entities, to act in their own behalf. That this might have had a positive effect on the self-esteem of at least some American Indians has not been definitively proven, but it can hardly be doubted. "Finally," Lurie has written, "although the new tribal constitutions were often inadequate to the tasks of self-government within the Indian communities, they served an extremely important function in allowing the communities to enter into contracts to deal with the federal government and the larger society." In short, Indians now had leverage within the American system that they had not enjoyed in any real sense since the administration of Andrew Jackson. Today, virtually every tribal government in existence has its origins in Collier's pragmatic vision. In 1971, Vine Deloria Jr. would call the Roosevelt years "probably the best years in American history for Indians."

World War II

In December 1941, when the Japanese struck Pearl Harbor, the population of American Indians was about 350,000. It would be only the very old, remote, and traditional among them whose lives would not be significantly changed by the next four years while the United States waged war in Europe and Africa and the Pacific—and at home. In all, some twenty-five thousand Indians served in the military. By 1944, 32 percent of the able-bodied Indian men were in uniform and under arms, some 7 percent of the entire Indian population, which is a highly impressive contribution. About an equal number were left behind on the reservations, and one reason was illiteracy. This would have a profound effect once the war was over, as would many other, more positive aspects of the Indian role in the war.

In addition to those serving as warriors, more than forty-five thousand American Indians worked in other ways in the war effort—half in mostly seasonal agricultural jobs, the rest in war industries. Of these, about twelve thousand were Indian women, most of them experiencing their first paid job, as were so many other American women at the time. A huge exodus from the reservations to urban centers resulted. Skilled and semiskilled Indians from throughout the West migrated to west coast cities and worked in munitions factories and related industries, in canneries and other plants. The Papagos and Pimas (now called O'odham) worked in the Arizona copper mines, which also attracted a number of Navajos and others. Numerous Sioux built air bases and military depots in the Plains states.

Another, less heralded contribution Indians made to the war effort had to do with their land. Extraction of oil and other minerals on Indian land took place as leases were quickly arranged through the Bureau of Indian Affairs. Several of the Plains reservations came to be used as gunnery ranges and for other military purposes. As a result of these uses and later failures to return lands to prewar status, significant portions of some reservations were permanently lost to the Indians. In addition, health care and education on the reservations suffered as BIA budgets were cut and staff left for the war effort.

The Bureau of Indian Affairs made a great deal of the Indians' contribution to the war, and the government brought Ira Hayes, a Pima marine paratrooper, back early from duty in the Pacific to help drum up enthusiasm for a war bond drive. Hayes was one of the six men who raised the flag over Mount Suribachi on Iwo Jima—surely the most remembered photograph from the war. His instant celebrity as a hero, as well as some racism he encountered on the tour, drove poor Hayes to alcoholism, and eventually a sorry life on skid row. Nor was the nation's service always positive for the other Indians who served, many of whom were having their first intensive experience in white society. Drinking and absenteeism were sometimes a problem for Indian work crews on the home front, who were also not accustomed to working under leaders who seemed to be martinets. Some, working close to home, would vanish simply for a family ceremony, regardless of the day of the week. Some were deeply hesitant to be photographed for their identification tags. There was also a bit of resistance to being drafted—usually due to a confusion about the status of Indians. A few Navajos insisted they could not serve, since the Treaty of 1868, by which they were located on their reservation after the Long Walk, forbade them from taking up arms. Some Iroquois claimed that they were not U.S. citizens but members of an altogether different and sovereign nation, and therefore should not serve. More often than not, these confusions were resolved and the Indians went off to war. Historian Donald Parman tells of one instance where a handful of Hopis simply refused to serve because they were pacifists, and were sent to prison for a year and a day. Upon their return they spoke so highly of the food and other accommodations that other Hopis asked how to get sent there.

On the other hand, Indians served in large numbers—in even greater percentages than other groups—and in all theaters of the war, typically alongside men and women of all other races. These wartime bonds were strong. In some instances, as in the Forty-fifth Infantry Division, as many as 20 percent of the troops were Indian (in this case mostly from Oklahoma and New Mexico). The most highly publicized Indian warriors had to wait until after the war for fame to come to them, for their mission was utterly secret. It came about when Philip Johnston, the son of a missionary on the Navajo Reservation, realized that to virtually anyone not brought up among Navajos, their language is utterly impenetrable. He helped develop a series of code words—such as "chicken hawk" for a dive bomber—that, when translated into Navajo, became a way of sending battlefield information in a wholly secure manner. The Japanese never broke the code. In all, some 420 Navajos along with a few other Indians were inducted into the Marine Corps and became the famed *code talkers,* the last remnants of whom are still elaborately honored at virtually any and all Navajo events, such as rodeos, fairs, and large ceremonial occasions. At an Indian youth rodeo in Ramah, New Mexico, in the 1990s, for example, all the Navajo vets sat in their uniforms in the front of the bleachers, and the first order of business for the rodeo announcer was to pay homage to one code talker and the other World War II vets present, then to the vets of later wars through the Gulf War, and finally to announce the singing of "The Star-Spangled Banner."

(It is often overlooked in the celebration of the code talkers that there were Hopi code talkers as well. In fact, some Comanche warriors served a similar function in World War I, though not as extensively as the code talkers of World War II.)

Not all that long after Ira Hayes helped raise the flag over Mount Suribachi, the war was over, ended by two vast mushroom clouds over Hiroshima and Nagasaki. Along with the rest of the American troops, American Indians returned to the United States to be demobilized. These were men who had served and suffered, who had saved the lives of white buddies and been saved by white buddies. They had caroused and drunk together on moments of leave, they had seen the world—whether it was Manila, in the Philippines, or Cairo or Paris or Rome.

They came home to the reservations as local heros. One Crow warrior, Joseph Medicine Crow, told anthropologist Peter Nabokov how he never thought about war honors as the four coups a Crow warrior of earlier times had to achieve in battle. But as he recounted his experiences in Germany to members of his tribe—surviving an attack that led him into the midst of an array of German foxholes and trenches, dynamiting some German artillery, knocking a German soldier off his feet and making him surrender, and finally breaking into a German compound and running off with some fifty German horses—his fellow Crows pointed out that he had completed the four coups and had earned himself the role of chief.

Being back home on the reservation, however, had its wrenching features. Returning vets were not allowed to drink without fear of being arrested. They were not, in many instances, allowed to vote, still being wards of the government they had fought under. On the reservations, there was practically no way they could find work that would pay as well as their military paycheck. Instead, they were greeted mostly by conditions of poverty and ill health. Even for those back home to whom some of the warriors had sent at least part of their paychecks, or who had worked in the fields or in the factories, the flush times were over. The nation had to retool, to accommodate hundreds of thousands of out-of-work former soldiers and war workers. Men took back the jobs that women had filled. It was a wholly different world after four years of war, and for the American Indians, it would never again be as it had been. Many Indians decided to live in the cities, to find jobs that military service had qualified them for. At the beginning of the war, some 7 percent of American Indians were urban dwellers. By 1950, this number would more than double, and it would keep growing at increasingly rapid rates until more than half of all Indians would live off-reservation. Many of these urban Indians would become less tribalized, identifying themselves not so much by clan or tribe but simply as Indians. That would be something new, something that Indians had never been able to bring off, even with the exhortations of Pontiac, or of Tecumseh and his brother, the Prophet. During the war, a number of Indian leaders had banded together to form the National Congress of American Indians, a group that would speak to the needs of all Indians, but even with that promising organization in business, pan-Indianism was not, at war's end, what could be called a movement. It was just happening here and there, on the ground. Few people in the rest of society—what is called the *dominant society*—took much notice. Most city dwellers would pass uncuriously by a building, on some side street in the city, called the American Indian Social Club or something similar. Life on the reservations went on below the radar of a new international power facing the exigencies and promise of the postwar atomic age. In about a decade and a half, though, Americans would suddenly become aware of the Indians in their midst.

Immediately after the war, most of the Indians returned to reservations. Navajos, for example, had been sent off to war with a ceremony and needed another performed, a cleansing Enemy Way ceremony, upon their return. Inevitably, facing the poverty and ennui on the reservation, some returnees would go the way of Ira Hayes. Many of those who returned to their reservations were determined to make a difference, to improve the lives of their people. Here, then, was a new generation of leadership, a large percentage of Indians who wanted better things for their people and who believed they knew how to accomplish that. After all, while the Roosevelt administrations had not come near to solving all the problems on the reservations, they at least made a deliberate effort to honor and strengthen Indian cultures. That would be something to build on.

Perhaps the major effect of the war years on Indian life was the creation of a powerful thirst for education. Indians who were illiterate had not been able to serve as soldiers, and this was a mighty incentive. But those who had served abroad and those in war industrial jobs became well aware that a comparative lack of education held Indians back. There were, for example, few Indian officers in World War II. Thousands upon thousands of Indian people returned to peacetime convinced that in order to deal with the white world, to enter it as those in cities did or to compete with it from the reservation—to understand the world of which they were inevitably and unmistakably a part— education was essential. With the GI Bill of Rights, many returning Indian soldiers were able to continue their education into colleges and vocational schools. All around the country, from Mohawk country to southern California, Indian people demanded education as never before. They demanded it for themselves and for their children.

Some Final Solutions

Even before the end of the war, ominous noises had begun to emanate from Washington and elsewhere. Western senators, including Senator Burton Wheeler, who had sponsored the Indian Reorganization Act in 1934, turned on John Collier and all his works, as well as most of the works of the New Deal. Mostly highly partisan Republican conservatives called for the repeal of the IRA, a return to allotment, and the abolishment of the Bureau of Indian Affairs. Some claimed to smell communism in the communitarian nature of tribal life, such as tribally owned lands. In the Truman presidency, they remained a highly vocal, even strident minority in the Senate and the House, but they were joined by the National Council of Churches, which publicly encouraged an end to the Collier policy of tribal cultural independence, which encouraged the pagan religious practices of the tribes. Soon after the war ended, a new word increasingly echoing a bipartisan consensus was heard: "termination." This term meant ending reservations and the federal government's trust obligations to the tribes. To Indian people, termination sounded very much like extermination. In 1945, there was enough support for this new policy idea (and so little support for his own policies) that Collier resigned as commissioner of Indian Affairs.

To be sure, now that the war was over and won, members of Congress took up the cudgels for an earlier idea, an Indian claims commission, or court, whereby all of the various Indian claims against the government for lands taken wrongly, for mismanagement of reservation funds, and for other lapses could be brought and settled once and for all. For most congressmen, this seemed only fair—especially given the great contribution Indians had made to the war effort. By then it had become fairly widely known that American Indians had contributed more sons to the military—proportionately—than any other ethnic minority in the nation. The idea appealed to those who believed in the rightness of letting the tribes remain tribes, for the awards to the Indians would help them finance economic development on the reservations. To those who favored termination, the commission and its awards would make palatable—if not to the Indians, then to the terminators' sense of justice—the withdrawal of the federal government from Indian affairs (by giving all its functions to the states). Indians would, after all, either be paid off or have their claims found not valid. One way or the other, it was expected that many of them would head for the cities and the BIA budget could be slashed in half, and eventually to nothing. A good deal of congressional rhetoric was expended from both points of view, all couched in terms of high purpose and the nobility of the red man. A South Dakota representative, for example, in his paean to the Indians, said that praise "is particularly due the Indians who have been wards of the Government, and who, when the testing time came, proved themselves staunch, true and courageous warriors for the cause of the United States."

Of course another reason, and perhaps the main one, for a claims commission was that it would absolve Congress of the annoying, politically controversial, and time-consuming business of voting on special judicial acts to let the Indians file their claims with the U.S. Court of Claims. The final House and Senate versions of the bill to create such a commission were shepherded through by a strangely matched pair—a Mormon lawyer named Ernest Wilkinson and the Interior Department's associate solicitor, a Jewish intellectual named Felix Cohen, who had single-handedly codified all the disorganized statutes, treaties, administrative rulings, and other instruments that impinged on Indian law generally into the *Handbook of Indian Law.* This soon became essentially the bible of Indian law and was used as such by even the Supreme Court.

When the Indian Claims Commission Act was eventually signed by Harry Truman on August 13, 1946, Truman's office released a statement that said this measure "removes a lingering discrimination against our First Americans and gives them the same opportunities that our laws extend to all other American citizens." Members of Congress positively warbled. "The most constructive piece of Indian legislation . . . during the past quarter of a century," said one. Another declared that it meant "the dawn of a new era for the American Indian."

The Indian Claims Commission Act established a commission of three men to be chosen by the president. They would hear any claim that any legitimate Indian group brought before them (but not individual claims or grievances) within five years of the passage of the act. Any claim dating back to the formation of the United States in 1776 could be brought before the commission: there was no statute of limitations. The commission would then settle all these claims by the end of the following five years. (Any claims arising after August 13, 1946, would have to be settled the old way, in the U.S. Court of Claims.) The only remedy available was money—in other words, a claim for land taken by the government from a tribe by virtue of fraud, say, could not result in the return of the land, but only payment for the loss. The amount of such payments, or awards, was to be determined by the commissioners. The act also provided for the right of appeal—to the Court of Claims and to the U.S. Supreme Court.

One of the most striking parts of the act (and one that alarmed the Justice Department, which would be defending the government) allowed the commission to compensate tribes for "claims based upon fair and honorable dealings that are not recognized by any existing rule of law or equity." This meant that the commission would hear moral claims as well as legal claims. For example, in previous suits, if a tribe had said that—whether by government agents' fraud or as a result of ignorance on the part of the Indians—the government had produced and the tribe had signed a treaty that paid the Indians an unconscionably low price for a land cession, the Court of Claims had ruled that that was a moral, not a legal, claim, and the Indians lost the suit. The "fair and honorable dealings" clause was included precisely to circumvent such rulings, and it would also be called upon in such matters as the wholesale shipment of the Chiricahuas—those who were guiltless by any definition, along with those who had been hostile—to twenty-seven years in prison camps.

As friendly to the Indians as the act was, it failed to take into account several important considerations. It did not provide that the commissioners should have any experience in Indian affairs, nor did it give anything by way of guidance as to how any of the claims should be settled. It was vague about the nature of accounting claims—such as mismanagement of reservation affairs by the government compared with the services supplied. It did not create a true investigative arm for the commission, and this along with other factors essentially meant that the commission would have to rely on information gathered by the tribes and their lawyers and the Justice Department. In other words, it would not act as a commission, listening to all and sundry sides and interlocutors something in the manner of Indian dispute resolution, but rather it would act as a court in which the adversarial system of Anglo-American law was the sole means of reaching the truth. Since most of the commissioners and other involved were, in fact, lawyers, this did not seem inappropriate, but it would have significant effects on the outcome of many claims as the years went by. Of course, five years—even ten years—was nowhere near long enough to settle the 850-odd claims that would be filed. The commission would struggle on until 1978. All but about fifty were over lost lands (indeed, many people erroneously called the commission the Indian *Land* Claims Commission). The remaining cases were over the government's role as a trustee of Indian moneys.

Even as the commission was gathering itself and alerting the tribes that they should file claims, the congressional faction in favor of termination was gathering strength, and the views of the Bureau of Indian Affairs were changing as well. As a response to the poverty and, importantly, lack of employment opportunities on the reservations, the BIA began a program of what came to be called relocation. Beginning on the Navajo and Hopi Reservations in 1948, the BIA moved Indians from their homelands to cities, providing them with transportation, some training and counseling, and subsistence funds until they got their first paycheck. The relocation program was expanded continuously from then on—to other tribes and to multiple cities from Los Angeles to Cleveland. By 1960, some thirty-three thousand Indians had been relocated by this program, but they were only part of the exodus. Many Indians, beset by the same problems that faced rural whites, voluntarily left the reservations for cities and the hope for a better life. By 1960, about 140,000 (or 40 percent of) American Indians lived in cities.

Ironically, given the attempts by nineteenth-century Californians to rid their state of "diggers," California has for several decades had by far the largest population of urban Indians. Today, of the 2.3 million people who identify themselves as Indians, about three quarters live in cities, the other quarter on reservations. About three quarters of all American Indians also live in the West. The trend to urbanization was well under way in the middle of the twentieth century and has continued at an accelerating rate.

Many Indians who relocated to the cities maintained ties with home, often going back for ceremonies and for other reasons, and this remains true. But relocation could be highly disruptive of tribal cohesion and loyalties. Intermarriage with Indians from other tribes, or with whites or blacks, attenuated one's tribal affiliation, as did the complex adjustments one had to make to adapt to life in the cities. There is, in fact, something called Indian time—many Indian people found strange (and still do) the way white people so frantically adjust their lives to a clock—and this was just one cultural difference that made adapting to city life (or indeed the white man's world) difficult. Regrettably, little study of urban Indians took place, so adaptations to urban life are not well understood to this day. After the end of World War II, anthropologists' attentions turned away from American Indians toward societies abroad, particularly in Africa and Asia. This was also a time when the notion of *acculturation* was in the anthropological air, but even so, most American anthropologists were not interested in the processes by which their erstwhile subjects were adapting to the new world of postwar American life.

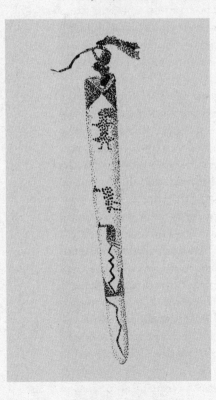

Havasupai scratching stick

(A tendency then as now in some quarters was to believe that the more acculturated Indian people became, the less they were truly Indian. In the 1970s, for example, the Havasupai Indians of northern Arizona found themselves the butt of this sort of thinking. They had long lived in a small horticultural village in a canyon tributary of Grand Canyon, a place graced with a beautiful river with several spectacular waterfalls. In summer, the Havasupais had traditionally moved up out of the canyon to the high ground to hunt and graze livestock. Their reservation did not include the lands above and they needed permission each year to go there. They requested that their former hunting grounds be added to their reservation and conservationists, particularly the Sierra Club, rose up in opposition to the Havasupais—and the club's own Native American Committee—fearing that if the tribe owned those lands, it might build a hotel on them and the conservationists would not be able to block it, not having standing to sue an Indian tribe. To ridicule the Havasupais' request, one noted Sierra Club official announced that he had visited the Havasupais down in their canyon and reported, "They aren't even real Indians. They have refrigerators and wear sneakers.")

Nineteen forty-eight also saw the passage of a bill establishing a grant program for higher education within the Bureau of Indian Affairs and the resolution of voting rights in two important states. Arizona, as noted earlier, refused Indians the vote because the state constitution excluded "persons under guardianship." In New Mexico, "Indians not taxed" were denied the vote. Two Mojave Indians sued in Arizona, and an Isleta Pueblo man sued in New Mexico. Courts ruled that both state constitutional provisions were unconstitutional. As the states fell into line on this issue, Indians would gain a considerable political clout in several western states, particularly South Dakota, Arizona, and New Mexico, where reservation Indians lived in significant enough numbers to be, on occasion, a bloc of swing votes in some state elections.

Voting rights came too late to save a large amount of Sioux land from being deliberately flooded. The Missouri River had flooded badly in 1943, and the Army Corps of Engineers proposed building fifteen hundred miles of levees below Sioux City and five major dams above the city. The Bureau of Reclamation joined in, and the upshot was that twenty-three reservations were affected, with the Sioux losing in all some 550 square miles of their most productive land to inundation, with nine hundred families (a third of their population) displaced. Similar loss of land and lifeways (in this case, fishing rights) occurred to the tribes living along the Columbia River—Yakimas, Nez Perces, Umatillas, and others. It was becoming ever clearer that Indians could not trust the federal government in all its many departments, manifestations, and bewilderingly contradictory initiatives, especially given that the BIA's duties were so at odds with Interior's other agencies. More and more, Indians began to realize that perhaps their real future lay with their own tribal councils—those governments that had come into being with reorganization—and with other Indian people.

On the other hand, as more and more Indians moved to cities, serious splits between urban and reservation members of a tribe could and did arise, none more crucial than that among the Klamath Indians of Oregon over the matter of termination, which was the federal government's last totally dictatorial effort to bring about a final solution of the "Indian question."

Termination

In 1947, under congressional subpoena, the acting commissioner of Indian Affairs explained how he had separated the Indian reservations into three categories. The first group consisted of the Flatheads, Klamaths, Menominees, Osages, Iroquois, and a few others. These tribes, he said, were sufficiently successful to no longer need federal assistance. A second group would need another decade before federal services could be withdrawn, and a third category of tribes would need an indefinite period of federal assistance.

Menominee dream guardian

As it turned out, this was the basis for a "kindly" compromise. With the advent of the Eisenhower administration in 1952 and with it Republican control of Congress, conservative Republicans led by Utah's senator Arthur Watkins were baying for the immediate abolishment of the Bureau of Indian Affairs and the withdrawal of federal funds from all the tribes. In his campaign, Eisenhower, the soldier, had praised Indian contributions to the war, and promised that they would be consulted about any change in Indian policy. This was not to be.

Instead, again with Senator Watkins carrying the flag, Congress passed House Concurrent Resolution 108, and Eisenhower signaled his agreement by signing it on August 1, 1953. A much less severe measure than what Watkins would have preferred, it called for an end of federal supervision over all Indians within the states of New York, Texas, Florida, and California, as well as the Flatheads (Montana), Klamaths (Oregon), Menominees (Wisconsin), and a few others. It said, as well, that all Indians should be subject to the same laws and have the same rights as all other American citizens. Various reform groups pointed out that the tribes had not been consulted about any of this. The new secretary of the interior said he would rectify this, later claiming (mendaciously, in an echo of Holm Bursum some thirty years earlier) that the tribes included in the bill were in favor of the measure.

Congress then began hearings—both houses jointly, led by Utah's Watkins—on the development of individual tribal termination bills. In all some sixty Indian groups were eventually slated for termination. Among the first to be terminated and the hardest hit by this policy were the Klamaths and the Menominees. Both dwelled in reservations that were heavily forested, and timber sales had rendered both tribes relatively prosperous. Both wound up hammered for their efforts.

The Klamaths were aboriginally settled on some 20 million acres in what is now northern California and southern Oregon, mostly forested high country. In 1864 the federal government negotiated a treaty that put the Klamaths on about a tenth of their original land, all in Oregon, where they would not be encroached upon. But at the same time other federal agents moved the Modocs and some Paiutes to the same lands. One upshot of the expectable intertribal conflict was that the Modocs broke out and went home, which led to the Modoc War in 1872, in which Captain Jack (as whites called the Modoc leader Kintpuash) and some fifty others held off a thousand troops for six months near Tule Lake, and cost the federal government half a million dollars. Captain Jack and three other leaders were eventually hanged.

When allotment came along in 1887, the Klamaths retained their unallotted land but over the years lost 70 percent of the lands that were allotted. Even so, per capita payments for timber sales made the Klamaths relatively well off. Meanwhile a considerable number of Klamath people moved to the cities, and when Congress in 1954 voted to terminate the Klamath Reservation, most of the city Klamaths were all for it, seeing that what remained of the tribal lands would be sold and per capita payments made to them as well as those who had remained on the reservation. The reservation Klamaths were opposed but the tribe was terminated. The standard federal programs due Indians were cut off, and the Klamaths became just another group of people who sought help from the local government if they needed it. In this, they were not surprisingly last in line. The lumbering income came to an end. The results were catastrophic: within a few years it was clear that infant mortality was rising steeply, along with alcoholism and deaths among people under fifty. Less than a third of Klamaths finished high school and three times as many Klamaths as non-Indians in Klamath County lived below poverty levels. Not until twenty years passed were the Klamaths able to reachieve federal recognition as a tribe, and by that time they were utterly landless.

The experience of the Menominees was not dissimilar. They had gotten their name from the Ojibways. It refers to wild rice, which, with maple sugar and sturgeon, traditionally made up most of the Menominee diet in the lake-filled woodlands of northeastern Wisconsin. Their extensive lands also became home for various other tribes—Winnebagos, Potawatomis, Sauks, and Foxes—and then, of course, white settlers. By 1880, more than a million settlers lived on what the Menominees considered aboriginal land. They survived allotment by arguing that their timber resources were needed to sustain them into the future. In 1935 they managed to sue the government for mismanaging Menominee forest resources, and in 1951 they were awarded $8.5 million as compensation. Then they learned they were among the tribes likely to be terminated. They asked for an immediate per capita payment of $1,000 against the compensation owed them, and in a bill authorizing this, Arthur Watkins slipped a provision terminating the tribe in three years. The tribe's general council believed it was simply approving the per capita payments and learned only later that they had voted for termination. In these times, only a few tribes in the nation had legal counsel, and most of them believed that the Bureau of Indian Affairs had the responsibility to look after their legal affairs.

In 1961, the Menominee tribal rolls were closed and the tribe became a corporation. Taxes had to be paid, and a once prosperous nation of Indians soon became the Wisconsin's poorest county as the corporation had to sell off its assets to survive. Tribal land, livelihood, and identity were gone. This disaster continued for more than a decade until a young Menominee woman, Ada Deer, began a grassroots movement to stop land sales and to regain federal recognition, which was accomplished in 1972. Ada Deer would in time become the first woman to serve as assistant secretary of Indian Affairs, a Clinton appointment.

As early as Eisenhower's second term, it had become obvious even to some of the hard-liners that the Indian tribes were simply not ready to have federal assistance withdrawn and their lands made subject to state and local laws and taxation. Democrats gained control of Congress, and men like Senator Mike Mansfield of Montana and Frank Church of Idaho controlled the various committees on Indian affairs. An antitermination tide began to rise. Conservative Barry Goldwater from Arizona defended the administration's policy of termination but said it was at best a long-range goal. New Mexico's senator Clinton Anderson, a staunch terminationist, changed his mind. A new secretary of the interior, Fred Seaton from Nebraska, promised that tribes had to understand and agree to termination or it would not take place. The Bureau of Indian Affairs, under a new commissioner, Glenn Emmons, developed a two-pronged plan of encouraging relocation but at the same time encouraging industry to locate on the reservations by various schemes such as tax breaks. The last termination bill was passed in 1962.

Overall, the immediate effects of termination had less sociological effect than the enormous migration to the cities at this time. Many thousands more people had to acculturate to city life than were dispossessed by the policy of termination. But termination had a far more potent and widespread symbolic impact. It was the ultimate putdown, an utter betrayal of trust responsibilities by the federal government. In taking note that the Bureau of Indian Affairs usually justified its requests to Congress for funds by saying it was working toward the goal of getting out of "the Indian business," Earl Old Person, a Blackfoot, testified to the Kennedy administration that trying to plan one's tribal future was hard if not impossible when the BIA constantly threatened to wipe the Indians out. "It's like trying to cook a meal in your tipi when someone is standing outside trying to burn the tipi down.

"So let's agree," he went on, "to forget the termination talk and instead talk of development of Indian people, their land, and their culture. . . . Why is it so important that Indians be brought into the 'mainstream of American life'? What is the 'mainstream of American life'? . . . Is it the same now as it was twenty-five years ago?"

Old Person went on to speak of the treaties Indians had signed, saying, "We do not demonstrate in the streets to get our rights. We feel we have rights guaranteed to us by these treaties and we trust the Government to respect these rights." As he spoke in 1961, the mainstream of American life was about to shift, and its currents were about to overflow the banks. And Indians would soon enough be taking to the streets.

CHAPTER SIXTEEN

RED POWER

Alcatraz and Earlier

On November 20, 1969, newscasts informed the American public that a group of eighty-nine Indians calling themselves Indians of All Tribes had taken over Alcatraz Island in San Francisco Bay, and that they intended to stay there until their demands were met. Alcatraz? Most Americans were either bewildered or amused. Why would *anyone* voluntarily go *to* Alacatraz, the Rock, the most feared name in the American penal landscape? Who were these Indians of All Tribes?

They were Sioux, Navajos, Mohawks, Cherokees, Ojibways, Puyallups, Yakimas, Omahas, and others—mostly young people—and they announced their intention to "reclaim" the island of Alacatraz and turn it into a center for Indian spiritual growth, ecological and native studies, and a museum. They referred to a nineteenth-century treaty the Sioux had signed granting the tribe rights to unused federal property on Indian land, and they claimed the island "in the name of all American Indians."

Several months later, the Indians of All Tribes released a statement angrily setting forth their grievances, saying, "We came to Alcatraz because we were sick and tired of being pushed around, exploited, and degraded everywhere we turned in our own country." Alcatraz, they announced, was a place where we "can beat our drums all night long if we want to and not be bothered by or harassed by non-Indians or police. We can worship, we can sing, and we can make plans for our lives and the future of our Indian people."

This kind of straight talk from Indians was something new to most people in the dominant society. However outlandish it might have seemed, there was no mistaking that the Indians on Alcatraz had taken it upon themselves to open a new era.

> We are a proud people! We are Indians! We have observed and rejected much of what so-called civilization offers. We are Indians! We will preserve our traditions and ways of life by educating our own children. We are Indians! We will join hands in a unity never before put into practice. Our Mother Earth awaits our voices. We are Indians of All Tribes!!!

Earlier in the decade, the Rock had been decommissioned as a penitentiary. Allies of the Indians of All Nations brought the occupiers provisions by boat, and the occupiers held powwows and news conferences. They held the island for nineteen months, their number swelling to as much as a thousand in the summer of 1970, and dwindling to fifteen the following summer, when they were escorted off the island by federal officials.

By simplistic standards, the occupation failed, since the island never became an Indian center or museum. On the other hand, most American Indians of the era and most historians agree that Alcatraz was the signal event in the rise of a new attitude among Indians and, on the part of the American public, about Indians. For practically an entire generation of Indians, it was the opening announcement that the long history of victimization was over, that Indian people intended to take their own destinies into their own hands, that being an Indian was something to be proud of.

What these American Indians were doing was taking advantage of the great upwelling of ethnic pride and assertion that came about in the sixties with the civil rights movement and washed over the nation in the seventies, changing the landscape of American politics and society probably forever. These were the decades inaugurated by the Civil Rights Act and marked by urban riots, the desegregation of schools and other public facilities, radical youth movements, hippies and LSD, the quagmire of Vietnam, huge marches on Washington, D.C., in protest over poverty and the war, and the assassinations of President

John Kennedy, Martin Luther King Jr., and Senator Robert Kennedy. Only months before Alacatraz, two black American Olympic medalists had scandalized the world by raising the fists of black power at the awards ceremony in Mexico City, and two Americans amazed the world by setting foot on the moon. President Richard Nixon, who had served as vice president during Eisenhower's eight years of Indian termination policies, was now president, promising, however improbably, a new era of cooperation between Indian tribes and the federal government.

Alcatraz, which Vine Deloria Jr. called the "masterstroke" of Indian activism, was not the first such act, but the most noticeable and the most noticed—and the most effective up to that point. The decade of the sixties had also seen the Indian version of the sit-in—a fish-in in the waters off Washington State, where the state ruled that off-reservation fishing by the Indians was illegal while the tribes said such fishing rights were theirs by treaty. One of the leaders of this event was a Makah, a member of a traditional fishing tribe whose reservation was on the northwestern corner of the Olympic Peninsula, a man who was an officer of a recently established pan-Indian group called the National Indian Youth Council. Like many other youth organizations, the NIYC was media savvy, militant, and a bit radical. It began using words and phrases borrowed from the other militant youth cultures—such as "Indian power structure" and "Uncle Tomahawks," and over the next several years it would stage a variety of attention-getting confrontations and protests. More fish-ins occurred—chiefly in Oregon and Washington—and they gained a good deal of sympathy from some liberals, most notably actor Marlon Brando and the black comedian Dick Gregory. Even so, these fishing issues received largely regional coverage.

One of the most widely admired features common in Indian cultures is the respect people have for the elders. So while the militant Indian youths could talk of Uncle Tomahawks, they could not bring themselves to the level of condemnation that many militant white youth movements regularly leveled against older generations. Even so, there were gaps among Indians. Many older Indian people generally were uncomfortable with the confrontational style, and reservation Indians were, as often as not, shocked and a bit dismayed by the behavior of their urban relatives. The National Congress of American Indians seemed all the more conservative in this period (at least by comparison), refusing for example to endorse the Poor People's March on

Washington in 1968, while many Indian youths from the NIYC joined in. Relocation had brought more Indians to the cities, and government efforts to keep Indian students in school and send them on to college had increased the Indian population on campuses. Even so, amid the continuing violence in the country at large and the increasingly loud demonstrations, the militant Indian events were comparatively low-key.

Meanwhile, the Kennedy administration had not really managed to arrive at its own Indian policy, except to try to foster more business investment on the reservations, and after the assassination, Lyndon Johnson made efforts to bring his War on Poverty with all of its many social initiatives like Head Start to Indian reservations as well. In 1968, Congress passed the Indian Civil Rights Act, what would seem to be an altogether benign piece of legislation, but like so many others, it served to muddy some of the waters in Indian country. (The militants at Alcatraz dismissed the Indian Civil Rights Act as mostly just talk. It hadn't, they said, changed the behavior of the dominant society.) Did the entire Bill of Rights in the United States Constitution apply to American Indians as U.S. citizens, or were there special circumstances that excluded them from some provisions? The 1968 act excluded Indians from the prohibition of established religion, since such tribes as the Pueblos were what could be called theocracies, and it was the intent of Congress not to intrude too far into such tribal affairs. Some tribes handled judicial matters in such a nonadversarial way as to make the guarantee of a jury trial inappropriate. As reasonable and as surprisingly responsive to Indian cultural ways as this act appeared to be, it was enacted with virtually no input from the Indians and was deeply resented by many for that reason—more of the same old business of the white society pushing their own answers to the "Indian question." As it turned out, this was the last major piece of national legislation on Indian affairs about which Indians would have so little say.

The year 1968 also saw the first sprouting of what would turn out to be the most militant of national Indian organizations, the American Indian Movement. It began in Minneapolis, devoted to obtaining needed services for urban Indians and also watching out for mistreatment of Indians by the authorities—something like the original purposes of the Black Panthers. Led by charismatic men like Dennis Banks and Clyde Bellecourt, two Chippewas, and soon joined by Russell

Means, a Sioux, it became a national movement that brought direct attention to such pan-Indian issues as economic independence, self-determination, political autonomy, and the education of Indian children. With each passing year, AIM became more noticeable, more angry, and more confrontational. While the last stragglers hung on at Alcatraz, Indian militancy was headed for its noisy, almost raucous heights. It would have both positive and tragic effects.

The Militant Seventies

Soon after Alcatraz, AIM took its highly symbolic protests to areas closer to the reservations. Protesting "many, many broken treaties," AIM and several similar groups that had sprouted all at about the same time occupied part of Mount Rushmore in South Dakota. Some Sioux leaders protested the protesters, calling them "out-of-state Indians." The same groups then mounted a Thanksgiving Day demonstration at Plymouth Rock that entailed boarding the *Mayflower II,* a replica of the original, to the dismay of some of the local Indians. The National Indian Youth Council, in 1970, mounted a highly public campaign against a Utah school for Navajos, charging it with racism, discrimination against the Native American Church, and brutality; and soon Indian student protests began elsewhere over a variety of issues, from school mascots and Indian hairstyles to more august matters. In these early years of the 1970s, AIM also led occupations of museums and local BIA offices. Two major efforts were soon to take place, both filled with symbolism and even dramaturgy and, as they got out of hand, felonies—all of which would gain sympathy from some, scare others, and draw new and forceful attention to the long and sad history of American Indian grievances. In both cases, AIM—now with chapters in many cities from Milwaukee to Denver—was the spark plug. It was a heady time, with young men now proudly wearing ribbon shirts and eagle feathers in their long braids, with the scenes of their militancy embroidered on blue jean jackets, instead of wearing what Mary Crow Dog, a young Sioux woman at the center of many of these demonstrations, would call, in her autobiography, *Lakota Woman,* "that hangdog reservation look."

Most of the youthful members of AIM who came from either the cities or the reservations were greatly influenced by the rebellious and often rough battles for civil rights that had erupted in many parts of society. They were often hard-drinking rebels, given to street talk as well as poetic invocations of the past. Many had been runaways, vagabonds, forced to become petty thieves, and they tended to scare the previous generation of Indians (though some of the most traditional elders on the Plains were entranced by the young militants). But the militants perceived that engaging in drunken barroom fights among themselves instead of the old raiding was not enough. As Mary Crow Dog would write, "You can't live forever off the deeds of Sitting Bull or Crazy Horse. You can't wear their eagle feathers, freeload off their legends. You have to make your own legends now. It isn't easy."

The first of the major national efforts was a cross-country caravan called the Trail of Broken Treaties. It marked a shift in strategy from addressing urban Indian problems to those of the reservations. Starting out in San Francisco in late 1972, the caravan was designed to arrive in Washington, D.C., just before election day to achieve maximum publicity. Along the way, a stream of typically beat-up, overcrowded cars would arrive at a reservation to collect more protesters and then move on, often bringing the twin schisms—generational and urban-rural— into sharper focus. On the Northern Cheyenne Reservation in Montana, for example, the children in school "were jumping out the windows," according to one teacher and tribal member. "AIM made a big impression." As sociologist Joane Nagel has chronicled, the older Cheyennes were less impressed. The AIM people did not know any dances, or any Cheyenne language, and were a bit scary to some of the Cheyennes. On the other hand, as tribal leader Ted Rising Sun recalled, "They fired off an automatic weapon. Most of us had been in combat in Korea and World War II. We'd heard automatic weapons. They didn't do anything for guys like us."

In due course, several hundred Indians arrived in Washington over a period of two days beginning November 1 to demonstrate outside the headquarters of the BIA. A good proportion of the protesters were younger reservation Indians who supported the red power movement and its heady programs. Indeed, there were so many protesters that housing arrangements were inadequate, one of the reasons why the demonstration changed from using the BIA steps as a forum to occupying the building, renaming it the Native American Embassy. The occupation lasted a week and was a major news story. The occupiers presented a twenty-point program for improving the lot of Indians, and various press releases detailing the unfortunate history of Indian-white relations, especially the failures of the BIA (which AIM and some others believed should be abolished, its functions turned over to other federal agencies). In the course of complex negotiations, the White House agreed to establish a task force to meet with the Indians to discuss their grievances, to recommend against any prosecution of the occupiers, and to pay for some of the caravan members' return trips.

On November 8, the protesters left, carrying with them boxes of what they called incriminating evidence, most of which was later returned. The building they had occupied was seriously damaged, which led several of the caravan's own leaders, along with other Indian leaders such as the National Congress of American Indians and the National Tribal Chairmen's Association, to deplore the action. But the Trail of Broken Treaties had some immediate effects: the commissioner of Indian Affairs was fired, and a new, higher-level post was created—assistant secretary of the interior for Indian Affairs—and filled by an Iowa Indian, Melvin Franklin. The BIA was in bureaucratic chaos, and for reasons that had nothing to do with Indian policy, the Nixon Administration at this time began dismantling the Office of Economic Opportunity, which, as a minor part of its efforts, had played a promising role on many reservations.

Three months later (almost to the day), AIM seized the nation's attention again, when two hundred armed members along with some locals took over the hamlet of Wounded Knee on the Oglala Sioux Reservation at Pine Ridge, South Dakota. It was February 7, 1973, and the symbolic nature of this occupation was lost on few Americans. Wounded Knee was known to many non-Indian Americans through a recent best-selling book by Dee Brown, *Bury My Heart at Wounded Knee,* about the nineteenth-century massacre there. The political nature of the occupation was far more complex, and few non-Indians understood much of it. The seizure of the hamlet was justified largely on the accusation that the Oglala tribal chairman, Richard Wilson, was corrupt and used tribal members as goons to keep the rest of the Oglalas down. Roadblocks were set up (and largely ignored as people came and went). Firefights broke out almost daily. Two hundred FBI agents and U.S. marshals descended on the town with heavy arms and helicopters, and squabbled among themselves. The occupiers also squabbled among themselves. The Oglalas, like many other tribal groups, were deeply and bitterly divided at this time. Many church groups came to the aid of the militants at Wounded Knee, as did several national organizations such as the Indian Rights Association, and several church members made efforts to negotiate peace amid the shooting.

The National Tribal Chairmen's Association opposed the occupation, believing that this was no time to deny an elected tribal council the right to govern, since that was something that had taken so many years, decades, even centuries, to obtain. The outspoken Mary Crow Dog would contemptuously call all the tribal chairmen half-bloods, meaning not real Indians, or "skins." The National Congress of American Indians, also fearful of the notion of a tribal government being overturned by urban Indians or other dissidents, joined in opposition. Middle-of-the-roaders among Indians complained that the issues pursued by AIM at Wounded Knee had little to do with the real problems on reservations, such as mineral rights, water rights, economic development, and health.

In the national media, the entire affair was made vivid (which it was) and romantic and fairly simple (which it wasn't). There is, after all, nothing that is romantic about gunfire, and firefights were common if typically ineffective. Mary Crow Dog gave birth to her first child as bullets flew overhead. The siege lasted for seventy days, resulting in the deaths of two of the Indian occupiers, the paralysis of one U.S. marshal, and the hamlet destroyed. Federal agents negotiated the final settlement directly with AIM, thus bypassing and diminishing the tribal government. By the time the siege ended, the media were long gone, the Wilson government was in place, and the occupiers were granted none of their demands except to obtain a federal commission to look into the 1868 treaties with the Sioux. In the aftermath, many AIM members spent much of the next years in court, on the run, or in prison.

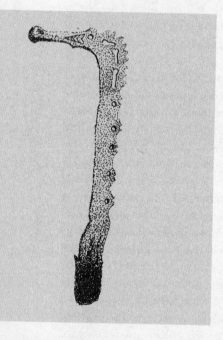

Ojibway antler drumstick

The net effect of the siege of Wounded Knee is probably incalculable. One observer, Tim Giago, a Pine Ridge newspaperman, complained that it was a disaster for the Oglalas themselves, who were left to clean up the mess, and whose plight was forgotten as the news media ran off to other stories. Their federal funds were cut, according to Giago, and litigation went against them. Others believed along with Russell Means that Wounded Knee was "the catalyst for the rebirth of our self-dignity and pride in being Indians." Both views are probably correct. In addition, the red power movement, of which AIM was the preeminent leader, forced Indians to focus all the more clearly on their own tribal as well as pan-Indian agendas. Many reservation Indians, for example, who had long complained bitterly about the incompetence (and worse) of the BIA, when faced by a serious challenge to its very existence, concluded that an incompetent government bureaucracy devoted entirely to Indians was better than no such office, with federal responsibilities to Indians spread around among a host of other agencies for which Indians would be a vanishingly small concern.

Surely, for an American public typically preoccupied with non-Indian affairs, these startling events proved that American Indians were alive and struggling for their rights. The number of celebrity supporters of Indian causes had swelled. A Harris poll showed that by far most easterners, midwesterners, and even westerners were aware of the event and supported the militants, while only in the South were most people against the militants. As a more immediately practical matter, by making proposals and demands that struck many (including many Indian people) as outrageously radical, the red power movement made more moderate demands and proposals seem all the more reasonable. Indeed, not long after Indians had showed up on Alcatraz, President Nixon issued a special message on Indian affairs in which he called for "self-determination without termination." He emphasized the "moral and legal" force carried by the agreements made between Indians and the federal government through history, and called for the strengthening of Indian autonomy without threatening the Indian sense of community. This message, delivered in July 1970, in fact heralded some beneficent actions on the part of the federal government that took place during the militant seventies. Whether most of them would have occurred without the bold and dramatic efforts of AIM and other militants is a question that may never be satisfactorily answered.

The dramatic days of occupations and grand causes were nearing their end. The last great red power event was the Longest Walk, in which hundreds of Indians walked from San Francisco to Washington. Symbolically it meant to bring attention to the historic dispossession of Indians from their homelands; on a political level it drew attention to the continuing problems Indians were experiencing. Unlike earlier events, it was designed as a peaceful, even spiritual demonstration, and signaled a new approach that Indian activists and supporters would make in the following decades, emphasizing the spiritual and communitarian lessons the dominant society could learn from the first Americans.

Meanwhile, AIM began to lose much of the support it had enjoyed in the white world, in part because it appeared to be falling apart. Two AIM leaders got into a quarrel on the Rosebud Reservation of the Sioux and one of them wound up shot and seriously wounded. Later, in 1975, a second shoot-out led to the deaths of two FBI agents, and Leonard Peltier, a Chippewa-Sioux security expert for AIM, and several other Indians were accused of the murder. He fled to Canada but was later arrested and tried in Fargo, North Dakota. An earlier trial of other AIM members for this murder had resulted in acquittal since all the evidence was circumstantial, but Peltier was convicted largely because of evidence that many legal experts believe was manufactured—a rifle in Peltier's possession at the time—and he was given two life sentences. His case and his cause continue to raise hackles on both sides to this day and will probably remain shrouded in controversy and murk for many decades to come. President Clinton's failure to pardon Peltier amid his flurry of last-minute pardons is seen by many Indians as standard bias by whites against Indians.

The AIM image was by this time seriously tarnished in the minds of many Americans. More tragedy was in store. In 1979, John Trudell, AIM chairman and the spokesman for the Leonard Peltier Defense Committee, made a rousing antigovernment speech in Washington, D.C. That night, February 11, his wife, his three children, and his mother-in-law perished in an unexplained fire on their reservation in Nevada. Rather than risk any further losses by AIM leaders, the national movement was dissolved. It continued as local autonomous groups to work on local Indian affairs.

One thing is certain about this era in Indian affairs: the leaders of AIM—city Indians like Dennis Banks, with his soft voice, hard-etched face, and braids wrapped in scarlet; Russell Means, with his nearly antic ability to stick pins in white pretensions—brought a charismatic presence to the "Indian question" that had not been seen since the heyday of horse culture on the Plains, and has not been seen since. During their moment in the sun, something else of importance had occurred, at least in part a result of their efforts. As Columbia University's Hazel Hertzberg has pointed out, a new public opinion "had been created in which sympathy for 'the movement' was expanded to include almost automatic support for the Indian causes that seemed allied to it." Between 1970 and 1980, the American Indian population would soar by 72 percent, a rise attributable to more than just birthrates. Many more people with partial Indian ancestry were now proudly claiming to be Indians on the census forms.

The Not-So-Militant Seventies

One nearly direct effect of the occupation of Alcatraz was a major triumph for a far-distant pueblo, that of Taos, in New Mexico, in a cause it had faithfully but fruitlessly pursued for sixty-four years. In 1906, Teddy Roosevelt included Blue Lake in the nearby Carson National Forest. The Taos people had been performing certain profoundly important ceremonies there since time immemorial, but lost exclusive access to the area. The ceremonies, however, were not something the Taos priests felt they could discuss with outsiders—many of the Rio Grande pueblos have kept their ceremonial life and other matters to themselves to this day—which made it all the more difficult to persuade the government of their importance to the tribe.

In the 1930s some Taos elders decided to take John Collier to Blue Lake to witness the ceremonies, but as they traveled up into the mountains, they grew uncomfortable with the idea, finally telling Collier that they simply could not let him be a witness. More than three decades later, another group of elders went to Washington, D.C., to talk about Blue Lake with a young U.S. senator who they intuited would listen. This was Fred Harris, a Democrat, of Oklahoma, whose wife, LaDonna, was a Comanche deeply involved in Indian affairs. Harris was greatly moved by the Taos men and convinced of Blue Lake's central importance as a sacred place. He introduced a bill returning the lake and the acreage surrounding it to the exclusive ownership of the tribe, based on the constitutional notion of freedom to worship.

At the time, the Nixon administration was having little success negotiating the Alcatraz problem and needed some victories that would express the administration's liberal outlook on race relations. LaDonna explained the Blue Lake matter to a friend who was interning at the White House, and she in turn spoke to Leonard Garment and John Erlichman, part of Nixon's praetorian guard. They spoke to the president. Soon enough Michigan's Robert Griffin, the Republican leader of the Senate, and other congressional leaders were behind the Harris bill.

Meanwhile, Clinton Anderson, New Mexico's senior senator and a Democrat, told his colleagues he was in favor of offering the Taos people a use permit, but had environmental objections to giving the tribe possession of the lake and the land around it. Without Anderson, Harris was told, it was no-go with the committee, so Harris gambled and announced, as was his right, that he would take the bill straight to a vote by the full Senate. With liberals like Edward Kennedy on the same side as the Nixon administration, the bill quickly passed both houses, and Blue Lake and a forty-eight-thousand-acre parcel of land surrounding it were once again in the hands of the Taos Pueblo. The president announced the reversion on December 15, 1970, saying that the bill represented justice, and respect for religion, and "a new direction in Indian affairs in this country, a new direction . . . in which there will be more of an attitude of cooperation rather than paternalism, one of self-determination rather than termination, one of mutual respect." Later, the Taos elders told Harris and his wife that they would be the subject of daily prayers at Taos for as long as they lived.

The seventies, turbulent and troubled, even chaotic, were also a time when American Indians had begun to seize the reins of their own destiny in many other ways. As early as 1967, at the instigation of several Indian leaders including Sam Deloria, former Indian Affairs commissioner Robert Bennett, and many tribal elders, the University of New Mexico School of Law founded the American Indian Law Center. At the time only about twenty-five Indians had law degrees in the entire United States. By the end of the 1990s, there would be thousands, graduated from New Mexico and many other universities and colleges, and these attorneys would take up Indian causes, tribal suits, and other legal matters with a profound understanding of Indian points of view as well as an ability to turn the Anglo-American legal system to Indian advantage. In 1969, the Navajo Nation founded Navajo Community College, the first reservation-based college run by

Indians since the Cherokee colleges of the nineteenth century, just as they had founded one of the first elementary schools run by Indians, the Rough Rock School, in 1967.

At the onset of the 1970s, there were some 792,000 American Indians, almost half of whom lived in cities. An American Indian Press Association was begun, a D.C.-based news service feeding pertinent stories to the hundreds of tribal newspapers then being published. Several tribes with considerable mineral wealth, led by Navajo chairman Peter MacDonald, formed the Native American Natural Resources Development Federation in 1974, the forerunner of a larger and more effective Council of Energy Resource Tribes, which would effect fairer royalty payments to the tribes in return for renewed or new mineral leases. Later, the Intertribal Timber Council was formed among timber-rich tribes to promote the wise use of their resources, and tribes in western Washington joined together to found the Northwest Indian Fisheries Commission to coordinate fishing policy, since earlier a federal district court had determined that treaties allotted those tribes up to 50 percent of the commercial salmon catch. The Menominees and most other tribes that had suffered termination were reinstated. In 1976, the Winnebago tribe of Nebraska won a court battle to stop the Army Corps of Engineers from flooding much of Winnebago land, and the Catawba Nation—now an incorporated tribe and perhaps the only eastern tribe to have an unbroken tradition of pottery making—began the Catawba Pottery Association, to make sure a new generation of potters kept the tradition alive after seven hundred years. The O'odham of southern Arizona won back the right to increase their water use for irrigating and farming their land, the ancient Indian practice that went back to the days of the Hohokam.

In 1973, the Supreme Court ruled that Indians had the right to be given preference for jobs at the BIA since that would encourage Indian self-government. By 1980, Indian employees at the BIA would rise from less than half to more than 70 percent of the total (which of course added to the number of Indians who did not want to see the BIA disbanded, as often called for by militant Indians and their supporters). In 1978, the Supreme Court both gave and took away in the matter of tribal sovereignty in a series of decisions that echoed like a series of gunshots. In one case, *Oliphant v. Suquamish Indian Tribe,* the court said that the Suquamish tribe had no jurisdiction over a white man whom tribal police had caught committing a crime and who had been tried in a tribal court. The question revolved, in part, around whether a tribe had always had the right to enforce its laws on others, or whether it was a right that had to be *awarded* to a tribe by Congress. Basing its decision (written by William Rehnquist) on a 1834 bill that had never actually been passed, the court said Congress had not awarded such a right to Indian tribes. Only a week after that decision, in *United States v. Wheeler,* the court said that the powers of tribes were inherent *unless taken away* by Congress. Then, two months later, in *Santa Clara Pueblo v. Martinez,* the Court said the Santa Clara tribal government could not be hauled into federal court for a sexual discrimination charge since the Indian Civil Rights Act did not provide a forum. That Indian tribal police and courts might not, after 1978, have known what on earth they were supposed to do would hardly be surprising.

Meanwhile Congress was responding to some Indian needs with legislation. The 1973 Comprehensive Employment and Training Act was designed to provide jobs for unemployed reservation and urban Indians. A consortium of administrators of Indian colleges lobbied successfully for the Tribally Controlled Community College Assistance Act of 1973, followed two years later by an act establishing the right of tribes to provide educational and other programs previously provided only by the BIA. In 1978, Congress passed the American Indian Religious Freedom Act, which expressed the right of Indians not only to preserve their religious traditions but to have access to those sacred sites that lay outside their reservations. This was really more of a statement than an act, since it had no teeth, no mechanism by which such sites could be preserved or made available to the tribes. That same year, Congress attempted to solve an old problem that plagued tribes over the years, especially those in the West.

It had become fairly common for Indian parents who were having difficulties of one sort or another bringing up children to place one or more of them in foster homes. Often these were white homes, and often far away from any other Indians. The Mormons pursued this placement with special alacrity. Often, the terms of these arrangements were not clear to the birth parents, and typically the tribe itself and even the extended families were not empowered to take any alternative action. In other words, as the Indian Child Welfare Act said, "an alarmingly high percentage of Indian families are broken up by the removal, often unwarranted, of their children." The act also accused states of being unresponsive to "essential tribal relations of Indian people and the cultural and social standards prevailing in Indian communities and families." So the act gave tribes more power over these kinds of arrangements and insisted that if states were involved they give precedence for foster care to the extended family or another foster home approved by the tribe.

In 1979, Congress also attempted to help a situation that had plagued Indian tribes even after Theodore Roosevelt had arranged the passage of the American Antiquities Act of 1906: the problem generally known as pot hunting. The pillaging of ancient Indian artifacts had in the meantime become an escalating problem, thanks to the ever-increasing value that collectors placed on such items as prehistoric pots, baskets, and religious icons, and even mummified human remains. In addition, high values made the theft of contemporary sacred objects such as Pueblo and Hopi katsina masks highly profitable. The Archaeological Resources Preservation Act made it mandatory that any excavating on public lands, including Indian lands or lands containing sacred Indian sites, could be undertaken only after a complete and complex permit exercise, which on Indian land involved tribal approval. Though this act was completely well-meaning, it too possessed little by way of teeth. National Park Service and other police units of the federal government made efforts to stop the unauthorized trade but they were given no special budgetary assistance to carry this out. The act tended to scare the casual pot hunter out of business, but hardened professionals simply learned to use more caution.

A far-reaching change in Indian policy occurred when the Department of the Interior issued new guidelines for the federal recognition of Indian tribes. At the time some 160 Indian groups still had hopes of gaining legal status as tribes, so that they would fall within the realm of the BIA and share in federal benefits. To be recognized, a group had to document its existence from the time of first European contact to the present and also prove that it continued to be an active community with some form of government in place. Such deliberations, once begun, usually dragged on for many frustrating years. Meanwhile, courts were busy restricting tribal sovereignty more and more to internal tribal affairs. For example, the question of criminal jurisdiction over nontribal members present on Indian land was ruled on by the Supreme Court in 1979. The tribes were not given jurisdiction. Exactly how a tribal government was to go about the business of governing was becoming so complex, so filled with legal thickets, that a tribe without legal counsel was largely out of luck.

For all of the militant action, the pride it gave to many, the widespread (even international) attention it brought to the plight and the goals of the American Indians, and despite the various congressional and other federal attempts to bring about a fairer, more mature deal for the Indians, they remained as a single group largely at or near the bottom of many of society's general measures of well-being. In 1980, in the realm of education, Indians had the lowest percentage of people with four years of college (7.7 percent) compared to whites, blacks and Asians, and the lowest percentage of people between eighteen and twenty-four with a high school degree (60.2 percent). Rural Indians had by far the lowest number of people over twenty-five with a fifth-grade education (3.4 percent).

Only among blacks did a greater number of families live below the poverty level. Among Indians, those on the reservations typically were worse off than the urban Indian population—though such measures do not include a large amount of bartering, gift giving, ceremonies, and other aspects of the more communal ways that tend to brighten the lives of reservation people. Forty percent of reservation Indians lived below the official poverty level, only 16 percent had electricity and refrigerators, only about half had telephones, and only about a fifth enjoyed running water and indoor toilets.

Compared to the total U.S. population, Indians were four times more likely to die of tuberculosis, six times more likely to suffer an alcohol-related death, not quite twice as likely to die by homicide, and a little more likely to die by suicide.

The Eerie Deliberations of the Indian Claims Commission

Originally planned as a five-year operation, the Indian Claims Commission was in business for three decades, finally closing its doors in 1978. In that period it decided claims brought by more than 170 tribes, and its few remaining cases were heard by the U.S. Court of Claims. Its life needed extending on five different occasions. The commissioners were selected less for their knowledge of Indian affairs than for political reasons—basically, the commissioners should not be all of one party. In its final incarnation, one commissioner was an Indian, the Lumbee Brantley Blue. One of the most important appointees was none other than Arthur Watkins, the termination champion who had lost his bid for a third term in the Senate. He was appointed by President Eisenhower and served as chief commissioner for seven years until 1967. The commissioners' deliberations went forward slowly and largely out of the public limelight. Indeed it is not likely that one out of a thousand Americans actually ever heard of the commission.

To begin with, as was true of the Court of Claims, the only redress the commission could award was money and not, for example, the return of contested lands. Most of the claims were for land lost by a tribe, band, or other recognized group of Indians, or land for which they had been paid an unconscionably low price. To make a claim, the group had to show it had (*a*) used and occupied (*b*) a tract of land with definite boundaries (*c*) exclusively of other tribes (*d*) from time immemorial. Problems arose with all these criteria. Who could make a claim? The act forbade claims by individuals. Early on, a coalition of California groups got together to register a claim, and it was thrown out since they were not a single tribe or band. A bright lawyer then arranged to bring suit by all the California tribes, and after some fretting and a higher court decision, it was agreed that the Californian Indians (all of them) were a "recognizable group of Indians." Henceforth, few claims were thrown out for the reason that the plaintiff did not qualify. After all, the purpose of the commission was to hear all the complaints and remedy them. If it turned tribes away from the process, they would wind up using the old system and tangle up Congress with attempts to get authorized to go to the Court of Claims.

There were other problems. For example, the Pawnees, first to have their complaint heard, had lived in large villages for part of the year and then hunted in a vast area including Nebraska and northern Kansas. How could the Pawnees prove they used all that land, occupied it, and did so exclusively? Indeed, they often ran into hunters and warriors from other tribes in the hinterlands of their hunting territory. There was a large overlap of tribal territories, which had often led to outbursts of warfare. Did friendly or hostile contested use of traditional lands wreck the exclusivity necessary for aboriginal title?

This knotty problem was solved by the creation of the sort of arrangement that apparently made most colonial operations functional—a mutual misrepresentation of fact. In short, the various tribes' lawyers agreed to draw lines on a map somewhere between two tribes' core areas and everyone simply agreed that the lines showed absolute and exclusive borders. This was, of course, mere fiction, as was the notion that such territories had existed from time immemorial. But this fiction was necessary for the claims to fit into the system of Anglo-American law. Another problem of this sort that turned out to be insoluble was the loss of bison: several tribes charged the U.S. with responsibility for the loss. But nowhere was there legal room for Indian tribes to own what Anglo-American law saw only as wildlife, basically free-ranging and unowned except by the United States. Such claims were thrown out.

Another slightly bizarre situation pertained to these deliberations. Since there were virtually no Indian lawyers in the years immediately after the Second World War, virtually all the cases were handled on contingency for the tribes by white lawyers who were approved (and to some degree aided) by the Department of the Interior. They were opposed by lawyers in the U.S. Justice Department—just down the street from Interior—who fought tooth and nail to throw out claims Interior wanted heard, and to reduce to a pittance the awards Interior wanted to be meaningful. These suits were slow to get heard and would drag on for years, even decades. White lawyers in Washington were carrying on in slow motion with hardly any participation or presence of any Indians, who were largely bewildered by the commission's proceedings. One proceeding that probably earned some guffaws from the tribal members was the refusal of the commission to entertain testimony by tribal elders about such things as the whereabouts of old hunting grounds. This was a court, after all, and not a forum for long oral accounts from (probably failing) memory about things that had taken place long before. On the other hand, virtually every working anthropologist in the nation who had any familiarity with one or another Indian tribe was called in to testify about such matters as the extent of aboriginal hunting grounds. Their information was valued, even though it was in almost all cases derived from the same old men whom the commission did not find reliable.

Other questions needed answering as well. What had the lost land been worth? Did the U.S. owe interest from the date of acquisition to the date of payment? The value of the land could be judged as what it was worth at the time it was taken, or what it had become worth since then. And it could be judged as what it was worth to the Indians themselves at the time of taking—this was the "nuts and berries" evaluation preferred, of course, by the Justice Department. If a gold mine was later discovered on the land, this argument went, Indians—say, the Chiricahuas, whose culture forbade grubbing around in the earth either for agriculture or for taking such things as gold from it—could not claim that gold mine in the value of the taken land. Lawyers for the tribes naturally disagreed. The problem of appraising a wilderness area by comparison with another wilderness for which no price had been assigned was also largely impossible, so government appraisers set a low value (six cents an acre, say), while tribal lawyers might claim $1.25. Faced with such huge variation, the commission typically and arbitrarily chose a figure somewhere in between. The point, of course, was to award the tribes *something,* but not so much that it would be too great a strain on the Treasury.

As for paying interest on such amounts, the commission soon was scared off by government attorneys who claimed at an early juncture that if interest were paid on the awards made so far, the bill would be $8 billion, and there were a hundred more claims to be heard. When the matter was appealed to the Court of Claims, it promptly ruled out the paying of interest.

Thus, the awards made had nothing to do with the usual judgments made in governmental taking of land under the Fifth Amendment, nor did they have anything to do with the cultural values Indian placed on their lands. In a case where a tribe was denied any compensation for, say, fisheries lost or the loss of land that was the actual home of a tribal deity, it might be compensated somewhat for gold deposits on its lands. One dissenting Court of Claims judge complained that "Indians are being denied payment for the most valuable de facto asset of which they were deprived and instead are being compensated for de jure assets they never could have reasonably supposed belonged to them. I am sure they will be greatly impressed with the wonders of the white man's justice."

In any event, the tribes mostly did get that *something,* and their acceptance of whatever award came their way signaled that the claim had been settled once and for all. When the Chiricahuas and others brought up the claim that they had not been treated fairly or honorably (one of the act's most celebrated grounds for complaint), there was simply no way the lawyerly minds of the commission or the tribes' lawyers could assess it. Finally the commission decided that if the government had done something bad to a tribe that it explicitly said in a treaty or other document that it would not do, then there would be grounds for redress. But it also decided that that had not happened, so no awards were made for dishonorable conduct on the part of the government. After all, they had never promised the Chiricahuas in writing or otherwise that the entire group would not be shipped off as prisoners of war. When the Chiricahua claim was appealed up to the Supreme Court, only one justice—William O. Douglas—voted for the tribe.

In addition to land claims, many tribes claimed that they had lost valued resources—actual money owed from rentals and leases that had been misinvested by the government, or natural resources like reservation timberland or income from such resources thanks to mismanagement by the government—and these were settled in an equally arbitrary manner.

In all, the commission awarded tribes $818 million in its thirty-one years. The Court of Claims, handling those claims left over in 1978, brought the total to $1.3 billion. This came to about $1,000 per American Indian. By contrast, the American citizens of Japanese ancestry who were interned during the four years of World War II were made eligible in 1988 for awards of $20,000, along with a formal congressional apology.

Each disbursement required congressional approval. In the earlier years, Congress ordered that the awards be made on a per capita basis, hoping that such payments to individuals would set them up for termination. But soon enthusiasm for termination dimmed in Congress, which attended to the Interior Department's recommendations that at least 20 percent of any award go to the tribe itself for making such improvements as were needed. In any event, most Indian tribes preferred to dole out the awards on a per capita basis, out of mistrust of the federal government. They felt that if they received money as a tribe, the government might reduce the governmental assistance to the tribe that year by the amount of the award. Also, there remained on many reservations a certain amount of distrust in the tribal governments' ability to spend the money wisely. They were still relatively new institutions in Indian country, and in some the leadership was considered too weak, while in some others it was a bit too strong. The Chiricahuas and the Mescaleros, now inseparable biologically or culturally, were a case in point. They received, in all, some $36 million, which amounted to about $11,000 per tribal member—far greater than the national average under the Indian Claims Commission Act. The tribal chairman from the 1960s till recently was Wendell Chino, who had already led the tribe into some ambitious forestry and ranching projects. With the commission's awards, the tribe built a luxury resort hotel and a ski lodge—and since then a casino. (Other money went to a scholarship fund.) But these were all tribally owned businesses. Many of the Apaches on the reservation complain that none of the award or the profits from the businesses have been of any direct benefit to the people of the tribe. More than 50 percent of the Apaches on the Mescalero Reservation lived below the poverty level well into the 1990s.

One of the more notable awards arising from the Indian Claims Commission and finally decided by the Supreme Court was a large payment to the Sioux for the loss of the Black Hills, which the United States had promised to protect for the Sioux in an 1868 treaty, but which had later been taken away for a pittance that was, in the 1970s, determined to be an unconscionably low price. In all, the award was more than $100 million, but the sixty thousand Sioux in eight relatively autonomous groups or tribes voted to refuse to accept the payment, believing that land is more important than money and that one day, somehow, they will get the land back, either by congressional action or, as many Sioux believe, on that day in the future when the white man will die out or otherwise disappear and the bison will return, and the Black Hills will once again be Sioux country.

One way to assess the accomplishments of the Indian Claims Commission (which at the time was the only organized and full-scale attempt by any nation that had colonized another people to make financial or other amends) is to look at it as a judicial body with judicial powers. It was unable to adjudicate satisfactorily the cases before it with established judicial doctrines and precedents (there were few applicable precedents), so it had to manufacture some largely fanciful information, and then award smallish sums of money based on a political understanding about the size of the Treasury and the response of Congress to draining it. In short, in creating the commission, Congress attempted to solve what it failed to see was a largely intractable *social* problem, not a legal problem, and the commission acted finally not as a real court or commission but as a politically oriented paymaster. Over the decades, the commissioners probably did the best they could, but the system simply was not going to solve the problems of Indians. Few mourned the commission's demise in 1978. Perhaps its greatest contribution was to reinvigorate many tribes as Indian people came together in anticipation of "my payment" and met regularly to hear news about the progress of their claims.

A Dispute Between Indians

It came as something of a surprise to many people, who were unaware of the ancient rifts between tribal groups that could still plague Indian affairs, when, in 1958, the Hopis and the Navajos sought and obtained congressional permission to sue each other. The dispute, which was over land, had been made all the worse over the years by the actions and inactions of the federal government. The government's attempt at a final solution led to yet more trouble, which would continue to fester until the matter was finally left to the two tribes themselves.

The original difficulty began only after Kit Carson rounded up as many Navajos as he could find and shipped them off to the concentration camp in Bosque Redondo in the 1860s. At that time Canyon de Chelly was about as far west as any Navajos lived, though occasionally after 1840, Navajos would raid Hopi settlements, chiefly for corn. (Before the Navajos, they were often raided by Utes swarming down from the Rockies.) In the 1860s, some Navajos who escaped Carson's roundup moved farther west to dwell in territory that the Hopis used for various ceremonial purposes as well as some grazing of cattle. The executive-order reservation of 2.4 million acres created for the Hopis by Chester A. Arthur in 1884 was created largely in response to Hopi complaints that they were getting crowded by Navajos. But as noted before, the language creating the reservation permitted the secretary of the interior to settle others within that reservation as he chose. Over the years many Navajo families moved into the Hopis' rectangular reservation.

In the 1940s, the BIA decided to treat the Hopi and the surrounding Navajo reservations as one administrative unit, dividing the entire area into nineteen grazing districts. The Hopi mesas, where the great preponderance of Hopis lived, were within a six-hundred-thousand-acre area called Grazing District Six. This was also during the BIA's main stock reduction program, which outraged both Hopis and Navajos. At this time, as well, the BIA moved various Hopis and Navajos around in an attempt to make district six more or less exclusively Hopi. From both sides there was resistance and encroachment.

Thus arose the request in 1958 to sue each other. Four years later a three-judge federal court settled (they believed) what was referred to as "the largest quiet title case ever tried," known as *Healing v. Jones*. The court ruled that district six was indeed exclusively for the use of the Hopis, and the rest of the larger executive-order reservation was a joint use area to be "shared and shared alike." For the most part and in practice, this meant Navajo people living throughout the joint use area and Hopis only in district six. The Hopis were deeply offended when the Navajos soon unilaterally granted a permit for coal exploration in the joint use area to a mining company that soon became Peabody Coal Company, and

Hopi katsina rattle

strip mining began. This was, of course, controversial: traditional Hopis and Navajos said it was defiling Mother Earth; progressive Hopis and Navajos were equally adamant that Mother Earth had put it there for the benefit of the people; environmentalists were convinced it was a sellout by Indians not worthy of the name; and so forth. Through various legal challenges the Hopi tribe forced the Navajos to make them party to the agreement and subsequent royalties, but this demonstrated fairly clearly that the two tribes were not likely to make a peaceful settlement out of the court's notion of joint use.

There soon arose a certain amount of pushing and shoving, with Hopis running Navajo sheep out of their exclusive area or impounding them. Eventually, recognizing that the problem needed a different solution, Congress took up the issue and in 1974 passed a bill providing that the joint use area be cut in half—one half for the Hopis and one half for the Navajos. The two tribes were to negotiate a new boundary, and if they were unable to do so within nine months, a federal mediator would draw the line. Thus about a year later, a judge drew a tortuous line more or less diagonally through the original rectangular executive order reservation. Neither side was satisfied—the Navajos said that nine thousand Navajos would have to be relocated and soon produced studies showing that this was cruelly stressful. The Hopis, only a handful of whom would have to move, felt that squatters had simply moved into their backyard and when a judge was asked to deal with the issue, he gave the interlopers half the yard. Both sides said they were losing the use of sacred sites. For a while the Hopi office of the BIA chartered a plane flown by a daring Walapai Indian pilot who would race along the new boundary line at an altitude of about fifteen feet to put the fear of the Great Spirit in any Navajo who ran his sheep on the wrong side. Wiser Hopi heads prevailed and the air sorties were soon called off, but occasional outbreaks of violence continued in these long empty stretches of sagebrush, the Hopis always pleased to point out to a visitor that the Hopi side of the line was noticeably greener.

The issue received a good deal of national attention, the press ineptly comparing it to the Israel-Palestine dispute (which tribe was Israel and which Palestine was not explained). Most public sympathy went to the Navajos, who not only had more people who would be relocated but a far more sophisticated public relations apparatus.

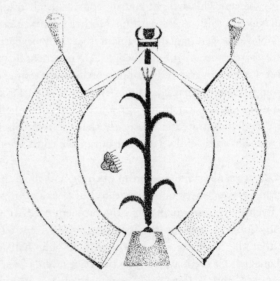

Navajo sand painting of the Corn Mother

For example, groups of wonderful-looking old Navajo women in traditional velvet blouses, long skirts, moccasins, and turquoise jewelry were trotted into the halls of Congress on a regular basis to explain their need for these ancestral lands. Hopi delegations, at least until the early seventies, always consisted of a few men in suits. A federal committee was impaneled to oversee the relocation process, and troubles continued to erupt. Hopis building the fence along the new border were occasionally shot at; Navajo women simply refused to move. There were demonstrations, sit-ins; numerous outsiders participated, both white and Indian, including members of AIM. Eventually public interest waned, and in all, some twenty-six hundred families were relocated, the great preponderance of them Navajos. When finally in the 1990s the matter was left to the two tribes to manage, the Hopis gave some two thousand Navajos a life estate in their homes on the wrong side of the line. The relocation and the land dispute are more or less finally resolved, but the bitterness—which began in the 1840s when Navajos began raiding Hopi villages and was only made worse by the actions and inactions of the federal government and the great phalanxes of white lawyers and bureaucrats and well-wishers who became involved over the decades—will almost surely persist for a long time.

There may have been a useful object lesson in this otherwise unsatisfactory affair—a lesson for the federal government and the dominant society to understand: there is no single "solution" to *the* Indian question. For all the pan-Indian impetus of the late twentieth century, and for all the shared history and difficulties and occasional triumphs of that ethnic group called Indians, they remain in fact many separate cultures, separate nations, and sometimes still uneasy neighbors.

CHAPTER SEVENTEEN

CURRENT EVENTS

In one sense, history begins exactly when the reader comes to the end of the word "now." On the other hand, if history is to be thought of as what historians do, or prefer to do, it cannot be up to the minute. Historians need a certain period of time to pass while they chew over events sufficiently to raise them above journalism and into the more measured and profound story that is the field they profess. By such measures, this account of a very long continuous collection of events could end here. It has, after all, already thrust its nose barely into the decade of the 1980s and sniffed what might be thought of as the beginning of a strong trend toward self-determination on the part of many Indian tribes. That would be a good, even promising note on which to end.

At the same time, many historians are greatly enamored of discrete eras—the Progressive Era, the Prohibition Era, and so forth. Such units of history claim to possess beginnings, middles, and ends, like all good stories. From that angle, the past two-plus decades demand discussion, for these recent decades have indeed witnessed what most likely will be seen as a new era in Indian history. For there has been a great surge of Indian creativity in the latter part of the twentieth century, not just legal and political creativity but in virtually all branches of culture. The story also will go on, and perhaps the most important message to be gleaned from these pages is that Indian history did *not* stop a long time ago—even though that was for centuries the plan shared by the devout, the cynical, the wise, the greedy, the kindly, and so many others who came here long after the Indians had arrived and created countless experiments in living in this new land. The arrival of non-Indians here led to multiple tragedies that have continued long after the non-Indians should have known better, and these clashes have called forth from many Indian people and tribes so multifarious an array of creative transformations of themselves that no single book, and not even a multivolume set of books, could chronicle them all. In October 1992, in Santa Fe, New Mexico, a number of Indian people gathered to offer what might be called an anticelebration of the five hundredth anniversary of Columbus's "discovery" of the New World. There was plenty of irony and cynicism expressed that day, as might be expected. Yet at one point a visiting Sioux who was unnamed in press accounts stood up and called for an actual celebration of the day by Indian people. He said they should celebrate the fact that, against all of the odds, for five hundred years Indian people, Indian cultures, and Indian spiritual beliefs had survived.

In a place like New Mexico one is constantly aware that the Indian peoples have accomplished more than survival. They have, in many instances, thrived. One sees candidates for state governor paying careful campaign attention to local Indian issues, for the tribal vote can be the difference between winning and losing. The state tourist bureau makes as much of the Indian presence in New Mexico as it does of all the state's ski resorts and other recreational attractions: here is Indian country, the real thing. Nationwide, thousands of galleries and shops make a living selling jewelry, baskets, pottery, and other Indian craft objects, and there is a flourishing trade in Indian fine art, such as easel paintings and sculpture. The market for southwest Indian crafts is so great—annual sales reach into the billions—that the market is constantly flooded with fakes from abroad. New federal laws now can and have put dealers in prison who knowingly sell fakes, or knockoffs as they are sometimes called. So elaborate are the dodges used by the fakers that a town in the Philippines renamed itself so that the silver-and-turquoise jewelry made there for the American market could be stamped "Made in Zuni."

An Indian presence, and one that is set forth by the Indians themselves, is now to be felt in the overall culture of America to an extent unseen before. While this presence is inescapable in the American Southwest, where most of the tribes remain culturally intact to a degree that is less common elsewhere, it is felt nationwide. A sculpture by the late Chiricahua Apache Alan Hauser is now to be seen in front of the United Nations building in New York, and his work is represented in the collections of most major art museums here and elsewhere. Hauser was both artist and teacher and helped to lift many Indian artists from the vernacular into the fine arts. American Indians have written numerous highly popular novels—Kiowa N. Scott Momaday won a Pulitzer Prize for *A House Made of Dawn,* and Leslie Marmon Silko's *Ceremony* is considered by many to be an American classic. Indian writers proliferate, many of them taking the classic form of the novel and turning it into their own Indian genre. For example, a young Flathead writer, Sherman Alexie, has emerged as a highly acclaimed novelist of national reputation; one of his novels, *Indian Killer,* is a uniquely Indian take on that nearly ubiquitous standby of thriller writers, the serial killer. Many readers in the dominant culture have become familiar with the age-old Indian character of the trickster, the shape shifter known as Raven or Coyote, among other identities. The trickster leads a creative, destructive, comic life all the more relevant to everyone in a world that seems to have gone a bit mad. National Public Radio now carries a weekly call-in program on Indian affairs. Intertribal powwows take place year-round in major eastern cities as well as small towns, reservations, and cities throughout the West. These are elaborate performances by dancers dressed in highly stylized, almost garish costumes, accompanied by the metronomic thunder of drums, and outlandish singing somewhere between a scream and falsetto that challenges the human larynx. The powwow, usually billed as a gathering of nations, is an important feature of pan-Indian identity. Indian-made movies like *Smoke Signals* are reaching out to ever larger audiences, and while eastern film critics held Kevin Costner's *Dances with Wolves* in elegant contempt, movie houses throughout the West literally overflowed with Indian families, who were delighted with the Indian actors, the authentic dress, the use of a real Indian language (Sioux, which most of the actors had to learn for the occasion), and a respectful if romanticized look at Indian life.

The Indian presence is felt all the more in the past decade as tribes—some little remembered—have taken shrewd advantage of federal and state laws to assert themselves again as political and economic players in American society. Not surprisingly, as many Indian tribes have taken steps toward self-determination, they have created controversy—as always—among the uncomprehending and occasionally even narrow-minded segments of the public. In a sense and to a degree, the shoe has been put on the other foot. The momentum is shifting. The question now is not so much whether the Indians will ever assimilate into American society and become mainstream Americans (whatever that means). They are learning to take what they want from American society without giving up their own identity. The question is becoming, how soon will the American public be able to accommodate in its capacious cultural and political body the existence of more than three hundred separate, independent, culturally unique, and determined entities called Indian nations?

One of the most unexpected arenas of Indian influence on the larger society of America and, indeed, beyond is the realm of religion. To begin with, in the seventies through the nineties especially, those who came to be known as New Agers were greatly influenced by the much-vaunted and in most cases very real spirituality of the American Indians. Looking for something beyond the cut-and-dried norms of everyday Western religions, New Age people discovered the healing power of crystals (long in use by tribal medicine men), prayer circles from the Plains (a circle of rock appeared on a red rock cliff overlooking Sedona, Arizona, a place where the local Indians had never used such devices), drums, feathers, and sweat lodges. All such Indian elements were happily and ecumenically worked into other themes, such as power vortices emerging from rock foundations, in behalf of world peace, and other newly invented rites, which tended to call forth ridicule from most people and annoyance or outright distaste from Indians, who thought their ancient ceremonies were being demeaned, even rendered less potent, by New Age mimicry. (On the other hand, it should be noted that many Indians were happy to fill the New Agers' needs for spiritual guides. Good money was made holding sweat lodges for whites. Indians even invented a little device of twigs and string and called it a "traditional Indian dream catcher," which soon became a must for any New Ager who wanted to sleep peacefully through the night.) As annoying as the New Agers were to most Indians, they were relatively harmless and good-natured groupies, certainly an improvement over religious fanatics bent on stamping out the sun dance or the Hopi katsina dances.

On the more sublime side, for most Indian people spirituality is a very real component of life, and it includes a noted reverence for the land that began to appeal to a much wider audience of environmentally involved and concerned people and, even, theologians as the twentieth century came to an end. The insistence by so many Indian spiritual leaders that Mother Earth needed to be tended to, indeed to be considered sacred, helped begin a growing movement in some Christian circles called creation theology. One of the much-traveled Indian spiritual leaders, Oren Lyons of the Onondagas, has spoken of such matters since the days when AIM and others were taking their messages to the public. "Leaders of the World," he said recently to a meeting of the United Nations, "there can be no peace as long as we wage war upon our mother, the earth. Responsible and courageous actions must be taken to realign ourselves with the great laws of nature." Invoking the spiritual powers of the universe and the natural laws that are the "essence of the spirit of life," Lyons and others made their points to numerous influential Christian religious leaders in the nineties. One of these, James Parks Morton, who had served as the dean of the Cathedral of Saint John the Divine in New York City, wrote in the year 2000, "And so it should come as no surprise that many of our great thinkers have begun to look back to the wisdom of the first peoples." He took note of how late Judeo-Christian theology had been in seeing the ecological crisis as "a disaster to God's sacred natural creation. . . . In Native American spirituality there is no such hard separation between Creator and creation, but rather a deep interpenetration of heaven and earth." Such commentary from a leading figure in the Christian ministry would have been hard to predict in the old days of allotment in severalty and termination, when the message of well-wishing educators and Indian policy makers was essentially "kill the Indian to save the man."

By the end of the twentieth century, Indian voices were being heard thoughout the land more clearly and in more ways than they had been since the time when Andrew Jackson set out to clear the East of Indian peoples.

The Rise of the East

By January 1977, the government of the state of Maine, some 350,000 residents, and an array of large private lumber companies and sawmills had been stunned by the news that the U.S. Justice Department was bringing a suit that could put more than twenty-two thousand square miles of the Pine Tree State into the exclusive hands of the Passamaquoddy and Penobscot Indians. There was nothing quiet about *this* quiet title case. For several months no municipality within the area—in all, two-thirds of the state's land area—had been able to issue bonds. Homeowners' titles were clouded. The Justice Department was employing terrifying words like "ejectments." Down-easters, as the people of Maine are often called, were at least metaphorically up in arms.

It took three years, but Maine finally reached an agreement with the two tribes and the federal government whereby the tribes dismissed their land claims and Congress appropriated $81.5 million to be put into trust funds for them. Of that sum, $54.5 million was available to the tribes to purchase land in the state—which resulted in the addition of about 150,000 acres—while the remaining $27 million would go in a permanent trust account, with the earnings available to the tribes to spend on whatever they saw fit. Both tribes proceeded to invest in off-reservation enterprises that employed both Indians and non-Indians, and they became a potent and even admired part of the Maine economy, potent enough for Harvard Business School to study the tribe's business strategy.

This astonishing development had its beginnings in the years shortly after the American Revolution when, under the Articles of Confederation, Congress wrote the Non-Intercourse Act, which insisted that a representative of the federal government had to be present at any arrangement whereby an Indian tribe ceded land to any other group or person. New York State and several others (as noted) nevertheless went happily ahead making treaties with Indians that called for the ceding of large tracts of their aboriginal lands, and got away with it until a Syracuse tax lawyer named George Shattuck got a bee in his bonnet about the cessions of land the state of New York had organized over the years with the Oneidas, an Iroquois tribe that had fought on the side of the American revolutionaries. Shattuck ran into jurisdictional problems: neither state nor federal courts in New York would listen to such a claim. Shattuck eventually took the case to the U.S. Supreme Court, asking not for the return of the land but for payments of rent by its occupiers for the previous two years. The Supreme Court ruled in January 1974 that since the Oneidas' claim was grounded in alleged violations of treaties and the Non-Intercourse Act, it should be heard in federal district court. The court went on, unasked, to point out that the Non-Intercourse Act was pertinent in all of the states, including the original thirteen.

Enter a young Ivy Leaguer just out of law school and working for the Native American Rights Fund. He learned that the Passamaquoddies had also fought for the Americans in the Revolution and had been promised protection of their hunting grounds by the Continental Congress. By 1794, disease had greatly reduced their numbers and the federal government abandoned them as it did many eastern tribes. So the Passamaquoddies were persuaded to sign a treaty with the commonwealth of Massachusetts (which included Maine in those days) by which they ceded virtually all their land but for a reservation on the Canada border of some twenty-seven thousand acres. Over the years this was nibbled away, and about a fourth of that reservation disappeared from their ownership. By 1970 the Passamaquoddies were seeking legal help to protect what was left—a reservation about the size of three New England towns—and found Tom Tureen.

In due course, after various jurisdictional squabbles, Tureen sued the federal government, demanding that it seek damages from Maine for the Indians. The Justice Department said that it had no right to sue for the Passamaquoddies since it had never recognized them officially as an Indian tribe. But the federal district court ruled otherwise and the Justice Department was ordered to sue for the Indians. The result was a huge money settlement, one that was far larger than those normally meted out by the Indian Claims Commission.

In 1976, at Tureen's instigation, the Native American Rights Fund (NARF) sued the federal government again on behalf of another New England tribe, one made famous by none other than Tecumseh, but for the reason that he thought it had vanished. "Where today," Tecumseh had asked, drumming up tribal cooperation to fight the white man, "are the Pequot? Where are the Narragansett, the Mohican, the Pokanoket, and many other once powerful tribes of our people? They have vanished before the avarice and oppression of the White Man, as snow before a summer sun."

Not quite. In the mid–twentieth century two old Pequot women lived on a 180-acre reservation in southern Connecticut. And a handful of descendants lived nearby, some among the remnants of the Narragansetts, and some unaware of or uninterested in their Pequot ancestry. In 1637, the Pequot population, already devastated by smallpox, was reduced to about a thousand in the Pequot War, fought with unsurpassed barbarity by the Puritans. The survivors were forced to sign a treaty that declared the tribe disbanded, its very name banned "to cut off the Remembrance of them from the Earth." About thirty years later, Connecticut (still a colony) atoned for this treatment by providing a two-thousand-acre reservation for the Western (or Mashantucket) Pequots. It was later reduced to less than a thousand acres, while the population fell to about 150. In 1855 the state's general assembly cut the reservation down to 180 acres, and three years later the reservation was home to nine Pequots.

In 1973, only one old woman lived on the Mashantucket Pequot reservation, Elizabeth George. Her grandson Skip Hayward, who was something of a ne'er-do-well and was probably more closely related to the *Mayflower* Haywards than he was to the original Pequots (he was one-sixteenth Pequot), found his life work when NARF appeared on the scene in 1976 and sued on the Pequots' behalf in federal district court in Connecticut. Hayward was soon tribal chairman, and in the early 1980s, state and federal legislation added twenty acres to the reservation and provided the Pequots with $900,000, of which $600,000 was available for buying land. It also extended federal recognition to the tribe.

The Pequots invested wisely, starting a bingo parlor, buying land (which became reservation land) near the main highway through southeastern Connecticut, and went on to build what was at the time the largest gambling casino in the United States, the Foxwoods resort, easily reached by the vast numbers of people living between New York City, Boston, and Providence, Rhode Island. Before long the casino, a multistoried resort that soars above the surround, was making a million-dollar profit per *day*. Not surprisingly the tribe drew many members back to Connecticut, building homes, offices, a fire station, steadily adding land, investing in research to strengthen (or some would say reinvent) Pequot traditions, and built a $193 million museum. It features a twenty-two-thousand-square-foot re-creation of a sixteenth-century Pequot village, based on extensive archaeological efforts financed by the tribe, not to mention more modern cultural artifacts such as the typewriter used by tribal chairman Hayward during the legal battles for federal recognition and payment for land lost.

The Pequot success has been accompanied, not surprisingly, by a great deal of sniping. Some have said the claim that the Pequots are a real tribe of Indians is fallacious: after all, some are clearly black and some are clearly white. The tribe's criterion is simply proof of descent from a Pequot woman who died in 1909. Others are outraged that the tribe was allowed to build the casino in the first place—the tribe had to overcome strong opposition from the state—and many others fret that the Pequots, now with their vast wealth, may become too strong a force in Connecticut politically as well as economically. And of course, from the outset, others in the gambling industry, like Donald Trump with his casino resorts in Atlantic City, New Jersey, have howled with pain about unfair competition from nontaxpaying casinos. Yet others are convinced that Indian casinos are sitting ducks to be plucked up by the mafia. Of course, there are large numbers of people who simply consider gambling sinful or dangerous and point to those who become addicted to it, while yet others simply cannot believe that real Indians—those paragons of spirituality and ecosainthood—would stoop to such a tawdry activity. Nonetheless, by the end of the twentieth century there were some three hundred tribes operating gambling casinos, with more to come. Revenues were estimated at some $10 billion in the year 2000 (the tribes are not obliged to make their revenues public).

The Pequots burst on the scene with such immediate notoriety and success that the onset of Indian gambling casinos is often associated with that tribe, but they were not the first. In the 1980s, the Cabazon band of Mission Indians sued the state of California, which had blocked the band from opening a casino. The Cabazon band were a part of the Cahuilla Indians, who aboriginally and still lived in the central part of southern California and, like many Indian groups, were avid gamblers themselves. Their casino would be in reach of the population of Los Angeles. The case reached the Supreme Court, which opened the way for casino-style gambling on Indian reservations in a decision in

1987. Many tribes, like many churches and civic organizations around the nation, already ran bingo parlors, but this decision opened the door to large-scale business. The following year, Congress passed the Indian Gaming Regulatory Act, a stated purpose of which was to keep Indian gambling facilities out of the hands of organized crime. (As of 2002, no instance of a mafia connection with any Indian gambling operation has been turned up, though rumors fly.) Another purpose of the act was to ensure that the tribes would be the primary beneficiaries of any such operation and that gaming would be conducted fairly.

It went on to confirm that type I gaming—minimal prizes at celebrations and ceremonies—and Type II gaming (basically, bingo) were to remain in the exclusive hands of the tribes. But type III—all other forms of gambling, like blackjack, roulette, and slot machines—called for a tribal-state compact that would negotiate the amount of money a tribe should pay the state from its gambling revenues. The compacts in turn needed to be approved by the secretary of the interior. The act also established the National Indian Gaming Commission to be an independent regulatory agency ensuring federal standards for such gaming.

Within the aboriginal lands of the Cahuillas lies posh Palm Springs, California. As it has turned out, the Agua Caliente band of the Cahuillas are the wealthiest group of Indians anywhere in the United States, and that is because they have managed against utterly astounding odds to maintain ownership of substantial chunks of land in the city of Palm Springs. The Palm Springs Reservation was established in 1875, then allotted, then reestablished in a checkerboard pattern in and around the town of Palm Springs in the last years of the nineteenth century. By the mid–twentieth century it appeared that the reservation had to be reallotted since the original scheme had been technically inappropriate. By the 1950s, there was thus a great tangle of old and new considerations, including rising land values. Much earlier in the century, the Agua Caliente band had only thirty-two adults, of whom ten were men, six of them not in a position to help. So the band turned their future over to the twenty-two adult women (although there was virtually no tradition of women in leadership positions). An all-woman tribal council handled the band's affairs until 1961, when a man was elected to the council. Legal and financial complexities of various sorts continued, but the band continued through the 1990s to hold firm, collecting rents on their lands as the city boomed, and by 1999 the band was comprised of 356 members, most of whom own allotted lands in the Palm Springs area that are worth, combined, in the billions of dollars.

Gambling

Almost immediately after the much-publicized success in Connecticut, what could be called Pequot envy broke out and Indian casinos proliferated. Aside from all the Sturm und Drang from well-meaning and ill-meaning whites that accompanied this astounding growth, gambling was an issue that often brought out factional disputes within the tribes—both before and during the planning stage, and after the casinos were in business. Traditionalists within tribes tended to fear casinos as destructive of tribal customs, spiritual life, and tradition. Progressive tribal members tended to see gambling as the only way out of a poverty-ridden existence that otherwise relied on the wayward policies of the federal government and the lackluster assistance doled out by the BIA. Some members of tribes with casinos complain that the gambling money is not benefiting them in any direct or indirect way. Outsiders opposed to gambling, or just Indian gambling, leap eagerly upon these complaints and point to the dissension casinos cause within tribes (as does virtually every other kind of initiative). Why, it is asked, are so many Indian people still living in poverty if they have casinos? This grave question is taken, with something less than perfect logic, as prima facie evidence that Indian tribes and casinos should not be mixed.

The Iroquois exemplify almost all such reactions. The Mohawks have had a violent history in this business, their warrior society taking up arms against state troopers in support of an illegal gambling operation on the reservation in 1989. But rumors of a secret pact between the tribal government and the state then turned the warrior society against casinos. Nevertheless, the Mohawks went on to build a casino on the Akwesasne Reservation, which lies athwart the U.S.-Canada border, and it has turned out to be a dud. The main enterprise there continues to be smuggling.

Meanwhile the westernmost tribe of the Six Nations, the Senecas, had long been considered building two casinos near Buffalo and Niagara Falls on land that the state of New York agreed to sell them for a token amount of money, by way of redressing old land grabs. The plans

Iroquois false face mask

have split the tribe, even families within the tribe. In particular, those who follow the "old religion" of Handsome Lake consider the notion of casinos a moral abomination. Tribal buildings have been illegally occupied. One casino supporter wound up getting shot—accidentally, it was ruled—by a casino opposer who was in fact the man's son. With each side at the other's throat and accusations of hoodlumism flying back and forth, the Seneca Nation of Indians voted on the question in May 2002. The most vocal tribal opponent of casinos, Susan Abrams, attempted to enter the tribal administration building on election day to oversee the vote count but was restrained by tribal marshals. The vote turned out to favor casinos by a mere 101 votes out of 2,058 cast. Tribal estimates had the Senecas receiving a billion dollars in casino profits over a fourteen-year period, with an additional $300 million being paid to New York State in that same period. Supporters saw it as a victory for those who wished to lift the people on the reservation out of poverty, one saying simply, "I'm sick of living in a trailer, that's all we've got. We can't do any worse." Others complained that making any sort of deal with the state of New York was an abridgement of the tribe's sovereignty, or as one said, "a slap in the face to the nation."

Unlike the Mohawks and their failed effort on the Canadian border, yet another member tribe of the Iroquois Confederacy, the Oneidas, built the Turning Stone Casino Resort in the town of

Verona, New York, and it takes in an estimated $167 million annually, with a high profit margin. As of late 2001, each enrolled Oneida member was receiving a quarterly check of $1,100, according to *The New York Times*. Even so the tribe is split between supporters and those who oppose it on various grounds, including the complaint that the quarterly disbursements are far too small for such a huge and profitable enterprise. Others oppose it as destroying traditional values. Accusations of mafia connections are bruited about. Meanwhile the Oneida chief executive of the casino has been quoted as saying, "Sometimes, people are sort of imprisoned in poverty so long that they begin to think the bars are there for their own self-protection."

By the turn of the century, New York State was in a mild state of hysteria again over the Iroquois. The Cayugas were awaiting a judge's decision on how much the state owed them for the illegal taking of sixty-four thousand acres back in the days when the state did not take the Non-Intercourse Act seriously. The Oneidas' claim of 250,000 acres—the languishing problem that set off the whole modern Indian uprising in the East—was being negotiated, with the possibility of a swap that would give the Oneidas a land base in the Catskill Mountains, not that far from New York City, where they would presumably erect another casino. The yin and yang of American political leanings—*The New York Times* and *The Wall Street Journal*—were seething and frothing editorially, saying it is one thing to put gambling in the boondocks, but please not so near New York City, and what, after all, of the mafia and the people who get addicted?

Perhaps the most alarming claim made by one of the Six Nations on New York State resources was that brought by the Onondagas, traditionally the keepers of the flame, who have pointed out that the land taken from them illegally under the Non-Intercourse Act includes the city of Syracuse. The tribe wants the Onondaga Lake, now polluted, cleaned up (it is considered sacred land) and have no intention of evicting people from their homes or taking over the city government. Instead, they will settle for other land elsewhere in the state, and for all anyone knows, they might build a casino there.

In fact, most Indian casinos are not the great cash cow that the Pequots' Foxwoods resort still is after about a decade of operation. Most casinos, since they have had to be built on reservation land, are located in rural and often quite remote locations. Those that do the best are, unsurprisingly, located near large population centers, such as the ones near major eastern cities, or Phoenix (the nation's sixth largest city), Albuquerque, and the like. By one estimate, all of the profits from gambling that Indians earn—after the costs of running the casino and all the associated services, including legal services to fend off continued attempts to scuttle them, plus paying a percentage of profit to the states as required by the tribal-state pacts—brings the average per capita income from gaming to about $3,000. (The vast majority of Indians earn no income whatsoever from gaming, however.) The number goes down considerably—almost a third—if the Pequots and a few other tribes are taken out of the mix as spectacular oddballs. Indeed, the Pequots and Mohegans—both in Connecticut—account for 20 percent of all Indian gambling revenues, or $2 billion a year between them.

A minority of Indian casinos outside Connecticut are doing spectacularly well. The Jicarilla Apaches of northeastern New Mexico and Sandia Pueblo, right next to Albuquerque, were doing well enough that between them in 1999 they offered the New Mexico State Highway Department some $19 million in interest-free loans to hasten the completion of a couple of state roads through the reservations, the state being in more than its usual budgetary crunch that year. Seeing neither the humor nor the irony in such an offer, one state senator complained that it sounded like a campaign contribution and even, he hinted darkly, something crooked. Meanwhile, some people smile as they drive by the Rio Grande pueblo casino emblazoned with the name Cities of Gold. Coronado was almost five hundred years early.

States can be expected to continue to snipe at Indian gambling casinos. Non-Indian gambling interests continue to say it is bad for their business, providing unfair competition with the likes of capital-intense riverboats on the Mississippi. In early 2002, the U.S. Supreme Court shut down a casino near El Paso, Texas, that was owned by the Tigua Indians. These are the descendants of the Indians who accompanied Antonio de Otermín out of Nuevo México when the Pueblos rose up in 1680. Like many tribes, the Tiguas were living in poverty when, in the early 1990s, they opened the Speaking Rock Casino Entertainment Center. Its closure will cost the El Paso area some twenty-two hundred jobs and a $60 million payroll, at the same time that the area has lost fourteen thousand jobs to military base closings and global competition. Half the tribe's twelve-hundred-odd members were unemployed before the casino opened; tribal unemployment was 1 percent when the casino closed its doors. The casino supplied the little tribe with more than $50 million a year for education, housing, and health care. The tribe, however, was formally certified as a tribe in 1987 by an act of Congress that also said the Tiguas and a few other tribes would need to abide by state gambling laws. Other than the Texas lottery, high-stakes gambling is illegal in Texas, which is why the Tigua casino was shut down. The tribal governor, however, assumes that the state wanted Speaking Rock closed because it competed with the state lottery as well as the forty-five thousand state-licensed slot machines.

On the other hand, since Indian gaming hit the scene, a number of states like New Mexico soon permitted slot machines at several of the state's horse racing tracks (which were already failing). Indian casinos appear to have put other, non-Indian entrepreneurs into what is euphemistically called gaming—all the more upsetting to those who disapprove of gambling on its face.

Historically, perhaps the most hypocritical frets of the dominant society over Indian gambling is about the people who become addicted. Many of the tribes with casinos have set up therapeutic programs to help their own tribal members who become addicted, but addiction to alcohol and fast foods (the latter contributing to a tremendous problem with adult-onset diabetes) is a far greater problem on the reservations. As for people in the dominant society who become addicted to gambling as a result of Indian casinos in their midst, most of them live in states that have racetracks, lotteries, and other outlets for the gaming urge. More than that, such complainers overlook the fact that Europeans who came to this continent deliberately got as many Indians as possible addicted to alcohol, one of the most devastating features of the last five hundred years of Indian history. There is an old adage about people living in glass houses.

With every step toward some form of sovereignty and self-determination on the part of an Indian tribe—of which the generation of a lot of money is a major one—there comes a backlash, at least locally. One favorite complaint is that in some tribes the benefits are not equally spread among all the tribal members but instead go to tribal businesses and leaders and their friends and relatives. On the other hand, there are many concrete examples of extraordinary benefits accruing to the tribes with successful casino operations. It is high time for the dominant society to recognize that so long as federally recognized Indian tribes operate within federal and state laws, what they do with their money from casinos or any other tribal projects is simply no outsider's business.

One of the Rio Grande pueblos least known to outsiders is Sandia Pueblo, which lies just north of the city of Albuquerque, New Mexico, and is home to about four hundred people. With the proceeds from gambling it has built a health center and medical-dental clinic for its members that the Kellogg Foundation cited as a model of rural health care. The Indians built a superior elementary school and may be the only community in the nation with a policy of zero tolerance for dropping out of school. A scholarship fund ensures that Sandia youths will be financially able to take their education as far up the scale as they can go. And like many tribes enjoying newfound income from gaming, they are aware that it is not likely to be a perpetual income source, and have begun a Southern Boundary Master Plan for economic development.

Plenty of roadblocks to economic development on Indian reservations exist, by the way, not the least of which are remoteness from urban centers and lack of infrastructure such as roads and communications systems. A less well known obstacle is the suspicion some private companies may have about the legal systems in place on reservations. Will they, for example, be responsive to the needs of a private business on such matters as liability? In 2001, the U.S. Department of the Treasury completed an exhaustive series of meetings throughout the country with the tribes and with private and public business and banking people to examine the obstacles and to create ways of overcoming them. Led by a Navajo planner, Rodger Boyd, whose city planning degree is from the Massachusetts Institute of Technology, this was not just another federal study by government bureaucrats but an open, free-ranging forum for Indian political and financial leaders and professionals from the private sector. It was explicitly not another attempt by the federal government to force economic development or policy changes on the tribes. Instead, it was designed merely to provide the tribes with information and analysis, and with access to financial and other economic institutions when and if the tribes wish it. While not necessarily earth shaking, the Treasury Department effort and the attitudes behind it would have been unheard of even as recently as the 1970s.

Water

Most of what remains now of Indian country is in the West, and in this large portion of the country, no single issue is more shrouded in controversy, confusion, and murk than water. No subject raises more hackles. No resource is ultimately more valuable. From time immemorial, water (or its lack) has been a major determinant of what sort of life Indians could and could not live in their particular parts of the continent. Water is what scientists call a limiting factor, and non-Indian society—especially in the West—has been pleased to ignore this aspect of water as huge farmlands have sucked aquifers nearly dry, enormous cities have metastasized across the arid landscape, and federal and state water managers have oversold the region's river flows with the same abandon with which airlines used to overbook their planes. In the West, only one river barely worth the appellation has not been dammed, this being the San Pedro, which trickles north out of Mexico into southeastern Arizona's old Apache country, and in a good year issues into that state's Salt River, itself a tributary of the once mighty Colorado. Today there are some added claimants to almost all of these waters.

Practically nothing makes many people in the West more apoplectic than hearing that an obscure endangered minnow that lives in one short section of a river has priority, when it comes to use of the entire river, over chili farms or ranches or urban sanitation or golf courses. It is almost as irritating when an Indian tribe points out, however softly, that its claim on a river's water comes ahead of all others. Many tribes are at play again in the fields of the Winters Doctrine, and not surprisingly with mixed results. The stakes in this particular game are extremely high.

Up until the 1970s, Indian tribes believed that the Winters Doctrine entitled them to all the water they needed for irrigation and other purposes. By way of asserting their tribal rights, for example, the pueblo of Santa Ana in New Mexico built a magnificent golf course in their arid lands along the Rio Grande. A tribal official confided that the Santa Anas had no interest in playing golf and did not expect to generate much income from it. They simply wanted to make it clear that they had a right to use enough local water to keep such an installation emerald green. Of course, it is far more complicated than that, and over the years from 1970 to century's end, Indians have lost six out of seven cases in which Winters rights were asserted. The losses arise (legally at least) from contradictory judgments and statutes that give "certain states" control of allocating water to Indian reservations. Some Indian tribes have contemplated the idea of selling (or leasing) their water rights, turning water into much needed cash, but they are now sophisticated enough in these arcane affairs to realize that making such a sale would require that some quantitative assessment be made of exactly how large or small an amount of water they have rights to. Under the circumstances, and in hopes if not expectation that the tide will turn one day in the courts, most of the tribes have concluded that it is best to leave the actual size of their rights ambiguous. In any event, the western tribes are now seen as players in this game, and are being treated in these matters with a deference that would have been unheard of a hundred years earlier. In an example of this deference, in 1999 the U.S. government gave an Indian tribe an unprecedented type of control over a region's water use.

The decision arose over two fish species, the endangered cui-ui and the threatened Lahontian cutthroat trout, both inhabitants of the Truckee River system that runs from alpine Lake Tahoe some hundred miles and three thousand feet downhill to the Pyramid Lake Paiute Reservation in Nevada. Along the way, water from two reservoirs must occasionally be released to benefit the fish, and the federal government gave the Paiutes the lead role in scheduling such releases. It is the first time the federal government has ever turned over the scheduling of such water releases when the water in question is not on reservation land. This may seem a small thing, a minimal kind of concession to a tribe's ability to manage such affairs, but it is the latest in a long battle the Pyramid Lake Paiutes had fought to obtain some control over their own destiny. Until 1990, federal policy for this reservation had been to encourage the Paiutes to farm, meanwhile allowing the state of California to withdraw increasing amounts of water from the Truckee system, which in turn diminished and even endangered Pyramid Lake as a fishing ground. In that year, with a regional drought compounding the problem, the federal government agreed to what is now locally called "the settlement." Federal policy for the region shifted dramatically to restoring the entire riverine system, including the tribal fishery and the spawning grounds for the two fish species that required federal protection. In short, it was a settlement that admirers saw as an effort to improve a local economy while respecting both the indigenous and other people *and* the environment and the various life forms in it. The Paiutes, asked to play a key role in any decisions on the use of the river's waters, were now a major player in the entire region. This was, in fact, a bit scary, for the Paiutes had till then remained a bit aloof from regional affairs. Some of their members thought they should not be involved; others pleaded that water is power. The Paiutes took on the role, and the decision in 1999 putting them essentially in charge of an important part of the management of the entire river system has only added to their newfound power. However incremental a step in the larger picture of tribal sovereignty throughout the nation, it is a far cry from what might have been expected a century earlier.

Sacred Matters

Probably no one besides the American Indians themselves, people engaged in Indian policy, and museum curators and anthropologists had heard of the Native American Graves Protection and Repatriation Act of 1990 (NAGPRA) until someone found Patrick Stewart's skull in the mud of an Oregon River a few years later. Of course it was not Patrick Stewart, though the forensic reconstruction of a face on the skull looked a lot like the star of *Star Trek* when photographed from one angle. That was the angle used in newsweekly cover stories, along with the announcement that this ancient, maybe first American was *European.*

It turned out that the man, called Kennewick Man, was not anything close to the first American, since he lived no more than nine thousand years ago; nor was he European (that was a slip of the anthropological tongue at the time of his discovery) but possibly Caucasoid, a category that includes such people as the Ainu, the aboriginal people of today's Japan—that is to say, Asians. Suddenly these dramatic remains of a very early American were withdrawn from study, and this is when most people first heard of what is a properly historic piece of federal legislation. NAGPRA requires that the Smithsonian and all other museums inventory their collections for all human remains (the Smithsonian reportedly housed the skeletal remains of some eighteen thousand Indians of one era or another) and all sacred artifacts and cultural material. Anything the tribes determine to be of cultural importance to them must be returned, or repatriated. In addition, the bill provides that Indian graves encountered in projects on federal and in some cases state land must go through a compliance process involving consultation with federally recognized Indian groups. For Indians, this is a landmark recognition of their cultural integrity. For archaeologists and anthropologists, it is a source of some consternation. NAGPRA has no force on private property.

Soon after Kennewick Man turned up, the several tribes of the Umatilla Reservation in Washington State claimed that the remains were ancestral, so they were stashed in a neutral place while some archaeologists and osteologists protested the tribal claim in federal court, counterclaiming that removal of the remains constituted a withdrawal of their right to pursue their own profession.

In 2002 the federal judge ruled that the four tribes of the Umatilla Reservation had no claim to these remains, being unable to show a direct biological or cultural ancestry. For that and other more technical reasons, the skeleton was turned over to the scientists. An important technical issue in this case is that the remains of Kennewick Man were found not on an Indian reservation (which is land held in trust by the federal government for the Indians) but on land owned by the government, in this case the Bureau of Land Management, and subject to the administrative control of the Army Corps of Engineers. Had Kennewick Man's remains been found on the Umatilla Reservation, there would have been no debate and no lawsuit.

It is unfortunate that so bitter a dispute occurred over the already overwrought topic of Kennewick Man. Not all tribes are eager to have such remains turned over to them: in California, most tribes cannot determine such questions of ancestry very well; and others cannot determine what clan might be involved, leaving "ownership" in doubt. At the same time, most museums and most archaeologists have become comfortable in the intervening years with the notion of repatriation of important Indian cultural materials to the Indians. The Smithsonian (in the form of the National Museum of Natural History) has a million-dollar-a-year program to facilitate the repatriation process, and however wistful many curators are, they see the reasonableness of the requirement. Most would agree with what Congressman Morris Udall said when NAGPRA was under discussion: the bill "addresses our civility, and our common decency. . . . In the larger scope of history, this is a small thing. In the smaller scope of conscience, it may be the biggest thing we have ever done."

Faced with similar if not equally as dramatic situations as Kennewick Man, yet other tribes are more likely to compromise. The Paiutes, for example, will not press their claim for the eight- or nine-thousand-year-old remains of a woman found years ago in Nevada's Spirit Cave, since her ancestry to them is by no means assured by archaeologists. Other tribes, more given to historical curiosity, claim such remains but want them examined by scientists to ascertain from them whatever can be known.

Constitutional or other legal issues aside, NAGPRA has established certain Indian concepts as the national standard, as legal scholar Rennard Strickland has pointed out. This Cherokee-Osage dean of the law school at the University of Oregon says that NAGPRA puts a great responsibility on the tribes to make sound judgments and requests, to establish a code that is "meticulously fair." The act, he goes on, "made understanding and preserving Native ways the official national policy."

To end this narrative now, with that thought ringing in the air, would be a happy choice—but not an honest one. For as Strickland and any other student of Indian history knows, the distance between national policy and local action is often very great, and often the federal government may, in its very vastness and complexity, entertain many policies on the same topic, some of them contradictory.

European Americans tend to categorize things in ways that either amuse or baffle many Indian people. For example, most of the members of Congress that passed NAGPRA no doubt would make a distinction between sacred objects used in church, such as a chalice, and a religious representation one might have in one's house, such as a painting of Jesus on black velvet hanging in the living room, which would be considered largely a secular item. Most traditional Indians would not make so clear a distinction. Most traditional Indian people in fact do not make a distinction between religion and, say, politics or economics or even gambling. For example, several southwestern and Plains tribes have long played a gambling game that the Navajos call a *shoe game.* People assemble in a large hogan and stay up the better part of the night playing this game, which involves guessing where a round object has been placed under a pile of dirt in one or another of four empty shoes. It is never played without a prior recitation of the story of the first shoe game, which determined whether all the animals would sleep at night or during the day—that is to say, part of the Navajos' creation story, which is the very essence of their religious view of the world. It is rarely if ever played without both team captains being medicine men, who in the course of the game exert their shamanic powers to win.

Most non-Indians do not look out upon the landscape and see spirits out there, spirits of such things as trees and rocks and lightning and wind. Indeed, such beliefs are considered by most Christians, at least, to be pagan and improper, even childish, and many conservative Christians today find such beliefs the work of the devil, just as the Puritans and the Spanish Franciscans and French Jesuits did five hundred years ago, in what one would like to think were less enlightened times. On the other hand, many traditional Indians find it peculiar, to say the least, that Christians and others can build a house for God, go there once or maybe twice a week, and whenever it seems like a good idea, proceed to tear God's house down and build another one with, say, a bigger parking lot, on the other side of town. If the gods reside in a mountain, it is not so easy to relocate them. For Indians, a sacred site remains sacred under most circumstances. On the other hand, a spirit or deity housed in such a place might decide to leave, and that has happened.

One of the most important deities of the Zunis in New Mexico is known as Salt Woman. She resided in a lake not far from the present town of Zuni but was evidently taken for granted by the tribe at one time, so she left, decamping to Zuni Salt Lake, about fifty miles away to the south. This is a lake located in volcanic country, with water seeping into it from an aquifer below. It contains some of the purest salt known anywhere. The salt is sacred to the Zunis and to surrounding tribes, even those as far away as the Mescalero Apaches to the southeast and the Hopis to the northeast. Over the centuries, distant and nearby tribes have worn paths to the lake to collect its sacred salt for their own ceremonials, and when one was on one of the paths, one went in peace even among enemies. The paths were like the calumet, absolute in their requirement of a time-out from any hostility. Today a large electrical utility from Arizona has leased New Mexico State land near Salt Lake, intending to mine coal there and use water from the aquifer to slurry it away. Hydrologists disagree, but a report made in behalf of the Zunis says that such water use could well drain Zuni Salt Lake. The Zunis worry: where would Salt Woman go then?

Places, geography, the land—this is sacred to many Indians. They tell stories about specific places that illuminate their ancient and sacred history and that, among other things, instruct their children in the proper way to live. They can merely refer to a place—a particular tree, or a bend in a stream—and bring forth the memory of a tale that embodies a hard-earned and complex wisdom. This is sacred wisdom and it is not seen to be different in any qualitative way from the fact that the landscape is also inhabited by spirits. It is the essentially pagan belief system in regard to the land—beliefs most other Americans do not much understand—that has let some European Americans form a new stereotype of Indians: they are all natural ecologists, holy tenders of Mother Earth and the guardians (if left to their own ways) of untrammeled wilderness. Some are and some are not, of course. From time immemorial, as this book has been at some pains to show, American Indians have engineered the land as best they could to serve their own purposes, and most of them were not mere traceless dwellers in the wilderness at the time of Columbus but village-dwelling agriculturalists. Yet a qualitative and quantitative difference unarguably exists between the onslaught of Western economic and technological prowess to make Ozymandian changes in the air, water, and land, and the biggest, most extractive mound-builder city ever built in North America. Indian views on the land have recently served as another needed incentive to all of us to be better stewards of the land and of living things. Even so, for all the progress Indians have made in the past decades getting their points of view better understood, very few examples exist like the return of Blue Lake and its immediate environs to the Taos Pueblo in the 1970s.

The Chumash Indians, reduced to a tiny fragment from a large group of village dwellers who inhabited a hundred miles of California coastline from Big Sur to Malibu for thousands of years, now need permits—from the likes of an air force base, an electric utility that runs a nuclear power plant, Canyon Diablo, and a private residential area—to approach lands sacred to the tribe. One of the most significant such places is Point Conception, which stretches out into the Pacific west of Santa Barbara. In 1912, a Chumash woman explained to an ethnographer that the soul of the departed can be seen beginning its journey to the afterworld, called Similaqsa, and one can hear the sound of this western gate closing after the departed soul. First, she explained, the soul

goes to Point Conception, which is a wild and stormy place. It was called Humqaq, and there was no village there. . . . There is a place at

Humqaq below the cliff that can only be reached by rope, and there is a pool of water there like a basin into which fresh water constantly drips. And there in the stone can be seen the footprints of women and children. There the spirit of the dead bathes itself. Then it sees a light to the westward and goes toward it through the air, and thus reaches the land of Similaqsa.

Today, a gated community of huge estates is interposed between the Chumashes and the gateway to Similaqsa. A guardhouse presides over the entrance, and the guard routinely turns away at least those living Chumashes who attempt passage without making special appointments.

Similarly, members of the San Carlos Apaches, in order to commune with the mountain gods on Mount Graham in southeastern Arizona, need to obtain a U.S. Forest Service permit and can be arrested for trespassing if they accidentally happen onto property that was given by the Forest Service, without benefit of an environmental impact study, to a consortium of astronomy organizations led by the University of Arizona and including the Vatican, which went on record as saying the Apache religion should be "suppressed." The church pooh-poohed the notion of any religious significance on the peak, where telescopes were to be built, by saying that it had found no physical evidence of religious activity up there, such as the foundations of a building like a church.

Many such sites are on federally owned lands, but federal policy seems to vary from place to place, even within regions. North of Mount Graham but still in Arizona, the San Francisco Peaks rise some twelve thousand feet into the sky, visible to most of the Hopi villages that lie ninety miles to the Peaks' east. The Peaks, part of the Coconino National Forest, are where the Hopi katsinas reside for half of each year when they are not dancing in the villages. The katsinas have had to share the upper regions since the 1960s with ski lifts snaking up the western side of the mountain. On the eastern side of the Peaks a pumice mine began to expand its operation in 1985 to cover an area of some ninety-five acres, an eyesore and yet another interference, as the Hopis see it, with the katsinas, who spend their time on the mountain rehearsing the bringing of rain. Then in July 2000, the Forest Service recommended to the Interior Department (which controls mining on all federal lands) that almost seventy-five thousand acres on the mountain's eastern slope be withdrawn from mineral use—including the pumice mine. In due course Interior came up with a million dollars for the mine owners and the pumice company gave up its claim. At a large gathering in August 2000 on the flanks of San Francisco Peaks to celebrate the official sealing of the deal, a former Hopi tribal chairman, Ferrell Secakuku, called it "the best day of my life." While the decision was celebrated widely among the tribes of the Southwest, it left behind a certain confusion as well, especially for the Apaches to the south. For the Forest Service's recommendation for the Peaks was exactly the opposite of the course it took on Mount Graham.

There seems no coherence to the federal government's approach to the issue of sacred Indian sites on federal land. An executive order in the Clinton administration directed all federal agencies to have care for such sites and to weight carefully any intrusion or destruction of them, but it had mixed results. The Native American Freedom of Religion Act enacted by Congress is all very well, but like many other such laws, it is largely toothless. In New Mexico, Congress mandated that a large area of mesa edge on the west side of Albuquerque be set aside as a national monument because its volcanic boulders bear more petroglyphs than virtually any other single place in the country. When developers found this land to be in their way, they enlisted Senator Pete Domenici to find a way to legally put a highway through the Petroglyph National Monument, a task complicated by the fact that no road can be built in a national park or monument unless it serves some major purpose there. The planned road was simply a throughway for a yet-to-be-created residential sprawl to reach downtown Albuquerque.

To defend the area, Bill Weahkee of the Cochiti Pueblo, one of five north of Albuquerque that considers the Petroglyph National Monument a sacred place, felt the need to write about it to the local newspaper—what he called "an unprecedented step," because most of the Pueblos choose to remain mute about their religious observances. Weahkee explained that the "ancient ancestors" held the site sacred because it "was born with Mother Earth's great labor and power"; he was referring to the volcanic vents, long since eroded into five remnants. The Pueblos, he went on, had used the area for gathering medicines and as a place to make offerings when hunts in the nearby mountains were complete. "It is here," he wrote, "that our Pueblo ancestors 'wrote' down the visions and experiences they felt." In the face of this insight, so bravely proffered by five groups of very private people, the U.S. Senate was persuaded to remove from the monument a strip of land that, oddly enough, coincided precisely with the strip where the road was wanted, and to donate it to the city of Albuquerque to do with as it wished. There the matter rested in the summer of 2002.

The list of such threatened sites goes on and on, a patchwork of conflicting attitudes and policies. In Wyoming a huge volcanic plug rises up from the surround, attracting rock climbers to its rugged and nearly vertical sides. It is called Devil's Tower, though the Plains Indians to whom it is sacred prefer to think of it by such names as Bear's Lodge. As Devil's Tower it became, in 1906, the first national monument to be established. June at Devil's Tower is a time of rebirth, of nesting birds and new plant growth; it is the summer solstice, when members of several Plains tribes come to make offerings and seek visions. In 1995, the National Park Service and the Indians who complained that climbers interfered with much of this (a vision quest, for example, requires solitude) agreed to promote a voluntary climbing ban in the month of June. Since then, the number of climbers in June has dropped from about thirteen hundred to some two hundred, these the clients of two outfitters who refuse to go along with the June climbing ban. One of these claims that climbing is his religion. The local Park Service people are powerless at this point to enforce such a ban but wonder if climbing would be permitted at all if they were starting over. Even so, eagles have returned to the tower to nest since the first June closure, and plants have returned that could not survive the annual trampling. Bear Butte in South Dakota, that place which was so important at the time the Cheyennes became horse people on the Plains, is now a state park, and only the inclusion of an unspoken agreement with a few Indian people working as employees of the park now keeps visitors from gawking at the Indian ceremonies that are carried out on its summit.

Every sacred Indian site seems to present a different problem. For example, several Plains tribes have begun to look seriously into setting up wind farms on their lands, a development that large numbers of alternative energy experts and environmentalists think would be an excellent contribution to a sensible energy system in the United States. A similar plan along the Columbia River in Oregon, however, is fiercely opposed by some members of the Cascade-Klikitat people, since the turning of hundreds of high-tech rotors would disturb the ancestral river people who lie below in the ground. It is difficult to see how a single national policy could be imagined, much less implemented, to deal with so complex a range of issues. Yet they all have one essential thing in common—the notion of freedom of religion.

In this realm of religious freedoms, which most Americans believe to be one of the linchpins of our democracy, the courts have been what might be called a bit jesuitical. A distinction is sometimes drawn between religious belief and religious practice. All Americans, even Indians, are legally and constitutionally free to believe whatever they wish. But if a large array of noisy campers are bustling around a shrine that is both sacred to some local tribe and happens to be on public land, that should not, courts have said, impair the Indians' prayers and communion with the spirits. Such a ruling would probably not be applied in the instance of a group of Indians bursting forth into a game of lacrosse in the nave of Saint Patrick's Cathedral during mass—and not just because Saint Patrick's is not on federal property.

Yet the government does have the right to actively block the actual practice of a religion under certain circumstances. In 1990, the same year Congress passed the Native American Graves Protection and Repatriation Act, designed to protect an important part of all native cultures, the U.S. Supreme Court delivered a rabbit punch to the only pan-Indian religion, the Native American Church. In the process, the Court threw the entire notion of freedom of religion as an unalterable right in the United States into jeopardy. (In some ways, it has been suggested, we are all Indians.) The case is known by the undramatic name of *Employment Division, Oregon Department of Human Resources v. Smith* (or *Smith II*) and it was one of numerous cases in which the Supreme Court had ruled on American Indian religious activities in the previous decade.

The first decision of the eighties pitted the Native American Church against the Navajo Tribal Council. From the time of Quanah Parker and the early use of peyote in religious rituals, its use spread widely throughout Indian country. A bill was introduced in Congress, the Hayden Bill, that would ban the use of peyote, taken to be a dangerous addictive hallucinogen. The bill failed but in 1918 practitioners sought to protect this new faith in Oklahoma by formally incorporating the Native American Church with the purpose of promoting "the Christian religion with the practice of the Peyote Sacrament." Indians in other states followed suit.

The peyote sacrament was typically part of an all-night ceremony that involved lighting a fire in a hole in the floor of the tepee in which such ceremonies, including individual prayers, usually took place. Songs, the consumption of the peyote buttons, and smoking ceremonial tobacco occurred, along with other rites, involving water and an eagle feather. In the morning a general discussion, the development of new songs, and then a grand feast all took place. Two strains of the Native American Church came into being, one of which emphasized Christianity, with peyote being the road to Christ, while the other was less focused on Christianity or not at all, and included worship of the Great Spirit and Mother Earth.

Peyote, of course, struck horror into a variety of people, who all took it as the equivalent of cocaine or LSD, and it has always been controversial for that. In fact, the peyote cactus does contain several alkaloids, in particular mescaline, that can in sufficient dosage produce mild hallucinations. On the other hand, in the Native American Church rites, where peyote is considered a deity, it produces for most a sense of well-being, of personal esteem, and its use has been documented by anthropologists and others as being an effective way for many Indian people who have been stripped of control over their destiny to regain a sense of self. The Native American Church has had well-documented success in treating alcoholism and drug addictions among Indians. On the other hand, the federal government classified peyote as a controlled substance on Schedule I. At one point, traditional Navajo medicine men, those who perform the long, often several-days-long healing ceremonies, grew alarmed at the spread of this new religion on the reservation and persuaded the Navajo Tribal Council to ban the peyote cult. The Supreme Court finally ruled in 1980 that the First Amendment did not restrict a tribal government from dealing with questions of religious freedom. In spite of that, the Native American Church has many adherents in Navajo land and the medicine men have since concluded that both the traditional Navajo ceremonial life and the peyote religion can coexist—in fact, many people comfortably practice both. (Indeed, many Navajo people have what might be thought of as a cultural bias in favor of religion per se. In the 1990s, a Navajo woman from Crystal, New Mexico, was baptized into the Roman Catholic Church while the rest of her family and friends sang Christian hymns that had been translated into Navajo. The woman, who was in her late eighties, was a member as well of the Native American Church and a traditional Navajo medicine woman.)

Before returning to the question of peyote in 1990, the Supreme Court produced eight more decisions impinging directly on Indian religion. In one case, they ruled that the Cherokees' desire to protect some land from expansion of the Tennessee Valley Authority was not sufficiently religious. Next they told the Navajos that the ceremonial importance of Rainbow Bridge was simply not indispensable enough to overrule the economic benefits of building a dam in Glen Canyon, which would put that huge adjunct to Grand Canyon under water, produce electricity and tourism, and put millions of people within a short walk of the previously hard-to-reach Navajo sacred site. In a case questioning promotion of tourism at Bear Butte in South Dakota, the Court opted for tourism. The Court then ruled that the Forest Service could go ahead and extend the ski lifts up San Francisco Peaks much closer to the upper realm, where the katsinas rehearse bringing rain to Hopi fields. Next, they told the Abenakis that each of their children had to have a Social Security number regardless of religious prohibitions; permitted a highway to be driven through numerous sacred sites in the Pacific Northwest, including an Indian cemetery used by several tribes, among them the Yuroks and Karoks; and then ruled that the Forest Service did not violate the First Amendment when it denied the Sioux a permit to create a religious and cultural community on some eight hundred acres of national forest land in the Black Hills.

It was after this bludgeoning of Indian religious pleas by the highest court that the matter of peyote came up again when an Oregon substance abuse program called ADAPT fired two men on its staff for using peyote in a Native American Church ceremony. The two men were a Klamath Indian, Alfred Smith, and a non-Indian, Galen Black. Both had overcome alcohol and drug problems via the peyote ceremonies. The state then refused the two men unemployment benefits, and they sued, with the case bouncing around, as legal scholar David E. Wilkins has written, like a yo-yo, reaching the Supreme Court, only to be passed back down the line and then up again to the Supreme Court. By this time, 1990, the Native American Church, the only formally incorporated Indian religious institution, had as many as half a million members. In fact, by the time the case reached the Supreme Court, Smith and Black and ADAPT had made a formal agreement saying that the religious use of peyote would not be taken as misconduct anymore, so the case was now what is called moot. Nevertheless, the Court majority, for which Antonin Scalia wrote the opinion, charged ahead like the bluecoats of old.

Earlier First Amendment cases had demonstrated that the government could bar—or "burden"—religious practices if it has a "compelling state interest" in doing so. In an argument from that doctrine (an argument that could not be followed by an ordinary layman), the majority compared the use of peyote in the Native American Church to the throwing of rice in weddings, and went on to say that the nation could not afford the luxury of questioning every state's efforts to control religious conduct within its borders. In a real sense, what Justice Scalia did was turn over the question of religious freedom to political regulation. Scalia's decision admitted as much: "It may be fairly said that leaving accommodation to the political process will place at a relative disadvantage those religious practices that are not widely engaged in; but that unavoidable consequence of democratic government must be preferred."

So much, as Indian legal scholar Rennard Strickland pointed out, for the Bill of Rights.

Of course, a lot of people were reminded of Felix Cohen's canary. In 1949, he had put it this way: for the dominant society, "the Indian tribe is the miner's canary and when it flutters and drops we know the poisonous gases of intolerance threaten all of the minorities in our land. And who of us is not a member of some minority?"

Conservatives and liberals and many in between reacted strongly to the Scalia decision. Jewish groups, evangelicals, Quakers, and Seventh Day Adventists, along with the National Council of Churches, the American Civil Liberties Union, People for the American Way, several national American Indian organizations, and fifty-odd constitutional scholars, joined several national American Indian organizations and signed a petition asking the Court to reconsider its opinion. The petition was denied.

Three years later Congress acted. It passed the Religious Freedom Reformation Act, which said the federal government has to offer proof that it needs to restrict any religious practice. It also has to show that its restrictive acts will be the least harmful way to restrict a practice. So minority religions appeared to be relatively safe—except those of the Indians whose special needs were not addressed by Congress. That left many contentious issues unresolved. To remedy this, Senator Daniel Inouye of Hawaii introduced an omnibus bill in 1994 called the Native American Cultural Protection and Free Exercise of Religions Act. Peyote was still a controlled substance, its use illegal in about twenty states. Indian prisoners in federal prisons were often denied the ability to practice their own rites. The use of eagle feathers and other animal parts was a murky area involving federal laws on endangered or threatened species and a host of other regulations. The issue of sacred sites was bereft of any particular federal policy and firm, much less enforceable, guidelines. Inouye's bill addressed all those issues, making it clear the use of peyote in traditional religious circumstances was legal, regardless of local or state laws. Inouye's omnibus bill failed passage. It was replaced by an act that simply legalized the use of peyote in the Native American Church, leaving all the other issues unaddressed.

Win a few, lose a few. Even such a phrase seems a bit Pollyannaish, given the still-grim demographic facts of Indian life. Poverty on many of the reservations is still a terrible, grinding problem, as are sheer ennui, alcoholism, suicide, unemployment, and poor health. A new stalker has also arisen, adult-onset diabetes. Obesity is now seen as a serious problem in virtually every segment of the American population, but nowhere is it more common than among Indian people, and particularly Indian youth. Even among the wealthier tribes and the most traditional, all these problems exist to one degree or another. Worse in some ways, some people with expertise in the matter project that by 2050, as few as thirty American Indian languages will still be spoken, most of them among the Iroquois and the tribes of the Southwest. Elsewhere the indigenous languages, the very core of an individual culture, will have given way to English and be forgotten. One hopes this is the sort of extreme prediction that comes in time to jump-start the process of remedy. Yet the remedy here cannot be national or even regional. It must be tribe by tribe, reservation by reservation. In too many cases, the rescue will have to be made by only one or two old ladies who still speak the original tongue.

It is dangerous down in any mine, and always a bit unpredictable, but for all the obstacles American Indians still face, the canary sings today with a far stronger voice than a century ago.

The Indians—after all—are still here.

Northwest coast cedar mask

BIBLIOGRAPHY
AND FURTHER READING

CHAPTER ONE: ARRIVAL

In the long course of writing this book, I have had the happy opportunity to collaborate with two men—one old friend, one new—on books that have greatly increased my understanding and appreciation for the deep past of the American Indians. One is a college roommate, David Leeming, who is a leading scholar of mythology around the world, and the other is James M. Adovasio of Mercyhurst College, who, however accidentally, became *the man* on early man in the New World. So I will list these collaborations first. Books that have been of equal importance to this chapter follow.

James M. Adovasio with Jake Page, *The First Americans* (New York, Random House: 2002). We fondly hope that this will be the definitive account for a while, putting to rest what has been a seventy-year faith in the primacy of Clovis Man as the first American, and replacing it with a more open field, beginning at least four or five millennia earlier—all this based chiefly on Adovasio's major dig at Meadowcroft Rockshelter in Pennsylvania.

David Leeming and Jake Page, *The Mythology of Native America* (Norman: University of Oklahoma Press, 1998). This was an attempt to look at American Indian mythology from a global perspective, showing where it fits on a psychological and literary level with other great world mythologies. This is not the tack usually taken by anthropologists or Indian tribes themselves, but it has the merit, among others, of rendering such tales more accessible to non-Indians, for whom the book is intended.

Books of American Indian mythology (which is another way of referring to their *own* religion and history) have proliferated. For this chapter I gleaned accounts from several, including most notably what amounts to the mother lode, Richard Erdoes and Alfonso Ortiz, *American Indian Myths and Legends* (New York: Pantheon Books, 1984); Leeming's and my book *God: Myths of the Male Divine* (New York: Oxford University Press, 1996); Peter Nabokov's *Native American Testimony* (New York: Viking Press, 1991), a book that is especially fascinating when discussing Indian-white relations; John Bierhorst's *Myths and Tales of the American Indian* (New York: Indian Head Books, 1976); Harold Courlander's collection of Hopi creation stories, *The Fourth World of the Hopis* (New York: Crown Publishers, 1971), a work the Hopis themselves prefer by far over the work of Frank Waters; and Paul G. Zobrod's *Dine Bahane* (Albuquerque: University of New Mexico Press, 1984), a brilliant translation of the entire Navajo creation story and history, what amounts to the great indigenous American epic.

A large number of archaeological works have been very useful in this chapter; I list only a few. Thomas D. Dillehay's popular review of South American archaeology vis-à-vis the first Americans, *The Settlement of the Americas* (New York: Basic Books, 2000) is accessible, thorough, and up-to-date and provides a good look at his pre-Clovis site, Monte Verde. Two other useful references are Robson Bonnichsen's *Who Were the First Americans?* (Corvallis: Oregon State University, 1999) and J. I. Mean and David J. Meltzer's *Environments and Extinctions* (Orono: Center for the Study of Early Man, University of Maine, 1985). James E. Dixon's story of mostly Arctic archaeology, *Quest for the First Americans* (Albuquerque: University of New Mexico Press, 1993), is a spritely personal account with a good deal of drama in a book that is also scholarly.

Vine Deloria's opinion on the first Americans comes from his book *Red Earth, White Lies* (New York: Scribner's, 1995), in which he takes on virtually all those aspects of the archaeological and earth sciences that have any impact on Indian views; one can say that Deloria is far more accurate and compelling when discussing Indian views than he is finding fault with science, which he does not really understand.

A bracing look at the nature of Indian history as such (bracing especially to someone starting out to write one) has been edited by Calvin Martin and is called *The American Indian and the Problem of History* (New York: Oxford University Press, 1987). Martin essentially sees the original sin of humanity in the invention of agriculture, and all but a few of the writers he assembled for this volume generally perceive Indian history as an area white folks will simply never understand. The historian James Axtell, whose books are cited in succeeding chapters, forcefully disagrees, as of course do I.

CHAPTER TWO: HUNTERS AND GATHERERS

One of the most useful collections of books on the Indians of North America in general, including their archaeological history, is the multivolume series published by the Smithsonian Institution, *The Handbook of North American Indians,* edited by William Sturtevant. This series has been invaluable to me throughout most of the chapters in this book; *California* (1978), *Northeast* (1978), *Southwest* (1979), *Southwest* (1983), *Great Basin* (1986), and *Northwest Coast* (1990). Jared Diamond's best-selling *Guns, Germs and Steel* (New York: W. W. Norton & Company, 1999) provides a fascinating overview of the effects on human societies in prehistory of many overlooked matters of geography and environment, including the notion that agriculture spread slowly in the Americas (compared to the Old World) since it had to spread north and south, which meant adapting to different temperature zones.

Adovasio's *The First Americans* (noted before) went into considerable up-to-date detail about the Pleistocene overkill notion. The prolific Brian Fagan's book *Ancient North America* (New York: Thames and Hudson, 1995) is a wonderfully rich, well-illustrated tour of the prehistory of this continent over a period of some fourteen thousand years, a volume he faithfully keeps up to date; and David Meltzer's *Search for the First Americans* (Montreal: St. Remy's Press, 1993; published in this country by Smithsonian Books) is a highly readable account of the early hunters and gatherers here.

In the 1990s, I was lucky to be invited to southern Texas by the Texas Archaeological Society, joining a number of archaeologists trying to obtain nutrition the old-fashioned way, which resulted in the section on hot rocks. Philip J. Dering's paper for the occasion, "Hot Rocks and Plant Processing: The Role of Earth Ovens in the Economy of the Lower Pecos," and LuAnn Wandsneider's 1996 draft article for the *Journal of American Archaeology,* entitled "The Roasted and the Boiled," were both of use in this section.

The story of Mondawmin is quoted here, with permission from David Leeming (and me), from our *Myths of Native America,* noted earlier.

CHAPTER THREE: HIGH SOCIETY

Brian Fagan's book *Ancient North America* (cited earlier) has splendid material on the mound builders, and Robert Silverberg's *The Mound Builders* (Athens: Ohio University Press, 1970) tells the long and wonderfully silly story of how the white amateurs and scholars dealt with these mysterious presences. The horse's mouth on the Hohokam culture is Emil W. Haury's *Hohokam* (Tucson: University of Arizona Press, 1976). There have been additional studies and reports since then, such as Bruce W. Masse's article entitled "Prehistoric Irrigation Systems in the Salt River Valley," in *Science* 214 (October 23, 1981), but Haury's on-the-ground overview still provides a wonderful big picture.

In this entire chapter Brian Fagan's previously mentioned book is very helpful. For a thorough study of the entire southwestern archaeological picture, Linda Cordell and George J. Gumerman's edited collection *Dynamics of Southwestern Pre-*

history (Washington: Smithsonian Institution Press, 1989) is another superior book. David Meltzer's book on the first Americans had some nice insights, as did Robert H. and Florence C. Lister's *Those Who Came Before,* an attractively illustrated book (Tucson: University of Arizona Press, for the Southwest Parks & Monuments Association, 1983). Highly reliable and particularly readable is Kendrick Frazier's updated *The People of Chaco* (New York: W. W. Norton & Company, 1999). Unlike many archaeologists, Frazier (who is editor of the *Skeptical Inquirer*) had the nerve to ask the Hopis and other Pueblo descendants of the people of Chaco what some of its more mysterious features could have meant. My own take on how the Chaco people might have interpreted events at the end of the Chaco phenomenon is a result of personal discussions with Emory Sekaquaptewa, of the Hopi Eagle clan, though he might well not agree with me. The material on the arrival of the Athapascans is largely from the Smithsonian's *Handbook,* though sources for this abound.

CHAPTER FOUR: MYSTERIES

The prophecies mentioned here derive from Leeming and Page's *Mythology of Native America,* Nabokov's *Native American Testimony,* and Courlander's *Fourth World of the Hopis,* cited earlier. The story about the Dalai Lama and the southwestern Indian leader is a personal communication to me from a friend and gallery owner in Santa Fe who was present, and the Norse material is from Fagan.

The material about smallpox and the other European pathogens derives from two general and two specific sources: Guy A. Settipane's *Columbus and the New World: Medical Implications* (Providence: Oceanside Publications, 1995) and Ann F. Ramenofsky's *Vectors of Death* (Albuquerque: University of New Mexico Press, 1987). Both set out the facts of the matter, as they are known, Settipane concentrating on the medical facts. Ramenofsky's book, which goes into the history of the controversy in ample detail, resulted from her adding her own archaeological analyses to the anthropological and epidemiological evidence of others by way of a reality check. William McNeill's *Plagues and People* (New York: Doubleday Anchor Books, 1998) is a world view of disease in history, and like Jared Diamond's book cited earlier, is full of wonderful insights. Barbara Tuchman's *A Distant Mirror* (New York: Alfred A. Knopf, 1978) describes the kind of psychological havoc such terrible plagues can cause, in this case on medieval Europeans, and my guess is that the American Indians reacted in an equally human manner.

Ernst and Johanna Lehner's *How They Saw the New World* (New York: Tudor Publishing Company, 1966) and Wilcomb E. Washburn's *Red Man's Land/White Man's Law* (Norman: University of Oklahoma Press, 1995) provide telling and often wryly amusing insights into what the Europeans made of the New World and its inhabitants. James Axtell's work (see later chapter sources) has given us some insights about the opposite.

The matter of cannibalism is naturally fraught with controversy. In the Southwest, Tim D. White's *Prehistoric Cannibalism at Mancos 5MTUMR-2346* (Princeton: Princeton University Press, 1992) is as formal, scholarly, and formidable as its title suggests. It is basically the forensics of cannibalism by a world-renowned osteologist. There have been numerous other accounts, such as that which appeared in the *New Yorker* some years back, written by Douglas Preston, in which Christy Turner (see Chapter One on Asian and Indian teeth) speculated that a gang of Mexicans burst into the Southwest and terrorized the population with this practice. Personal communication with Marsha Ogilvie, a blind osteologist of Albuquerque, gave rise to the explanation that much of Christy Turner's evidence may in fact be the result of witchcraft executions. The account of cannibalism from the Northeast is to be found in Frederick Drimmer's *Captured by the Indians* (New York: Dover Publications, 1961).

CHAPTER FIVE: THE SPANISH

Officially entering what is called history with this chapter, I should bring attention to other general or overall histories that I found invaluable for both details and perspective. Notably, in addition to the Smithsonian's multivolume *Handbook* (talk about misnomers), I found myself referring throughout this writing to the two North American volumes of Bruce Trigger and Wilcomb E. Washburn's four-volume set, *The Cambridge History of the Native Peoples of the Americas* (New York: Cambridge University Press, 1996). The two editors roped in a host of specialist experts in different eras, and the set is an invaluable reference while being exceptionally good reading for such a work. I also have been greatly helped both with an overall sense of the passage of these events and with specifics by Susan Hazen-Hammond's *Timelines of Native American History* (New York: Berkeley Publishing Group, 1997), Frederick E. Hoxie's *Encyclopedia of North American Indians* (Boston and New York: Houghton Mifflin Company, 1996), and Carl Waldman's *Atlas of the North American Indian* (New York: Facts on File, 1985). Another companion throughout the writing of this book is a yellowed 1976 Bantam paperback edition of Alvin M. Josephy Jr.'s *The Indian Heritage of America,* first published in 1968 by Alfred A. Knopf. Josephy is one of the earliest of modern historians to take on this long story from the standpoint of the American Indians and he remains one of their grandest champions.

An exceptionally rich compendium of learned and often quite surpising views of the long period of contact is Peter C. Mancall and James H. Merrell's *American Encounters* (New York: Routledge, 2000). If one had to read only one book about the initial contacts made between Europeans and American Indians, this book, with its panoply of historians reporting on their active research in this area, would be a wise choice.

For the early *entradas* of the Spanish into the worlds of the American Indians, David J. Weber's *The Spanish Frontier in North America* (New Haven: Yale University Press, 1992) is an invaluable one-volume overview, replete with excellent details as well. The Spanish efforts in Florida (and environs) are well told in Charles Hudson's *The Southeastern Indians* (Knoxville: University of Tennessee Press, 1976) and archaeologist Jerald T. Milanovich's *Laboring in the Fields of the Lord* (Washington: Smithsonian Institution Press, 1999), which dwells chiefly on the relations between the Indians of Florida and the Catholic missionaries.

The first eighty-odd years of Spanish colonization of what is now New Mexico, decades that finally erupted in the Pueblo Rebellion of 1680, are much studied, but they and the rebellion are amply covered in the following books. Fray Angelico Chavez, a Franciscan, wrote movingly of the Spanish experience in this new part of the world in *My Penitente Land* (Santa Fe: Museum of New Mexico Press, 1993), and he is, for reasons not difficult to understand, more sympathetic to the Hispanics than the Indians. Andrew L. Knaut's *The Pueblo Revolt of 1680* (Norman: University Press of Oklahoma, 1995) is the best one-volume account of the causes and events of the rebellion, though not everyone agrees with him over the proximate and ultimate causes. Joe Sando, a Jemez Pueblo member, writes of the rebellion and the rest of Pueblo history from the inside, in *Pueblo Nations* (Santa Fe: Clear Light Publishers, 1992). Alvin Josephy's profile of the mysterious spark plug of the rebellion, named Popé, stands out in his early book *The Patriot Chiefs* (New York: Viking Press, 1961). I have chosen to make more than is usual of the rebellion since it is little mentioned and less known outside of the Southwest, and as the only time any Indians ever ran some settled Europeans out of the territory, it deserves to be more widely appreciated. Indeed, the entire experience of American Indians and the Spanish typically get short shrift in histories of American Indians, which mostly look at this long story from the vantage point of the eastern seaboard.

The entry of the Spanish into the country of the Pimas and Papagos (now known collectively as the O'odham) is well told in Edward H. Spicer's classic *Cycles of Conquest* (Tucson: University of Arizona Press, 1962), which was a landmark book in many ways. It forcefully introduced the notion of acculturation into the minds of anthropologists and remains one of the best studies of this process throughout the southwestern Indians' experience of Spanish, Mexican, and then American rulers. The First Man story of the Pimas (Akimel O'odham) is to be found in Nabokov's previously cited work.

CHAPTER SIX: THE FRENCH AND THE ENGLISH

Books by two of the towering figures in the study of Indian history today, James Axtell and Richard White, served me especially well in this chapter (and others). Axtell's volumes, published by Oxford University Press, are wonderful human accounts of real human lives and attitudes: *The Indian People of Eastern America* (1981), *The Invasion Within* (1985), and *Beyond 1492* (1992). Axtell is the only historian I ran across who spent some time talking about Indian humor, and for this alone he should get a special medal. Richard White's astounding book on the Indians of the Great Lakes region and their relationships with the French, *The Middle Ground* (New York: Cambridge University Press, 1991), may be the most important single book in this entire field in the past several decades, describing the invention by both sides of what amounted to a coherent (if short-lived) new culture.

Yet another leader among Indian historians is Colin G. Calloway, editor of *After King Philip's War* (Dartmouth: University Press of New England, 1997), a book full of fresh insights into the Indian world in New England. My old colleague Russell Bourne's book on that war, *The Red King's Rebellion* (New York: Atheneum, 1990), put me in mind, among other things, of how rare it is that a superb editor can also be a superb writer. For those great movers and shakers of colonial America, the Iroquois, I have relied heavily on Daniel K. Richter's *The Ordeal of the Longhouse* (Chapel Hill: University of North Carolina Press, 1992).

For the Powhatan tribes, which experienced another kind of Englishman, I relied on Helen C. Rountree's *The Powhatan Indians of Virginia* (Norman: Oklahoma University Press, 1989) and a less known study by a youthful Lewis R. Binford: *Cultural Diversity Among Aboriginal Cultures of Coastal Virginia and North Carolina* (New York: Garland Publishing), written as a collegiate thesis in the 1950s and published in 1991. Binford remains the most towering theoretical archaeologist in the world, stirring controversy wherever he alights, and he was personally very helpful to me in the original thinking about this volume. The multiple invasions of the English—all four separate ones bringing different kinds of Englishmen, including, finally, the formidable Scots-Irish, and each with a different impact on the Indians with whom they interacted—is lengthily and valuably examined in David Hackett Fischer's *Albion's Seed* (New York: Oxford University Press, 1989). Separate essays in Mancall and Merrell's compendium were especially helpful in this chapter.

For better or worse throughout this book, I have been more interested in the implications of the different styles of warfare (European and Indian) than in recounting the endless bloody battles and campaigns. There are innumerable books on this aspect of Indian history, and many of the major battles (a very few of which are looked at herein in some detail) are amply described elsewhere. In this chapter, looking at military strategies and techniques, I am indebted to Armstrong Starkey's book *European and Native American Warfare, 1675–1815* (Norman: University of Oklahoma Press, 1998) for straightening out a number of common misperceptions. Also, the great military historian John Keegan had at least one useful (to me) insight in his *Fields of Battle* (New York: Alfred A. Knopf, 1996).

CHAPTER SEVEN: THE FRENCH CONNECTION

Nabokov's *Native American Testimony* provided the story of the arrival of the French into the lives of the Winnebagos, a story originally collected by Paul Radin, the anthropologist. Winnebago history is well summarized by Nancy Lurie in the Smithsonian's *Handbook*. The rest of this chapter is based largely on White's *The Middle Ground* and two other volumes of almost exact contemporaneity with White's. In *A Country Between* (Lincoln: University of Nebraska Press, 1992), Michael N. McConnell traces the emptying and then the filling of the Ohio Valley with refugee tribes, which settled into republican villages made up of people from various tribes. In *Indians, Settlers and Slaves in a Frontier Exchange Economy* (Chapel Hill: University of North Carolina Press, 1992), Daniel H. Usner explores the French colonies of Louisiana and the polymerization of separate elements—French, Indians, and blacks—into a unique gumbo. Fischer's *Albion's Seed* provided material on the devastating (in most cases) arrival of the Scots-Irish on the frontier. To pursue these invaders across the country into the period of the mountain men and on to California, with continuing effect on the Indian populations, a highly readable and surprising book is Bil Gilbert's *Westering Man* (New York: Atheneum, 1983).

CHAPTER EIGHT: INVADING THE PLAINS

The Cheyenne story about the race between the four-footeds and two-footeds can be found in various sources, but I am indebted to Ruth Rudner for my own favorite version, which she recounted in *Sacred Lands of Indian America* (New York: Harry N. Abrams, 2001). For tracking the Cheyennes (and others) as they moved out onto the Plains, I followed Douglas B. Bamford's *Ecology and Human Organization on the Great Plains* (New York: Plenum Press, 1988). A fine historical overview of the Indians of the Plains is Paul H. Carson's low-key account *The Plains Indians* (College Station: Texas A&M Press, 1998). For anthropological and historical insights I learned (relearned, as a matter of fact) much from Robert H. Lowie's old classic *Indians of the Plains*, which I had the pleasure of reprinting in a Natural History Press edition in 1963, as well as the work of John C. Ewers, especially his lucid essays collected in *Plains Indian History and Culture* (Norman: University of Oklahoma Press, 1997). Richard White's essay in Mancall and Merrell's previously cited volume, *American Encounters*, shed new light on Plains warfare, especially that of the Sioux. The primary focus of this chapter derived from Elliott West's *The Contested Plains* (Lawrence: University Press of Kansas, 1998), which delves into not only the dramatic history of Cheyenne responses to the new ecological situation they faced moving onto the Plains, but also the price they had to pay. West's book, more than any other I have read, captures the heady exhilaration of these times—the dreams, visions, drama, and tragedy on all sides.

CHAPTER NINE: WORLD WAR AND A NEW NATION

James H. Merrell's account of the Catawba experience in his and Mancall's *American Encounters* formed the basis of the Catawba discussion here. King Haglar's complaint about the destructive effects of alcohol, one of thousands lodged by Indian leaders, is from Nabokov.

Fred Anderson's *Crucible of War* (New York: Alfred A. Knopf, 2000) is a wholly winsome account of the so-called French and Indian War that pins its beginnings—at least by way of satisfying a story's requirement for a beginning as well as an end—on the explosive character Tanaghrisson, the Catawba-Seneca guide for young George Washington. Other books consulted heavily for this warlike period include Roger L. Nichols's *Indians in the United States and Canada* (Lincoln: University of Nebraska Press, 1998), a smooth comparison of Indian policies in the two countries through time; Colin G. Calloway's *The American Revolution in Indian Country* (New York: Cambridge University Press, 1995); and Anthony F. C. Wallace's *Jefferson and the Indians* (Cambridge: Harvard University Press, 1999). To round out a sense of how dreadful life could be in this period for Indians and Europeans, Elizabeth A. Finn's *Pox Americana* (New York: Hill and Wang, 2001), detailing the virulent outbreaks of smallpox during the American Revolution, provides grisly insight.

The digression far to the west into California is based in part on the Smithsonian *Handbook* and in particular on Robert H. Jackson and Edward Castillo's *Indians, Franciscans, and Spanish Colonization* (Albuquerque: University of New Mexico Press, 1995). I feel obliged to confess that with this chapter, the story of the American Indians heads so far "south" that chronicling it up to the middle of the twentieth century became the most depressing research and writing assignment I have ever taken on.

CHAPTER TEN: REMOVAL

For Tecumseh's role as a pan-Indian leader, I relied chiefly on John Sugden's thorough modern biography, *Tecumseh: A Life* (New York: Henry Holt and Company, 1997), with important insights gained from Alvin Josephy's previously cited *The Patriot Chiefs* and from Gregory Evens Dowd's essay in Mancall and Merrell.

For the postcontact history of the southeastern tribes I found Hudson (previously cited) helpful, along with James W. Covington's *The Seminoles of Florida* (Gainesville: University Press of Florida, 1993) and Leitch J. Wright's *Creeks and Seminoles* (Lincoln: University of Nebraska Press, 1986). Thornton Russell's demographic history *The Cherokees* provided many useful facts, while Rennard Strickland's account of the events surrounding removal put a personal face on it. I am indebted in many more ways than can be properly cited in a bibliography to this Cherokee-Osage (with some Scot) legal scholar and historian, and in particular for the deeply moving view of the removal period embodied in much of his work, including "Genocide at Law: An Historic and Contemporary View of the Native American Experience," *University of Kansas Law Review* 34 (1986). Here again, Washburn (1995), Nichols (1998), and Mancall and Merrell (2000) provided useful insights, as did David Lavere's *Contrary Neighbors* (Norman: University of Oklahoma Press, 2000), which is a fascinating account of the interaction between the tribes local to what became the Indian Territory and those who were relocated into their midst.

CHAPTER ELEVEN: AN AMERICAN SOUTHWEST

The Listers' previously cited book provides some of the story of Narbona's invasion of Canyon de Chelly; the rest one can hear, as I did, from a Navajo-guided tour into Canyon del Muerte. Hopi history of this period is nicely recounted in Harry C. James's *Pages from Hopi History* (Tucson: University of Arizona Press, 1974), and Sando (1992) reports on the Rio Grande pueblos of the time. Peter Iverson's *The Navajo Nation* (Albuquerque: University of New Mexico Press, 1981) is the best source of postcontact Navajo history. The material on the Chiricahuas derives from research for a book I happily coauthored with lawyer Michael Lieder, a history of the Indian Claims Commission with the Chiricahuas as a focus, *Wild Justice* (New York: Random House, 1997). For the Paiute account I relied on Robert J. Franklin and Paula A. Bunte's volume *The Paiute* (New York: Chelsea House Publishers, 1990), along with the Smithsonian *Handbook*.

The continuing tragedy in California is chronicled in all the detail this writer could bear in the Smithsonian's *Handbook*.

CHAPTER TWELVE: THE LAST OF THE GREAT HORSEMEN

The best and most accessible battle history of the so-called Indian wars of the Plains is National Park historian Robert M. Utley's *The Indian Frontier of the American West* (Albuquerque: University of New Mexico Press, 1984.) For the highlights of the black divisions' campaigns on the Plains and in the Southwest, William H. Leckie's *The Buffalo Soldiers* (Norman: University of Oklahoma Press, 1967) remains the standard, with the Buffalo Soldiers' accomplishments put in a larger black perspective in William Loren Katz's pictorial history *The Black West*

(Seattle: Open Hand Publishing, 1987). My main guide to the style and implications of Plains warfare was Robert Wooster's compact volume *The Military and United States Indian Policy, 1865–1903* (Lincoln: University of Nebraska Press, 1988). West (1998) and an older book by Stan Hoig, *The Sand Creek Massacre* (Norman: Oklahoma University Press, 1961), provided the details of that event. Bruce Hampton's *Children of Grace* (New York: Henry Holt and Company, 1994) is one of the most recent accounts of the Nez Perces' effort to escape into Canada, and the account of the last free-ranging days of the Chiricahuas comes from the Lieder and Page book already cited. (Going from the tragic to the ridiculous, I wrote an alternative history novel about what would have happened if the Apaches had won, called *Apacheria* [New York: Ballantine Books, 1998].)

CHAPTER THIRTEEN: THE RESERVATION

For accounts of the reservations, particularly in the early days, one needs to cast a wide net. Mine turned up the following books that were of particular help. Some of this material comes from accounts of legal case histories, since it is largely through such complaints that one can glean the state of affairs at the time. Much of the material herein on the humanitarian movements derives from Wilcomb E. Washburn's volume in the Smithsonian *Handbook* (*History of Indian-White Relations,* 1988.)

Two books mentioned in the ethnography section are John C. Cremony, *Life Among the Apaches* (New York: Indian Head Books, 1991), and Randolph B. Marcy, *The Prairie Traveler* (Cambridge: Applewood Books, 1988). For the ethnography section, particularly useful were Frank Hamilton Cushing's *Zuni* (Lincoln: University of Nebraska Press, 1979); Wallace Stegner's biography of John Wesley Powell, *Beyond the Hundredth Meridian* (Lincoln: University of Nebraska Press, 1953); and Gordon R. Wiley and J. A. Sabloff's *A History of American Archaeology* (New York: W. H. Freeman and Company, 1993). For more on Stevenson's informant and on the role of the *berdache* in much of Indian society, Will Roscoe's *The Zuni Man-Woman* (Albuquerque: University of New Mexico Press, 1991) is a good place to start. Legal considerations were derived from Charles F. Wilkinson's *American Indian Sovereignty and the U.S. Supreme Court* (Austin: University of Texas Press, 1997).

The Chiricahua and Mescalero experience on the reservation are drawn from the splendid oral history compiled by Eve Ball, *Indeh: An Apache Odyssey* (Norman: University of Oklahoma Press, 1988). An excellent overview of the Indian reservations in general is German geographer Franz Klaus's *Indian Reservations in the United States* (Chicago: University of Chicago Press, 1999), and another good specific study of reservation life is Richard J. Perry's *Apache Reservation* (Austin: University of Texas Press, 1993). The school experience I quoted was from interviews conducted by James Wilson for his book *The Earth Shall Weep* (New York:

Atlantic Monthly Press, 1993). Once again, Iverson is the reliable guide to Navajo history. Porcupine's account of the prophet Wovoka is quoted in the helpful collection by Wayne Moquin and Charles Van Doren, *Great Documents in American Indian History* (New York: Da Capo Press, 1973).

CHAPTER FOURTEEN: THE PROGRESSIVE ERA

In addition to numerous previously cited volumes, including Franz (1999), Lieder and Page (1997), Nichols (1998), Sando (1992), Stegner (1953), Washburn (1988), and Wilkinson (1997), this chapter benefited especially from Donald L. Parman's *Indians and the American West in the Twentieth Century* (Bloomington: Indiana University Press, 1994) and Francis Paul Prucha's *Documents of United States Indian Policy* (Lincoln: University of Nebraska Press, 1990). Walter Nugent's *Into the West* (New York: Alfred A. Knopf, 1999) provided helpful material, particularly on the rise of tourism in the Southwest.

CHAPTER FIFTEEN: WATERSHED

In this chapter, previously cited works have supplied me with virtually all the data and insight. They include Iverson (1981), Lieder and Page (1997), Nichols (1998), Parman (1994), Pruchka (1990), Washburn (1998), and Nabokov (1991). My wife, Susanne, somewhat inadvertently found herself in the midst of the controversy over the Havasupais and, siding with the tribe, was promptly fired by the Sierra Club from her job as head of the club's national committee on Native American affairs, but not before the club had wired every member of the U.S. Congress to pay no attention to anything she said.

CHAPTER SIXTEEN: RED POWER

In addition to the books listed for Chapter Fifteen, material for this chapter came from Joane Nagel's invaluable study *American Indian Ethnic Renewal* (New York: Oxford University Press, 1996), Rennard Strickland's insightful essays in *Tonto's Revenge* (Albuquerque: University of New Mexico Press, 1996), and the contributors to a book I edited, *Sacred Lands of Indian America* (New York: Harry N. Abrams, 2001). What may well be the most articulate account of the great militant events of this era is the poetic, tough, and moving account by Mary Crow Dog in her memoir (with Richard Erdoes), *Lakota Woman* (New York: Harper Perennial, 1990), and I have quoted from her for this chapter. My wife and I were present at Hopi (and Navajo) during much of the most public uproar over the Hopi-Navajo land dispute. I am on record in Susanne's and my *Hopi* (New York: Harry N. Abrams, 1982) as finding the Navajo position on this matter greatly overwrought.

CHAPTER SEVENTEEN: CURRENT EVENTS

In addition to the list that applied in the two previous chapters, a number of volumes assisted in the continuing story. The Pequot story has been covered in journalistic detail in Jeff Benedict's *Without Reservation* (New York: HarperCollins Publishers, 2000) and Kim Isaac Eisler's *Revenge of the Pequots* (New York: Simon and Schuster, 2001). On the matter of peyote and the Native American Church, Joe W. Martin's *The Land Looks After Us* (New York: Oxford University Press, 2001) was helpful, and David Aderle's classic study *The Peyote Religion Among the Navaho* (Chicago: University of Chicago Press, 1982) was invaluable—which is, of course, why it is considered classic. Here again, the contributors to the previously cited *Sacred Lands of Indian America* provided much background and many stories for this chapter. My guide on NAGPRA is James M. Adovasio and his account in *The First Americans,* cited for the first chapter of this volume. The Treasury Department's recent study (2001) was produced by the Community Development Financial Institutions Fund and is called *The Report of the Native American Lending Study.* Some of the story of the Pyramid Lake management plan is to be found in Fergus M. Bordevich's *Killing the White Man's Indian* (New York: Doubleday Anchor Books, 1996). Finally, I am indebted to Rennard Strickland in this chapter as well, in particular for his article "Indian Law and the Miner's Canary: The Signs of Poison Gas," *Cleveland State Law Review* 29.

SOME ACKNOWLEDGMENTS

Most of the nonfiction books I have written have been collaborations, but even in a book like this one, with a single author, the result is a collaborative effort. Those at the Free Press who have striven to make this book as good as it could be are thanked herewith: My editor, Bruce Nichols, who, if patience is the supreme virtue, is supremely virtuous, waited far longer than he originally imagined for this book to turn up on his desk. He was then good enough to give every word his gentle and wise attention. Not only that, but he and I discussed and rejected series of unsuitable phrases until, jointly, we came up with the book's title. Casey Reivich in his office also caught me napping a few times, and has seen to more scheduling and other details than I can imagine, as well as ramrodding most of the roundup of photographs for this volume (which was a hell of a lot more complicated than you would imagine). I am most grateful to Chuck Antony for giving the book a thorough and rewarding dose of copyediting, and to Edith Lewis for seeing to all of its editorial treatment as it made its way through production. Finally, it looks so elegant and readable thanks to designer Karolina Harris.

In terms of an overall sense of how Indian people and the rest of us Americans should interrelate, I bow to Ruth Frazier, for several decades the president of Futures for Children and a great-hearted, ferociously devoted, properly ribald supporter of anything helpful to the lives and dreams of Indian children.

I am grateful to the editors of the Zuni newspaper the *Shiwi Messenger,* who gave permission for the use of the anonymous student's poem in the front of the book. I freely borrowed from a long (and never written down) list of sources for the little drawings sprinkled here and there in these pages. They were not intended to represent the most important artifacts of Indian cultures, or the best known. Instead, they were objects that for the most part simply caught my eye and would, I hoped, provide a mostly osmotic sense of the diverse creativity of Indian people without making too big a deal about it, while visually lightening the accumulation of so much text.

Having stood all this time upon the shoulders of so many giants, I find myself awed by the amount of scholarship that continues to be done in Indian history. We are all, I think, greatly blessed by the work of the scholars. As noted elsewhere, I have availed myself of much of their work to produce this volume, which I hope leads many of its readers back to them in a continuing exploration. This book benefited greatly through reviews of its first draft by Jim Adovasio and Rennard Strickland, neither of whom are in any way responsible for any place where it has strayed from the true path.

Of course, none of this could take place without the Indians themselves, and to them I bow with humility and the utmost goodwill, as well as with apologies to the many tribes who did not find their way into this necessarily abbreviated one-volume account of their long residence here.

In this kind of work as in most other matters, I am unashamedly dependent on my wife Susanne.

Wooden mat creaser, Ozette

INDEX

ABOUT THE AUTHOR

Jake Page is a former editor of both *Natural History* and *Smithsonian* magazines and author of numerous magazine articles and books on topics related to American Indian history, culture, and art. With his wife Susanne, he produced the classics *Hopi, Navajo,* and *Field Guide to Southwest Indian Arts and Crafts* and edited *Sacred Lands of Indian America;* most recently he collaborated with James M. Adovasio on *The First Americans.* Page lives in New Mexico's Indian County.